HARDPRESS.NET
HOME OF HARD-TO-FIND BOOKS

Gleanings and Reminiscences
by Frank Thorpe Porter

Address:
HardPress
8345 NW 66TH ST #2561
MIAMI FL 33166-2626
USA
Email: info@hardpress.net

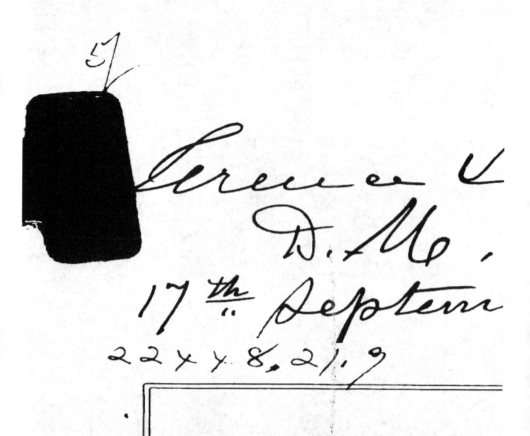

5

Terence V[...]
D. M[...]
17th "[...] Septem[...]
22 x y. 8, 21, 9

Subscriber's Copy.

GLEANINGS

AND

REMINISCENCES.

DUHALLOW CASTLE

THE ANCIENT STRONGHOLD OF THE MacDONOGHS (M'CARTHYS).

GLEANINGS

AND

REMINISCENCES.

BY

FRANK THORPE PORTER, A.M., J.P.,

BARRISTER-AT-LAW,

AND FOR UPWARDS OF TWENTY YEARS A MAGISTRATE OF
THE HEAD OFFICE OF DUBLIN POLICE.

" Scire tuum nihil est, nisi te scire hoc sciat alter."—PERSIUS.

DUBLIN:

HODGES, FOSTER, & CO., GRAFTON STREET.
1875.

To

CAPTAIN LUKE JOHN HENRY ALEN,

Of Wellington Road, Dublin,

The direct representative of a family mentioned in the 2nd chapter,

𝕿𝖍𝖎𝖘 𝖁𝖔𝖑𝖚𝖒𝖊,

As an acknowledgment of

His sterling and disinterested friendship,

is

inscribed.

PREFACE.

In submitting the following pages to the consideration of the public, I am influenced by a desire to extend the appetite which is so greedy in devouring fiction to some morsels of fact.

Several of my narratives refer to incidents which, in their disclosures, might occasion disagreeable feelings to the parties or to their kindred. In such cases, I shall adopt fictitious names; but in all the details offered to the reader, I shall include nothing which I do not firmly believe or personally know to be *strictly true*. To the former class must be referred several anecdotes derived from parental lips, and referring to years previous to my birth. In a theatre, the performers are neither applauded nor hissed from behind the scenes. The judgment which they have to encounter is that of the audience. As a literary manager, I shall leave each tragic or comic incident to the unbiassed opinion and criticism of my readers. I shall occasionally have to encounter the danger arising from allowing a great culprit to escape, or a virtuous and estimable individual to undergo misfortune. In this respect the writer of fiction possesses a vast advantage. He can lavish every worldly blessing on the deserving, and allot the direst punishments to vice and crime. But when we have to deal with stern realities, we may regret the occurrence of a fact which leaves guilt undetected and innocence in deep affliction. I can, however, safely assert, upon the experience of a long professional and official life, that vice seldom attains to great worldly prosperity, and that worth and integrity are rarely subjected to utter destitution.

It is difficult to classify anecdotes or reminiscences which are not connected with each other. The course I propose to adopt is to lay before my readers the narratives which I have derived from sources anterior to my birth, from lips truthful and occasionally humorous, but now silent for ever. I shall reserve, as far as possible, my own personal recollections for the latter part of this publication, in the hope that the amusement and information obtained from others, may soften the critical reader to an indulgent reception of the portion peculiarly connected with myself. I may remark that some anecdotes in which my name is introduced have been very extensively published in several periodicals. I accord to their authors my willing testimony as to their great imaginative power, for in the statements concerning me there is not one word of truth. My friend, Mr. Fitzpatrick, in his recent productions of "The Sham Squire" and "Ireland before the Union," has mentioned me as the source from which he derived the particulars of a few incidents in those interesting works. His unexaggerated correctness forms a strong contrast to the flippant fictions of others. However, when my name is brought before the public, in reference either to fiction or fact, it affords me some apology for appearing *in propriâ personâ.*

F. T. P.

CONTENTS.

———•———

GLEANINGS AND REMINISCENCES.

CHAPTER I.

LONERGAN'S CASE—OLD PRISONS.

ALTHOUGH it is probable that I may bring before my readers an incident or two of a more remote date, I shall commence with the narrative of an alleged crime and its supposed punishment, which has been adverted to by Sir Jonah Barrington in his "Personal Recollections," Vol. I., page 52, and in the description of which he has lapsed into considerable inaccuracy. According to him, the name of the person chiefly concerned was "Lanegan;" but in that respect there is a positive error; for by examining the records of the Crown Office, (Ireland,) I find the name, as my father had frequently stated to me, to be "Lonergan." He was a young man who had been educated at the school of the Rev. Eugene M'Kenna, of Raheny, in the County of Dublin, and from that establishment entered Trinity College, Dublin, in the year 1773. During his undergraduate course, he resided with Mr. M'Kenna, and acted as an assistant in the school. In 1777, having finished his University studies, he became a tutor in the family of Mr. Thomas O'Flaherty, of Castlefield, in the County of Kilkenny. That gentleman was

B

singularly unfortunate in having married a woman of most depraved tendencies. She engaged in a intrigue with Lonergan, and on the 28th of June, 1778, Mr. O'Flaherty died under circumstances which occasioned the arrest of Lonergan, on a charge of having poisoned him. The woman evaded arrest and escaped to a foreign country. Some time must have elapsed between the commission of the crime and the apprehension of the accused party, for it was not until the Summer Assizes of Kilkenny, in 1781, that Lonergan was arraigned for *Petit Treason*, the offence being considered by the law, as it then existed, as more aggravated than murder, inasmuch as he was in the domestic service of the man whom he was alleged to have destroyed. He succeeded, on certain legal grounds, in postponing his trial; but in the ensuing term a writ of *certiorari* issued, and the indictment was removed to the Court of King's Bench. A trial at bar was held on November 12th, 1781, the jury having been brought up from Kilkenny. The prisoner was convicted, and sentenced to be hanged and *quartered* on the 24th of the aforesaid month, and the sheriffs of the City of Dublin were directed to have the sentence carried into effect. At the time of his conviction, the prisoner declared that he was innocent of the crime; but he admitted that he bought arsenic at the instance of Mrs. O'Flaherty, who, according to his statement, told him that she intended to use it in destroying rats. He did not deny the imputation of an adulterous intrigue with her. The Rev. Mr. M'Kenna did not forget his former pupil and assistant. He visited him in prison, testified to his character in very favorable terms at the trial, and, after condemnation, was assiduous in preparing him to meet his impending doom with Christian resignation.

He determined to attend him to the termination of his
sufferings, and to pay the last duties to his remains.
M'Kenna was married to a cousin of my father, and he
was on terms of the closest intimacy with our family.
My father resided in Skinner Row, (now Christ Church
Place,) Dublin; and at the period to which this narrative
refers, he was in the prime of life—tall, vigorous, and
active. He was also serjeant of the grenadier company
of the Dublin Volunteers. He had known the unhappy
Lonergan during the peaceful and comparative innocent
days that the latter had spent at Raheny. He pitied the
miserable fate of the culprit, doubted his guilt, and sympathized with the worthy man whose pious solicitude
and friendship still sought to console the spirit that was
so soon to pass away. On the evening before the execution, M'Kenna remained with the condemned as long as
the regulations of the prison permitted. He then betook
himself to my father's house, where he proposed to stay
until the earliest hour of the morning at which he could
be admitted to the gaol. Having mentioned that he
would not fail to attend Lonergan to the consummation
of his fate, in compliance with the culprit's request, he
was informed by my father that he should also be at the
execution, for that owing to the paucity of regular troops
in Dublin, the sheriff had made a requisition for a guard
of the Volunteers, and that the grenadier company were
to attend at Baggot Street, (the Tyburn of Dublin,) to
which place the prisoner was to be escorted from Thomas
Street by a troop of cavalry.

Accordingly, on the 24th November, 1781, Lonergan,
having briefly but very distinctly denied any participation
in the crime for which he was condemned, was hanged by
the withdrawal of the cart from beneath the gallows to

which the halter was attached, and although he received no drop, his sufferings did not seem to be very acute. He almost immediately ceased to struggle, and life appeared to be extinct. The weather was extremely inclement; and when the body had been suspended for about twenty minutes, the sheriff acceded to a suggestion that it might be cut down. There was some difficulty in getting at the rope so as to cut it with a knife. M'Kenna remarked this to my father, who, drawing his short, slightly curved, and very sharp hanger, directed the cart to be backed towards the body. Then, springing up on the cart, he struck the rope where it crossed the beam, and severed it at once. A coffin was brought forward from a hearse which was in waiting. The sheriff directed the cap to be removed, and the body to be turned with the face down. Then he handed a sharp penknife to the executioner, who made two incisions across each other on the back of the neck. This was considered a formal compliance with the portion of the sentence which directed "quartering." The body was then left to the care of the faithful friend, M'Kenna, who directed it to be placed in the hearse and conveyed to his house at Raheny. On the 26th, a funeral, very scantily attended, proceeded to Raheny churchyard. M'Kenna had the coffin lowered into a very deep grave, and the burial service was read by the parochial clergyman. Persons were engaged to watch for a few nights lest any attempt should be made to exhume the corpse for anatomical purposes. In two days after the funeral my father received a note from M'Kenna, in consequence of which he immediately proceeded to Raheny. On his arrival he was pledged to secrecy and co-operation. He willingly assented, and having been conducted into a small apartment in the upper part of the house, he there beheld alive, although greatly debilitated, the man whom, at Baggot Street, he had cut down from the gallows. On the night of the 30th November, he brought Lonergan into Skinner Row. There he kept him concealed for upwards of a week, and then succeeded in shipping him for Bristol. From thence he proceeded, unsuspected and uninterrupted, to America, where, under the name of James Fennell, he lived for a considerable time, and supported himself by educational pursuits. His resuscitation was attributed to the rope having been unusually short, to his being swung from the cart without receiving any perpendicular drop, and especially to the incisions in his neck, which produced a copious effusion of blood. Lonergan stated that on being suspended, he immediately lost any sensation of a painful nature. His revival was attended with violent and distressing convulsions.

OLD PRISONS.

Before I proceed to the details of some other narratives, I trust that my readers will not censure me for submitting to their perusal incidents connected with real or imputed crimes, and asking them to accompany me, even in imagination, to prison scenes. There is scarcely a novelist of celebrity that has not frequently introduced his readers to such places, and generally without exciting any repugnance to his description of them, or to the narratives which they supply or the subjects they suggest. Although the prison may disappear and be replaced by other structures, even of a different character, its ideal existence continues, and perhaps outlasts those that arose on its foundations or in its vicinity. In Paris, the Bastille is spoken of as if it still existed. The name is inscribed on omnibusses, and the cab-driver asks no further explanation when ordered to

drive " a la Bastille." A house within a short distance of
the place where it stood displays on a sign-board a view of
the old fortress-prison ; and few strangers pass it during
the day without pausing to gaze on the picture of a building to which history refers so many fearful incidents,
exaggerated nevertheless most enormously by the unscrupulous revolutionists who introduced a " reign of terror "
of greater extent, and more sanguinary atrocity, than the
records of all the state prisons of France could supply.
The Chateau of Vincennes is an existing building ; visited
more for the memories of the past than for the attractions
of the present or the hopes of the future ; and few visitors
leave it without gazing on the spot where, at midnight, the
hapless Duc D'Enghien received the fatal volley and filled
an untimely grave. Many prisons in England are associated
with local traditions or historical events highly interesting ; but the lapse of time and the habitudes of a people
exceptionally romantic have deprived them of an extensive
popular appreciation. The Tolbooth of Edinburgh and the
building of the same designation in Glasgow have derived
a lasting fame from the pen of Scott ; and whilst the
English language exists, the readers of the " Heart of
Mid-Lothian " or " Rob Roy " will have the Tolbooths
vividly impressed on their imaginations. There are anecdotes connected with the old prisons of Ireland, many of
which would afford most ample subjects for the writer of
Romance, whilst even their simple details would fully
verify the adage that " Fact is stranger than Fiction." I
shall now proceed to a narrative which refers to a period
more than a century past, but in which, as to names and
dates, the crown-office records of the time fully agree with
the statements which I have heard from the descendants
of some of the most respectable characters connected,

but in no discreditable manner, with the circumstances detailed.

There may still be seen on the right hand side of the road leading from Dublin through Mount Brown to Inchicore, a small portion of a granite wall which formerly was in front of "Old Kilmainham," the common gaol of the County of Dublin. That building was considered one of the worst prisons of the kingdom, in consequence of its insufficient size and lax discipline. Swift is said to have been, in his youthful days, a frequent, although not a criminal visitor at this old gaol ; and there, perhaps, in the conversation of its inmates, he acquired much of the coarseness and indelicacy which mar the wit and vigor of his productions. I shall, however, most willingly and scrupulously abstain from offering to my readers any specimens of the language of such a time and place, when the building echoed with drunken revelry, and the sufferings of a prisoner were aggravated by indecent buffoonery or ribald jests. To my narrative such expressions are neither necessary nor ornamental.

CHAPTER II.

VESEY AND KEOGH.

On the 15th of February, 1743, a gentleman named James Vesey, who held a commission in the army, was returning to Dublin from a southern county where he possessed a respectable landed property. The facilities which now exist for the safe and prompt remittance of money were then almost unknown, and he had with him upwards of eighteen hundred pounds in specie. He was so unfortunate as to be stopped on the road at Castleknock, and robbed of the money, his watch, and its appendages. The highwayman who opened the door of the post-chaise had an associate who kept at the horses' heads, and could not be recognized. After the perpetration of the crime, the traveller proceeded on to Dublin and apprised the authorities of his loss. A vigilant search terminated, after a few days, in the apprehension of two brothers named Martin and Sylvester Keogh. They were men of a sinister reputation, who resided near Rathcoole, and spent more money than they could be supposed to have acquired honestly, being the occupiers of a thatched house of humble dimensions, and a neglected farm of six or seven acres. On being brought before a magistrate, Martin Keogh was fully identified by Mr. Vesey, as the man who, pistol in hand, opened the door of the chaise and despoiled him of his property.   Against the other there was no criminating evidence, and after a detention of some days, he was discharged.   The closest search after the money terminated unsuccessfully, not a guinea could be found.   Martin Keogh was committed for trial at the ensuing commission of *Oyer et Terminer* for the county of Dublin, and was there convicted of the robbery, on the positive and undoubtedly true testimony of Mr. Vesey.   Sentence of death was passed, and the doomed felon became an occupant of the condemned cell at Old Kilmainham, from the dreary precincts of which he was to issue at the end of twenty-one days, to die upon the gallows.   Mr. Vesey's leave of absence had been extended until the result of the trial left him free to proceed to England to join his regiment; and he departed from Dublin without any other satisfaction for his eighteen hundred pounds than what might be derived from the impending punishment of the delinquent.   He had ample opportunities for seeing Martin Keogh during the preliminary proceedings and in the progress of the trial, and the figure and features of the highwayman remained indelibly impressed on his memory. Soon after Mr. Vesey's arrival in England, he proceeded to encounter the dangers and privations of protracted foreign service; he attained the rank of Captain, and his regiment formed a portion of "the terrible English column" on the memorable field of Fontenoy, the 11th day of May, 1745.

It is unnecessary to introduce here any lengthened or distinct description of the obstinate valor with which the English advanced, thinned, but undismayed, by the concentrated fire of the French artillery, and unbroken by the repeated charges of veteran troops led by the most chivalrous of a gallant nobility.   They were not broken until assailed by the Irish Brigade, who rushed upon them with irre-

sistible fury.   Then, penetrated and scattered, the column
became completely' disorganized, and subjected to fearful
slaughter by the impetuous Irish and exulting French.
Captain Vesey remained on the field of battle.   He had
been wounded, almost simultaneously, by two balls, and
also received a blow from the butt of a musket, which reduced him to a state of utter insensibility.

Louis XV. was present at Fontenoy, and in the hour of
victory displayed the only virtues which, in his character,
were associated with many great vices.   He was generous
and humane, and at once directed that the wounded English
should receive the same care as was bestowed on his own
soldiers.   Considerable numbers were conveyed to Lille,
where surgical skill and the soothing attentions of religious communities and kind-hearted inhabitants effected
numerous recoveries.   Captain Vesey was soon conva-
lescent.   During his illness, several officers of the Irish
Brigade forgot he was an enemy, but recollected that he was
their gallant and suffering countryman, and from them
he experienced the courtesy of gentlemen and the sympathy of friends.   Amongst them was the Count de
St. Woostan, an officer in the regiment of Berwick, who
was acting at Lille in a capacity similar to that of town-
major in an English garrison.   One evening, at the
Count's quarters, the conversation turned on the various
incidents of the battle in which they had been so recently
engaged, and an officer remarked that Vesey owed his life,
in all probability, to a private in Berwick's regiment, who
procured assistance to convey him from the field whilst in
a state of insensibility, and manifested the utmost anxiety
for his preservation.   This elicited a very natural remark
from Vesey, that it was extraordinary the man had never
since approached him, either to evince any satisfaction at

his recovery, or to claim a recompense for his services. On further enquiry, he ascertained that the soldier's name was Martin Vaughan, and that he was in the garrison of Lille. On the following day he proceeded, accompanied by the Count, to seek out the man to whom his safety was ascribed, and found that he had been sent, on escort duty, a short distance from the town. The Count, thereupon, left directions for Martin Vaughan to present himself at his quarters on a certain evening. The soldier attended accordingly, and was ushered into the presence of the Count and Captain Vesey, the latter of whom felt inclined to distrust his own senses when he beheld Martin *Keogh,* whom he believed to have been, for more than two years, mouldering in a felon's grave. Suddenly, however, the idea occurred that a recognition might be irreparably injurious to the man who had recently rendered him such material service. He felt at once that Keogh's escape from the ignominious fate to which he had been doomed was like an interposition of providence, highly beneficial to both of them. He approached the man and briefly expressed his thanks for the care to which he ascribed his safety. He then tendered him twenty *louis d'or,* but the gift was at once respectfully declined. The soldier appeared greatly agitated, and exclaimed—" No, Captain Vesey, not a penny of your money will I ever touch again."

The Count remarked the expression, and observed— " Why, Vaughan, it would appear that you have met the captain before you took service with us."

" We have met," said the soldier; " he knows when and where; he will tell you what he knows, but he does not know all. Ye are two gentlemen on whose honor I can rely, and I shall tell you all on one condition."

"Excuse me," said the Count, "my curiosity is not so intense as to make me desirous of a confidence disagreeable either to Captain Vesey or to you. You have been a good soldier, in every respect, since you entered the regiment. I have known you only in that capacity. I have no wish to be informed on any previous transaction."

"And I pledge my hand and word," said Vesey, "that I shall never allude to you except as the man to whose humane exertions I am indebted for my life."

He extended his hand to the soldier, who respectfully pressed it between his own, saying—"Let it be so, I am fully satisfied." He saluted the Count and departed.

In about two months after an exchange of prisoners was effected. The Count and Vesey parted with mutual regret and assurances of lasting friendship. A few minutes before they parted, the Count mentioned that he had procured for Vaughan the grade of sergeant. Vaughan asked and was granted an opportunity of bidding the Captain a respectful farewell. The military operations of the English were for some time extensive and diversified; and during eleven years Vesey did not revisit Ireland. He had been in India and in America; and he again became a prisoner to the French in 1756, when the Duc de Richlieu captured Minorca. There he again met with the Count de St. Woostan. Their friendship was renewed, and Vesey, who had attained to the rank of colonel, obtained permission, upon parole, to visit Paris, whither the Count was proceeding with despatches. He casually enquired for Vaughan, and was informed by the Count that soon after their parting at Lille, Vaughan's brother, Sylvester, had arrived from Ireland, and joined the regiment. He was killed at the battle of Raucoux, where Martin was severely wounded, and had consequently become an inmate of the

Hotel des Invalides. There Colonel Vesey again saw the man, whose escape from an ignominious death had often occasioned perplexing conjectures to his prosecutor. The old sergeant evinced great pleasure at the Colonel's visit, attended him through the establishment, and having conducted him into one of the arbors, which the veterans of the Invalides have, from the very commencement of the institution, cultivated with peculiar care and taste, he offered the Colonel a seat under an agreeable shade, and requested him to listen to a narration of the escape which had been effected from Old Kilmainham. " I need not now, sir," he added, " ask any condition from you, for the man who arranged the affair is dead. No one can now be injured by the disclosure. I have bitterly mourned the disgraceful act that subjected me to capital punishment, which I only escaped by flying for ever from my native country, and which also led to the loss of my poor brother, whom I persuaded to join in it and some other similar deeds. God knows my heart. I would willingly make restitution of your property, but I shall never possess the means. It was a great consolation that I was able to do you a little service after Fontenoy, and I felt a certain happiness in receiving your forgiveness when we parted at Lille."

" My good friend," said the Colonel, " as to the affair at Castleknock, I would wish you never to mention it again. I have, however, a great curiosity to know how you managed to avoid the fate which, to say the truth, I thought you had undergone."

" We took the money, sir," said Martin, " and placed it in a strong canvas bag. We hid it in neither house, garden, nor field, but in a deep part of the river Liffey, below the Salmon Leap. There was a stout cord from the bag to a heavy weight, so that it might be easily caught by a drag.   Well, I was convicted and sentenced, and there were four others condemned at the same Commission, and we were all to be executed on the same day. One was a forger, and three were housebreakers.   We each occupied a separate cell in the condemned yard.   It was a horrible place, for I well recollect that on each side of the yard a full length figure of Death was painted,* holding in his skeleton hands a scythe and hour-glass ; so that wherever our eyes turned, we were reminded of our hapless condition and coming sufferings.   The gaoler came in two or three times daily, whilst our cells were open, and I soon remarked that he took very little notice of the others, but spoke pretty often to me.   On the fifth or sixth day after my sentence, I was in my cell, counting my days, and trying to count my hours ; making pictures in my despairing mind of the cart and the crowd, and cringing as if I already felt the slippery noose of the soaped halter closing round the creeping flesh of my neck ; thinking of the happy days of innocent childhood, and feeling some consolation in my misery that my brother had not been condemned ; that I left no wife or family, and that both my parents were dead, and spared the shame and sorrow of their son's public execution.   This was the state of my mind when the gaoler entered the cell.   He closed the door, and addressed some kind expressions to me, hoping that I was resigned to the great change that was impending, and enquiring if he could do anything for my comfort or consolation.   In a stout but low tone I replied, that I would rather get rid of the business without being

* This gratuitous cruelty did not cease when Old Kilmainham was taken down.   Similar disgusting figures have been seen by me, on the door and walls of the condemned yard, in the present county gaol.—F. T. P.

hanged at all. He closed the door, and sat down on the block-stool, and we remained silent for a few minutes; but there were looks passing between us ; we were reading each other's hearts. At length he said—'Have you the money ?'

"'It is safe, every guinea of it,' I replied 'but useless to me and to every one else, if I am to stay here for the few remaining days of my life. Moreover, I could not give it all, for there would be very little use in going out of the prison if I had not the means of going far and going fast ; but I have fifteen hundred pounds for a friend, who would be a real friend.'

"'Mr. Vesey is gone,' said the gaoler, 'we are perfectly secure from any observation or interference on his part; I am running a great risk, but I shall try the chance. I am, I admit, in great want of money. Give me fifteen hundred pounds, and I will allow your brother to pass through my rooms to the top of the prison, and to bring a rope ladder with him. He can descend into the yard, and there he will find a key in the door of your cell ; this can be done at twelve tomorrow night ; and you may be far away before nine the following morning. Your brother will be here to see you by-and-by, you can arrange with him, but there is no time to be lost.'

"'My brother' I replied, 'shall have nothing to do with the business, except to bring the money, I shall not cross the wall, I must go out by the door, I must be let out, or I stay until I am disposed of along with the rest.'

"'It is impossible,' said the gaoler.

"'It is not impossible,' I replied, 'but very easy, if you can get a little assistance. I must be sick, very sick ; fever, gaol fever, is to be my complaint ; I must die, and be sent out in a coffin.'

"'No,' said he, 'there must be a real corpse. I think it can be managed, but I cannot have more than a thousand pounds for myself, the remainder of the money must be divided between two other persons, on whose co-operation I feel certain that I can fully rely.'

"We agreed upon the plan, and for several days I was really sick, made so by artificial means—spirits, laudanum, tobacco, and other things were used in various ways. Half of the stipulated sum was brought by my brother, and paid to the gaoler in the condemned cell. The other men were removed to another part of the building. At length *I died,* you understand; and on that night a corpse was introduced into my cell by the gaoler himself. It was of my size, and was procured from the neighbouring burial ground of the Hospital fields, vulgarly termed *Bully's Acre;* but unlike the generality of such disinterments, it was to go back there again, and to be buried in my name. I was informed that there would be an inquest on me; but as I had died of putrid, spotted fever of the most infectious description, it was not likely that the coroner or the jury would view my body, unless at the greatest possible distance. I assisted the gaoler to arrange the supposed corpse of myself, placing the face to the wall, and then I was quietly let out upon the high road, after having paid the balance of the fifteen hundred pounds. My brother who had brought the money, was in waiting, but we soon separated. He thought it would prevent suspicion being raised if he attended the funeral of my substitute; and I set out on foot, taking the road to Wicklow, and stopping in the morning to have a little rest and refreshment at Loughlinstown. About the time of my funeral, I was passing Coolagad, near Delgany, and was alarmed by a pack of hounds crossing the road close to where I was walking. There were some riders following them whom I knew, but they were too much engaged in the sport to think about, or even to look at me. I proceeded by Wicklow and Arklow to Wexford, and there I got a passage to Jersey. From that island I was taken by a smuggler to St. Malo, on the supposition that I was extremely anxious to join the Irish Brigade. My life was now safe from the hangman, but I had much trouble and suffering to encounter. I was suspected of being a spy, although I could not speak a word of French; and the possession of some of your guineas was a great crime in the eyes of those who wished to get them for themselves. At Chartres I met a fellow-countryman, who was in Berwick's regiment, and at his instance I enlisted to get rid of the annoyance I was suffering, and to avoid the poverty which I saw approaching, and which was certain to overtake a stranger, whose only resource was military service. I took, on enlisting, the name of Vaughan, which was that of my mother's family. I have again to express my deep sorrow for the wrongful act I committed, and *I hope you will never regret that I was not hanged.*"

Colonel Vesey parted with Martin Keogh, *alias* Vaughan, in the kindest manner, and was soon after enabled to proceed to England. His military career was terminated by a wound at the capture of Quebec, in 1761, which incapacitated him for further service : he died at Bath in 1776. The Count de St. Woostan accompanied the gallant but much calumniated Lally-Tollendahl to India. He possessed his confidence, shared in his dangers and subsequent persecutions, but eventually, freed from every imputation, restored to the rank and emoluments of colonel, he died at

c

Amboise, in 1782.   His name was Alen, and he belonged
to a family which, located at St. Woolstans near Celbridge,
in the county of Kildare, occupied high position in Ireland
previous to the reign of Elizabeth, and from a collateral
branch of which the ducal Howards of Norfolk derive the
additional name of Fitzalen.

Martin Vaughan married, in 1758, a *blanchisseuse de fin,*
who had a comfortable dwelling and profitable business in
the *Rue de Bellechasse,* Paris.   His name disappears from
the register of the Invalides, in 1769.   His escape from Old
Kilmainham protracted his existence twenty-six years.   It
was effected by means which would not be practicable in
any prison of the British Empire at the present time.
Officials have become more respectable, and their integrity
is protected from temptation by the intervention of a vigilant superintending authority, unknown at the period to
which the foregoing narrative refers.   It will, in all probability, occur to the reader that the two persons whose
co-operation the gaoler considered as indispensable in
effecting the escape of Martin Keogh, were the coroner of
the county and the medical officer of the prison.   Such a
conclusion is almost inevitable.   Still, a similar project
could not now be accomplished by a similar combination.
There have been, however, some inquests held in the same
county (Dublin) which seriously compromised the coroner
of the time and the medical man habitually employed by
him, but none of them originated in a prison.   It is right
to state that they occurred anterior to the appointment of
the present coroners and of their respective immediate predecessors.   I shall recur to them in a subsequent page or
two, when I come to the narration of some extraordinary
incidents entirely within my personal knowledge and recol-

lection. As yet I have placed no female character prominently before my readers. I shall proceed to introduce
one ; and however I may distrust my own powers of description, I feel that the mere facts which I shall detail
will not prove uninteresting, especially as they refer to her
whom I may term the heroine of the story.

CHAPTER III.

MARY TUDOR.

LONGEVITY, although desired by almost all human beings, is a subject of contemplation to very few. We attach, in general, a greater interest to an aged tree or an antique building, than to a venerable individual whose life may connect with the present time the stirring period of the American war of Independence or the awful period of the French Revolution. It is, perhaps, better for ourselves that as we attain old age we should meet with respect and care, without being sought as close companions by our juniors: we thus become habituated to think more on those who have gone before us, and of our own approach to that solemn moment which is to quench the socket-glimmer of earthly existence. Nevertheless, we occasionally meet with some whose mental faculties have not yielded to the attacks of time, in proportion to the effects produced by his inexorable hand upon the corporeal frame, and whose society is sought by many who observe that they can, even in the years of senectitude, revert to their early days, and seek to enjoy the pleasures of memory by detailing to others the scenes through which they have passed, and the points of character they have noted. Such a person I can truly designate my father to have been. His frame was robust, and his general health very good, even after he had attained to fourscore years. Accident had rendered him lame, but his mind and memory were strong, and his disposition affable. Whilst he perfectly recollected the past, he evinced a warm interest in the present; and almost immediately after the opening of the Great Southern and Western Railway of Ireland, he sped from Dublin to Cork and back, merely to contrast the five hours' performance of the "Iron Horse" with the four days' journey of his early years. It was a great gratification to him to take a slow drive through Dublin, and recount to his companions, of whom I was generally one, the former appearance of places, and the habits and peculiarities of their occupiers; but no part of the city called forth his recollections more strongly than the locality of Christ Church Place. He never mentioned it by its present name; with him it continued "Skinner Row;" and it was no small pleasure to him to remark that the house in which he had lived and prospered at the beginning of the present century, was still remaining, whilst the entire of the opposite side of the "Row" had disappeared. He regretted the change even whilst he admitted the advantage of the alteration; but he could not refrain from reinstating in his imagination, and describing, the narrow-fronted houses within eighteen feet of the opposite dwellings, rising to a height which effectually precluded even half-an-hour's sunshine from reaching the thoroughfare. His mind reverted to the former tenants, jewellers, silversmiths, and booksellers, by which trades the "Row" had been monopolized; and it was more agreeable to him to recollect Dick Tudor, Tom Delancy, Jemmy Wilson, and many others, cleaning their windows and sweeping their shops, than to remark that such avocations, in the present day, had ceased to be incumbent on even the junior apprentices, and had devolved upon menial servants.

One evening he was enjoying the society of two or three convivial friends. He had taken a drive that day, accompanied by me, and had halted so long in Christ Church Place, that the hackney carmen might almost have suspected that he meditated an invasion of their stand. He enjoyed his drive and his dinner, and having attained to his second glass of whisky-punch, he commenced, at the instance of his companions, the narration of one of his " Skinner Row " reminiscences.

Dick Tudor was a goldsmith and jeweller. He had the reputation of being the wealthiest man in the locality. He neither lent nor borrowed. His intercourse with his neighbours was very limited. He was a widower, and had an only child, of whom he was excessively fond. His tastes were in his business; he had a love for his art, and would execute a beautiful design for a smaller comparative profit than would satisfy him for second-hand plate or mere repairs; but his affections excluded every other worldly object, and were concentrated in his daughter, Mary Tudor.

She was about eighteen years of age at the time to which the commencement of the narrative refers, and, although reared in a city, was as simple and unaffected in her manner as if her life had previously been passed on mountain heather or in mossy dell. She was a brunette of perfect features, and small but symmetrical figure. Her disposition appeared to be gay, and almost puerile, and none would suppose that in a trader's daughter, whose jocund smile and sparkling eyes seemed to seek and spread mirth around her, there was a latent intensity of feeling, and a determination of character, worthy of the noblest cause or of the highest lineage.

Skinner Row had its attachments, jealousies, and little

diplomacies as fully as ever they existed even in more important localities. In one respect, it possessed a material for civic intrigue greater than could be found in any other part of Dublin in the last century. The Row commanded, in the Common Council, one seat for the Stationers' Guild, and two for the Goldsmiths. As to those objects of ambition, there was a certain fixed understanding—there should be no division outside their own precincts, and the members chosen should be men of the Row. Amongst themselves, intrigues, insinuations, or open opposition might be freely practised; but once they had determined on the man to be supported, every vote should go to him. Dick Tudor and James Wilson were the goldsmiths chosen for the Common Council, and the distinction thus conferred excited great envy in the mind of of Tom Delancy, whose discontent was kept fully alive by his son, not on account of civic honours, but because young Christian Wilson had contrived to stand between him and the sun in the rays of which he wished to bask, namely, the eyes of pretty Mary Tudor.

Old Tudor and James Wilson were friends, not very intimate, but perhaps liking and respecting each other more on that account. Tudor's daughter and Christian Wilson were lovers, and the infrequency of their meetings only rendered their occasional interviews more delectable. The neighbours observed the attachment of the young people before their parents suspected its existence; but the moment Tudor perceived a preference evinced by his daughter for young Wilson, he sedulously endeavoured to prevent all future communications between them. He became suddenly anxious that Mary should visit some relatives in the County of Wexford, about whom he had for years expressed no interest. He thought change of air

would materially serve her health, although no other eye
could notice the slightest indication of illness, or even
delicacy of constitution.   Accompanied by an elderly
female attendant, she left Dublin by a conveyance termed
Good's Long Coach, which the proprietor, William Good,
advertised as the perfection of cheap and expeditious
travelling.   It left the Ram Inn, Aungier Street, Dublin,
on each Monday morning, at an early hour, so as to
ensure reaching Wicklow town on the succeeding night.
Tuesday saw the vehicle achieve a further progress to Gorey,
and on Wednesday evening it reached Wexford.   It returned to Dublin in the three succeeding days, and thus
enabled the public to have a cheap, safe, and comfortable
communication, to and fro, between two places about
ninety English miles asunder, within the short space of
six days.

Three or four weeks elapsed, and Tudor mentioned, in
answer to some kind enquiries, that Mary was enjoying
herself wonderfully at Kilmore, in the County of Wexford,
and that she had written him a very interesting description of the Saltee Islands, St. Patrick's Bridge, and the
Lady's Island.   She was very comfortable with a worthy
cousin and his wife, both arrived at an age which made
them appreciate a life of quietude.   They were very kind
to her, and they had no family or nearer relations than
himself and Mary.   Her visit was likely to lead to considerable advantages.   He would never have disclosed his
daughter's temporary residence if he had not believed
Kilmore to be as difficult of access to Christian Wilson as
Madeira or Malta would be to a gallant of the present
time.   The lover was a youth of very peculiar character—
clever and active, but rash and inconsiderate.   Having ascertained that the smacks which traded between Wexford

and Dublin, if favored by a fair wind, could make the run in a few hours, he determined on seeing Mary Tudor. His father had allowed him as a perquisite the profits arising from making "balloon guineas" into rings, and he had thereby acquired a few pounds, as it was a very prevalent custom for females of the humbler classes to invest a guinea in a ring, and carry their money on their fingers. Savings-banks were then unknown.

Christian informed his father that he wished to go, for a few days, to a friend in Drogheda, and obtained his consent. He left home in the evening, ostensibly to go by the mail, but he sojourned to Hoey's Court, and was seen there in company with some young men whose characters were unknown, or worse. They left Hoey's Court about ten o'clock, and Wilson betook himself to Sir John's Quay, and went out of the river in the smack "Selskar," of Wexford, on the night-tide. After midnight Dick Tudor's workshop was robbed; but the guilty parties did not all escape. Two were apprehended leaving the premises, and were recognized as having been seen in Christian Wilson's company in Hoey's Court for some time after his own father supposed him to have left Dublin for Drogheda. A letter was posted to the latter place, and, to old Wilson's astonishment, he received a reply that his son had not gone there. Where was he?

Whispered malice is most intense. Delancy and his son added assertion to suspicion, and revelled in the idea of a broken-hearted father, and a disgraced, degraded son, being forced by the awkward circumstances, magnified and industriously disseminated, to abandon, one, the coveted representation of the Goldsmiths' Guild, and the other, the pursuit in which all the affections of his heart and the energies of his mind were concentrated—the love of Mary Tudor.

In a few days Christian Wilson returned to Dublin. His father's reproaches were fierce and unmeasured, and became a perfect storm of rage when the young man refused to state where he had been, or for what purpose he had left home. Old Tudor aggravated the quarrel between the father and son, by accusing them of a design to entrap his daughter into a clandestine union, to which James Wilson replied that he would sooner transport his son than consent to his marriage with Tudor's daughter. The circumstances of the robbery were fully investigated. They did not directly inculpate Christian ; but enough appeared to sully his reputation, and to prove that he was not sufficiently guarded in his associations. Old Delancy expressed his good-natured regret that the son of one "Wainscot man"* should be strongly suspected of robbing another. Young Delancy, with affected benevolence, expressed his *sincere* gratification that Christian had not been *caught ;* and there were not wanting some kind-hearted individuals to convey his observations to the unhappy subject of them. The young men casually met in Christ Church yard ; an explanation was demanded ; and the demand was answered by the sneering remark, that the affair explained itself. Christian was maddened by his rival's taunts, and gave Delancy a fearful beating. A blow or fall produced concussion of the brain. The assailant had to fly ; and his father determined to send him, banished and unforgiven, to the West Indies, consigning him to the care of a relative who had been for several years in Barbadoes.

* In the old " Tholsel" or Guildhall of Dublin, members who had served the office of Sheriff, or who represented the Guild of Merchants, occupied the centre of the Council chamber. The members representing incorporated trades sat next the wainscot. They had the reputation of being the most independent members of the Corporation.

Mary Tudor received a letter written at Liverpool, and announcing the immediate departure of Christian Wilson for his tropical destination. In it he simply stated the circumstances which led to his expatriation, and renewed his vows to her of deep affection and fidelity. The young woman at once determined on departing from Kilmore; and on her arrival in Dublin placed Christian's letter in her father's hands. She insisted on the examination of the master and crew of the Selskar; and they proved that they dropped down the river with Christian on board, two hours before the time of the robbery. But this was not all. The guilty parties confessed that the young man was not with them, and accounted for having sought his society in Hoey's Court, for the purpose of eliciting some information as to Tudor's premises into which they were desirous of effecting an entrance. Young Delancy had recovered. Tudor and James Wilson had been reconciled; but Christian had sailed in the ship " Hyacinth," of Liverpool, and he must see Barbadoes before he can become aware of Mary's truth and her determined exertions to remove all aspersions from her lover's character.

The " Hyacinth " never reached her destined port. Her fate was conjectured, but was not ascertained, as it would be in the present time of superior arrangements in agency and communication. Her owners received their insurance as for a total loss, and James Wilson believed that his hapless son had been entombed in the ocean.

At the commencement of the war between England and her revolted colonies of North America, two commissioners were sent out, in the hope that differences might be reconciled and peace restored. The Earl of Carlisle and Mr. Eden, (afterwards Lord Auckland,) were proceeding on this mission in a frigate, and after having encountered very stormy weather, they fell in with a boat in which were several persons, reduced to the utmost extremity by hunger and fatigue. They were rescued, and recovered their strength by rest and nutrition. All, except one, were sailors, and they were, perhaps very summarily, added to the frigate's crew. The landsman was of a melancholy temperament, although young and naturally strong. He was, however, of an humble and unpresuming manner, which did not indicate vulgarity or ignorance. He expressed a desire to make himself useful, cleaned some watches for the officers, and kept the plate of their mess in proper order. Curiosity induced Lord Carlisle to accost him, and the communication resulted in several acts of kindness on the part of the nobleman, which were respectfully and gratefully, and perhaps it may be said, gracefully, received. His Lordship's interest in the poor shipwrecked fellow increased; and on their arrival in America, he obtained for his protegè, from Sir Henry Clinton, an ensigncy in the army.

Meanwhile Christian Wilson was forgotten in Skinner Row by all except one. They had "mourned him dead in his father's *house*." His family never adverted to his fate, for the subject was of painful recollection in more senses than one. But Mary Tudor, although she seldom spoke of Christian, would not admit that he was dead. Suitors for her hand were numerous, but to none would she give the slightest encouragement, and Delancy soon discovered that indifference was too mild a term to describe her feeling towards him. Some years had passed. Her father had attained complete senectitude, but was still sound in mind and hale in body. He lived happily with his daughter, who consulted his wishes on every subject, except his anxiety to see her married in comfort and respectability before he died. She had attained to her twenty-fifth or twenty-sixth year, and she was particularly intimate with the family of the person from whom this narrative is derived. In fact, it was her only intimacy, and in her intercourse with them she frequently avowed her conviction that the " lost one" would return.

One morning a note was received by my father, requesting him to call, as soon as possible, on the writer, at the Queen's Head Hotel in Bride Street. He repaired to the place appointed; and in consequence of what there occurred, he had interviews next morning with Richard Tudor and James Wilson, and prevailed on them to accompany him to Cork Hill, about 11.30 a.m., and there he pointed out to the astonished and delighted old men Captain Christian Wilson, of the 60th Regiment, marching his company to relieve the guard at Dublin Castle.

The tale concludes. The lovers met and were united. Old Tudor was rich; his closing years were happy. Wilson retired from the army after he had attained the rank of Major, and settled on a property in a southern county, where the descendants of him and Mary Tudor are living in independence and respectability.

This narrative has been closely criticised. It has been asked, Did the hero of the tale keep his very existence concealed so long, and why? Suspicions have been expressed that the lovers had some communication or correspondence. Whatever conjectures may be entertained, they need not be canvassed here. The reader may form his own opinion. Much was said on the subject, and something was even sung. The following verses are a portion of a lyric attributed to a Mr. Rooney, a basket-maker in Fishamble Street. The Tholsel guard, to the somnolent tendencies of which an allusion is made, were in number about a dozen. They were dressed in blue with orange facings, and armed with pole-axes. An alderman of the time sarcastically described them as " selected for their age and infirmities, and not required to be awake unless at their meals."

" Some folk averr'd a bird was heard
    To Mary's casement nigh ;
And from its throat there thrill'd the note,
    He 's coming by-and-by.

" Some said there came, with war-worn frame,
    A vet'ran grenadier,
Who spoke of one that led him on
    Through battle's fierce career.

" Some said between them both had been
    Of love notes not a few,
But this was clear, he did appear,
    And wed his maiden true.

" Through Skinner Row the toast must go,
    And our cheers reach Christ Church Yard,
Till its vaults profound send back the sound,
    To waken the Tholsel guard.

" Here 's to their health in peace and wealth ;
    May Death, that bold intruder,
A long while pause ere he lays his claws
    On such as MARY TUDOR."

CHAPTER IV.

THE BIRTH OF A WORD——A LETTER OF INTRODUC-TION——THE HONOR OF KNIGHTHOOD.

I HAVE mentioned in the narrative respecting Lonergan, that my father was a member of the corps of Dublin Volunteers, and that he was serjeant of the grenadier company. Many of his comrades were living within my memory, and I could name five or six who derived great gratification from reverting to the period when the citizen soldiers of Ireland were enrolled in thousands for the purpose of resisting an invasion which was threatened by the French. The reviews, parades, and convivial associations of the Volunteers afforded many agreeable recollections ; and I have heard from different narrators the same account of what may be termed the birth of a word which originated in Eustace Street, Dublin, upon the same day that ushered into this breathing world the oldest and highest of rank amongst the Irish nobility.* I indulge in a hope that my readers may consider the circumstances under which a word was added to our language as curious or interesting, especially when they are apprised that it was not taken from any other language, ancient or modern, and yet it has become ubiquitous.

* These expressions refer to the late Duke of Leinster, who has died since I wrote them.—F. T. P.

On the 21st of August, 1791, news had arrived in Dublin that Her Grace the Duchess of Leinster had given birth to a young Marquis of Kildare. To all ranks of society the intelligence was welcome, but especially to the Volunteers. The Duke was the general of that force in his province, but his own corps, of which he was colonel, was the Dublin one. Along with the announcement of the accouchement of the Duchess, came an intimation, that the corps would be expected at Carton on the happy occasion of the christening. The opportunity for paying a compliment to their commander was hailed by the citizen-soldiers with the utmost enthusiasm, and there was a numerous gathering of them, to learn the particulars and to consider their arrangements, at a tavern in Eustace Street, Dublin, kept by a person named Bennett, and known as "The Eagle." The evening had, as might be expected, a convivial termination. Several who had attained to high civic dignities were amongst those assembled; and there was also present Richard Daly, the proprietor and manager of the Smock Alley theatre, who had an extraordinary propensity for making wagers in reference to incidental matters, however unimportant. In the course of the evening some casual opinions were expressed on the histrionic powers of an actor named Sparkes, who was then drawing immense houses in Daly's theatre. One of the Volunteers, named Delahoyde, expressed his surprise that such crowds should run after Sparkes, and remarked that his popularity was more the result of fashionable caprice than of histrionic merits. "He is, in my opinion," added the speaker, "just what the French would term *un fagotin.*" "And what is the exact meaning of that word?" asked Alderman Moncrieffe. "There is, perhaps, no one word in the English language which conveys its meaning exactly," said the interrogated party. " If I could give an English word to signify a low, vulgar mountebank, I should not have employed the French term." "Then," observed Daly, " why do you not make a word and send it into circulation ? You should not feel aware that our language was deficient in expression without being charitable enough to supply its want, especially as it costs nothing to make a word." " But," rejoined the other, " how could I ensure the reception of a word into general use ? It might be characterized as slang, or remain unnoticed and unadopted ; it might be as difficult to obtain currency for a word, or more so, than it was to pass Wood's halfpence."

" Dick," said Alderman Moncrieffe, " suppose you try your own hand, as you think the matter so easy. I would leave it to your own ingenuity, but I fear you will find it very difficult to induce the public to take your word. If they took some of your *assurance* it might be an advantage ; you have plenty to spare."

" I thank you, Alderman," replied Daly. "I did not suppose that so much wit could come from the neighbourhood of the Tholsel."

" Oh !" said Moncrieffe, " it has strayed up to us from the theatre, where it has lately become scarce. But, Dick, why have you chatted so long on this and other subjects this evening without offering a single wager ? Come now, start a bet."

" I shall not use a phrase or make a word," said Daly, " in disparagement of Sparkes, from whom I have derived much pleasure and profit ; but I shall bet you twenty guineas, and I propose our friend and captain, who is also your brother alderman, I propose John Carleton as the judge or arbitrator between us, that within forty-eight hours

D

there shall be a word in the mouths of the Dublin public, of all classes and sexes, young and old ; and also that within a week, the same public shall attach a definite and generally adopted meaning to that word, without any suggestion or explanation from me. I also undertake, as essential to the wager, that my word shall be altogether new and unconnected with any derivation from another language, ancient or modern. Now, Alderman, what say you to taking my word or winning my money ?"

" I shall not take your word, Dick, but I propose winning some of your money. I shall put five guineas in the wager, provided the present company take up the balance, and let the winnings be spent on the evening of the first parade day after our return from the christening of the young Marquis of Kildare."

The company were joyous, and the proposal of the appropriation of the proceeds to festivity induced a speedy acceptance of the remaining liability. The terms were reduced to writing, and deposited with Carleton. Daly looked at his watch and took his departure. It happened to be a Saturday evening, and he reached the theatre a short time before the termination of the performance. He immediately procured some lumps of chalk, and a dozen or two of cards. Upon each of the cards he wrote a word. It was short and distinct, and at the fall of the curtain he required the attendance of the call-boys, scene-shifters, and other inferior employées of the concern. To each of them he gave a card and a piece of chalk, and directed them to perambulate the city until daybreak, chalking the word upon the doors and shutters of the houses. His directions were diligently obeyed, and on the Sunday morning the doors of shops, warehouses, and even private dwellings appeared to have one word conspicuously chalked on them. The timid were alarmed, lest it indicated some unlawful or hostile intention, but these apprehensions were dissipated by the fact of its universal appearance. One, as he issued from his dwelling, conceived that it was meant for a nick-name for him; but he immediately changed his opinion on seeing it on his neighbour's premises also. It could not be political, for all parties were treated the same way. It was manifestly not a mark on any religious persuasion, for all denominations were chalked alike. It was not belonging to any known language, nor could a word of any meaning be formed by the transposition of its letters. Still the universality of its appearance excited the curiosity of all, and formed a subject for public conjecture and general conversation. After a few days the general conclusion was, that the word was a hoax, a trick, a humbug, a joke. However, it was not forgotten. The parties to the wager, which Dick Daly was adjudged to have won, have all disappeared, but I have heard several of them narrate the particulars as I have stated them. The hands by which the word was chalked have all mouldered into clay, but the term that owed its birth to the Eustace Street wager has become almost ubiquitous. It is heard in India, Australia, the United States, Canada, or the Cape; in fact, wherever the English language is spoken. The word is QUIZ.

It may not be inopportune to mention here that I related the foregoing account of the origin of the word "quiz" one day in, I think, the year 1832, at the table of Cornelius Lyne, the facetious and convivial barrister of the Munster Circuit, where he was designated, in contradistinction to the old Irish chieftain, " Con of the hundred *battles*," " Con of the hundred *bottles*." Amongst the guests was a gentleman named Montgomery, who resided in Belfast. On hearing my story, he remarked that a quiz has occasionally produced a reality. He proceeded to tell us that when James Madison was President of the United States, a young man connected with one of the most eminent houses in Belfast, thought fit to make an American tour. Having crossed the Atlantic, he passed upwards of eighteen months to his perfect satisfaction. On his return he was greatly pestered by one of his fellow-townsmen, a pushing, plausible, self-sufficient kind of fellow, for letters of introduction to some American friends, the applicant declaring his intention of visiting all the principal cities of the Union. At length the solicited party replied to an urgent entreaty, by declaring that there was no one with whom he felt himself warranted to take such a liberty except his friend Madison. "The President!" exclaimed the importunate teaser; "why it would be invaluable." Acceding to his request, a letter was written commencing with "My dear Mr. Madison," and conveying the assurance, that the attentions which the writer had received would never be forgotten, and that the recollection of such kindness emboldened him to introduce a friend, in the hope that he would be received with even a portion of that urbanity which had been experienced so agreeably, and remembered so gratefully, by his ever faithful and obliged, &c., &c. The traveller departed, and a considerable time elapsed before he reappeared in Belfast. When he returned, his first visit was to the author of the valuable introduction. "My dear friend," said he, " I presented your letter at a public reception. The President was more than polite, he was extremely cordial. I was invited to several delightful parties, and received the utmost attention. It was, however, very extraordinary, that when I called to pay my farewell visit, he asked me several questions in reference to your personal appearance, remarking that you had lapsed from his recollection." This was not so very surprising, for the President had never seen the man whose letter of introduction for the other had been a thorough quiz. At the conclusion of the anecdote which my narrative had elicited from Mr. Montgomery, Tom Moylan, Mr. Lyne's nephew, contributed another. He remarked that the Belfast man had only quizzed a President, but a Dublin man had completely humbugged a king. When George the Fourth was reigning, a Dublin medical doctor wrote a book. He had a copy splendidly bound for presentation, and then went to London, to the royal levee, where he handed a card to the lord-in-waiting, on which his name appeared as attending to present his work on a certain professional subject, *and to receive the honor of knighthood.* The lord-in-waiting thought that all was right; the king thought so, too. The Dublin doctor knelt down, the king took a sword, gave him the slap of dignity, and bade him arise Sir Thomas ———. After the levee, and when the newspapers had published the knight-hood as one of the incidents of the day, there were some enquiries about the recipient of the distinction. Who had recommended him? Of what minister was he the pro-tegè? But they were all too late, the knighthood had been conferred. People could only laugh. Canning was reported to have said, that he supposed the doctor claimed the honor by *prescription.* Although I was not personally acquainted with the medical knight who was the subject of Tom Moylan's anecdote, I have a perfect recollection of him for several years before he was dubbed a "Sir." He resided in St. Peter's parish, Dublin, and was very prominent in the old agitation times antecedent to Catholic Emancipation. At the vestries there could not be a rate or cess proposed to which he had not an amendment or direct negative to offer. On one occasion, at a very crowded parochial meeting, he complained to Archdeacon Torrens, who was presiding, that the vestry-room was too limited a place for such an important discussion as that in which they were engaged. " I move, reverend sir," said he, "that we adjourn *to the churchyard.*" " My dear doctor, replied the archdeacon, very quaintly, " you will have us there time enough."

CHAPTER V.

A MILLIONAIRE.

I SHALL revert to old Skinner Row in reference to the career of an individual which may be said to have commenced there about the year 1782. The incidents which I shall detail are not of an amatory or very sentimental nature, but nevertheless, truly extraordinary. To a Dublin, or even an Irish reader, it is unnecessary to offer an assurance of their truth, or to mention the individual's name. Only one error in reference to him has had currency, and that to a very limited extent. It arose, in all probability, from envy or malice, and consisted in describing him as a person of very imperfect education, of plebeian manners and disposition, and of almost menial avocations. He might have been truly described as well-informed, unaffectedly courteous, unobtrusive of his own opinions, and tolerant of the opinions of others, whilst his business transactions were marked by diligence, integrity, and intelligence. The proprietor of a very extensive establishment in a central situation in Dublin, where bookselling and auctions of libraries were carried on, had advertised for an assistant; and the situation attracted the attention of many competitors, of whom the individual alluded to was one. He was young and active, and sought a personal interview with Mr. V. the advertiser. He was

informed that the latter had gone up to Skinner Row, to my
father's house, where he would be engaged for upwards of
an hour. The applicant hurried off to the narrow, crowded,
and inconvenient locality. The footway was dispropor-
tionally raised above the carriage road, and at the very door
of the house to which he was going, he accidentally slipped
and fell. In a disabled condition, he was raised and carried in, and it was ascertained that his ankle was dislocated.
His sufferings excited great sympathy. He was conveyed
to a bedroom, and surgical aid was procured. Mr. V.
manifested great interest in the young man, and came
frequently to see him. After several weeks elapsed his
cure was effected, and the situation which he sought was
given to him. He expressed the deepest gratitude to my
father for the kindness he had experienced, and the acquaintance which commenced in the painful accident referred to, ripened ultimately into a very close intimacy.
He gained the confidence of Mr. V., who conferred many
marks of his esteem, and on the retirement of that gentleman from business, he became, to a great extent, his
successor. All his undertakings prospered, and he acquired
the reputation of being extremely wealthy. A rúmor
was circulated that, between the leaves of some books
which he had purchased, he had found several bank notes
of considerable value, but that report was groundless. In
addition to extensive bookselling, he had formed a connection with the house of Bish and Co., of Cornhill, by which
he was enabled to do a profitable business in bills on
London amongst the Dublin traders, for at that time the
facilities of letters of credit were very little known. He
also dealt largely in the tickets and shares of the State
Lotteries which, three or four times in the year, stimulated
the community into legalized gambling. One evening in

the year 1794, my father had occasion to call upon him, and found him unusually dissatisfied. He said that Bish's people had made a great mistake in sending him several whole tickets instead of quarters, eighths, or sixteenths, and that three tickets had been left on his hands, involving a loss of sixty pounds. There was not sufficient time to communicate with London before the drawing day, and he could only warn them against committing a similar error on the next occasion. However, in about a week after, my father ascertained that the mistake had eventuated in one of the tickets turning out a prize for twenty thousand pounds. Bish was no longer censured by the man whose wealth, previously considerable, had received a great and unexpected augmentation. The writer of fiction would hesitate before he would adopt a young man lying on the flagway of a city in which he was a complete stranger, with a dislocated ankle, as the material for a future *millionaire*. The person to whom this narrative refers was not English, Irish, or Scotch. He was a Manxman, who left his native island to seek in Dublin, what he most completely found, a fortune. He died a member of Parliament for an Irish county. Three of his sons attained to similar positions, and one of them was elevated to the House of Peers. Their positions were honorably and worthily acquired.

CHAPTER VI.

THE SHIP STREET DIAMOND——SECOND-HAND PLATE
——THE SILVER SLAB——LAW'S WINDOW——OLD
NEWGATE.

I HAVE already mentioned that old Skinner Row contained a considerable number of establishments belonging to goldsmiths and jewellers. Pre-eminent amongst them was one kept, in the early part of the present century, by Matthew West, who realised an ample fortune there, and attained to high civic distinctions in Dublin. His concern was celebrated for an extensive assortment of jewelry, and for the tasteful and correct execution of orders specially relative to the setting of precious stones. When such were brought to be cleaned, arranged, or set, the owner was required to state the value which he attached to the property, and to sign such statement on the back of the receipt given for the articles. Mr. West gave considerable employment, especially in gem-setting, to a man named Delandre, who occupied the upper part of a house in Great Ship Street, in front of the ground on which the church of St. Michael le Pole formerly stood, and over the yard of which the windows of his working-room opened. A narrow passage led from the street under the house to a building in the rere, and a high wall separated this passage from the old cemetery. The top of the wall

was thickly studded with broken glass, to prevent tres-
passes. In the year 1811, a gentleman called on Mr.
West, and produced a diamond to which he attached considerable value, and which he wished to have set in a
peculiar style. His order was taken, and a receipt was
given for the stone, with an endorsement of its value at
£950. Delandre was sent for, and received the diamond,
with directions for the setting, and with an injunction to
be expeditious. He took it to his work-room, and, the
weather being very warm, the window close to his bench
had been opened. He was using heavy pressure of the
diamond against the material in which it was to be set,
when either the tool or the gem slipped, and the latter
flew out of the opened window. Instantly alarming his
family, he watched the passage and the yard until means
were adopted to prevent the entrance of any strangers.
Then the passage was swept, and the sweepings were
sifted. The surface of the old cemetery, for a considerable
space, was similarly treated, the top of the wall was
brushed carefully, and a tombstone in which a fissure was
observed was raised and examined; but all the searching
was fruitless. Finally, Delandre had to betake himself to
Mr. West, and communicate the disastrous loss of the
valuable jewel. Extraordinary as was the statement, Mr.
West did not discredit the workman, in whose probity he
placed great confidence. He undertook to afford constant
employment to Delandre and to his son, but stipulated that
an insurance should be effected on the life of the former,
and that weekly deductions should be made from their
earnings, so as to provide for the premium on the insurance policy and form a reserve for the value of the
diamond. Delandre scrupulously observed his engage-
ments. He had full employment from West, and although

he was working, as he termed it, "for a dead horse," he kept his hands busy and his heart light. Each year lessened his liabilities, and at length, having paid for the diamond, he received an assignment of the policy of insurance, for the ultimate benefit of his family. He had grown old and rather feeble, but still, in conjunction with his son, attended industriously to his trade. Mr. West had died, and I, who had been a schoolboy when the diamond was lost, had become a magistrate of the Head Police Court of Dublin. In my younger days I had often heard of the Ship Street diamond, and the various accounts of its loss were occasionally exaggerated immensely in reference to its size and value. In 1842 some much needed repairs were in progress at the rere of Delandre's dwelling. Whitewashing and plastering were intended, and the top of the wall between the yard and passage was to be re-glassed. Old Delandre had gone out to buy some provisions, and on his return he was accosted by one of the workmen who had been removing the glass from the wall, and who showed him a *curosity* which he had found. Delandre did not require a second look to satisfy himself that it was the long-lost gem. Amongst the glass which had been on the wall there was the neck of a pint bottle, which had been placed in the plaster with the mouth downwards, and it had formed the trap in which the diamond had been caught on falling from the window. Delandre gave the finder a liberal reward; but with a laudable anxiety to remove all suspicion of a sinister nature from himself, he had the discovery of the diamond made the subject of a solemn declaration, which the finder subscribed before me in the Head Police Court. The loss of the gem had been eventually highly advantageous to the man, by whom it was at first very naturally considered a great calamity. It had induced him to adopt a life of strict economy and industry, which easier circumstances would not have suggested or enforced.

SECOND-HAND PLATE.

The same Mr. West to whom the last incident referred had a handsome private residence in Harcourt Street, and he was known habitually to place an unlimited confidence in the care and discretion of his wife, to leave large sums in her custody, and to approve of or acquiesce in the investments to which she might apply such moneys. Her management fully justified his confidence, and he made no secret of the course he had adopted or of the satisfactory results it produced. In 1817 he had arrived one morning in Skinner Row, when a livery servant, of very stylish appearance, entered and inquired, " Had Captain Wilson been there ?" Mr. West replied that " he had not the pleasure of knowing Captain Wilson ;" and then the servant stated, that " his master, Captain Marmaduke Wilson, intended to purchase some plate, and had ordered him to go to Mr. West's, and await his arrival there." He added, " He is a fine-looking man, but he has lost his right arm at Waterloo. I have to deliver a message in Dame Street. You will easily know him when he comes ; and please to tell him that I shall be back in about ten minutes." The servant departed, and very soon after his master made his appearance. A complete *militaire,* he displayed moustaches, a Waterloo ribbon, and a frogged frock-coat; but the right sleeve was empty from the elbow, and the cuff was looped up to the breast. He inquired for the servant, and seemed a little dissatisfied at the fellow's absence. He then proceeded to inform Mr. West that he was about to fix his residence on a property which he held in the county of Monaghan, and that he wished to unite economy with respectability in his domestic arrangements. He had heard that Mr. West's stock of second-hand plate was very ample, and wished to purchase some on which the crestings could be obliterated and the Wilson crest substituted, producing at the same time a silver snuff-box, on which a crest was engraved, with the initials of Marmaduke Wilson beneath it. The servant had returned, and accompanied his master through the warerooms, conducted by the proprietor, who succeeded in displaying tea services, salvers, &c., which met with Captain Wilson's approval, provided the prices were lower. The demands were reduced considerably, as the customer urged that it was a dealing for " cash down." The charges amounted to one hundred and forty pounds, when the Captain said " he would not go any further for the present," and requested Mr. West to have the plate packed in a basket which the servant had brought, in order that Mrs. Wilson might see the articles before the crests were altered. The silver was directed to be treated as he desired, and he then turned to Mr. West and said, " You must be my amanuensis, and write the order to Mrs. Wilson for the cash. I shall send my man for the money, and when he brings it, you will let him have the basket." Mr. West took the pen, and wrote, at the Captain's dictation—

" DEAR MARIA,
        " I have bought some second-hand plate, of which, I think, you will approve. Send me, by bearer, £140."

He added—" Just put my initials, M. W. Is it not very curious, Mr. West, that our initials are the same?"

He then took the pen in his left hand, and made a rough kind of small semicircle in the left-hand corner, which he designated his private mark. "Now," said he to the servant, "make all haste to your mistress, get the money, and fetch it here. I shall wait until you return, for you have not far to go." The servant departed, and the Captain remained for about twenty minutes, and seemed very impatient at the fellow's delay. He expressed an opinion that perhaps his wife had gone out, and said that he would take a car and see what caused the delay, adding, "When he brings you the cash you can let him have the hamper." The Captain then departed. The servant did not come for the plate, and it remained packed and ready for delivery on the arrival of the purchase money. Late in the afternoon Mr. West went home, and having dined, was asked by his wife "What second-hand plate was it that you bought to-day?" "I bought none," he replied, "but I sold some, and it was to have been taken away at once, but I suppose it will be sent for to-morrow." "And why," enquired Mrs. West, "did you send to me for one hundred and forty pounds? Here is your note, which a servant in livery brought, and I gave him the money."

The swindle was complete. The basket was never called for, nor could the defrauded party ever obtain any trace of the Waterloo Captain or of his livery servant. The reader need not suppose that the veteran delinquent was minus an arm. He was "made up" for the part which he was to play in the deliberate and deeply-planned villainy, and in all probability he had both his hands in full use, to take off his moustache and frogged coat in a few minutes after leaving Mr. West's premises. The transaction excited much interest and some merriment. It afforded a subject for one of Burke Bethel's jokes. He said that whether the captain reappeared or not, he could never be designated otherwise than as *off-handed* in his dealings with Mr. West.

THE SILVER SLAB.

There was another Dublin establishment in the gold, silver, and jewelry trade, and also belonging to a Mr. West. It was in Capel Street. I may mention an incident connected with it of a very extraordinary nature. There were mills at Chapelizod, near Dublin, kept by a Mr. M'Garry, in which he had very powerful machinery for rolling metals. He was frequently employed to roll silver for Mr. West. In the year 1829, a silver slab, valued at £27, was delivered to his carrier at Capel Street, and the usual receipt was given for it. The slab was to be rolled into a silver sheet; but when the vehicle in which it had been placed arrived at Chapelizod, the article was not to be found. In appearance it was not bright, having lain in store for some time after being cast. Advertisements and enquiries failed to discover it, and Mr. M'Garry paid its value to the owner. In 1845, it was brought to a silversmith named Chapman, on Essex Quay, and offered for sale. Chapman stopped the article, and gave the bearer of it into custody. On an investigation before me, it appeared that a shoemaker who lived in Leixlip had found it on the road and taken it home with him. He never suspected that it was silver. He considered it to be pewter or zinc, and it was used for the purposes of a lapstone for sixteen years. How the person in whose possession it was found had ascertained its real quality did not appear, but he had purchased it from the shoemaker for half-a-crown. West's and M'Garry's books coincided as to the nature of the article, its value, and the time of its loss.

The old slab was adjudged to M'Garry, who at once sold it to Chapman for the price he offered, £22. The shoemaker expressed deep, and certainly sincere, regret that he had never suspected the real value of his lapstone. His only consolation was, that the roguish fellow who induced him to sell it for half-a-crown, lost two shillings and sixpence by the bargain.

LAW'S WINDOW.

Whilst shops profusely stocked with articles of the precious metals and with costly jewels attract affluent and even extravagant customers, they also afford immense temptations to thieves and swindlers. No establishment in Dublin was superior in any respect to that in Sackville Street belonging to Mr. Law. On each side of the entrance there was a window, consisting of a single sheet of glass, inside of which a most magnificent display of costly plate, gems, and watches tacitly demanded and obtained the admiration of all spectators. In the year 1847, and in the afternoon of a pleasant May day, an elderly gentleman stood at the window next the corner of Eden Quay, and gazed with delight on the various splendid and tasteful productions inside. He had an umbrella, which he carried beneath his arm in a horizontal position, and with the ferule end unluckily too near the costly sheet of glass. A young fellow came rapidly running along the footway, and violently jostled the respectable admirer of the splendid contents of the window. The glass was smashed by the point of the umbrella, and the mischief resulting from the collision only imparted greater celerity to the jostler's movements. He fled down Eden Quay, and was almost instantly out of sight. Mr. Law was in his shop, and along with some of his assistants seized on

E

the proprietor of the intruding umbrella.   The old gentleman demurred to the imputed liability, and ascribed all the mischief to the ruffian who had rushed against him.   Law was persistent, and demanded nine pounds for his fractured glass.   He threatened to give the old gentleman in charge to the police.   The latter became very indignant and excited, used extremely strong language, and even applied opprobrious epithets to those by whom he was detained. He said that he was a stranger, just arrived from England, to transact some affairs of importance connected with the purchase of extensive properties in the west of Ireland. He warned Law that he would bring an action, and look for ample damages, if he were not permitted to depart. He stated his name to be James Ridley, and that his residence was in Lincoln's Inn Fields, London.   Finding that Law was about to send for a constable, he produced a Bank of England note for £100, and told the "obdurate scoundrel" to take the cost of his window out of that, but *at his peril.*   Law disregarded the threat, deducted nine pounds, and gave £91 to Mr. Ridley, who departed, vowing vengeance.   However, no proceedings were instituted, and subsequent enquiries after James Ridley in Lincoln's Inn Fields resulted in no such person being known there. *The £100 note was a forgery.*

OLD NEWGATE.

Towards the close of the last century, a gaol for the city of Dublin was built, and its appearance had a great tendency to deter any person from incurring the liability of becoming an inmate.   Its soot begrimed-walls and rusty portal completely falsified its designation of Newgate, and its front constituted a considerable portion of a locality, the aspect of which suggested no idea of verdure, although

it was called Green Street. It was a place replete with
fatal memories, very few of which are worthy of being
evoked, and it has been completely taken down. The sons
of the gentleman who was governor more than fifty years
ago were my schoolmates, and my associations with them
made me acquainted with some incidents which may be
worthy of narration. When Oliver Bond was under sentence of death for treason; and whilst there was the
strongest probability that the law would take its course, he
was permitted, during the day-time, to occupy an upper
apartment, the door of which was partly of glass. Mrs.
Bond was as much with him as the rules of the prison
allowed, and was sitting in the room on the day when Mr.
Michael William Byrne was executed as a united Irishman.
The fatal procession had to pass close by the door of
Bond's apartment; and as it approached, Mr. Byrne remarked to the sheriff, that Mrs. Bond would be greatly
shocked by seeing a person pass to that scaffold on which
her husband expected to suffer. Mr. Byrne then suggested
that they should stoop and creep noiselessly by the door, so
as to escape her observation. His wish was complied
with, and on reaching the drop, he turned to the sheriff,
and remarked, with an air of great satisfaction, "we
managed that extremely well." This spontaneous solicitude to spare the feelings of an afflicted female, will aptly
class with that of the gallant Count Dillon, who was one
of the earliest victims of the Reign of Terror in France, and
who, when he arrived at the guillotine, was requested by a
female fellow-sufferer, to precede her, upon which the
preux chevalier saluted her with courtly grace, and stepped
forward, saying, "anything to oblige a lady."

In one of the back yards of Newgate, to the right of the
entrance, was the place of confinement for the condemned,

the walls of which exhibited initials, sometimes entire names of unhappy occupants. One, who suffered the extreme penalty of the law nearly sixty years ago, for forging notes of the Bank of Ireland, pencilled the following lines on the door of his cell :—

> "Unhappy wretch, whom Justice calls
> To bide your doom within these walls,
> Know that to thee this gloomy cell
> May prove, perhaps, the porch of Hell.
> Thy crimes confest, thy sins forgiven,
> Mysterious change ! it leads to Heaven."

It is to be hoped that the soul of the poor prisoner experienced the " mysterious change " which his untimely fate led him so fully to appreciate.

CHAPTER VII.

GONNE'S WATCH.

IN the year 1810 a manufacturing goldsmith of high respectability, named Gonne, lived in Crow Street, Dublin. His establishment was noted for the superior execution of chased work, especially in watch cases, and he had occasionally extensive orders from the house of Roskill, of Liverpool, the reputation of which for watches and chronometers, was then, as it is still, extremely high. Mr. Gonne indulged himself in the purchase of a splendid gold watch of Roskill's best make, and prided himself greatly on the possession of an article not to be surpassed either in exquisite ornamentation or accuracy of movement. He was fond of pedestrian excursions, and his hours of relaxation were frequently devoted to a ramble along the low road to Lucan, which is certainly not inferior in picturesque scenery, to any other of the many beautiful localities in the vicinity of Dublin; but on one night Mr. Gonne came home greatly disgusted with his promenade, and avowing a determination never again to set foot on *that nasty road*. He did not bring home his beautiful watch, and it transpired that a man, of small stature, had disturbed an agreeable revery by requesting to be accommodated with whatsoever money Mr. Gonne had in his possession, and that he also expressed great admiration of his

watch and insisted on the immediate delivery of that article.
The propinquity of a pistol to Mr. Gonne's breast, induced
a speedy compliance with the disagreeable demand.   On
his arrival in Dublin, Gonne declared that he had been
robbed by *a little tailor*.   He stated that the fellow's features were concealed by a veil, and that as soon as he got
the watch and a small sum of money into his possession,
he managed to ascend the wall of Woodlands demesne
with surprising agility, and on it he seated himself *cross-
legged*.   He then addressed the victim of his depredation
by name, and assured him that his watch should be safely
kept, and that an opportunity should be afforded for re-
deeming it for ten pounds.   Gonne apprised the authorities
of the outrage which he had suffered.   He declared that
he never, to his knowledge, beheld the robber before ; that
he did not recognise his voice, but felt satisfied that he was
a tailor, from the manner in which he sat on the wall.   An
experienced peace-officer who heard the description, agreed
with Gonne that the delinquent was a tailor, and added
that he knew the man.   It appeared that there was a little
knight of the thimble, of most remarkable activity, named
Flood ; he was of dissipated habits, and was known at the
racket-court in John's Lane, where his play was most
astonishing.   He rarely missed a ball, and none would encounter him in a match of rackets, unless at very great
odds.   Flood was sought for, but was not forthcoming.
Several of the provincial towns were searched in vain, and
it was supposed that he had left the country, when he was
apprehended, almost in the act of committing a highway
robbery on the Rock-road, which at that time constituted
a portion of the City of Dublin.   His haunts were discovered and searched, and several articles of value, supposed
to have been acquired by highway robbery, were found.

There was a case quite sufficient for the conviction of Flood in the affair for which he was apprehended; but it was deemed expedient to investigate several other charges, and amongst them the robbery of Mr. Gonne, who minutely detailed all the circumstances of his disagreeable adventure on the Lucan Road, but he could not identify the prisoner. He was then directed by the divisional magistrate of police, before whom the case was pending, to pass round to the rere of the bench and view a number of watches which were in a drawer, of which the magistrate had the key. His watch was not amongst them. Flood was committed for trial, and sent to Newgate on two other charges, but the robbery of Mr. Gonne was not considered one on which an indictment could be sustained.

At the period to which this narrative refers, there was in Ireland a Lord Lieutenant belonging to the highest rank of nobility. His tastes and amusements were rather unlike those of his successors. His personal undertaking was quite sufficient for the disposal of three or four bottles of claret after dinner. He was so good a judge of whisky-punch as to impart to Kinahan's LL its peculiar designation and much of its popularity amongst " choice spirits." He dined at Donnybrook fair, *upstairs in a tent,** visited John's Well in its pattern days, took oyster suppers at " Queen Casey's " cellar in Britain Street, patronized an occasional cockle party at Dollymount, superintended

---

* The proprietor of this tent was a person named Cheevers. Having received an intimation, a few days before the fair, that the Lord Lieutenant would, with a select party, dine in his tent, he had it constructed with a lofting or first-floor, and a flight of steps, by which the Viceregal party ascended to their repast. On the succeeding days, whilst the fair lasted, the elevated apartment which had been honored by his Excellency was crowded to excess, and Cheevers received an ample remuneration for his very original project.

matches of single-stick in the riding school, witnessed
what was then termed the "Royal Sport of Cock-fighting"
in Clarendon Street; and his fingers were no strangers to
"the gloves." But his favorite amusement was harmless
and graceful. He played rackets frequently in John's
Lane, and took great pleasure in witnessing a match well
contested by first-rate players. At the time of Flood's
detection, his Excellency was making a tour through the
south of Ireland, and after an interval of a few weeks, he
returned to Dublin, to receive some English visitors of
distinguished position and convivial tendencies. Amongst
them was Lord Sydney Osborne, who prided himself upon
his skill at rackets, and who on the day of his arrival
stated at the viceregal table, that he was open to play
"any man in the world" for a thousand guineas. His
Excellency immediately took up the wager, and engaged
to find a successful competitor for his noble guest. It
was stipulated that the match should be played within
three weeks, at the racket-court of the Kildare Street Club.
On the following morning the Lord Lieutenant proceeded
to John's Lane, and apprised the marker of the racket-
court that he wished to find a little fellow whom he had
frequently seen there, and whom he described as the most
expert player that had ever come under his observation, as
one who had distanced all his antagonists, but he had
forgotten his name.

"My Lord," replied the marker, "I think your Excellency means Flood."

"Yes, yes, I now recollect the name; I want him particularly, for I have wagered a large sum on a match between him and an English gentleman, and if he wins, I
shall reward him amply."

"Murder! murder!" exclaimed the marker, "your Grace

must lose. Flood can't play your match, *he is to be hung on Saturday.* He played rackets well, but he played some queer tricks, too. He used to go looking for watches and purses on the roads outside Dublin, and he was caught at last, just near Merrion churchyard. Baron George tried him, and he was found guilty. The judge told him to expect no mercy, so he is to die at Newgate on Saturday."

" 'Tis a d———d business," said his Excellency.

" Indeed it's likely to end that way," replied the marker, "for he was rather loosely conducted, and now he has but a very short time to make his soul."

His Excellency departed greatly disconcerted; he felt that he had been too hasty in his wager. His thousand guineas appeared to be hopelessly gone, and he could not bear to think how Lord Sydney Osborne would chuckle at a walk over. He dined that day in Stephen's Green with his very intimate friend, Sir Hercules Langrishe, to whom he took an opportunity of communicating his unpleasant predicament. To his great surprise, Sir Hercules did not appear to think that there was much difficulty in the matter, and he even intimated his willingness to back Flood for a hundred or two. " There is no danger," observed the baronet, " of a change of ministry; you will be Lord Lieutenant for some years; so the sooner you give Flood a pardon, and set him to practise for the match, the better chance for your wager."

" Could there be a memorial got up in his favor?" suggested his Excellency.

" It would not be advisable," replied Sir Hercules; " it would make the affair a public topic. No, that would not do; just send over a pardon to-morrow; let Flood come to me. I shall procure liberty for the fellow to practise at the Shelbourne Barracks, and he also can get into the court at the club at early hours, as it is there that the match is to be played."

It was soon known that Flood was saved. The motive was left to public ingenuity to discover, and, consequently, every reason except the true one was assigned. It was supposed by many that he had given some valuable information about a recent mail-coach robbery; but in the meanwhile, he had been made aware of the high opinion entertained of his skill as a racket-player, and the expectations that he would win the match.

Full of gratitude for having been rescued from the gallows, he promised to win, and redeemed his promise. His noble antagonist was an excellent player, but in hand, eye, and agility, the tailor was greatly superior. The nobleman became agitated and lost his temper, which was speedily followed by his money. His aristocratic feelings were not, however, outraged by even a suspicion of the fact, that he was defeated by a little tailor, who, if the law had been permitted to take its course, would have "shuffled off his mortal coil" in front of Newgate; and who had been liberated from the condemned cell only for the purpose of liberating a thousand guineas from the pocket of a duke's brother.

His Excellency gave Flood fifty pounds and some good advice, suggesting a removal from Dublin and even from Ireland; but Flood was for some time unwilling to depart. He remained in a city where he could only be known as "the unhanged one," and where his character could not be retrieved. His trade was useless. He could not obtain any employment. His money was soon exhausted, and he had an insuperable objection to recur to his former habit of taking nocturnal strolls in quest of watches and purses. Unwilling to give the law another *lien* on his neck, he at length determined to leave Ireland as soon as he could obtain means of crossing the Channel. Mr. Gonne was rather surprised by receiving a visit from him, and still more by the request of a couple of pounds. The indignation of a man who had been robbed of his watch and money exploded at once. He assured Flood of his sincere regret and deep disappointment at the gallows having been shamefully defrauded of its due. He then informed him, in terms more plain than polite, that he could not expect any contribution on the voluntary principle, but that a reasonable expenditure would be willingly incurred to procure a halter, if its application to Flood's neck was guaranteed. The "unhanged one" bore all this very meekly, and said that he had a simple and intelligible proposal to make, namely, that Mr. Gonne should lodge two pounds in the hands of a certain person on condition that the money should be restored if the watch was not recovered by its owner; but if the article was obtained for Mr. Gonne, Flood was to receive the deposit, to enable him to leave Dublin for ever.

This offer was acceded to, and the cash was lodged with Jack Stevenson of St. Andrew Street. Jack was a man of very extensive connections. He had nephews and nieces in abundance; and whenever any of them wished to retire plate, jewels, or trinkets from the vulgar gaze, Jack, like an affectionate uncle, *advanced*, and took charge of the valuable articles. He adorned the space between his front windows with the ancient crest of Lombardy, three golden apples; and his transactions with his relatives were of such a particular nature, that they were recorded *in duplicate.* He had known Flood in his early days, before he had become an adept either in racket-playing or robbing. He consented to hold the money subject to the specified conditions; and then Flood and Gonne proceeded to the last place to which it might be imagined that the steps of the former would be voluntarily directed, namely, to the Police Office, where he had been charged, and from whence he had been committed. There he told Gonne to remain at the exterior door; and, as the Office was about to be closed for the day, he desired him to ask the magistrate when he came out, what was the exact time. Gonne complied with this direction, and His Worship readily, but rather too hastily, produced a watch. No sooner was it displayed than its appearance elicited the most disagreeable oath ever sworn before the " worthy justice," for Gonne instantly exclaimed, " By. G——! that 's .my watch."

Gonne obtained his watch, and was with great difficulty persuaded to refrain from bringing the transaction under the notice of the Executive. The system by which the magistrate managed occasionally to possess himself of a valuable watch or some other costly article, consisted in having two or three drawers wherein to keep the property found with highwaymen or thieves. If the prosecutor identified the delinquent, he was then shown the right drawer; but if he could not swear to the depredator, the wrong drawer was opened.

The magistrate to whom this narrative refers, was dismissed in a short time after, for attempting to embezzle fifty pounds. I wish, for the honor of the profession of which I am proud to be a member, to state that he was not a barrister. Flood was afterwards for many years the marker of a racket court at Tottenham Court Road, London. He judiciously and wittily changed his name to *Waters*.

CHAPTER VIII.

THE MAJOR.

I SHALL now advert to another Police magistrate whose name I need not refrain from mentioning, inasmuch as although his unpopularity was unparalleled, his name has never been associated with any imputation of a dishononrable or debasing tendency, such as was manifested in reference to Gonne's watch. Henry Charles Sirr was for many years Town-Major of Dublin; and through the insurrection of 1798, and during the outbreak of 1803, he was peculiarly energetic and most unscrupulous in the exercise of his powers as a magistrate of Police, in which capacity he continued until his death in 1841. He was detested by all those to whose opinions he was opposed, and whose designs and acts he was engaged in repressing or punishing. He was not respected by those of a contrary tendency; for he unnecessarily and continually engaged personally in enquiries, searches, and arrests, which a proper appreciation of his magisterial position would have induced him to leave to his subordinates. He was accustomed, during the insurrectionary times, to traverse the streets of Dublin or the suburbs, with some special attendants following at a short distance. He carried pistols, and was also provided with a short heavy bludgeon. If a suspicion crossed his mind in reference to any person whom he casually met, his usual practice was to knock the individual down, and then to ascertain if he had secured the right man. He was of considerable although indirect advantage to his colleagues and successor; for, during his official career, the acts of his colleagues, if of an unpopular tendency, were attributed to the example he afforded, or to his supposed suggestions. His successor was judged by the contrast, and his faults were considered as venial mistakes, whilst the Major's acts were only remembered to be stigmatized as wilful misdeeds. His courage has been doubted, but the imputation of cowardice is not fairly sustained. It arises from the prejudice which satisfied itself that he could not possess any good quality. His conduct at the apprehension of Lord Edward Fitzgerald did not evince either courage or cowardice. He entered the room after the conflict had commenced, and fired the fatal shot, in all probability, to save the life of his associate. He frequently, and without any necessity, risked his personal safety, and there is no sound reason for believing that he was of a pusillanimous nature.

In 1798 Sirr received information that a young man of most respectable family, who had involved himself in the insurrectionary movement of the period, had arrived in Dublin, and was concealed in the upper room of a house in Bull Alley. The Major proceeded, attended by several of his myrmidons, to the place, and entered a house on the right hand side from Bride Street, the lower part of the premises being a butcher's shop. He went up to the front two-pair room, and there surprised the accused party lying on a bed and partly undressed. He held a pistol to the young man's head, and commanded him to arise and surrender. The mandate was complied with, and the captive apparently submitted to his fate. He arose and asked permission to wash his face and hands, which was accorded and he then put on his coat, which the Major had previously ascertained to have no weapons in the pockets. Suddenly the prisoner made a spring, throwing himself bodily against the window, which yielded to his force, and out he went. Sirr shouted and dashed down stairs, greatly impeded by his own assistants who were hurrying up on the alarm. The poor fellow who had adopted so desperate an expedient, met, in his fall, a clothes pole, and then came on some wooden shed work which projected over the front of the shop; the latter was rather crazy and gave away. He sprang to his feet unhurt, darted down the alley, and escaped by one of the numerous passages with which it communicated. Sirr hastened down to the Coombe, turned out the Poddle guard, and searched the neighbourhood, but without success. When the British government, after the campaign of Waterloo, formed some regiments of lancers, they procured two Austrian officers, of ascertained capability, to impart a knowledge of the lance exercise to those regiments. One of the officers was the Bull Alley jumper. He took an opportunity of renewing his acquaintance with Sirr, and jocosely apologised for having terminated their previous interview so suddenly and unceremoniously.

Sirr was once tricked into making himself instrumental in carrying out the punishment desired by an outraged father against a profligate son, and it occurred also in the unhappy year of 1798. There was a wealthy bookseller residing on Lower Ormond Quay, who had a son, his only child, bearing the same Christian name. Mr. Patrick W——, the father, was very indulgent. Mr. Patrick W——, the son, was extremely vicious. His time was chiefly spent in society of the most objectionable description, and he was not particular as to the means whereby he made his father's money available for his licentious pleasures. He had been absent from the paternal roof for some weeks. His father had vainly sought to discover him, when he unexpectedly met him in the street, and directed a storm of well-merited reproaches on the young reprobate.

Young Pat stood submissively attentive to his parent, and allowed him to vent the first burst of his wrath, and when old Pat closed his impassioned complaints by peremptorily ordering him to go home, he mildly replied, " I was going there, sir, to try if you would admit me ; I own it is more than I deserve, but give me one trial more before you cast me off: give me one more trial and you shall not regret it."

"You young villain ! where have you spent the last month ? "

" I spent it as badly as I could, except the last week, and during that time I have been with Mr. Luke White, at Woodlands."

" At Woodlands ! " exclaimed the astonished old man, " Is it with Luke White, my oldest, my most valued friend, you have been ? "

" Yes sir. This day week I was walking in Stephen's Green, and Mr. White met me. I sought to avoid him, I own that, but he called after me, took me aside and expostulated with me about my habits and associates. He told me that I was breaking your heart, and that I must reform my life. He said that he grieved, as did all your friends, over the coming ruin of your hopes, and that he was determined, if possible, to avert it ; that you were his esteemed, respected, and highly valued friend. He then proposed that I should go out to him that evening to Woodlands for a week, and that in the peaceful retirement of that residence, he would try to bring me to a proper sense of duty to a worthy father. I yielded to his remonstrances, and accepted his invitation; and having spent the week with that excellent gentleman, I was going, by his direction, to throw myself upon my knees before you, and implore your forgiveness."

"Oh!" exclaimed old Pat, "may heaven's choicest blessings be showered on him, my real, true friend, who felt for my misery, and has relieved it. Come, Pat, my darling boy, all is forgiven and forgotten. Happiness is in store for us both. You will be my pride and comfort. I can die contented if my eyes are closed by a son whom I leave respectable in conduct and character."

Father and son proceeded home; and old Pat immediately sought all means to convince young Pat of his faults having been condoned. He was informed of the business transactions then pending; and his father handed him a cheque for a considerable amount, and directed him to proceed to the bank, and pay some bills which were due that day.

Young Pat departed. He did not return; and the notary's messengers called in the evening with the unpaid bills. The miserable parent was only able to discover that his son had been seen, during the afternoon, in most disreputable society. Next morning old Pat waited on Mr. White, and thanked him most warmly for his exertions to reclaim the young reprobate by his advice and expostulations. "If anything could have produced a good effect on him," exclaimed the agonized father, "it would have been your advice, your example, and the contemplation of the sweet scene and happy family to which your invitation last week——"

F

" My dear sir," interrupted Mr. White, " there is a great delusion on your mind. I have not seen your son, nor have I had any communication whatever with him for more than twelve months."

The old gentleman staggered to a seat. A terrible convulsion shook his frame. Then supervened that which is fearful to witness in woman, but doubly horrible in man, hysterical tears and sardonic laughter. At length the fit terminated. Old Pat arose and took his leave. He walked away with surprising energy, and his countenance assumed a calmness beneath which was concealed nothing less

" Than the stern, single, deep, and wordless ire
   Of a strong human heart, and in a sire."

Old Pat sought a private interview with Major Sirr, and confided to him strong suspicions that young Pat was compromised with the United Irishmen, and that if closely and properly interrogated, he could disclose a great deal, especially as to some depôts of pikes and other weapons intended for insurrectionary purposes. He affected to stipulate for the utmost secrecy as to the Major's informant, protested that he regarded the rebels with the utmost horror and detestation, and that he had no idea of favoring a change in public affairs detrimental to those who, by unremitting industry, had realized property. He suggested that his son, when arrested, should be brought to the Custom House, which, at that time, was in Essex Street, and directly opposite to his own residence on Ormond Quay. Sirr entered into his views, complimented him on his prudence and loyalty, and took immediate measures for the arrest of young Pat, who, when captured, was delivered to some of " Beresford's Troop," to exercise their inquisitorial talents in eliciting all he knew about men whom he had never seen, and as to designs of which, in all probability, he had never heard. The young man was perfectly free from all political or religious influences. Beau Brummell might as justly have been accused of complicity in the designs of revolutionary *sans culottes*, as young Pat of any sympathy with other pursuits than the midnight orgies and debasing revels of the worst of both sexes.

In the Custom House yard he was interrogated, and his denials only produced louder and sterner demands. Truth, strict truth, issued from lips to which it had been hitherto a stranger. The triangles stood before him, and all his protestations of innocence were uttered to ears worse than deaf. He was stripped, tied up, and lashed until he swooned; then taken down, and recalled to a sense of existence by restoratives, only to be put up again, until, at last, he lay before his torturers, a lacerated and semi-animate frame, incapable of enduring further suffering. They cursed him as an obdurate, callous villain, from whom nothing could be extorted; and whilst his terrific punishment was in process of infliction, his father was looking on, from the window of his residence. The wretched youth was conveyed home, and a considerable time elapsed before he was sufficiently recovered to proceed to America, whence he never returned. His father made no secret of the means he adopted to punish young Pat and to trick the Major.

Sirr was occasionally humorous. He announced to one of his acquaintances the fate which was expected to befal Theobald Wolfe Tone, in the laconic phrase—"Mr. Tone is to a-tone to-morrow in the front of Newgate." Galvin, the hangman, having applied to Sirr for his interest and recommendation to procure a small pension, laid before him a memorial, which he was desirous of having forwarded to Government under the Major's auspices. In it the veteran executioner submitted that for many years he had acted as finisher of the law in the County and City of Dublin, with frequent visits for professional purposes to towns on the Home and the Leinster circuits. That age and infirmities were rendering him incapable of continuing his public duties; and that he humbly besought a small pension for the support of his declining years. " Tom," said the Major, " you should have stated in your memorial that during your official career you discharged your duties *to the perfect satisfaction of all parties concerned.*" " I thank you, Major," replied the stupid old wretch, " I'll get it altered, and put *that* in." One of Sirr's colleagues, a barrister, was remarkable for speaking in a low voice, and with a great lisp. He was indebted to the Major for the nickname of " Mississippi."

At a funeral in St. Werburgh's churchyard, and close by the vaults in which the body of Lord Edward Fitzgerald had been deposited, the Major was present. After the interment, a Mr. S.——, whose person was invariably extremely slovenly, approached him and remarked, " I suppose, Major, that you cannot be here without thinking of Lord Edward."

" My friend," was the reply, " I am at present thinking of you, and wondering from whence you derive such an ample supply of soiled shirts."

In 1831, during Earl Grey's administration, Sirr attended meetings convened in favor of Parliamentary Reform, and moved resolutions of the most liberal tendency. He voted at the city election for the Reform candidates, and was twitted by the late Thomas Ellis for having deserted his party and forgotten his principles. His answer was simple and true—" I am totally unchanged ; I have always supported *the Government*, and I shall continue to do so."

When the piers which form Kingstown harbour were in course of construction, the supply of stone was derived from immense quarries at Killiney, and conveyed along a tramway, on which, near the quarries, there were slopes down which the loaded waggons required no impelling power, but rather to be restrained, by breaks, from acquiring a dangerous velocity. Major Sirr was fond of collecting natural curiosities, especially of a geological nature ; and he frequently visited Killiney in quest of spar formations, which were occasionally found there. He was by no means niggardly in his dealings with the spar finders ; but still he could not conciliate them into a feeling of kindness or respect. One day he was proceeding up the tramway slope when the discharge of artillery at the Pigeon House fort attracted his attention. He turned and looked in the direction of the firing, just at the moment when a train of loaded wagons was about to descend. Being right before them, he would have been utterly destroyed in a moment, but the breaksman saw his perilous situation, and applied the requisite pressure, stopped the train, and saved the Major. Several persons witnessed his danger and the prompt means by which it was averted. On the transaction becoming known in the quarries, there was an immediate strike. All work was stopped, and a determination was unanimously avowed to insist on the dismissal of the breaksman. No specific complaint was preferred against the individual whose expulsion was required. The Harbor Commissioners deputed Mr. Hickman Kearney to enquire into the grounds and reasons for such an extraordinary demand. He went to the quarries and called on the workmen to come forward and explain the

cause of their animosity to the breaksman. The only
reply was that " he should go." It appeared, on reference
to the clerk of the works, and to the overseers, that the
obnoxious man was honest, sober, diligent, and attentive
to his duties ; and it was strongly urged that no accident
had occurred at the slope since his appointment, and that
he had, by his presence of mind and promptitude, saved
Major Sirr's life. This produced a general exclamation
of " That's the reason he sha'nt stay amongst us. What
business had he to save the Major ?" The poor breaksman
would have lost his employment, but for an old and influential workman who interfered in his favor, and induced
the others to forgive him, *provided he faithfully promised
never to do the like again.*

The Major was peculiarly unpopular amongst the hackney carriage drivers, and yet he was not a severe judge of
their delinquencies, for he dismissed nearly half the complaints preferred before him, and the average of his fines
was three shillings and sixpence ; still, they hated him ;
and although he preached to them very many little sermons in the carriage court, and occasionally sought to
impart Scriptural knowledge to their minds, the benighted
"jarveys" detested the magisterial apostle. At last the
" Major" died. His illness was very brief, and his indisposition commenced in a covered car. He drove home
to the Lower Castle-yard, and never rallied, but sank in
a few hours. The story was circulated that he actually
died in a covered car ; and for some time after his decease,
I was occasionally treated to the hearing of complaints
preferred by covered car-drivers against outside carmen,
for usurping their turns, and defrauding them of their
jobs. It was, and is, very unusual for carmen to summon members of their own body ; but in the cases to

which I refer there was a peculiar grossness assigned to
the offence. " Yer worship," the plaintiff would exclaim,
" I would not mind him *stumping me,* but he roared out
to the people that were going to hire me that my car was
the very one the owld Major died in, and yer worship,
I could 'nt be expected to forgive that."

~~~~~~~~~~~

CHAPTER IX.

COMMITTALS——A BARBER WANTED——DWYER THE
REBEL——AN EXTRAORDINARY INQUEST——SER-
GEANT GREENE'S HORSE——CHRISTY HUGHES——
THE POLICE CLERKS——RECORDER WALKER——THE
POLICE STATUTES——PREAMBLE——A BENEFIT SO-
CIETY CASE——POLICE RECRUITS——A BORN SOL-
DIER.

IT is pleasing to observe decided improvements in institutions of importance to the community. In the time of
Major Sirr, the coarsest language was addressed from the
bench of the police courts, not only to prisoners on serious
charges, but to persons prosecuting or defending summonses. If a magistrate of police were now to apply
terms of abuse, even to the most disreputable characters,
he would most certainly be severely censured, or perhaps
dismissed. The personal characters of the present magistrates of Dublin ensure the observance of the strictest
propriety in their courts. I may remark, also, that imprisonment cannot now be inflicted in the reckless manner
formerly adopted. On the day when my magisterial functions commenced, I called for a list of the existing committals to the Dublin prisons from the Head Office. I
was astonished to find that one man had been detained

for the previous fifteen years, another for thirteen, and a third for ten, in default of sureties, to keep the peace, and be of good behaviour. I ordered the immediate discharge of those persons, and two of them expressed great dissatisfaction at being thrown upon the world from which they had been so long estranged. These committals were signed by Major Sirr. There is no danger of persons being now sent to prison, and forgotten there; for if such a committal were sent, through ignorance or inadvertence, the Board of Superintendence would soon draw attention to the fact of a prisoner's subsistence being charged on the public for an illegal or unreasonable period. At the time when the committals to which I have alluded came under my notice, I happened to meet with some reports from a Governor of the Richmond Bridewell addressed to the magistrates of the Head Police Office during the time when that prison was under their exclusive control and supervision. In one of these documents, the writer states the building to be in good repair, and perfectly adapted for the safe custody of its inmates, and that every ward was in a clean and wholesome condition. He proceeds to describe the good effects produced by the use he made of a barber, who, for riotous and disorderly conduct, had been committed for two months with hard labour. He had not put the delinquent to stone-breaking or oakum picking, but employed him in shaving and hair-cutting of the other prisoners, the effect of which was to improve their appearance, and to impart cleanly tendencies. He then expresses his regret that the barber's term of imprisonment had elapsed, and that the prisoners had become less cleanly-looking from remaining unshaven and uncropt. He terminates the report by earnestly and most respectfully suggesting to "their worships" to avail themselves of the first opportunity that may offer for committing *another barber for the longest term in their power.*

For some time after my appointment to the magistracy, Alderman John Smith Fleming was my senior colleague at the Head Office. He had a very vivid recollection of the rebellion of 1798, and was secretary to his uncle, Alderman Thomas Fleming, Lord Mayor of Dublin in that year. Amongst other anecdotes of that period, I have heard him relate that Dwyer, one of the insurgent chiefs, had prolonged his resistance for some months after the insurrection had been generally quelled. In the mountains of Wicklow, with a few but faithful followers, he evaded every exertion for his capture. Mr. Hume, of Humewood, near Baltinglass, was particularly anxious to secure Dwyer. He was the commander of a corps of yeomanry, and a magistrate of the County of Wicklow, which he also represented in Parliament. Of very extensive influence, he easily procured the co-operation of the civil and military authorities of his own and of the adjoining districts. Still Dwyer was not to be had. At length an arrangement was made that the yeomanry corps of the western portion of Wicklow should assemble, at an early hour on an appointed day, at Humewood, and should set out to scour the country, exploring every recess, and leaving no place, on hill or plain, unransacked for Dwyer. Yeomanry from Wexford, Carlow, and Kildare were to move on preconcerted points, so as to intercept the fugitive if he should attempt to shift his quarters. A day was wholly spent in a most fatiguing search. It seemed as if Dwyer had transformed himself into a bird, and flown beyond sight or reach. However, in a short time, Mr. Hume received an intimation, that if Dwyer's life would be spared, and that he would be permitted to leave the country, he was willing to surrender. With the assent of the Government, Mr. Hume acceded to this offer. Dwyer was brought to Dublin, and the required undertaking and consequent immunity from punishment were acknowledged before the Lord Mayor. The outlaw was kindly and generously treated by Mr. Hume during the few days which preceded his departure for America; and at a final inverview Mr. Hume said—"Before we part, Dwyer, will you tell me how you avoided capture on the day that we scoured the whole country in search of you?" "Sir," replied Dwyer, "I had information of your intentions, so I went to Humewood on the night before, and when the yeomen were paraded on your lawn, before they started in search of me, *I was looking at them from your hay-loft.*"

For some years previous to 1842, the number of persons "found drowned" in the County of Dublin was much greater than might be expected either from the extent of the population or the nature of the locality. It was indeed true that one canal, the Grand, extended along the greater part of the southern boundary of the Irish metropolis, and another, the Royal, was similarly situated in the northern direction; but although these canals afforded great facilities for the termination of human existence, whether by suicide or accident, the cases of drowning were far more numerous than could be fairly attributed to violence, intoxication, lunacy, or carelessness. It would also seem that the southern canal was much more destructive to human life than the other, and that the bank which was in the county possessed some attraction for the corpses, for they were almost always taken out at the county side. It happened on the 11th of March, 1842, a few minutes before 10 o'clock, a.m., that a young man named Kinsella, who was employed in a distillery at

Marrowbone Lane, was proceeding, after his breakfast, from his residence at Dolphin's Barn to resume his work, when, on approaching the canal bridge, he was stopped by a constable, who informed him that the coroner required his attendance, as a juror, on an inquest that was about to be held on the body of an old man, just taken out of the canal. Kinsella vainly expostulated against the detention. He was told that it would be a very short business, for there were no marks of violence on the corpse; it would merely be a case of "found drowned." The man was accordingly sworn on the inquest, and the coroner having informed the jury that they were required by law to view the body, they were conducted to the apartment where it lay. As soon as Kinsella beheld the corpse, he rushed forward, dropped on his knees beside it, seized the stiff and frigid hand, and exclaimed "My father! my poor, dear father! We buried him on this day week, decently and well, in the Hospital Fields. He had no business in the canal; and *them old clothes* never belonged to him; he never wore a stitch of them." The coroner and the doctor vainly endeavoured to persuade Kinsella that he was mistaken; and his recognition of his parent produced an enquiry, which resulted in bringing to light some very extraordinary practices on the part of the county functionary and his medical satellite. They were paid by public presentment, according to the number of inquests held; and they had recourse to the expedient of having bodies disinterred, clothed in old habiliments, and thrown into the canal. Such bodies were almost always discovered very soon, and were taken out on the county side of the canal, to swell the coroner's next presentment for inquests on persons who were "found drowned." A crush from a passing barge afforded an additional profit, as the bruises constituted a plausible reason for a *post mortem* examination, and thereby doubled the doctor's ordinary fee. The coroner and his associate were convicted of conspiring to defraud, and consequently were deprived of their functions. It must be acknowledged that, if their mode of procuring inquests was not honest, it was certainly novel and ingenious. If the practice had been known in the days of Hamlet, it would have furnished an additional reason for his exclamation :—

" To what base uses we may return, Horatio."

In the year 1842, and for several subsequent years, by an arrangement with my colleagues, I undertook the magisterial duties connected with the licensing and regulation of job and hackney vehicles, and the adjudication of complaints in the carriage court. At the time when I assuumed those duties, Richard Wilson Greene (whose high legal acquirements ultimately obtained for him the position of Baron in the Court of Exchequer) was in very extensive practice at the Bar. An issue from Chancery was sent to be tried at one of the principal towns on the Leinster Circuit, and he was specially retained for one of the parties. A very efficient reporter, named Christopher Hughes, in whose character there was great comical eccentricity, was employed to take down, in short hand, the trial of the issue. Early in the succeeding term, it was arranged that a consultation should be held at the house of the senior counsel, in Leeson Street, and Mr. Hughes was requested to meet Mr. Greene at the Courts, with his notes, and to accompany him to the consultation. The appointed time had nearly arrived, when Greene and Hughes hurried off from the Four Courts. Having passed out to the quay, the former hailed an outside car, on which they sat beside each other, and the driver was ordered to make all possible haste to Leeson Street. The horse was a fine-looking animal, but he stepped high and was very slow. Mr. Greene urged the driver to hasten on, and after two or three expostulations, he remarked to the Jehu that the horse was unfit for a jaunting car, although he was large and strong, but that he would suit well for a family carriage. The driver, a lad of eighteen or nineteen years of age, exclaimed, " Bedad your honor is a witch!" "What do you mean?" asked Mr. Greene. " Oh," replied the carman, " I mane no offince, but yer honor is right about the baste; that's what he is. I'll tell yer honor a saycret. The baste is a carriage horse belonging to one Counsellor Greene, and the coachman has a hack-car and figure on Bride Street stand. He ginerally manages to have something the matther with one of the horses, and that gives him an opportunity to get a good deal of work out of the other in the car." Although Mr. Greene was very angry at what the driver had communicated, he did not disclose that he was the owner of the horse. He whispered to Hughes, and requested him to give the driver his name and address, but to leave him unpaid. When they arrived at Leeson Street, Greene at once entered the house of the senior counsel, and warned the servant against telling his name to the carman. Hughes had a scene, and was treated to a copious supply of opprobrious epithets, but he did not pay, and merely gave his name and address. He was summoned, at the owner's suit, before me; and when the case was called the proprietor of the vehicle, in very energetic terms, demanded exemplary costs against the defaulting hirer of his car. His denunciations were suddenly interrupted by the appearance of Mr. Greene; and there was abundant merriment, of which I had a full share, when it transpired that the learned Queen's Counsel had hired a hack-car drawn by his own horse. The coach-man ran out of court, and I afterwards heard that he never applied for wages or discharge. The incident attained great publicity, and afforded much amusement in "The Hall" amongst the long-robed fraternity. One day Greene said to some of his brethren that he believed the fellow had left Dublin, but that he was strongly tempted to send the police in quest of him. "Send your horse," observed the facetious Robert Holmes, "for he is best acquainted with *the carman's traces.*"

Mr. Hughes, whose name appears in the preceding anecdote, deserves to be noticed upon his own merits. He was frequently engaged in reporting proceedings in the Police Courts, and we never had occasion to impute any in-accuracy to his statements. He was always ready to assist any of his brethren of the "press-gang," and to suggest a palliation or excuse for their casual errors. I frequently indulged him with permission to sit in the magistrate's room whilst he was transcribing his notes, and I have been often amused with his remarks and state-ments, which were strictly true, and in which he never concealed his own professional expedients or mistakes. He mentioned that he was directed to go to one of the dinners of the Malachean Orphan Society, where O'Connell pre-sided, but having indulged in his potations at a luncheon, he forgot the requirement for his services at Mrs. Mahony's great rooms in Patrick Street. "I slept," said he, "until about 11 o'clock, and then I recollected myself, so I went quietly to the office and got the file of the previous year, and, with a little alteration, it did for the day's dinner as well." He often mentioned what he designated his greatest mistake. He described it thus :—" On the con-cluding day of George the Fourth's visit, in 1821, he went to Powerscourt, where he got a splendid reception from the noble proprietor. Lord Powerscourt had caused reservoirs to be constructed above the waterfall, in order that when his Majesty went to see it, the sluices might be drawn, and a tremendous cataract produced. I went down in the morning and viewed the place, and minutely noted all the preparations. I then drew on my imagination for a description of a second Niagara, and put into the mouth of the royal visitor various exclamations of delight and surprise. I sent off my report, and it appeared in due time, but unfortunately the king was too much hurried by other arrangements, and did not go to the Waterfall at all, but drove direct from Powerscourt House to Kingstown, where he embarked. I have been often quizzed for my imaginative report, but, nevertheless, I stated what the King *ought* to have done, and what he *ought* to have said, and if he did otherwise, it was not my fault."

I was extremely fortunate, at my accession to magisterial office, to find myself provided with clerks who could not be surpassed in diligence, integrity, or intelligence. I shall particularize Messrs. Pemberton and Cox. The former was the son of a previous chief magistrate, at whose instance he was appointed. The latter had been for several years in America, and had been engaged by Jacob Philip Astor in forming the settlement of Astoria, in Washington Irvine's description of which he is most favorably mentioned. He was a man of great literary taste, and was an accomplished linguist. Their performance of official duties never required from me, nor to my knowledge from any of my colleagues, the slightest correction or reproof. Pemberton was a solicitor, and was promoted in 1846 to the Clerkship of the Crown for the

King's County. He had been many years before an assistant to Messrs. Allen and Greene, the Clerks of the Peace for the City of Dublin. I shall have to notice hereafter some amusing incidents connected with Cox, but shall give precedence to a few anecdotes derived from Pemberton, and arising from his acquaintance with the old Session House in Green Street, and the records there, to which, I suppose, he had full access.

Towards the close of the last century an aid-de-camp of the then viceroy was indicted, at the Quarter Sessions, for the larceny of a handsome walking-stick, and also for assaulting the gentleman who owned it, and who was, moreover, a Frenchman. The transaction arose in a house of a description unnecessary to be particularized. An affray took place, the Frenchman was kicked down stairs, and lost his cane, which was alleged to have been wrested from him by the aid-de-camp. The charge of larceny was absurd, and the grand jury ignored the indictment. But the assault could neither be denied nor justified, and the traverser submitted, pleaded "guilty," and was fined five pounds. That punishment did not cure his propensity for beating Frenchmen and taking their *sticks.* On the 21st of June, 1813, he beat Marshal Jourdan at Vittoria, and captured his *baton;* and on the 18th of June, 1815, at Waterloo, he beat the greatest Frenchman that ever lived, Napoleon Bonaparte. I do not feel justified in naming the delinquent aid-de-camp, and perhaps the reader may think it quite unnecessary that I should.

More than half a century has elapsed since the office of Recorder of Dublin was held by Mr. William Walker, whose town residence was in Lower Dominick Street. One day a groom, in the service of a Mr. Gresson, was tried before him, for stealing his master's oats. The

G

evidence was most conclusive, for the culprit had been detected in the act of taking a large bag of oats out of his master's stable, which was in the lane at the back of the east side of Dominick Street. When the prisoner was convicted, the Recorder addressed him to the following effect:—" The sentence of the Court is, that you are to be imprisoned for three calendar months ; and at the commencement of that term you are to be publicly whipped from one end of *that lane* to the other, and back again ; and in the last week of your imprisonment, you are to be again publicly whipped from one end of *that lane* to the other, and back again ; for I am determined, with the help of Providence, to put a stop to oat-stealing in *that lane.*" His worship's emphatic denunciation of oat-stealing in *that lane,* arose from the circumstance of his own stable being the next door to Mr. Gresson's.

The same civic functionary was a great amateur farmer. He had a villa and some acres of land at Mount Tallant, near Harold's Cross, and prided himself upon his abundant crops of early hay. On one occasion he entered the court to discharge his judicial duties at an adjourned sessions, and was horrified at hearing from the acting Clerk of the Peace (Mr. Pemberton) that there were upwards of twenty larceny cases to be tried. " Oh!" said he, " this is shocking. I have three acres of meadow cut, and I have no doubt that the haymaking will be neglected or mismanaged in my absence. In a few minutes, he inquired in an undertone, " Is there any old offender on the calendar?"

" Yes," was the reply, " there is one named Branagan, who has been twice convicted for ripping lead from roofs, and he is here now for a similar offence, committed last week in Mary's Abbey."

"Send a turnkey to him," said the Recorder, "with a hint that, if he pleads guilty, he will be likely to receive a light sentence."

These directions were complied with, and the lead-stealer was put to the bar and arraigned.

"Are you guilty or not guilty?"

"Guilty, my lord."

"The sentence of the court is that you be imprisoned for three months. Remove him."

Branagan retired, delighted to find a short imprisonment substituted for the transportation that he expected. As he passed through the dock, he was eagerly interrogated by the other prisoners—

"What have you got?"

"Three months."

"Three months—only three months!" they exclaimed; "Oh! but we're in luck. His lordship is as mild as milk this morning. It's seldom that he's in so sweet a humor."

"Put forward another," said the Recorder.

"Are you guilty or not guilty?"

"Guilty, my lord."

"Let the prisoner stand back, and arraign the next."

Accordingly, the prisoners were rapidly arraigned, and the same plea of "Guilty" recorded in each case. Presently it was signified to his lordship that the calendar was exhausted. All the thieves had pleaded guilty.

"Put the prisoners to the front of the dock," said he; and they were mustered as he directed. He then briefly addressed them—

"The sentence of the court is that you and each of you be transported for seven years. Crier, adjourn the court."

Branagan had been thrown as a sprat, and had caught

the other fish abundantly. This incident might afford a useful, or perhaps it should be termed, a convenient suggestion, to other judicial functionaries, especially on circuit when there is a crowded dock.

When Mr. Pemberton received the appointment of Clerk of the Crown for the King's County, Mr. Cox, who had been for several years the second clerk in the Head Police Office, succeeded to the chief clerkship. He possessed very extensive knowledge of the world, and was highly educated. Many incidents connected with him are worthy of being recorded. I may mention here that the Police Laws of the Irish Metropolitan district are, to the highest degree, complex, voluminous, involved, and perplexing. In the English Metropolitan district two statutes regulate, one the Police Force, and the other the Police Courts. In Dublin we have a statute passed in 1808, another in 1824, a third in 1836, a fourth in 1837, a fifth in 1838, a sixth in 1839, a seventh in 1842, and an Act in relation to public carriages, which may also be termed a police statute, in 1848. They contain three hundred and sixty-six sections, and may be designated as disgraceful to the several executive governments which have left them unconsolidated and uncodified. When the 5th Vic. sess. 2, Chap. 24, passed, it recited the other Acts to which I have alluded, and then its preamble proceeds to heap or bundle them all together in the following terms :—

" Be it therefore enacted by the Queen's most Excellent Majesty, by and with the advice and consent of the Lords Spiritual and Temporal, and Commons, in this present Parliament assembled, and by the authority of the same, that the said recited Acts of the forty-eighth year of the reign of King George the Third, of the fifth year of the reign of King George the Fourth, of the session of Parliament holden in the sixth and seventh years of the reign of King William the Fourth, of the first year of Her present Majesty's reign, and of the sessions of Parliament holden respectively in the first and second, second and third, and third and fourth years of Her present Majesty's reign, and this Act, shall be construed together as one Act ; and that all and every the enactments and provisions therein contained shall apply and extend to this Act, and to all Convictions, Warrants, Distresses, Proceedings, and Things, made, taken, or done in execution of this Act, as fully to all intents and purposes as if the same were herein repeated and re-enacted, save in so far as such enactments and provisions are inconsistent with or contrary to this Act, or as such enactments or provisions may be altered by this Act, or other enactments or provisions made in lieu thereof."

Mr. Cox commented on this farrago by observing that " its framer would have an easy death, for that if he was affected with ague, or even if he were hanged, he would be too lazy to shake in the former or to kick in the latter case." In the blank leaf of a bound copy of the Police statutes, the following was written in reference to the preceding quotation :—

" The preamble saith the forty-eighth of George the Third is one, that must be tack'd to another Act, the fifth of George his son. Then whilst you're at it, just take a statute, the sixth and seventh session, of him who did own the British throne, the next in due progression. Then the first of the reign of our present Queen, and then the first and second ; the next that occurred was the second and third, then the third and fourth is reckoned. All these in fact, to the present Act, you must fasten tight as leather. There may be flaws in many a clause, but, take them all together, it must be your plan, as well as you can, to deal with your numerous doubts, or be the employer of some shrewd lawyer, to shew you their ins and outs. If your puzzled brain, you rack in vain, until you fume and curse ; if they bother you, why they've bothered me too, so take them for better, for worse."

There were, and I suppose still are, many complaints preferred before divisional magistrates, at the Police Courts, in reference to claims on Benefit or Friendly Societies, for allowances in cases of sickness, or for money payable to members or their representatives, under family visitations. Whenever any summonses on such subjects were disposed of by me, I called for the transaction and account-books, and required them to be produced at the commencement of the proceedings. On one occasion a quire of copy paper, stitched in a cover of brown, in a condition absolutely dirty, and in which the entries were irregularly scrawled, was handed up to me. I strongly censured such a slovenly mode of recording their proceedings as very discreditable. On hearing the complainant, I considered that the case was very well suited for an arbitration, and the parties. offered no objection to have it so disposed of; but they disagreed on each of the other societies which were suggested for the purpose of deciding it. However, one of the persons concerned said, that he would be satisfied to leave the matter entirely to Paddy Flannery, whom he saw present, and whom he considered "the most knowledgable man in all Dublin on such a business." The others concurred, and I directed Mr. Cox to indorse on the copy of the summons a reference by me, with the consent of the parties, of all matters in dispute between them to the aforesaid Flannery. I proceeded with some other business; and the indorsement having been made, I signed it without any hesitation, and it was given to the late Mr. Charles Fitzgerald, who was concerned in the case, but in whose honor and probity all parties who knew him fully confided. In a day or two after, I was talking to him, during a few minutes of leisure, and he showed me the indorsement which I had signed. It was as follows :——

" This Benefit Society, which keeps no proper book, evinces impropriety deserving a rebuke. As further litigation on each part they decline, no other observation is requisite on mine. 'Tis left to Patrick Flannery to judge of every fact, and in whatever manner he thinks right they're bound to act. My order I reserve until he makes out his award, and when he does, at once I will the rule of Court record."

Dr. Ireland was, for many years, the principal surgeon of the Dublin Metropolitan Police. He had to inspect the recruits, and satisfy himself of their size, health, mental capacity, and bodily strength being suitable to the service in which they proposed to engage. Cox said that the Dublin Police was, in one respect, very like to Howth Harbor, as no one could get into either without passing "Ireland's Eye." When the railway was being made from Dublin to Wicklow, he said that its course through the County of Dublin was extremely inharmonious, for it went first to a Dun-*drum*, proceeded to a Still-*organ*, and then attained to a *Bray*.

Mr. Cox came into the Police Court one morning after the custody cases had been disposed of. He brought forward an elderly female whom he stated to be desirous of making a statutable declaration before me, and which she had brought already drawn. There was a peculiar expression in his countenance as he suggested that I might, perhaps, be pleased to peruse the document previous to its official reception. It was made under circumstances which I shall briefly mention. A young man named Dempsey thought fit to embrace a military life, and enlisted in the 97th Regiment. He did not give his paternal name, but adopted the maiden name of his mother, and was enrolled as Peter Moran. He served for some years in India, but died there from the effects of sun-stroke. Some arrears of pay and a share of prize-money were due at the time of his decease; and his widowed mother applied, as next of kin, to obtain the amount. The War-Office authorities did not understand how Peter Moran came to be the son of Anne Dempsey. The declaration to which Cox slyly drew my attention was intended to afford an explanation of the grounds on which the claim was preferred, and it, moreover, afforded an instance of a martial disposition being as early in its inception as the birth-acquired tendency of poetic inspiration. The declaration was as follows :—

" Police District of Dublin }   I, Bridget Carey, of Fade Street, in the
      Metropolis, to wit,   } City of Dublin, widow, do hereby solemnly declare that I am a midwife, and have been such for the last thirty-five years ; and I further declare that about twenty-seven years ago, I attended Anne Dempsey who was then living in Little Longford Street, in her confinement, and, with God's assistance, I then and there *safely delivered her of the soldier in dispute ;* and I make this declaration for the information of the Secretary-at-war, and the other authorities of the War Office, &c."

Cox remarked, with an assumption of gravity which was irresistibly comic, " I suppose, your worship, that it is not necessary to describe the uniform or accoutrements in which ' the soldier' made his natal appearance." The document was retained by me, and another was substituted, in which the deceased was not accorded the distinction of having been " born a soldier."

CHAPTER X.

MENDICANCY.

I THINK that some useful information may be blended
with amusement by offering to my readers a few anecdotes
in reference to mendicancy and the laws intended for its
repression. Two persons were charged before me at the
Head Police Office, in 1843, with begging in the public
streets. One was detected in Castle Street and the other
in Palace Street. They were male and female, and stated
themselves to be brother and sister. Neither denied the
commission of the offence. Having been searched at the
station-house, the man was found to have £300 in his possession, and the woman had £180. I do not recollect what
names they gave, but I am sure they were not the real ones.
They were committed, each for a calendar month, with hard
labor; but during the period of their imprisonment their
subsistence was charged on the rates of the city of Dublin,
and the £480 were returned to them at their discharge.
I have been informed that the law of Scotland authorises
the support of vagrants, when committed to gaol, to be
defrayed from money found in their possession. If such
be the case, I would suggest to our Irish Members to
have the law of this country, in cases of vagrancy, assimilated to the Scotch system as quickly as possible.

Very soon after the occurrence which I have mentioned,
a gentleman who resided at Kingstown, arrived there by

train between seven and eight o'clock, p.m. He was walking up the Forty-foot Road, when he was accosted by a man of humble but decent appearance, who kept by his side whilst addressing him. "I came out, sir," said this individual, "early in the day, on an appointment with Mr. Herbert, of Tivoli Terrace, as he promised to let me have a few pounds that he owes me ; but I found that he had to start suddenly for Bray on some particular business, and he left word for me that he would be back about ten o'clock, so I have to wait : and I declare, sir, that I had only enough when I left home to get a return ticket, and I have not had a bit to eat since morning. Might I ask you for as much as would get me a crust of bread and a mug of milk." On reaching George's Street, the gentleman handed him a sixpence, and received the expression of an earnest prayer for his earthly prosperity and eternal happiness. On the following evening, the gentleman arrived at the same time, proceeded up the same road, and not being recognized, was accosted by the same person, who told the same tale, concluding with a wish for "the crust and mug of milk." A constable happened to be in view, and the hungry applicant was arrested and charged as a vagrant beggar. He had two ten-pound notes and three of five pounds, with eighteen shillings in silver and copper coin. The vagrant stated his name to be Richard Bryan, and a most extraordinary document was found on him. It was soiled and partly torn, but it was signed, "Your loving brother, John Bryan," was dated, "Borris, August 30, 1843," and contained a suggestion which was fully acted on, and which I could not allow to escape my recollection. Here it is :—

"We have got in the barley all right, and we are going at the oats to-morrow. I had to lend the horses to-day to Mr. Kimmis. I couldn't refuse, for you know he is a good warrant to obleege us when we want a turn. Nolan is bothering about the rent. He is very cross. You must see and make it out for him, *if you were even to beg for it.*"

One month's imprisonment, with hard labour, provided the mendicant with some " crusts " and " mugs of milk " at the cost of the county. The delinquent did not, I be- lieve, resume his solicitations within our district. The office sergeant who escorted him, with some other pri- soners, to Kilmainham, told the clerk at Kingstown on the following morning, that Mr. Bryan stigmatized my decision as " most uncharitable and disgusting."

I did not find medicancy so persistent in any part of the police district as in Kingstown. If a vagrant was brought up and punished for begging in Rathmines or the Pembroke township, or if the detection occurred at Inchi- core, or in the most respectable parts of the city, it was not at all probable that the beggar would be soon found again in the same locality. The Kingstown vagrants, as soon as they were discharged from Kilmainham, generally started off to return and resume their solicitations at the piers and jetty, or about the streets and terraces, which were more devoted to healthful recreation than to profes- sional or commercial affairs. I have no doubt that mendi- cants from distant places receive more at Kingstown or Bray, from visitors whom they recognize, or who recognize them, than would be given to them if both parties were at home. A lady with whom I was personally acquainted, and whose family residence was near Carlow, has several times, in my presence, given sixpences to beggars who belonged to her own neighbourhood, and I have heard her tell them that Kingstown was a better and more lucky place for them than ever they would find Carlow to be. I shall close my observations on street begging, by deliberately stating from my personal and official experience, that not one penny can be given to any mendicant on our thoroughfares in real, efficient, and merited charity. I would now warn my readers against another kind of begging, which avails itself of very systematic and elaborate means, and sometimes displays considerable educational acquirements, namely, written applications to charitable individuals to alleviate dire distress or succour unmerited misfortune. I know that this system is extensively practised in London, and I have heard that it is reviving in Dublin. I use the term " reviving" because it was completely crushed here in 1844 by the intelligence and activity of the detective division. At that time it was discovered that a confederacy of impostors had been formed in Bridgefoot Street, and that the members of this nefarious association were levying contributions on all in whose dispositions they had ascertained charity and credulity to be united. Forty-one of them were arrested and brought before me, and I committed them for trial on charges of " conspiring to defraud, obtaining money under false pretences, and forgery at common law." They were, however, consigned to Newgate, exactly at the time when the State prosecutions against O'Connell had been commenced ; and it was the received opinion in police quarters that they owed their escape—for they were not prosecuted—to a feeling on the part of the attorney-general of that period, that all his attention was demanded in bringing down the eagle, and that none of his energies could be spared to scatter a flock of kites. But they were not relinquished by the detectives, and were brought in detail under the castigation of the law until the confederacy was broken up. Their begging letters and petitions were addressed to all whom they considered likely to yield the slightest attention to their requests. These productions were termed in their slang "*Slums.*" One impostor represented that she was a clergyman's widow, with four female children, the eldest only eleven years of age; that her pious, exemplary, and most affectionate partner had died of malignant fever, contracted whilst whispering the words of Christian consolation to the departing sinner, and imparting the joyful assurance, that the life flickering away, the socket glimmer of a mere earthly light, would be rekindled in a lamp of everlasting duration and unvarying brilliancy. That resigned to her suffering, and adoring the hand from which she had experienced chastening, she was not forbidden to hope that the blessed spirit of charity would be manifested in her relief, and in shielding her helpless, artless babes from the privations of distress in their infancy, and from the still more fearful danger of being, in advanced youth, exposed to the snares of sin and its depraving consequences. A contribution, however small, addressed to Mrs. ——, at No. — Bridgefoot Street, Dublin, would, it was respectfully hoped, be accorded by Lord ——, or Mr. or Mrs. ——, whose well-known, though unostentatious benevolence, must plead the poor widow's apology for such an intrusion. Another was an unfortunate man, who for many years had earned a respectable livelihood as a commercial agent, and supported a numerous and interesting family by his industry and intelligence, but having unfortunately been in the County of Tipperary, when a contested election was in progress, he unguardedly expressed a wish for the success of the Conservative candidate, and although not a voter, he was set upon by a horde of savage ruffians, and beaten so as to produce paralysis of his lower extremities, and that now nothing remained for him but to entreat the humane consideration of one who could not, if the public testimony of his, or her generous disposition, was to be credited, refuse to sympathize with a parent whose helplessness compelled him to witness, with unavailing anguish, the poignant miseries of the offspring he had hoped, by his honest exertions, to have supported and reared, without submitting to the galling necessity of soliciting that aid which nothing but the most absolute destitution could reconcile him to implore. A *military lady* announced herself as the widow of color-sergeant Robert Maffett, who having served faithfully for twenty-three years, the four last having been in India, had been severely wounded in a decisive battle in Scinde, and when invalided and pensioned, was unfortunately drowned at Blackwall, in consequence of the boat which was conveying him ashore being accidentally upset. That she and her eight poor orphans had no resource on reaching her native city, where she found that all her relations had died or emigrated, and where she was friendless and alone, but to throw herself upon the charitable feelings of one whose character emboldened her to hope that the humble appeal of the soldier's widow, for herself and her poor orphans, would not be unavailing. These and a thousand other *slums* were manufactured in Bridgefoot Street, alias Dirty Lane, not an unsuitable name for the locale of such proceedings, and they were invariably accompanied by lists of subscriptions, and magisterial or municipal attestations, admirably got up in the first style of forgery. In the first case to which I have adverted, the " hapless widow " succeeded in getting five pounds from the Lord Chief Justice of Ireland, (Pennefather.)   In the instance of the " military widow," Lady Blakeney was lightened of three pounds.   Another *slum* was circulated by a scoundrel who represented himself to be the son of a gentleman in the south of Ireland, of an old family, and of the pristine faith; that he had been educated at Louvain, had an ardent wish to become a Catholic clergyman, and that one of the most distinguished dignitaries of that church was inclined to ordain him, but his father had died in debt, without leaving him the means of providing even the most humble outfit for such a vocation. One of his missives produced the effect of relieving an alderman's lady of five pounds sterling, which the excellent and worthy matron piously suggested might be useful in providing the embryo priest *with vestments.*

This confederacy was not confined to Dublin. Its branches extended through Leinster, Connaught, Munster, and in almost every important town in England its connections were established. It is, however, very curious that the Scots and our Northern countrymen were left comparatively free from its attacks. Why? Is it because the rascally crew conceived the natives of Scotland and Ulster to be more cautious or less benevolent than their respective Southern neighbours? The reader may judge for himself; but swindlers are not, in general, very wrong in their estimate of character or disposition.

The head-quarters of the society were in an obscure country town in an inland county of Ireland, and there the *materiel* of the association was seized, according to my recollection, in April, 1844. There was found at the source of their system, a chest of very elegant manufacture, and containing, in compartments, admirably executed counterfeits of the public seals of Cork, Waterford, Limerick, Sligo, Drogheda, Dublin, Liverpool, Bristol,

Hamburg, Havre, and New York. These were used to seal forged certificates and attestations, which were transmitted for use to more populous places; but the seals were cunningly kept in a remote, and for a long time, an unsuspected locality.

CHAPTER XI.

CARRIAGE COURT CASES—DUBLIN CARMEN.

WHEN I assumed, by an arrangement with my colleagues, the regulation of the public vehicles, and the disposal of complaints in the Carriage Court at the Head Office, I announced my inflexible determination to cancel the licence of any driver who was proved to have been drunk whilst in charge of his vehicle on the public thoroughfare. I required the fullest proof of the offence, to which I awarded the highest punishment. I am happy to say that such cases were by no means frequent, but there were some, and they generally occurred at funerals. A Rathfarnham carman was summoned before me and was convicted, not only on the clearest evidence, but by his own admission. He was about my own age, and I remembered that when I was about eighteen years old, I was one day swimming in a quarry-hole at Kimmage, where the water was at least twenty feet deep, and was suddenly seized with very severe cramps in my left leg. I kept myself afloat and shouted for help, but I was unable to make for the bank, when a young fellow who had been swimming, and was dressing himself, hastily threw off his clothes, plunged into the water and pushed me before him to the side of the quarry. He saved my life, and I now beheld him in the person of the convicted carman. I related

H

the circumstance from the magisterial bench, and then cancelled his licence, and remarked to those who were assembled, that when I treated the preserver of my life so strictly, others could not expect the slightest lenity at my hands if they transgressed in the same way. The poor fellow left the court in great dejection, and when my duties for the day were over, I dropped in to my friend Colonel Browne, the Commissioner of Police, and mentioned the circumstance to him. He said, " You cancelled his licence, but I can give him a new one, and he shall get it to-morrow." The licence was accordingly renewed without causing me the slightest dissatisfaction.

Most of my readers are aware that the Richmond Bridewell, which is now the common gaol of the City of Dublin, is situated near Harold's Cross; and that on its front is inscribed, " Cease to do evil. Learn to do well." A carman named Doyle, who lived at Blackrock, was summoned before me on charges of violent conduct, abusive language, and extortion. He was a man of very good character, and the complainant was a person of the worst reputation, who had been convicted of several misdemeanors of a very disgraceful nature. Frauds and falsehoods were attributed to him as habitual and inveterate practices. He was sworn, and then he described Doyle as having been most abusive and insulting in his language, as having threatened to kick him unless he paid much more than the rightful fare, and as having extorted an extra shilling by such means. The defendant denied the charges totally, and declared that the accusation was false and malicious. He then asked me to have Inspector O'Connor and Sergeant Power called and examined as to the complainant's character, and whether he was deserving of being believed on his oath. From my own personal knowledge of the complainant's reputation, I willingly acceded to the demand, and desired that the required witnesses should be called from the upper court, where they were both attending. Whilst we were waiting their appearance, Doyle made a speech ; it was very brief, and I took it down *verbatim ;* he said :—

" Your worship, if I get any punishment on this man's oath, it will be a wrong judgment. The Recorder knows him well, and he would'nt sintence a flea to be kilt for back-biting upon his evidence. He has took out all his degrees in the Harold's Cross college ; and if, instead of sending me to the Cease to do evil hotel, you had himself brought there, the door would open for him of its own accord, for there is not a gaol in Ireland that would refuse him. He swore hard against me, but thanks be to God, he did not swear that I was an honest man, for there is nobody whose character could stand *under the weight of his commendation.*"

On the evidence of O'Connor and Power, I dismissed the charge, and subsequently spoke of the case, and repeated Doyle's speech, in festive society. When Boucicault produced his interesting Irish drama of Arra-na-pogue at the Theatre Royal, I was one of his gratified audience, and was greatly surprized at hearing the speech which had been originally delivered before me in the Carriage Court by the Blackrock carman, addressed to the court-martial by Shawn-na-poste, to induce a disbelief of the informer by whom he was accused. I subsequently ascertained that it had been given to Boucicault by one who could fully appreciate its originality and strength, my gifted friend, Dr. Tisdall.

The Dublin carmen are far from being faultless, but, as a class, I found them generally very honest. Whilst I discharged the carriage business, I knew instances of considerable sums of money and articles of value, which had been left in their vehicles, being brought in and delivered up to the police. I do not know how such property, if unclaimed, is now disposed of; but in my time, I invariably, after the expiration of twelve months, had it delivered, subject to charges for advertising, &c., to the person who brought it. I may mention one very extraordinary incident. Before the opening of the Great Southern and Western Railway, the Grand Canal Company ran passenger boats to the towns of Athy and Ballinasloe. A boat for the latter place left Portobello each day at two o'clock. A Rathmines man, who was owner and driver of a covered car, was returning home one morning about 11 o'clock, when he was hailed, in Dame Street, by a respectably dressed man, who engaged him to drive about town, and to be paid by the hour. The hirer stopped at several establishments and bought parcels of woollen, linen, plaid, and cotton goods, as also a hat and a pair of boots, for all of which he paid in cash. There was merely room for the hirer in the vehicle along with his ample purchases. Finally, he directed the driver to go to Portobello, adding that he intended to leave town by the passage-boat at two o'clock. When the car arrived at the end of Lennox Street, the driver was ordered to stop. The hirer alighted and told the driver to go round by the front of the hotel and wait for him at the boat. The order was obeyed, and the carman waited until the boat started, but the hirer did not appear. The driver apprized the police of the circumstance, and, at their suggestion, he attended the two boats which left on the following day, but no one came to claim the goods. They were brought to the police stores and advertised, the hirer was described and sought for in various hotels and lodging-houses, but without any result. It was ascertained at the establishments where the parcels were purchased that they cost twenty-seven pounds, and the carman ultimately got them on paying some small charges. He had not been paid his fare, nevertheless he was not dissatisfied. A rare case amongst his fraternity.

When it was proposed to have a hackney fare for sixpence, "for a drive with not more than two passengers, direct, and without any delay on the part of the hirer, from any place within the municipal boundary to any other place within the same," I refused to sanction such a regulation. I considered that it would, in many instances, be a most inadequate payment for the employment of a vehicle. I suggested that the fifteen municipal wards should form three districts of five wards each, and designated, Southern, Middle, Northern. I proposed that a drive entirely in one of those districts should be a sixpenny fare, that from South or North to Middle, or *vice versa*, should be eightpence, and that North to South, or *vice versa*, should be tenpence. My suggestions were not even considered, for the carmen published advertisements that they were desirous of giving cheap locomotion to the people of Dublin, but that the magistrate refused to allow them to take small fares. I sent for the "runners," as the attendants on the stands were termed, and told them that I should no longer object to the sixpenny fare which was proposed. I added that it was the carmen's own act, and, to use a homely phrase, "as they had made the bed, nothing remained for me but to compel them to lie in it." The by-law was no sooner in operation than numerous cases of its violation were brought before me. I fined each, if I thought it fully proved, in the maximum penalty of two pounds. One delinquent was extremely urgent to have a smaller penalty inflicted. I recognized him as having been present when I used the phrase which I have quoted, and reminded him that he had been fully warned. He replied, "Yes, yer worship, we did make the bed, and you promised to make us lie in it, *but we never thought that it would be so heavily quilted.*"

I held that any stop or deviation from the direct line between two places, at the hirer's instance, voided the sixpenny contract, and entitled the driver to additional remuneration. I often availed myself of a sixpenny lift, and was once taking one in which I passed the Shelbourne Hotel, in front of which there was a "hazard," or branch stand for five or six cars or cabs. It was considered very objectionable for a disengaged vehicle to stop alongside a hazard and thus obstruct the carriage way. I observed a jarvey committing this offence, and desired my driver to "hold a moment." I said to the offender, "If a constable takes your number for obstructing, you will not escape for less than ten shillings." I then bid my man to go on. He replied, "Yes, yer worship, and it would serve that fellow right to have him punished, for he is after putting your worship in for *another sixpence to me.*"

Two of my daughters had gone to make some purchases at the establishment of Messrs. Todd and Burns, in Mary Street. They were engaged to spend the afternoon at a house in Leinster Street. Rain was falling, and the elder beckoned to the driver of a covered car who happened to be passing. They got into it, and desired him to go to No. 14 Leinster Street. When they arrived, the elder let her sister pass before her into the house, and then she offered a sixpence to the carman. He declined to take it, and said that she should give "the father or mother of that." She asked how much did he demand? and the reply was "a shilling at least." She then said that she would get half-a-crown changed in the house, and bring him a shilling, but she added "that she would speak to papa about it." "Musha, who is papa?" said he. "Mr. Porter," was the reply. She went in, got the change, and came back with the shilling, but he was gone. He preferred giving her a gratuitous drive to having my opinion elicited in reference to the transaction.

A cavalry regiment, if I recollect rightly it was the "Scots Greys," occupied the barracks at Island Bridge in 1854. One day an outside jaunting-car was waiting in the barrack-yard, and the driver was standing on the step. He was a few yards from the quarters of a Captain B——, who was reputed to have a private income of £15,000 per annum. The officer was amusing himself with a little gun, which discharged peas and leaden pellets by detonating caps with greater force than the captain was aware of. He shot at the carman, and the pellet passed through his overcoat and reached his back, giving him a smart blow, but without penetrating the skin. The driver was looking round, and expressing his displeasure, when he received a second shot which, striking the calf of his leg, lodged in the flesh. He instantly whipped his horse, drove rapidly away, and betook himself to the Meath Hospital, where the shot was extracted. He summoned the officer before me, and when the facts were stated, I expressed an opinion that the act was most unjustifiable, that a wanton and very severe assault had been committed, but that I thought it originated more in a spirit of foolish fun than in any wish to injure the complainant, and as it was a misdemeanor, the parties might come to an understanding, which would render further proceedings unnecessary.

The captain accosted the carman—" Will you take one hundred pounds ?"

" Of coorse, I will, yer honor, and I'll never say another word, even if you war to shoot me agin."

Two fifty-pound notes were handed to the delighted complainant, who then said to me—

"The business is settled, yer worship, and I can only say that whin I was hit, although it gave me a great start, I felt satisfied it was a *rale gintleman* that shot me."

I advised the captain to discontinue the sport of jarvey-shooting. Cox complimented him on his generosity, adding that he ought to have got a large covey of such game for the price he paid. I regret to add that the money did not improve its recipient. He lapsed into habits of idleness and drunkenness, lost his licence through misconduct, and was reduced to complete destitution.

A gentleman, who lived in Baggot Street, came to Exchange Court one morning for the purpose of reporting that his coach-house had been entered, as he believed, by means of false keys, and that a set of cushions, adapted to an outside jaunting-car, had been abstracted. He described them as white cord material with green borders and seams. A detective mentioned that he had seen cushions of the description on a car which had been brought for inspection, and the licence of which had been suspended on account of its unseemly condition. The car was then in Dame Street, and a further enquiry eventuated in the discovery on it of the articles which had been supposed to have been abstracted. The owner of the car was a brother of the gentleman's servant who had lent his master's cushions to pass the inspection. The car licence was cancelled ; but I believe that similar tricks were frequently played on similar occasions.

For upwards of ten years I have been estranged from the Dublin Police Courts. I cannot speak as to the habits and characteristics of the carmen of the present time. I have already stated that, according to my experience and recollection, they were honest and sober. I can add that I knew many instances in which members of their class manifested generosity, kindness, and courage. A man belonging to New Street stand went to the fair of St. Doolagh's, and expended his savings in the purchase of a fine-looking horse that appeared in a sound condition, but on whose leg there was a slight scar. In about a week after the fair, the beast exhibited some very extraordinary symptoms, and at last became most furious and unruly. He dashed into a shop window, and injured himself so much as to make it necessary to kill it. It was the opinion of a veterinary practitioner that he had been bitten by some rabid animal, and had taken hydrophobia. The other carmen promptly subscribed a sum sufficient to defray the damage done to the shop, and to procure another horse for the man who vainly sought to ascertain the former owner of the one that he bought at St. Doolagh's. I am aware that previous to the establishment of the fire brigade in Dublin, the drivers on a car-stand would leave two or three of their number to mind their horses and vehicles, and apply themselves to work the engines and extinguish fires in their vicinity. Many acts of heroism on the part of carmen have occurred on our quays and at Kingstown, in saving, at their own imminent risk, persons in danger of drowning.

Having noticed some very good qualities, I must remark on the scarcity amongst them, according to my experience, of veracity. When a carman was summoned by a constable he almost invariably met the accusation by a direct contradiction. If called on to answer for being shabbily dressed or dirty in his apparel, he bought or borrowed a good suit of clothes, shaved, put on a clean shirt, and stated boldly to me that he was just in the same attire when the policeman "wrote him." If the summons was for being absent from his beast and vehicle, he insisted that he was holding "a lock of hay" to his horse all the time. If the complaint was for furious driving, the defence was that "the baste was dead lame, that it was just after taking up a nail, and was on three legs when he was 'wrote.'" If it was alleged that the horse was in a wretched condition, and unfit to ply for public accommodation, he expressed his surprise that any fault should be found with a horse that could "rowl" four to the Curragh and back without "turning a hair." Whatever statement was made for the defence, it evinced imaginative power, for the plain, dull truth was hardly ever permitted the slightest admixture in the excuse offered. Mr. Hughes, whom I have mentioned in some earlier pages, was in the carriage-court one day, on an occasion when an old man named Pat Markey, formerly belonging to the Baggot Street stand, made a statement utterly at variance with all probability, and directly opposed to the evidence adduced against him : however, on the prosecutor's own showing the case was dismissed, as the charge was not legally sustained. On leaving the court, Hughes asked Pat why he did not tell the truth at first, as it would have been better for him ; upon which the other exclaimed—"Musha, cock him up with the truth! that's more than ever I towld a magistrate yit." A delinquent seldom mentioned the offence for which he was punished ; he generally substituted for it the inducement which led to its commission. If he went into a tobacconist's, and while he made his purchase, his horse moved on, and was stopped by a constable, who summoned the driver, the latter when asked what he was fined for would reply, "for taking a blast of the pipe." If, on a Saturday evening, he betook himself to a barber's shop to have the week's growth taken off his chin, and incurred a penalty for being absent from his vehicle, he said, "the polis wrote him" for getting himself shaved. And on Sunday morning, if a devotional feeling prompted him to get "a mouthful of prayers," whilst his beast remained, without any person to mind it, upon the public thoroughfare, he expressed his indignation at a consequent fine "for going to Mass."

I found it impossible to adapt the law, as it existed in my time, so as effectually to compel the carmen to keep themselves in cleanly, respectable attire, or their vehicles in proper order. When summoned and fined, their comments evinced the inutility of the punishment. I have said to one, "Your car has been proved to be in a most disgraceful state, and I shall fine you ten shillings." The reply has been, "I thank yer worship, shure *that fine will help me to mend it.*" I have told another that I would suspend his licence for a month; but this only elicited a request for an order to admit him and his family to the poorhouse during the suspension. If the complaints preferred by the police did not effect much good, those brought forward by private individuals were, in their general tendency, and as a class of cases, decidedly injurious. When extortion, violence, insolence, or an infraction of duty provoked an aggrieved person to summon, the usual course was for the delinquent to send his wife to the complainant's residence, or sometimes to borrow a wife, if he had not one of his own, to beg him off. In the case of a young lad being the offender, the intercession was managed by his mother, whether the maternity was real or pretended. The afflicted female beset the door, and applied to all who passed in or out "to save her and her childher, or her poor *gorsoun*, from the waves of the world," that Mr. Porter was a "rale Turk," and if the poor fellow was brought before him, he would be destroyed "out of a face." A riddance of such importunities formed no slight inducement to forego the prosecution, and consequently the majority of such cases were dismissed for the non-appearance of the complainant; but sometimes the fellow who had been "begged off" came forward, stated that he was ready to answer the summons, and insisted on his loss of time being recompensed by costs. I must admit that I always complied with such applications, and I have enjoyed frequently the vain remonstrances of the forgiving party, who, for his mistaken and expensive lenity, acquired nothing but the wholesome warning not to summon a Dublin driver without appearing to prosecute.

Although the carmen were rather fond of getting more than their fare, they became the dupes and victims of dishonest and tricky employers, and, to use their own term, were "sconced" much more frequently than was generally supposed. The Four Courts constituted, in my time, the frequent scene of such rascality. There was seldom a day in Term that some poor carman was not left "without his costs" by a plausible fellow, who alighting at one door, and passing through the hall, went out at another, leaving the driver with the assurance, that "he would be back in a minute," to find that he had been employed, for perhaps an hour or two previously, by a heartless blackguard, who desired no better fun than "sconcing" him. I believe that a regulation has been since adopted which authorises a driver engaged by time to require payment in advance. I consider it a very great improvement.

CHAPTER XII.

A GRATUITOUS JAUNT——THE PORTUGUESE POSTIL-
LION——MISCELLANEOUS SUMMONSES.

A YOUNG woman who was servant in a house in Harcourt
Street in which two students resided, had an altercation
with one of them, which eventuated in a summons and a
cross-summons before me. It appeared that the young
man had imputed dishonesty to her, and she had been
very indignant and abusive towards her accuser. He
called his fellow-student as a witness, to prove that the
girl threw a bottle at him, and that she freely used the
terms of swindler, blackguard, &c. The charge of dishonesty was unfounded, and the encounter between the
parties terminated without any personal injury to either,
but the damsel cross-examined the witness in reference to
a transaction, and elicited a mode of procuring a jaunt
across the city, which I hope that I shall not lessen the
reader's interest in my observations and reminiscences of
the Dublin carmen by briefly detailing. The woman
acquired the knowledge of it by having overheard a conversation between the young men.

They had been invited to an early evening party at
Summer Hill. They were not inclined to walk such a
distance, and neither of them found it convenient to pay

for a vehicle.   At last the one who subsequently complained of being termed a swindler and blackguard said that he would get a covered car without payment.   Accordingly, having walked to the nearest "hazard," he desired his comrade to get into a car, and also seated himself, he then directed the driver to proceed "to Santry."   "Santry!" exclaimed the astonished jarvey; "is it joking you are?   D——l an inch I'll go to Santry to-night.   Get out of my car if you plaze, the baste is tired, and I wont go."   "My good fellow," was the answer, "I shall not get out, and you may as well get on at once."   "By gorra, if you don't get out, I'll pull you out," said the carman. "If you lay a finger on me," answered the occupant, "I will resist you as well as I can, and I shall prosecute you for an assault."   It was a bad business.   The carman changed his tactics.   "Why, yer honor," he mildly urged, "it is an unrasonable thing to ax a man to go to such a place even in the day time, for there's nothin but murdher and robbery on that bloody road, an' if I *do* go, we'll be all kilt, and you'll be robbed into the bargain ; shure you haven't right sinse to think of such a jaunt." "My friend," said the fare, "there may be something in what you say, but I shall call at a house on Summer Hill and get firearms for myself and my companion, and with two case of pistols I fear no robbers."   The carman grumbled, but he had a sturdy customer, so he mounted his seat and drove on.   When they came to Summer Hill he was desired to pull up, and the two sparks alighted, assuring him that they would immediately procure the arms and resume their journey.   As soon as they were inside the hall-door, the jarvey plied his whip, and rattled off as fast as he could, congratulating himself that he had escaped a drive to Santry, and leaving the two scamps to enjoy the joke of having got a gratuitous jaunt from Harcourt Street to Summer Hill.

There was at the time of my appointment to the magistracy, a car proprietor in Dublin, whose name was Bittner. His father had been a sergeant in the King's German Legion, had been invalided, and died in Dublin about the year 1810, leaving one son, who was then sixteen years of age. He was tolerably educated, intelligent, cleanly, active, and well-looking. A gentleman who was in delicate health, engaged the lad as his personal attendant, and was soon after advised by his physicians to betake himself to the south of Europe, in the hope of checking the progress of pulmonary disease. Lisbon was the only available place to the invalid, and he proceeded there, along with his youthful servant. He lived in Portugal for nine or ten years, and was so well satisfied with the care and attention of Bittner that he left him a legacy of £250. The gentleman's body was directed by his will to be interred in Dublin, whither it was conveyed by the faithful domestic. Bittner did not squander his money, neither did he become inactive. He was fond of horses, and of equestrian exercise, and engaged in the service of the late Mr. Quin, of Bray; then the proprietor of an extensive hotel and first-rate posting establishment. The romantic scenery of Wicklow was then, as it must ever be, highly appreciated, and Quin's chaises conveyed many visitors to the varied and numerous scenes of picturesque beauty. On one occasion Bittner was directed to bring a chaise to the door, to take two foreign gentlemen through the Glen of the Downs, and on to Dunran. The travellers were quite unacquainted with the English language, and in the hotel, had recourse to signs and self-attendance as much as possible. They got into the chaise, having

previously pointed out on a map to Mr. Quin, the route
they wished to take.   On arriving at the gate of Dunran,
they made signs to stop the vehicle, and alighted.   They
then began to bewail to each other, their ignorance of
English, and their consequent inability to acquire information as to the scenery, residences, and other particulars
usually interesting to tourists.   They spoke Portuguese,
and Bittner immediately accosted them in their own
language, told them that he would procure a person to
mind his horses, and that he would then take them up to
the " View Rock," and conduct them to each of the many
places worthy of their observation.   They expressed the
highest gratification, and availed themselves of his services.
As they proceeded, he told them that Mr. Quin's was the
greatest and best regulated establishment *in the world.*
That there were postillions kept there who had been
procured from every European nation.   The French
postillions had gone with a party of their countrymen to
the " Seven Churches," and two Germans and one
Italian had left, early in the morning, for the Vale of
Ovoca.   The Spaniard was gone to Luggelaw.   " I,"
said he, " am the Portuguese postillion, I am delighted to
have you, and can take you to all the beautiful places in
Wicklow, but I am afraid that I shall soon have to leave
this employment, for we hardly ever have a Portuguese
gentleman at the hotel, so my chances are very poor."
The travellers, driven by Bittner for about a-week, went
to all the delightful scenery of Wicklow, and when
departing, gave him a couple of sovereigns.   In about
three months after, Mr. Quin received a parcel in which
there were two nicely bound volumes, and a complimentary letter, sent from Lisbon by Don Pedro Cabrito.
With some difficulty he got the letter translated, and also

a couple of pages which had been turned down to attract his attention. He was then made aware that the Portuguese traveller accorded the highest praise to the comfort and elegance of his establishment, and also to his anxiety to convenience his foreign visitors, by keeping postillions, who, in the aggregate, were acquainted with *all European languages.* The book also made honorable mention of the " Portuguese postillion," Bittner. The latter, as I have already stated, became a car proprietor. His vehicles were cleanly and neat, his drivers well conducted, and a complaint against him was of very rare occurrence. On one occasion, after I had heard an explanation from his driver, he asked my leave to say " a word or two," to which I replied, " With pleasure Mr. Bittner, I shall hear you, provided you do not speak Portuguese." " Oh! your worship," said he, " I see you know that story. I suppose Mr. Quin told you." His supposition was correct.

A FEW HYPERBOLES.

One of the clerks in the police-court of Liverpool got leave of absence in, as I best remember, 1845. He came to Dublin with some other young Englishmen for a few days of recreation. Curiosity induced him to visit our police-courts, where our clerks received him with fraternal courtesy. He told Mr. Cox that he and three others took an outside car, for a suburban drive. It happened to be on *Corpus Christi* day, and they were going along Rathmines road, just as the religious procession incident to the festival was moving round the extensive court outside of the Roman Catholic church there. They directed the driver to stop, and then stood up on the seats to obtain a full view. Almost immediately one of them exclaimed,

I

"Well, that beats the devil!" The carman touched his hat to the exclaimer and replied, "Yes, your honor, that's what it's for." I have heard the late Judge Halliburton (Sam Slick the clock-maker) say, that he asked a carman what was the reason for building the Martello towers? and that the interrogated party told him, "he supposed it was, like the round towers, *to puzzle posterity.*"

The Spaniard, who described the rain as so heavy, that "it wetted him to the marrow," was not so poetical or forcible in his hyperbole as some of our jarveys have been. I recollect reading in a little work, published many years ago, and entitled "Sketches of Ireland," that when a gentleman complained of the choking dust of the Rock road, and declared that he did not think it possible for a road to be so dusty, his driver remarked, "It's thrue for yer honor; but this road bates all others for dust, for, *by all accounts, there was dust on this road the day after Noah's flood.*" A lady who resided at Chapelizod was wont to give a carman whom she frequently employed a glass of grog, along with his fare, at the conclusion of each engagement. However, she became too sparing of the spirits, or too generous of the water, but the grog eventually became so weak, that its recipient criticised it, of course with an oath, by asserting, that "if you threw half-a-pint of whisky over Essex Bridge, you might take up as strong grog as that at the Lighthouse."

MISCELLANEOUS SUMMONSES.

According to my recollections of the summons cases of a police-court, apart from carriage complaints, I feel justified in remarking on the mild and forgiving tendencies of the men, and the vindictive rancour of the women of Dublin. From recent conversations with police functionaries, I am disposed to believe that the present time differs in no material respect from the past. The man claims the protection of the law; " he has no desire to injure the parties he complains of, but he wants them bound to the peace, just to keep them quiet." The woman wants " the coorse of the law," and to have her adversary chastised and kept from killing the whole world, like a murdhering vagabone as she is; it 's no use in talkin', but the street will never be quiet until she gets *some little confinement* just to *larn* her manners." Summonses for abusive language, or as the fair complainants term it, " street scandal," are, perhaps, the most numerous cases as a class; and on the hearing of them, there is frequently elicited an amount of vituperation beyond anything that Billingsgate could attempt to supply. In almost every case a total absence of chastity is imputed as a matter of course; and if a foreigner would only believe both sides of a police summons-book, he would be forced to the conclusion that chastity was a virtue rarely found amongst the lower order of Dublin females. Yet the very contrary is the fact: furious in their resentments, uncontrollable in their invectives, and inveterately addicted to assassination of character, they are, in general, extremely chaste; and attest the value they attach to female virtue by invariably imputing its absence to their opponents. Sometimes, indeed, a novel term of reproach arouses volcanic fury, and an eruption of indignation is excited by the most extraordinary and unmeaning epithet. I cannot forget a fish-vendor from Patrick Street vociferating to me, that if her enemy was not sent off to Grangegorman *at wanst*, her life and her child's life (for she was *enceinte*) would be lost. " But what did she say?" was my query. " What did she say! yer worship, what did she say! Why she came down

forenenst the whole world at the corner of Plunket Street,
and called me "a bloody ould excommunicated gasometer."
I may mention that as female invective generally ascribed
incontinency to its opponent, so the male scolds—happily
not very numerous—had their favorite term of reproach;
and when they wished to destroy a man's reputation, they
designated him—a thief?—no; a robber?—no; a murderer?—no; they satiated all their malignity in calling him
"an informer."

Disputes between manufacturers and their artisans or
workmen were very rarely the subject of magisterial investigation. There was, however, one case disposed of by me
in which a comparison was instituted of a most extraordinary nature. A journeyman summoned an employer
for abruptly dismissing him, without giving him, according
to the usage of the trade, "a week's notice or a week's
wages." I shall not mention the name, residence, or trade
of the defendant; but I must say that his countenance
exhibited the greatest obliquity of vision that I ever
observed in a human face. All the trite phrases commonly applied to squints would fail adequately to describe
the tendency of his eyes to avoid seeing the same object at
the same time. He admitted having summarily discharged
the workman, and alleged that the complainant had totally
spoiled an article which he had been directed to make in a
hexagon form, and conformable to a pattern supplied, and
had produced a piece of work in which shape and proportion had been totally disregarded. The complainant
insisted that the work had been properly done, and in
complete conformity with the model, and he asked why
it was not produced, so that I might judge, by viewing it,
whether it deserved to be condemned as crooked and
shapeless. I suggested a postponement of the case, and

the production of the condemned article. The defendant, who was rather excited, replied, " Your worship, I was so vexed when it was brought in, that I threw it out of the window of the finishing room into the yard, and it was smashed to pieces, but I am ready to swear, in this or any other court, that *it was as crooked as the two eyes in my head.*" The laugh in which I indulged, at hearing this comparison, was lost in the risibility of all present. I suggested that the parties might come to an understanding, and that the complainant might be afforded another opportunity of making an article perfectly conformable to the pattern, and without any resemblance *to anything else.* This was agreed to, and they departed reconciled.

CHAPTER XIII.

DOGS—WHIPPING YOUNG THIEVES—GARDEN ROB-
BERS—REFORMATORIES—APOLOGIES FOR VIO-
LENCE—TRESPASSERS ON A NUNNERY.

THE statute, passed since my retirement, to enforce and
regulate the registration of dogs, has relieved the magistrates from having to dispose, in the course of each year,
of some hundreds of summonses against the owners, or
reputed owners of dogs which were found " roaming at
large on the public thoroughfare, without log or muzzle."
In my time, I never found a summons in reference to a
dog, at the instance of a constable, entered indiscriminately
with other complaints. If the first case was a canine one,
I might feel assured that it would be followed by forty or
fifty others of the same description, and that the dogs
would monopolise the day. It appeared to me that the
police were occasionally directed to give special attention,
for two or three days, to the unlogged and unmuzzled
curs, and thus produce what our clerks used to term " a
dog board." The appearance of a male defendant was
extremely rare. The persons complained of were generally working tradesmen or labourers, who, on receiving a
summons, directed the wife to attend the court, as they
could not afford to lose their time. When a defendant
was called, his female substitute, eager to have the first

word, answered to the man's name; but what she said referred to the animal. A mere listener might imagine that the defendants were either guilty of some atrocious offences, or were subjected, unheard and untried, to a fearful, fatal doom; for instance—

" Call James Foley."

" He's drounded, yer worship, we drounded him off Wood Quay, the very evening that we got the summons, he was'nt logged or muzzled, but he is dead now, and the policeman 'ill never see him again."

" You are fined two and sixpence."

" Oh ! yer worship, that's very hard, and he dead."

" Call Peter Casey."

" He's hung, sir; he was very owld and stupid, and had'nt a tooth in his head, so we hung him, not to be bother'd with him any more," &c.

" Call Patrick Dempsey."

" Plaze yer worship, he's dead, and if the polisman knew him, he'll know that he's dead. We had him hung and got him skinned, and I have his skin here to show you."

Perhaps another case would disclose the appalling fact, that Denis Reilly was " *pisened* by a young doctor that we got to sponge his nose with some Prooshun stuff, and it kilt him." Such calamities have been averted from the Foleys, Caseys, Dempseys, and Reillys of the present time, and the magistrates have been relieved from having to listen to such murderous details from the lips of the gentler sex by the magical effect of canine registration.

WHIPPING YOUNG THIEVES.

In a few years after my appointment, a statute passed authorising the infliction of corporal punishment on boys convicted of thieving. The Act empowered us to order the offender to be flogged, if we were of opinion that his age did not exceed fourteen years. There was a lad named Lowry, who was an inveterate thief, and who received five or six castigations by my directions. The instrument employed was a birch rod, with which a constable gave the delinquent six heavy lashes. As soon as Lowry appeared before me, he seemed to disregard the details of the charge preferred. There were no protestations of innocence, no admissions of guilt; but the moment he entered, he commenced the loud and continued assertion, "I'm beyant fourteen, I'm beyant fourteen." On each occasion I differed from the opinion so forcibly enunciated, and ordered the application of the birchen correction. Finally, he withdrew from my quarter, and restricted his delinquencies to the B and C divisions. I was informed that he expressed his disgust at my decisions by saying— "If I was to live until I got as grey as the owld rascal himself, he'd still insist that I was not beyant fourteen."

One day there were a number of packages lying in a heap on the floor of a shop in Parliament Street, and rather near the entrance. A label upon each stated the contents to be three pounds of tea, of the finest quality, offered by the proprietor of "The Golden Teapot" to his respected customers, at the unprecedented low price of seven shillings. The parcels were covered with bright tin foil, and had on each end a large seal in red wax. A detective passing at the opposite side of the street observed a boy stoop forward, just inside the door, and possess himself of one of the packages of "splendid tea." The young thief was seized at once and brought before me, in about five minutes after he had stolen the article. I ordered him to be taken down stairs, to have six lashes administered, and to be discharged. I then directed the office messenger to run over to the establishment, and tell them to send some person to claim the property. On his return he said that the people were making fun of him, and laughing at the result of the young thief's attempt. I then raised one of the seals slightly with an office knife, and found that the parcel was a *dummy*, made up for show, and that the contents were sawdust. I told the messenger, when I had closed the seal with another touch of wax, to take it down and give it to the delinquent on his departure, as the owners had not claimed the property. The whipping was just over, and the sufferer issued forth, having under his arm the cause of his punishment, and for which it was to become his consolation. I was standing at the window, and just as he passed the external rails, he stopped suddenly, and proceeded to examine the package. Instantly he tore the cover, and flung up the contents. The pain of the flogging seemed to return with augmented force, and he screamed forth the most vituperative comments on my decision. "It wasn't tay at all. I was beat for sawdust, and there's no law for that. I'll get a letter wrote to the Lord Leftennant, you owld rascal, and he'll larn you the differ between sawdust and tay." Inspector O'Connor told me that the case was very fully discussed amongst the young thieves, and that the general conclusion was, "not to be too ready to steal parcels out of shops, without knowing what was inside of them."

GARDEN ROBBERS.

My immediate predecessors generally resided in Dublin, and they were considered by the proprietors of orchards and gardens in the rural portion of the district, as too

lenient to depredators of fruit and vegetables. At the
time of my appointment, there was no safety for such
crops unless they were closely watched, and during the
night, the discharge of firearms, to deter marauders, was
almost continuous in Dolphin's Barn, Kilmainham, Harold's Cross, and Crumlin. Any cessation of strict vigilance was certain to produce consequences which might
be fairly termed calamitous to those whose fruits and
vegetables were depended on for the maintenance of their
families. There were many persons who followed garden
robbing as their avocation, and the injuries inflicted by
them frequently extended to the succeeding year. If
they feared interruption, they would tear or cut the
branches of the larger fruits, and entire gooseberry and
currant bushes would be abstracted, to be picked at leisure.
Small fines or short imprisonments had totally failed to
check such offences. At the time to which I refer, I resided at Roundtown, and although I had gardens and a
fine vinery there, they were never spoliated, so that in
adopting towards fruit-stealers stronger measures than
they had previously experienced, I was not actuated by
any personal feeling. However, I had the birch very
liberally used amongst the boys, and the more mature
offenders were, when convicted by me, deprived of any
opportunity for continuing their depredations on the growing or ripening productions of the season. Personal
motives were, nevertheless, sometimes ascribed to me,
even by those who were highly pleased with my decisions.
A very extensive orchard and garden at Harold's Cross
were entered by three habitual thieves, and they were captured whilst hastily filling two sacks with the choicest
apples, pears, apricots, &c. They had taken the sacks
from premises adjoining, and I convicted them of two

distinct offences. Each was sent for four months to Kilmainham, with hard labour. Mr. Cox was engaged in drawing the informations and committals, when the proprietor exclaimed, in a tone of the highest gratification, "Oh! Mr. Cox, is it not a blessing from God that we have now got a magistrate *who has a garden of his own?*"

Two musicians belonging to a regimental band were observed one night to cross a wall at Inchicore, into a garden abounding with every description of choice fruit. The police were quietly apprised of the offence, and the delinquents were apprehended coming out of the premises precisely at the place where they had entered. They were both Germans. Their pockets were crammed, and each had a handkerchief containing as much as could be bundled in it. They had not taken a peach, apricot, or plum; even the pears and apples were disregarded; and the produce of their daring raid consisted entirely of *onions*. I committed them for a week, and they were dismissed from the service by the regimental authorities.

REFORMATORIES.

Previous to my retirement from magisterial duty, the offence of fruit-stealing had greatly diminished, and I believe that it does not now attain one-tenth of its former frequency. When the magistrates were empowered to send juvenile thieves to reformatories, corporal punishment ceased to be administered. I preferred having a boy flogged and discharged to sending him to prison, to be kept, at the public expense, in baneful associations. As soon, however, as a reformatory became available, I transmitted the juvenile offenders, after a few days' imprisonment, to the care and instruction which, in all those institutions, have produced most beneficial results. My first consignment to Glencree Reformatory was made under circumstances rather extraordinary.

I was invited by my kind and valued friend, the late Mr. George Evans, of Portrane, to spend a week at his hospitable mansion. Arrangements were made by me with my colleagues to admit of my absence for that time, and that I should take the duty on the Monday of the succeeding week. Accordingly, I came to Dublin from Donabate by an early train, and commenced the custody cases about ten o'clock, a.m. A constable prosecuted a lad whom he had met on Rathmines Road about four o'clock on that morning, carrying a coarse bath-sheet, in which two check shirts, three pairs of cotton socks, and a washing waistcoat were wrapped. The prisoner was charged with having those articles in his possession, they being "reasonably suspected of having been stolen or unlawfully obtained." I called on the prisoner to account to my satisfaction how he came by them. He declined any explanation, and produced a laugh in court by saying "that I would know time enough." I ordered him to be imprisoned for a week, and then to be transmitted to Glencree for three years. On my return home to Roundtown in the evening, I was told that my bath-sheet, nightshirts, &c., had been stolen on the previous night from a bleaching-line in the back yard, over the wall of which my first envoy to Glencree had managed to clamber. The articles did not remain long in the police store.

APOLOGIES FOR VIOLENCE.

Soon after my appointment to office, an election occurred, and the city of Dublin was keenly contested. I received an order to proceed, on the nomination day, to Green Street, to take charge of the civil force there, and to report myself to the returning officer, the High Sheriff. I had consequently, in my official capacity, to present myself to my own brother, the late Joshua Porter, and I continued during the election, which was protracted as long as the law allowed, ready to quell any riotous demonstration. My brother was not fortunate enough to please all parties. His arrangements of booths and selection of deputies were denounced as having been made in a partial spirit, and the mob vociferously expressed an anxiety to be actuated in their treatment of him by the greatest of Christian virtues, for they unanimously agreed that it would be a "charity" to pelt him, if any opportunity offered to make a liberal subscription of stones for the purpose. He was escorted each day to and from the court-house by a strong body of police, and he remained in it until the termination of the proceedings in the evenings. There was usually, during the election, a troop of hussars stationed in Halston Street, at the rere of Newgate, and a party of police was distributed between them and King Street, North. One afternoon, just at twilight, I walked out of the court-house, and as soon as I got to the steps, a crowd in King Street uttered a yell of animosity, and sent a volley of stones at me. I was not struck by any of the missiles. The police moved towards the mob, and the latter receded a few yards, but remained together. I walked towards them, and loudly informed them, that if they renewed their attack, I had the " Riot Act" in my pocket, and would instantly read it, and rep y by a discharge of carbine bullets. There was no further demonstration on their part, and I returned to the court-house. In a few minutes, I was departing for home, when I was accosted by a carman named Smith. He asked me, " Would I take a covered car ?" and I replied in the affirmative. He brought me home; and on discharging him, he said that the people had directed him to try "if he could get to say two or three words to me." He then conveyed to me the most extraordinary apology that could emanate from a mob for an attempted outrage. "Yer worship, I was tould to tell you that there wasn't a man or boy among them would throw anything at you or any other of yer magistrates, but whin you came out on the steps, in the dusk of the evening, they really thought that you were THE HIGH SHERIFF."

I may mention that being in London in 1849, on official business, I was invited to dine at the Mansion House at an entertainment given by the Lord Mayor of that year (Sir James Duke) to the judicial authorities, metropolitan magistrates, &c. I had the honour to sit beside Chief Baron Pollock, and in conversation with him and two or three others in my proximity, I narrated the preceding anecdote. He said that the apology tendered to me was not more ridiculous or absurd than one which had been offered by some of those engaged in the "No Popery" riots of 1780, connected with the name of Lord George Gordon. There was a house in Charles Street, from the precincts of which morality was totally estranged, and it was thoroughly devastated by a furious mob. Some of those concerned in wrecking it were subsequently arrested, tried and convicted of the offence. When brought forward for sentence, the judge gave them to understand that the reputation of the premises afforded no justification for their violence, nor could it be alledged in mitigation of their punishment. Two or three of them exclaimed, "that if they had known what the house really was, they would never have attacked it; but they had been told, and fully believed, that it was *a Nunnery.*"

TRESPASSERS ON A NUNNERY.

In twelve or eighteen months after the festive occasion to to which I have referred, I accompanied a friend to visit two of his daughters, who were pupils at the Loretto Convent, Rathfarnham. Mrs. Ball, the aged and respected Superioress, gave us a very kind reception. We were conducted through the gardens and conservatories. On returning to the house, we were plentifully served with refreshments. In the course of conversation, my friend expressed his regret that so much hostile feeling should exist against conventual institutions. I remarked that it was not at all so intense as it had been in the previous century, when in London the mere reputation of a house being a nunnery was considered by the populace as fully sufficient to justify its destruction. To the best of my recollection, the Superioress observed—" I hope that those who entertained such hostile feelings lived long enough to repent of them. I think that the various classes of society are coming to a better understanding, and I expect great progressive improvement. Here we have not suffered the slightest annoyance for more than thirty years, and the only matter of which we had to complain was not very serious. Shortly after this establishment was founded, two young fellows, who resided in the neighbourhood, formed a design to entice two very handsome and rich young ladies to elope with them. They provided ladders, climbed into the trees which overhung the wall, dropped notes at the feet of the lasses, and were for a time incessant in their amatory pursuit. However, a communication with the guardian of one and the parents of the other, and the consequent authoritative expostulations, produced a satisfactory effect. They promised to relinquish their project, and as a token of their sincerity, sent us their ladders. I believe they repented of having given us any trouble, and they implicitly kept their promise. One of them is now a colonel in the army, and the other is *a magistrate of police.* Mr. Porter, let me request you to have some more fruit and another glass of wine." I admired the kind and forgiving sentiments of the Superioress, and felt very grateful for her courteous hospitality, but I had no idle curiosity to know the names of the two ladder lads to whom her observations referred.

CHAPTER XIV.

TERRY DRISCOLL'S FICTION—BRIDGET LAFFAN—
SAILORS—FISHER.

I SHALL now revert to magisterial reminiscences, and notice an anecdote originally published in the *Warder* newspaper, as a portion of a letter signed " Terry Driscoll," which was the *nom de plume* of a well-known facetious and imaginative contributor named Jackson. It purports to be a report of observations addressed by me to a female who was repeatedly charged with being "drunk and disorderly." It states that Mr. Porter said to the delinquent that her frequent intoxication was always accompanied with indecent language and personal violence, so as to render her a public nuisance and a plague to the police. He then adjudged her, in default of solvent security for her good behaviour, to be committed for one calendar month, which time should be sufficient to bring her to a proper state of reflection on the past, and a disposition to reform her habits, and to curse Whisky. To this she is represented to have replied, " That she had no fault to find with Whisky, nor would she ever curse it, but from the bottom of her heart she could wish *bad luck to Porter.*" To this anecdote several English periodicals have afforded extensive publicity, and I have merely to say that it is altogether a fiction.

K

BRIDGET LAFFAN.

There is, I believe, still living in Dublin, a woman named Bridget Laffan. I would readily wager that since 1841 she has been the subject of more than two thousand committals, in which drunkenness, violence, abusive language, indecent expressions or behaviour, and occasional mendicancy, constituted the offences. Shortly before I retired, she was brought before me charged with intoxication, and with three distinct assaults; one being on a constable in the execution of his duty. I told her, the cases having been fully proved, that on each of the assaults she should go to prison, with hard labor, for two months, which would relieve the public and the police for the next half year from one who had become an intolerable pest and disgrace to the community. When I directed her to be removed, she exclaimed that " she had got no fair play, and had not been allowed to say a word for herself." I then said that she was at liberty to speak, if it occurred to her that there was any favorable circumstance in her case either as a defence or mitigation. Her reply was short and peculiarly argumentative.

" It 's an unrasonable thing to sind me to Grangegorman for six months, and to call me a pest and disgrace to the 'varsal world. If it wasn't for me and the likes of me, that gets a bit disorderly whin we have a drop, and kicks up ructions now and then, there ud be very little call for polis magistrates and polismen, or such varmint. It 's creatures like me that 's yer best friends, and keeps the bread in yer mouths, and all we get for it is jailing and impudence."

SAILORS.

During the considerable time in which I discharged magisterial duties at the Head Office and also at Kingstown, I cannot recollect that more than five or six charges were preferred before me against sailors. When the Ajax was stationed at the latter place one of the crew stole some clothes and other articles from several of his shipmates. The thief was detected on shore with some of the property in his possession, and was summarily convicted before me, and imprisoned, with hard labor, for six months. I notice this case on account of the discontent which, I was credibly informed, the treatment of the delinquent produced amongst the crew. It is generally believed that the abolition of corporal punishment was anxiously desired by our sailors ; but in reference to the instance of thieving which was disposed of by me, it was regarded on board the ship as almost tantamount to the forgiveness of the delinquent. The opinion was most freely expressed that the fellow should have been sent on board, tried by court-martial, *and flogged.* It was the only offence of a mean and disgraceful nature that I ever knew to be charged against a blue-jacket.

About twenty years have elapsed since " La Hogue " frigate came into Kingstown. One of the crew, as fine-looking a young man as ever I saw, came on shore and indulged too freely in strong potations. It required two or three constables to effect his capture and lodgment in the station-house. Next morning he was brought up before me, and the circumstances of his intoxication and resistance were in course of statement by one of his captors, who occupied the witness box, whilst the prisoner stood directly opposite to the bench, with the ship's corporal, who had been sent ashore to look after him, standing close beside him.   I said to the sailor, " If you wish to put any question to the constable, you are at liberty to do so, and if you feel disposed to say anything for yourself, I am ready and willing to hear you." He stood silent and downcast, when the ship's corporal nudged him and said quite aloud, " Speak up for yourself like a man, the magistrate is a good gentleman and is ready to hear you." The prisoner replied in a desponding, but perfectly audible tone, " It's no use, that fellow (pointing to the policeman) will swear anything, and the old chap will believe him." There was loud and general laughter at the estimate formed by the tar of the constable and of the magistrate. I discharged him, without prejudice to informations and a warrant, and told the ship's corporal that the warrant should not be sent on board. I consequently restricted the sailor to remain in his vessel during her stay at Kingstown, which was for about another week.

From the same ship a sailor came ashore attired in his best clothes and with seven pounds in his pocket. He was decoyed into a disreputable place, where, by the administration of whisky and snuff, he was rendered insensible. A detective observed a woman leaving the house, and carrying a bundle. He allowed her to proceed to the railway terminus, at the entrance of which he arrested her. The bundle contained the seaman's clothes, and the female searcher got a five pound note and two sovereigns secreted in the culprit's *chignon*. The police did not inform the sailor of the clothes and money having been found. They dressed him in some old ill-fitting habiliments, and he looked most lubberly in his attire, and also deeply dejected at the supposed loss of his clothes and cash. His sadness was at once dissipated by the contents of the bundle being produced, and the bank-note and sovereigns completed the restoration of his spirits. There was, however, one small article missing, and in reference to it he made an earnest request of me, and accompanied it with *an alluring offer*, in the following terms :—

" Your honor, my clothes are all here and my money is safe too. I only miss a little blue hankecher with white spots, I had it from mother when we last parted ; and it's dog's usage I'll get from her if I haven't it at our next meeting. If you send out a smart chap or two in search of it, I think it will be easily got, and if it is, I'm d——d but I'll stand anything that you and your people choose to call for, all round."

A summary conviction, with six months imprisonment, of the woman with whom the clothes and money were detected, terminated the proceeding. The kerchief was not sought for, and we had "all round" to content ourselves without the proffered libations.

FISHER.

One of the most extraordinary characters of the many who came under my frequent magisterial notice, was a man named Fisher. He was the most inveterate and incorrigible drunkard that was to be found in Dublin, perhaps I might truly say, in the Empire. He had been educated, as I heard, in Stockholm, and acquired a proficiency in several European languages. He had also considerable classical attainments. His intemperance had ruined his commercial interests, and precluded his employment by others, even in very subordinate capacities. Occasionally he would be taken and kept almost as a prisoner in the concerns of an extensive timber merchant, arranging with the Norwegian or Danish people engaged in the delivery of cargoes. A suit of clothes and a pound or two would be thus acquired, but in a few minutes after his liberation he would assuredly be found in street or lane, hall or entry, dead drunk. He was never violent, abusive, blasphemous, or indecent, and as his senses returned, he became courteous and submissive. By the police he was generally pitied, and when a constable was obliged to state that he found " Mr. Fisher " drunk on a thoroughfare, he almost invariably added that he was *very quiet.* The magistrates were not severe on the wretched creature, and in general, the ruling in reference to him was deferred until the close of their sitting, (four o'clock,) and then the charge sheet was marked, " Dismissed with a caution." If there happened to be a paucity of cases, we were not disinclined to allow Fisher to address the bench, and state the grounds on which he expected or solicited exemption from punishment. He never "worshipped" us, but invariably named the magistrate, with the prefix of " My dear." I recollect a short speech having been made by him before myself, which excited my surprise and admiration from its purity of diction and the combination of interesting ideas it evinced. The charge against him was " Drunk on a public thoroughfare," and the constable stated that he found Mr. Fisher lying on the steps of a hall-door in Peter Street, fast asleep, and having been aroused, he was very drunk, but perfectly quiet.

"My dear Mr. Porter," said the prisoner, " I acknowledge and regret my lapse from propriety—

' Facilis descensus Averni.'

I have, however, been severely punished. I reclined on

the steps where your constable found me, and immediately
I sank into a slumber which, had it lasted for ever, would
have afforded me a blissful immortality. Sweet visions of
the past, retrospections of youthful joys, untainted by
the errors and cares of the present, monopolised my
imagination. A mother's lips were pressed to mine.
A father's smile gladdened my heart. I had clasped a
sister's hand, and a brother's arm encircled my neck.
The home of my childhood arose before me, and the garden, with which my earliest recollections were associated,
appeared in luxuriant, vernal beauty. The strong hand of
your officer, firmly but not rudely applied, dispelled the
delightful scene in which I was entranced, and recalled me
to the sad reality of captivity and degradation. Have I
not already suffered enough to justify the clemency which
I implore?" The wretched man was cautioned and discharged.

Having been brought before me on four successive
mornings, I told him that I would not permit his coming
so frequently, and that I adjudged him to pay a shilling,
or to be confined for twenty-four hours. Thereupon he
replied, " I regret, my dear Mr. Porter, that on this occasion you do not manifest your usual equanimity. I acknowledge my fault, but I am not worse to-day than I
was yesterday or any of the previous days. Moreover, I
must respectfully submit that you are greatly mistaken in
your remarks as to my *coming* so often. I never *came*
before you or any magistrate. I was always *brought*. If
the police will leave me as they find me, I shall never
complain of their want of attention, nor shall I ever in-
trude on your presence. Strike off that paltry shilling,
and let me depart once more." I told the constable to
remove the prisoner, upon which he exclaimed, " If you

are obdurate, and insist on marking a penalty, put five shillings on the sheet.   It will look more respectable, and there is just the same chance of its payment."

Fisher continued a hopeless, persistent drunkard. With natural talents of no mean order, and with educational acquirements from which great and varied advantages might be expected, he lived despised and ridiculed, and afforded to those under whose occasional observation he came, a melancholy but certain proof that when a man's habits render him his own enemy, he becomes incapable of deriving any benefit from the friendship of others.   On a winter's night in, I believe, 1856, Fisher betook himself to a limekiln in Luke Street.   He lay down too near the edge and fell asleep, never to awake again in this world. Suffocated by the fumes of the kiln, his corpse, after an inquest and verdict of "accidental death," was consigned to a pauper's coffin, and was ultimately made a subject for anatomical demonstration.   His fate was truly melancholy, but some salutary reflections may be derived from contemplating the final consequences of habitual and unrestrained intemperance.

CHAPTER XV.

A DUPER DUPED.

I SHALL now proceed to relate a magisterial reminiscence in which the only fictions are the names of the parties, and I trust that at the termination of the narrative, my readers will agree in the moral which I shall attempt to deduce, that the person who commences a cheating game is not to be pitied, if, at the close, he finds himself the only loser.

Twenty-five years have elapsed since, in an aristocratic family, in a central county of Ireland, a young woman was residing in a capacity rather difficult to define. She was somewhat above a menial and below a governess, neither the companion of her employers nor the associate of the servants. Her educational attainments were very limited, and her industrial power was of little value, for she was of small frame and delicate constitution. The care of two children was deputed to her, and all services necessary for their health, comfort, instruction, correction, or amusement were expected from Elizabeth Jones.

She had enough to do, but she did not think so. Her life was monotonous, her tastes were not congenial to the circumstances and persons amongst whom she was placed. A native of Wales, far from her kindred, and prevented by her position from forming, amongst her own sex, a friendship, or even an acquaintance to which she could attach any value, her only resource was to fall in love,—and a few casual attentions from an officer of constabulary quite overcame poor Elizabeth Jones.

> " He dazzled her eyes, he bewilder'd her brain,
> He caught her affections so light and so vain."

He perceived that he was loved, and pretended a reciprocal feeling. He promised, and vowed, and swore that she should be his wife, and he deceived her.

Richard Gilmore was sorely annoyed when Elizabeth Jones suggested very strong reasons for the immediate observance of his solemn promise of marriage; but he refused compliance, and sought to convince her that their union would only ruin him without saving her. She addressed her remonstrances to deaf ears. Marriage was out of the question, and she found herself a ruined, friendless creature, with the certainty of a speedy and disgraceful expulsion from the house in which she had for some years humbly earned her subsistence. However, she vented no reproaches; she only upbraided with a tear, and communicated her determination to depart and carry her sorrows to some distant locality. Of this intention Richard fully approved; and he congratulated himself on the prospect of being so soon delivered from any future annoyance on the part of Elizabeth Jones. She fixed the time for leaving her situation, and requested a last interview with Mr. Gilmore, at an early hour, before the inmates of the house were stirring. Richard was punctual. She opened a writing-desk, and informed him that she had come to the resolution of releasing him from every promise on his part, from every claim which she could advance then or at any future time, on one condition: she only required his written pledge, upon his honor as an officer and a gentleman, that he would never seek to renew his acquaintance with her, or even pretend to know her if they met. To this he joyfully acceded, and placed the required document in her hands; but his curiosity induced him to enquire as to her motive in seeking such a solemn written undertaking.

"Richard Gilmore," she said, "I was prostrated by acute and increasing misery, but a door of escape from total disgrace and destruction has been opened. I can never be happy, but I may have some opportunity for reflection, and ultimately, my mind may become somewhat tranquil. I shall soon be a mother. I am about to depart from Ireland for ever, and shall fix my residence in a retired part of England, and there, in the garb and under the designation of a widow, I shall devote myself to the care of the child of whom you are father, but for whom, I only insist and have stipulated with you, that you shall never disgrace your offspring by disclosing its paternity, and never remind me by your presence of the degradation to which, by your falsehood, I have been reduced."

"But," said Gilmore, "your means are scanty, and for a time you must be incapable of any industrial pursuit or exertion. I can give you some pecuniary assistance; it is my duty to do all I can to alleviate your sufferings. I deserve your reproaches, and would gladly do anything to prove that I am not so utterly heartless as you think me."

"No, Richard Gilmore; not a farthing would I receive from you, if it were to save me from starvation. To you I owe my ruin, but with you I have no further communication; and I shall never allow you to think that I have compromised my wrongs for money, or taken a price for my character. Moreover, I may now tell you that I shall not want your assistance; and as I feel that you dare not break your written undertaking, you may read this."

She placed in his hands a letter, of which the following
is a copy, substituting fictitious names :—

" Abergavenny, June 14th, 1847.

" MISS ELIZABETH JONES,

"Madame, I hasten to apprize you of the death of your lamented
aunt, Miss Rebecca Jones, who expired yesterday morning, after a very
short indisposition.   The respectable deceased applied for my professional
assistance about three weeks since, in the settlement of her worldly affairs.
For some years she had lived in great seclusion, and was extremely averse
to any communication with your brother; she would never see his wife.
In fact, her relatives seem to have been disliked in proportion to the
proximity of their residence; and it is to your long absence from her that
I ascribe the preference which she has evinced towards you, on which I
offer you my respectful congratulations.

"By your aunt's will (which is in my possession) she has devised to you
several freehold interests in and adjacent to this town, producing about
£300 per annum; she has also bequeathed to you £2,000 secured by
mortgage on the property of Mr. Deacon, of Aberystwith, and a bond of
Mr. Edmond Morgan, of Cardiff, for £1,100.

"I hope, Madame, you will feel that in the capacity of your respected
relative's confidential adviser I have not been hostile or even indifferent to
your interests; and I beg to assure you that, if your affairs are entrusted to
my care, I shall make every exertion to justify the preference that I
respectfully solicit.

"I have the honour to be, Madame,
"Your obedient, humble servant,
"DAVID WYNNE, <i>Solicitor.</i></div>

"PS.—Mrs. Wynne desires me to convey, with her respects, a request
that, if you visit Abergavenny, you will honor her and me by becoming
our guest during your stay."

"Good heavens !" exclaimed Richard Gilmore, " how
delighted I am, my dearest Lizzie, at your good fortune.
I shall fully and faithfully observe my pledge; but before
we part, consider well whether you should not use your
altered circumstances for your own comfort, for the complete prevention of every future pain and difficulty, and
above all, for the sake of your unborn offspring. If I

could, without absolute ruin, have redeemed the promise which my passion produced, you should never have had occasion to upbraid me. I loved you fondly, dearly; and it is in your power to give me an opportunity of proving, whilst we live, a faithful and devoted husband."

"Ah no!" said Elizabeth, "our marriage could never be happy; we would be mutually miserable. You would never respect her whom, in her supposed poverty, you scorned; and our union now would be as much the subject of scandalous comment as if you wedded me this day openly at the church of Castle——."

"If you marry me, my darling Lizzy, I shall adopt means to prevent exposure, or even suspicion. You shall leave this place immediately, go up to Dublin, and take a lodging in one of the small city parishes, where few Protestants reside. I shall obtain leave of absence, follow you to Dublin, take out a licence, and after a short stay I shall return and effect an exchange to a remote county, where I can present you to society as my wife, without any suspicion being entertained that our union has been too recent for your reputation. There your child can be born without any stain on its birth, or any cloud on its future prospects. Come, Lizzy dear, forget and forgive; I am still your own fond Richard."

He seized her hand, her struggle was slight, his arm encircled her waist, and on her lips he imprinted the seal of his future truth and of her present forgiveness. In two days Elizabeth Jones was lodging in Nicholas Street, Dublin, and in about a week Richard Gilmore was married to her in the church of St. Nicholas. The wedding was very private and quiet, the only witnesses being the man in whose house they lodged, his wife, and two young persons whose attendance they procured.

Three or four days elapsed, and Richard Gilmore accosted his bride. " Lizzy," he said, " I cannot delay my return to duty beyond another week. I have already made application for an exchange ; but before I return to the country, I think it would be well if I went over to Wales and regulated the future receipt of your rents, and also ascertained how the money due by Deacon and Morgan is circumstanced. If they pay five per cent. punctually, we shall be very comfortable. I have calculated that, with my pay, we shall have near £600 a-year. I shall buy a nice jaunting-car and———"

" You need not trouble yourself, Richard," said Mrs. Gilmore, very solemnly, "about my property in Wales. In fact, I have just taken a leaf out of your own book, and if the perusal is disagreeable, it is not to me that the authorship should be imputed. You made me a promise of marriage, you broke your word, and refused to save me from disgrace and misery. I procured a letter to be written about property that never existed, and made you believe that it was your interest to marry her whom your affection or sense of honor did not suffice to shield from destruction."

" You infernal Jezebel! you lying profligate! debased and degraded you shall be. I shall never live another hour with you. I shall never give a farthing to save you or your brat from starvation."

" I thank you, Mr. Gilmore, for myself and my coming brat. Thank heaven, you cannot say my bastard. You know what course it best answers you to take, but———"

Richard Gilmore was gone. Presently he was heard descending the stairs, and in a few minutes more the landlady announced to Mrs. Gilmore that her husband had departed, having first paid the lodging rent for the coming week, and having relinquished any further tenancy.

Mrs. Gilmore heard this intelligence with surprising calmness, and replied by informing the landlady of Mr. Gilmore's position, and of the place where he was stationed; adding that she would stay for the time for which the rent was paid, and that then, when she would be really destitute, she would go to THE WORKHOUSE. She imparted a good deal of confidence to the landlady, whom we shall name Mrs. Canavan, and who, seeing that she would not lose anything, gave Mrs. Gilmore her utmost sympathy. Mrs. Canavan was a fair specimen of human nature; for we never refuse our sympathy to our unfortunate fellow-creatures when we are not asked for anything more.

In another week Mrs. Gilmore proceeded to the South Dublin Union Workhouse, and there informed the admission committee that her husband was a constabulary officer; that his income was about double the reality; that he had some private property and great expectations; and that she, on the eve of her *accouchement*, was deserted by her husband, and compelled to become an inmate of the workhouse.

The committee admitted the applicant, registered the admission, and brought the case before the Board of Guardians on the following Thursday, when they obtained a ready sanction to prosecute Mr. Gilmore for deserting his wife, and leaving her, as a pauper, chargeable on the rates. A summons bearing my signature issued, and the constabulary officer appeared at the police-court. The marriage was proved, as were the circumstances of the desertion. On the part of the Guardians a demand was made for the immediate committal of the delinquent, to be imprisoned, with hard labor for three months. Richard

Gilmore escaped a formal conviction by paying the expenses already incurred, and undertaking to allow twenty shillings weekly for his wife's maintenance. All parties left the police-court; but in an hour or two after the case had been heard, Richard Gilmore returned and applied to me to have Elizabeth Jones, calling herself Gilmore, apprehended on a charge of bigamy. He alleged that she had been married in Wales about four years previous to her marriage with him, and that her husband, Thomas Jones, was still living. His assertions were made on statements which he had received from others. He had no legal evidence of the charge, and I refused to issue a warrant for the apprehension of the alleged bigamist, but he determined to persist in the accusation. He seized on his wife in the public street, and gave her into the custody of a constable on a charge of felony. On the following morning he stated on oath that he had been informed, and fully believed, that the prisoner had been married to one Thomas Jones in a parish church near Carnarvon; that said Thomas was still living; and he further swore to the marriage of the prisoner with himself in the city of Dublin. He asked for a remand, and stated that he expected to produce witnesses from Wales to prove his charge. I remanded the accused for six days, and Richard left Dublin by the next Holyhead packet in quest of evidence to convict his wife. Before she was removed to prison she sent to me a short note, in which she implored me to direct that no person should be permitted to see her in the prison unless at her own request; and further, that on the day for resuming the investigation, she should be placed amongst a number of females, and that the witnesses should be required to identify her from amongst the others. I considered those requests to be fair and reasonable, and directed that they should be complied with. Richard Gilmore returned to Dublin the day before the resumption of the case. He brought over two witnesses, and sought at the prison to give them a view of the accused, but they were denied admittance. On the appointed day Elizabeth Gilmore was brought from the prison, and placed in the carriage-court with about a dozen of other females, amongst whom was Mrs. Canavan, her Nicholas Street landlady, who manifested great interest in her sufferings, and great indignation at Richard Gilmore's attempt to transport an innocent creature whom he had vowed to love and cherish. Without separating the prisoner from the other women, I proceeded to swear the first witness, one William Jones, who stated that he was a parish clerk of some unpronounceable place in Wales; that he remembered the marriage of Thomas Jones and Elizabeth Jones, and he produced the registry; he recollected the matter very distinctly, the more so from the parties being both of the same name as himself. I directed him to look at the women present, and to point out the one whom he had seen married at the time mentioned in the registry if she was amongst them. Mr. Jones walked to the group, viewed all the women, and very deliberately placing his hand on Mrs. Canavan's shoulder, identified her as the culprit. He was instantly electrified by a burst of abuse, delivered in an accent acquired much nearer to Patrick Street than to Penmanmawr.

Mrs. Canavan's vocabulary was too copious to be select. I do not think that I could have restrained her, and I admit that I allowed her a latitude from which I derived some amusement. She descanted on the propriety of "cropping the ears"* of perjured parish clerks, but gave

* Cropping the ears was in former times a punishment for perjury.

L

up that idea as, on full consideration, it appeared too mild a treatment for the Welshman. She proceeded to assure him, that there was not a gaol in Ireland that would refuse him admission; and that in no place of such a description could he meet with anyone worse than himself. She appealed to my benevolent tendencies to have the Welsh fellow transported at once, upon the grounds that it would be "a charity;" and she descanted on the physiological defect in such a parish clerk having been born without handcuffs, suggesting an artificial amendment of the natural deficiency. She thanked Mr. Jones for the pleasant news, that she had one husband in Dublin and another in Wales, and assured him that he might expect some very particular attentions from the Dublin one in acknowledgment of his testimony.

> " And still she talked, and still the wonder spread,
> That one small tongue could utter all she said."

The parish clerk was overwhelmed with confusion, but Richard Gilmore persisted in his charge, and demanded the examination of his remaining witness. Accordingly, a Mrs. Edwards was sworn. She deposed that the Thomas Jones mentioned in the registry was her brother. She had not been present at the marriage, but was satisfied that her brother was living, for she had seen him at Swansea about a month previous, at which time he was proceeding to America as supercargo in a merchant vessel. On further examination, she stated that she was aware that Thomas and Elizabeth Jones had separated within the last two years, and this put an end to the case, for a reference to Gilmore's information showed that his acquaintance with the prisoner commenced nearly three years before their marriage. I remarked that the only allegation fully and clearly proved was the marriage of Mr. Gilmore to Miss Jones in the church of St. Nicholas; and it only remained for me to discharge the prisoner, to congratulate the parties on the removal of all imputation on the legality of their union, and to wish them many years of connubial happiness. Richard Gilmore did not manifest the slightest gratitude for this kind expression; he left the court without asking his wife to accompany him, but she was not compelled to betake herself again to the workhouse. Her weekly stipend was continued. Soon afterwards a són was born, and he is now a confidential employé in an extensive mercantile establishment in Dublin. I do not believe that he ever sought his father, or that his father ever took the slightest notice of him. Wishing him prosperity and happiness, I hope that he may never be necessitated to engage in any correspondence or enquiry relative to his mother's property in Wales. She resided for a considerable time in one of our southern suburbs, and latterly affected no secrecy as to the means which she adopted to effect her marriage. In the year 1858, I expressed, in some conversations with a medical man of her acquaintance, a wish for the particulars, and a copy of the letter which I have given to my readers was enclosed to me by post, without any accompanying condition, or even an indication of the quarter from whence it was furnished.

CHAPTER XVI.

WHO THREW THE BOTTLE ?——EXCISE AND CUSTOMS CASES.

In the " Dublin Annals " given in Thom's Almanac and Official Directory, it is stated in reference to the year 1822, " Riot in the theatre, on the Marquis of Wellesley, the Lord Lieutenant's first visit thither, during which a bottle was flung into his Excellency's box."

At the time referred to, I had not attained a profession, and my magisterial position was twenty years distant. I have, however, a very distinct recollection of the affair, as I was seated about the centre of the pit during the riot, and I have to notice that the statement in the Dublin Annals is incorrect. It contains, perhaps, the only inaccuracy that can be found in that voluminous and comprehensive publication. No bottle was flung into the viceregal box, but a rattle was thrown, which struck the front of the box, fell inside, and was raised and held up to the view of the audience by the Lord Lieutenant himself. A bottle was thrown from one of the galleries, and it struck the curtain in the middle with such violence, as to form a kind of bay for itself, and it slipped down on the stage, close to the foot-lights, and was taken up unbroken by the leader of the orchestra.

Prosecutions for riot were instituted, and amongst others a man named Henry Hanbidge was indicted. To him was imputed the throwing of the bottle, and some persons swore informations to the effect, that they were in the middle gallery, and that the bottle was cast from the upper gallery to the centre of the curtain. The proceedings for riot were ineffective. There was no conviction.

When I became a magistrate, in casual conversations with Pemberton, Cox, and others, the "bottle and rattle riot" formed a topic. They said that the assertion of the bottle having been cast from the upper gallery was generally disbelieved. It was, in fact, regarded as an impossibility. Major Sirr and Alderman Darley went one morning, whilst the prosecutions were pending, to the theatre, bringing a large hamper of bottles, and accompanied by some active and powerful peace-officers, who were directed to throw bottles from the upper gallery to the curtain, but not a bottle reached even the orchestra. The roof of the theatre sloped forward and downwards, and the elevation required to send the missile to the curtain invariably smashed it against the ceiling, and distributed the broken glass about the pit. The Major and Alderman came to the conclusion that the riotous bottle had been cast from the boxes or lower gallery.

In about ten years after the affair at the theatre, the house of Sir Abraham Bradley King in Dame Street was consumed by fire. The conflagration commenced in the lower part of the premises, in which there was a great quantity of stationery. The first and second floors were almost immediately in flames. The catastrophe occurred on a Sunday morning. No fire brigade was then organized, no fire escapes had been provided. A man was in the top front room, and he had no access to the roof. A fearful death appeared to be his inevitable fate, when another man emerged from the roof of a neighbouring house, carrying a rope of six or seven yards in length, at one end of which he had formed a running noose. He stood on the narrow parapet over the window, and let down the looped end to the poor fellow, whose only chance of escape depended on the sheer strength and steadiness of an individual. The rope was fastened round the waist of him whom the flames were fast approaching, and he was carried along by the intrepid fellow whose courage and humanity excited him to risk his own life to avert destruction from another, until the window of the adjoining house was reached, and the rescue was completed. This heroic act was accomplished by Henry Hanbidge.

I had been ten or twelve years in office as a police magistrate when I was applied to by a poor old fellow who was suffering acutely and completely debilitated by rheumatism, to sign a recommendation for his admission to Simpson's Hospital. The applicant was Henry Hanbidge. I most readily complied with his request, and told him that I would insert a few observations on his noble achievement at the fire in Dame Street. He expressed the deepest gratitude for my disposition to serve him. When I was giving him the document, I said, "Now, Hanbidge, might I ask you who threw the bottle?" He replied, "I did, your worship." I asked him "from what part of the house was it thrown?" "From the upper gallery, your worship. A friend and I had emptied the bottle, and I ran my stick into the neck, and shot it straight to the curtain off the stick." My predecessors had not thought of such a mode of projection.

EXCISE AND CUSTOMS CASES.

During my tenure of office I had an undesirable monopoly of the cases brought forward for infractions of the Excise laws, and also an ample share of imputed violations of the statutes regulating the Customs duties in the City and County of Dublin. The barristers who preceded me as magistrates of the Head Police Office, had, in consideration of such business being disposed of by them, an addition of £105 to their salary; but when I was about a month in office, I was favored with a communication that, without prejudice to the continuance of the work, I was to be exonerated from the trouble of receiving or acknowledging the usual pecuniary remuneration. The proceedings instituted by the Excise were, almost invariably, of an uninteresting character. I only recollect one which I consider worth recording in these pages. The premises of a maltster were visited by a revenue officer, and in one of the rooms he observed that a board of the floor was rather loose under his step. He raised it, and found a shoot which led to another floor in adjoining premises, which were apparently untenanted, and in which a large quantity of fresh malt was in process of drying. The principal workman in the maltster's employment dropped on his knees, implored mercy, and said that he would confess all. He then stated that he had made the communication for the purpose of stealing his master's malt, and that he had taken away all that was found by the officer in the adjoining store. He produced from his pocket a key for the external door of the building in which the malt was found. The maltster escaped the infliction of a very heavy penalty, but the workman was convicted on his own confession of stealing the malt, and was sentenced to twelve months' imprisonment. I subsequently was informed that during his confinement the man whom he had robbed (?) supported his family most comfortably, and as soon as the culprit terminated his incarceration, *he was received back into the maltster's employment.*

As to the infractions of the Customs laws, my cases all consisted of tobacco or brandy, and the seizures were, in almost every instance, effected immediately on the arrival in port of the respective ships. I believe that the intelligence of smuggling ventures being on board was almost always furnished by those from whom the contraband articles were purchased, or by the attendants in taverns or liquor shops, before whom unguarded conversations might have occurred, and in some instances from both sources. According to my recollection, the great majority of detections occurred on board vessels coming from places belonging to the British Crown. Jersey contributed largely to the contraband traffic, Gibraltar afforded an occasional venture, and the timber ships from the British provinces in North America were frequently made available to the illicit importation of tobacco. A fine brig from St. John's, New Brunswick, named, as well as I can remember, "The Hope," arrived in Dublin in the summer of 1852. She was boarded in the bay by some officers of Customs, to whom the master stated that his cargo was exclusively timber. No other description of goods was mentioned in the vessel's papers. The officers proceeded to raise some boards at the foot of the cabin stair, and took out a large quantity of Cavendish tobacco. They then entered the cabin and removed some other boards, finding an abundance of tobacco which had been there concealed. The master was arrested, and having been brought before me, I remanded the case, by the wish of all parties, for a week.

The revenue authorities did not institute any proceedings involving the condemnation of the brig, but they sought the conviction of the master, who was adjudged by me to pay two hundred pounds, or in the default of such payment, to be imprisoned for six months. His wife had been the companion of his unfortunate voyage, and their separation, on his committal to prison, was extremely sad. He was a fine-looking young man; I think his name was Harris, and he stated that he belonged to St. John's. The wife was also a native of that place, and I never beheld a woman who, in my opinion, surpassed her in personal beauty. Moreover, she was very near the time when to the designation of " wife " the term " mother " would be added. Whilst I condemned the man I deeply commiserated the woman, and all who witnessed their parting sympathized in her affliction. At the Richmond Bridewell, he was treated with much kindness, and was frequently allowed access to the gardens, to which, as well as to his prison-room, his wife was constantly admitted. There was a young man confined at that time at the instance of some of his relatives. He was a very extraordinary person. In him great literary attainments were combined with imaginative power: he had a mind which could

> " Give to airy nothing
> A local habitation and a name."

He sometimes lapsed into excessive intemperance, during which he exhibited such violent tendencies as justified a committal for two months in default of substantial bail. This imprisonment brought him into association with Harris, the tobacco smuggler. They became confidential friends. At this time about two months of the smuggler's

term had expired, and his fellow-prisoner expressed an
anxiety that they should both be liberated together. Harris
could not perceive how such a wish could be accomplished,
but the other thought it perfectly feasible. He prepared
a memorial to the Commissioners of Customs, which he
desired Harris to sign, and it was forwarded forthwith.
In a few days I received a letter from the solicitor of the
Customs, and with it the memorial. The Commissioners
expressed their willingness to have three months taken
off the term of the smuggler's incarceration, provided that
the committing magistrate did not object to such a commutation. I immediately forwarded the fullest approval
of such lenity, and having read the memorial, I returned
it to the solicitor. I regret that I did not keep a copy of
it, for it was a document which I feel myself incompetent
to describe in terms suitable to its merits. In refined and
elegant language it acknowledged the commission of the
offence and the justice of the punishment inflicted. It declared a determintaion to abstain in future from every wilful
infraction of the laws, and implored the commiseration
of those to whom it was addressed for the misery to which
the memorialist was reduced, even though it had originated
in his own misconduct. His young and affectionate wife,
who had accompanied him from her native country, had
been unable to withstand the pressure of their misfortunes,
and had gone to an early grave in a strange land, being
attacked by premature childbirth. He had not even the
mournful privilege of assisting at the interment of his
beloved consort and her offspring; but from the gloomy
precincts of a penal prison he besought the authorities to
come to the merciful conclusion that he had suffered
enough.

Half of his imprisonment was abrogated, and the time

of his discharge was at hand. I was about to leave the police-court on an afternoon, when I was informed that a lady earnestly requested an interview for a few minutes. To this application I acceded; and the fair visiter, having apologized for her intrusion, proceeded to inquire—

" If you please, sir, will you kindly inform me whether my husband's time of imprisonment is to be calculated from the day of his arrest or from the day of his trial ? "

I asked the name of the lady, and she replied that she was Mrs. Harris. I remarked that " I was agreeably surprised, as I had seen it stated that she was dead."

" Oh, sir," she exclaimed, " that was put in the memorial by Mr. ———— without even my husband's knowledge. However, I lost my little baby. But I hope that you will not tell that I am alive." I then informed her that her husband's term commenced from the date of his conviction, and she retired. I did not feel it necessary to give any publicity to Mrs. Harris's continued existence.

When the Ajax man-of-war was stationed at Kingstown, the officer in command frequently exercised his crew in warlike operations. In the year 1844, as well as I now can recollect, he announced his intention to have a mimic attack made on the ship, by boats, at night. A vast number of persons assembled to behold a spectacle intrinsically grand and peculiarly novel to a Dublin public. The operations commenced about ten o'clock, and continued for upwards of an hour. Signals of alarm were displayed by numerous lights of various colours, and they were succeeded by tremendous discharges of artillery and musketry, above which the cheers of the supposed combatants were frequently audible. At length the assailants retired, and the Ajax remained intact and triumphant. The spectators were most enthusiastic in their applause of the bloodless conflict, which certainly was most deserving of public admiration.   However, it afterwards transpired that during the sham battle in the harbour, some extraordinary operations were effected in the vicinity.   A smuggling vessel landed a cargo of tobacco close to the Kingstown end of the eastern pier, but outside the harbour. The venture was completely successful, and several days elapsed before the revenue authorities received any intimation of such a daring proceeding.   The cargo was conveyed away partly by rail, partly by road, and it was reported that almost the whole of it was transmitted to Limerick, but nothing tangible resulted from enquiries or searches.   On the same night another cargo was landed on Dalkey Island, and hastily concealed amongst the rocks.   It was supposed to have been brought by a consort of the craft which had made the other run.   On the following day, a man, apparently of the seafaring class, gave information to the Customs that he knew where there was a large quantity of contraband tobacco concealed, and that he was willing, for the usual remuneration, which I believe was nearly half the value of the commodities, to conduct them to the place.   He accordingly took them to Dalkey Island, where they found the tobacco.   It was subsequently rumoured, and I believe the rumour was well-founded, that he was the master of the vessel from which it had been landed; and as one cargo had been successfully smuggled, and the vessels had got away in safety, the reward, incident to discovering the other cargo, was sufficient to pay the prime cost and expenses of the two ventures, and to realize a considerable profit on the whole transaction.

Lest the favorable issue of the illicit speculation which I have last narrated should have the effect of encouraging or even suggesting to any individual any connection with such traffic, I would say that I noticed the successful issue of the enterprise as an extraordinary and exceptional incident. Detection is generally the result, with forfeiture of the goods, fine, or imprisonment. About four years before I retired from office, a young man, who had a fine fishing boat at Howth, and who was engaged to be married, went off to Jersey, and freighted his craft with tobacco and brandy. A revenue cutter was sent to meet him, and he was captured within view of his native hill. His vessel forfeited, his cargo seized, himself a prisoner, and utter ruin substituted for his dazzling but delusive hopes, he lapsed into the extreme of despair, jumped overboard, and perished. His fate should deter, more than a casual and extraordinary escape should encourage, an infraction of the revenue laws.

CHAPTER XVII.

JOHN SARGEANT——THE MAGISTERIAL OFFICES——TWO
MURDERS — ONE REPRIEVED — DELAHUNT'S
CRIMES.

I SHALL now present a magisterial reminiscence which
derives its greatest interest from antecedent occurrences,
the first of which brings me back to 1821, the year in
which George the Fourth visited Ireland. If I become a
little diffuse in my recollections of the period, it is because
they are strongly impressed on my memory and extraordinary in their nature. Nothing could exceed the
universal homage tendered to the king. If it has been
termed " servile adulation" by some, I am not prepared
to insist on a complete exoneration of our national character from such an imputation. I was then an undergraduate of the University of Dublin. On the day of the
Royal entry, we, the students, possessed ourselves of the
railings in front of the College, as affording an excellent
view of the procession. The rails were freshly painted,
and produced a most piebald appearance on our hands and
clothes, (blue coats with " welcome" buttons, white waistcoats and trousers.) We rubbed some of the paint off
our hands on the faces and clothes of each other previous
to proceeding to the Castle with the University Address.

On entering the upper yard from Cork Hill, we marched
to the right by the footway, and had an opportunity, of
which we availed ourselves, of pulling the white caps off
some of the cooks and scullions who were viewing us from
the two lower windows in the farthest corner of the yard.
We jostled each other up the staircase, and during the
reading of the Address, amused ourselves by climbing on
each other's shoulders by turns in order to have a better
view. Some of us, amongst whom I was one, suggested
rather loudly, that cakes and wine would be acceptable.
This produced a counter suggestion from some officials
of our immediate retirement from the State apartments.
On reaching the hall, I observed the porters and other
attendants sternly expelling a tall female who was dressed
in deep black. She appeared in great affliction, but was
accorded no sympathy. No one thought that anyone else
had a right to be sad when the King was in Ireland. I
subsequently saw the " woman in black," at the review in
the Phœnix Park, vainly endeavouring to approach the
Royal presence. I was a spectator of the various public
demonstrations during the Royal sojourn, and enjoyed
the exciting pageantry as anyone of my age and temperament might be supposed to do. I pass, however, to the
day of the king's departure, the 3rd of September. On
the morning of that day, the place of his embarkation
was Dunleary, but on his arrival he changed its designation into "The Royal Harbour of Kingstown." He entered his barge very near the place where the commemo-
rative column stands, and close to the inner end of the eastern pier. The " woman in black" somehow managed to
get very near. She endeavoured in vain to address him,
and just as the Royal barge was shoving off, she rushed
forward, holding a paper in her hand, and, in her frantic

haste, was precipitated into the water, from which, however, she was speedily rescued.   The king saw enough of
her exertions and mishap to excite his curiosity, and ordered her communication to be received and laid before
him.   It was a petition imploring the Royal mercy for
her husband, who was then under sentence of death in a
southern county, for burning his house with intent to defraud an insurance company.   Her prayer was favourably
considered.   An act of clemency appeared peculiarly suitable to the termination of the Royal visit, and the sentence on John Sargeant was commuted to transportation.

At the time to which I refer there was a considerable
portion of Kilmainham prison appropriated to the reception of convicts under sentence of transportation ; and in
a short time after the successful exertions of the "woman
in black" at Kingstown, John Sargeant was transmitted
to Kilmainham, there to remain until a sufficient number
of convicts were congregated to form a living freight for a
transport ship, and to transfer the future advantages of
their patriotic exertions to a southern hemisphere.   I use
the term "patriotic" in the same sense as the accomplished pickpocket, Barrington, applied it in a prologue
spoken by him previous to the performance of a play at
Sydney by a company consisting exclusively of transported
thieves—

> " True patriots we ! for be it understood,
>   We left our country for our country's good."

At the time of Sargeant's arrival at Kilmainham, I had
a very near relative who was a member of the committee
or board which superintended the gaol, and I frequently
accompanied him to the prison.   Sargeant was a person
of considerable educational acquirements.   He managed
to ingratiate himself with some of the authorities of the

convict depôt, especially with a Dr. Trevor. He was frequently employed in copying documents, which business he discharged most satisfactorily; and I have often seen him thus engaged. When the other convicts were sent off, some pretext or excuse was made available for retaining him, and after the expiration of two years, he succeeded in obtaining a pardon, and was released from confinement. The "woman in black" did not witness his liberation; she had previously succumbed to that fate which crime inflicts most severely on those whose love clings to unworthy and guilty objects, even in suffering and disgrace; love which, like the ivy, will embrace a ruin with greater tenacity than it would if the structure stood in its pristine strength or in renovated beauty.

About three years more had elapsed, and I was residing in London, attending the number of terms requisite for a call to the Irish Bar. At Gray's Inn I was an adept in all the duties then requisite for an admission to the status of a learned barrister-at-law, and indeed I brought to their inception no slight qualifications. I could decant old crusted Port wine without a funnel, my carving was considered faultless, and the salads of my dressing would gratify the palate of Apicius Cœlius. In that society there was far greater intercourse between the Bar and the students than I ever observed at our King's Inns. I frequently derived great pleasure and, I believe, no slight advantage, from the conversation of those whose deep research and matured experience qualified them to utter words of wisdom and suggestions of prudence to their juniors. I was fond of attending the courts, and criminal trials possessed for me a peculiar attraction. One day I sat close to two barristers whom I had occasionally met previously. They spoke with great interest of a trial

M

which was expected to be held at the Old Bailey on the following morning, and suggested to me to be present at it, and I followed their advice.   The prisoner was alleged to have been concerned in various frauds, but the specific offence for which he was tried was for obtaining upwards of £800 under false pretences and representations, and by means of forged documents.   It appeared that a West Indian Creole, Mr. D——, had arrived in London some months previous, possessed of an immense fortune.   He indulged in habits of extravagance most frivolous and ostentatious.   He fell into the error of considering fast society good society, and formed acquaintances and established confidences which a very moderate share of discretion would have made him avoid.   Mr. D—— had seen a lady, a member of a noble family, whose ancient lineage connected them with the most remote periods of English history, and in which gentle blood was thoroughly united with personal worth.   Mr. D—— became deeply enamoured, and made no secret of his admiration, but he could not procure an introduction.   His tropical temperament spurned all patience and prudence, and an Irish gentleman, Mr. John Sibthorpe, took him under his guidance and protection, and promised to realize all his visions of matrimonial bliss.   Sibthorpe advised that the lady's maid should be approached, and enlisted, with an ample bounty, in the Creole's service, and that she might be induced, in a short time, to convey letters to the adored one, who could not long continue indifferent to the suit of an amiable, wealthy, and disinterested lover.   The bait was swallowed.   One hundred sovereigns were confided to Sibthorpe to be transmitted to Kitty, and a note in reply, purporting to be written by her, acknowledged the Creole's generosity and promised her best exertions.

More money was sent and more notes were received. The lady was described as expressing a lively and grateful interest in the man who had manifested such an attachment. This encouraging communication produced a most respectful but ardent letter from the lover to the lady, and a further douceur to the maid. In due time Mr. D—— received a note couched in terms most favourable to his suit, and professing to be written by the fair hand which he panted to possess. Enraptured beyond expression, he imagined himself at the summit of his wishes, when he casually and suddenly learned the afflicting intelligence that the lady's nuptials with a noble suitor were fixed for an early day. Unable to restrain his feelings, he rushed into her paternal hall as she was about to enter her carriage, and kneeling before her, besought her pity for a broken-hearted man to whom she had kindly written. Mr. D—— was interrupted in his expostulations by being kicked out of doors by the footmen, and he soon discovered that Sibthorpe had forged the correspondence on the part of both maid and mistress. The delinquent was apprehended, prosecuted, and convicted. I heard him sentenced to two years' imprisonment with hard labor, and as he stood at the bar I had no difficulty in recognising the object of anxious solicitude to "the woman in black," the pardoned incendiary, the profligate John Sargeant.

In two or three months after the trial of this swindler, I returned to Ireland, and engaged in professional pursuits, to which I devoted my attention for about twelve years. I then became a magistrate of police. In 1844, I was doing duty in College Street Police Court for the late Alderman Tyndall, who was suffering from severe indisposition. An application was made to me by a director and secretary of one of the principal banks in the city, I think it was "The Royal." They were accompanied by their solicitor, and it appeared that a bill of exchange for £100, purporting to be the acceptance of a gentleman of high position in the county of Wicklow, had been tendered for discount on the previous day, and that they had ascertained it to be a forgery. A close description was given of the accused, who had been told to call at the bank at two o'clock. An information was sworn and a warrant issued, and the delinquent was apprehended in the vestibule of the bank, whither he had the audacity or folly to proceed on his nefarious design. On being placed before me, he stated his name to be John Sharkey, and that he had recently returned from Oporto, where for several years he had been employed as a clerk in an English house engaged in the wine trade. I remanded the case for the production of the alleged acceptor, and during the intervening time very conclusive evidence was obtained as to the body of the bill having been written by the prisoner. At his final committal, I told him that, although I never before had any magisterial cognisance of him, I had no difficulty in recognising the person whom I had seen convicted at the Old Bailey, and who had previously been an inmate of Kilmainham, after having the sentence of capital punishment commuted to transportation. The latter punishment was subsequently awarded to him in Green Street, and thus, as far as I am aware, was closed the career of Mr. John Sargeant.

THE MAGISTERIAL OFFICES.

My magisterial office was held for twenty years and four months. During that time I was a Justice of the Peace for the city and county of Dublin, and for the counties of Meath, Kildare, and Wicklow. The division appurtenant to the Head Office comprised, at the time of my appointment, (in January, 1841,) about one-half of the southern moiety of Dublin, in which were contained the poor and very populous districts known as "The Liberties." In about six years after, we were required to supply a magistrate daily to the Police Court at Kingstown, for the discharge of the business incident to the townships of Kingstown, Blackrock, and Dalkey; and in about three years later, the entire of the Metropolitan Police district south of the Liffey was assigned and consolidated into one division, in which my two colleagues and myself had to discharge the magisterial duties. Persons apprehended in the police district for offences committed in other parts of Ireland were brought before us to be remanded or transmitted, according to circumstances. I mention these particulars to enable my readers more fully to appreciate the extraordinary fact, that during the period which I have specified there never was brought before us an individual charged with a capital offence. I do not mean to induce an impression on the reader's mind that our locality was free from crimes of magnitude. Two murders occurred in our division during the time referred to, but in each case the culprit was committed by the coroner.

One of them was in the city, and the other in the county portion of our district. The former case was the deprivation of a wife's life by the hand of her husband. He was a house-painter, a journeyman bearing an excellent character for knowledge of his business, industry, honesty, and strict sobriety. She was the daughter of a tradesman in Rathfarnham, and her person was exceedingly comely. Very soon after marriage, she lapsed into

habits of the grossest intemperance, so as to acquire the
soubriquet amongst her neighbours of "the drunken
beauty." She was a frequent, though involuntary, visitor
to the police court for having been found "drunk and
incapable" in the public streets. One evening her husband found her completely intoxicated, and he discovered
that his best clothes had been pawned to furnish the
means for her inordinate indulgence. She replied to his
complaints and reproaches in abusive and opprobrious
terms, until exasperated beyond the control of reason, the
unfortunate man seized an old sword-stick which happened to be at hand, and with that weapon he pierced her
eleven times through the body, three of the stabs perfo-
rating the heart. Curiosity led me to visit the scene of
the sanguinary termination of a union which commenced
in ardent love, and might have lasted long and happily, if
every hope of domestic peace and enjoyment had not been
subverted by intemperance. I was present at the inquest,
which resulted in a verdict of "wilful murder" against the
husband. He was subsequently convicted at the Commission Court, and received sentence of death. I exerted
myself in procuring memorials to the Executive for a
commutation of the capital punishment, and in an interview with the Chief Secretary and the law officers I
argued that the multiplicity of the wounds inflicted on
the wretched woman denoted a sudden burst of uncontrollable passion, and not a premeditated design of deliberate and malicious destruction of life. I expressed an
opinion that one mortal stab would indicate more malice
than could be inferred from the eleven furious blows.
My representations were received with courteous attention, and the applications for mercy were acceded to ; but
the unfortunate man died in the Richmond Bridewell in

less than six months after the transaction. His heart was broken. I may mention here, that whilst I was a crown prosecutor on the Leinster circuit, and during my tenure of magisterial office, I never knew of an application for mercy to be made to the Executive that did not receive the fullest and fairest consideration, and I believe that all the Governments of which I have had any knowledge or experience were equally desirous to avail themselves of any opportunity for tempering justice with mercy.

The other murder which occurred in our division was perpetrated in December, 1841, by a young man named Delahunt. In the character of this culprit there was an amount of cool, dispassionate, and deliberate predilection for crime, surpassing any details in the pages of the "Newgate Calendar," or the "Archives of the Parisian Police." About one year previous to the last-mentioned date, a poor Italian organ-grinder was found lying close to the wall of Rathfarnham demesne, on the roadside near Rathfarnham bridge. His throat had been cut, and a belt which he usually wore round his waist, and in which it was supposed that his scanty savings were stowed, had been taken away. A man named Cooney, a tinker, had been seen in the immediate vicinity of the place, and he had been taken into custody on suspicion, by the constabulary. An inquest was being held, when Delahunt accosted Colonel Browne, the Commissioner of the Dublin Metropolitan Police, in the Castle yard, and told him that he (Delahunt) had seen the murder committed. The Colonel immediately directed one of his sergeants to take the man out to the coroner, as the offence had been committed in the county, and outside the police district. On being produced at the inquest, Delahunt swore that he had seen Cooney murder the Italian. A reward of twenty-five pounds had been advertised for the conviction of the perpetrator of the fearful assassination, and that accounted for Delahunt's promptitude in offering his testimony.   On the trial of Cooney at the ensuing commission, the jury disbelieved Delahunt, and acquitted the tinker.   I am satisfied that they arrived at a proper conclusion, and I strongly suspect that if Delahunt really knew anything about the crime, it was owing to himself being the perpetrator.

In about four months after the trial of Cooney, there was a contested election in the city of Dublin, at which it was deemed expedient to utilise the canvassing abilities of a considerable number of coal-porters.   These energetic advocates of liberty took considerable liberties with such voters as they found recusant to their wishes, or even tardy in complying with their demands.   They were provided with hackney cars, and provided themselves with cudgels. Individual resistance or even indifference to their behests occasioned very forcible applications to the heads and shoulders of any elector, and when they brought him to the hustings, his attention was invited to a reserved body specially stationed in the vicinity of the polling booths from whom he was informed that he might expect very strong censures on his want of patriotism, if he voted on the wrong side.   After the election, some prosecutions were instituted for threats and actual assaults on voters, and there was one case in which a retired military gentleman had been dragged from his bed in a state of illness, and violently assaulted with cudgels.   A reward was offered for the discovery and conviction of his assailants, and Delahunt at once came forward.   He pointed out, on the quay, six coal-porters as the guilty parties, swore that he had heard them directed to go to the gentleman's residence and bring him to the poll, and that he followed them and witnessed the entire transaction. They were committed for trial at the Commission Court, and there Delahunt most positively identified the six. One of them had a large hare-lip, and the party who had been assaulted swore that the fellow with the split lip was not present at the outrage. Another of the accused established the fact, by the evidence of constables and turnkeys, that he had been convicted on the day previous to the attack on the voter, and that he was in gaol for drunkenness and disorderly conduct at the time when Delahunt swore to having seen him assaulting Captain C———. The six coal-porters were acquitted, and Delahunt's sanguine expectations of an ample reward were completely disappointed.

On the 20th of December, 1841, a little boy named Thomas Patrick Maguire, eight years of age, was playing with some other children in Blackhall Row. The children were of the humblest class, and Maguire was bare-footed. Delahunt, having previously ascertained his name, and that he lived with his mother in Plunket Street, told him that he had been sent to bring him to her. The poor boy went with him, but was not brought home. Delahunt took him to a distant part of the city, and called at his (Delahunt's) brother's lodgings in Little Britain Street, where he stated to his sister-in-law that Maguire was a stray child whom the police had given into his care to take home. He sharpened two knives at his brother's, and after his departure with the child, one of the knives was missed. In the meantime, he brought the little fellow across the city, bought some cakes for him, and took him into a lonely lane in the suburbs, close by Upper Baggot Street, and there between seven and eight o'clock in the evening, he cut the child's throat. In a very short time, the body was found, and taken to a police-station in order to have an inquest held.   Delahunt reappeared, and stated that he had passed 'the end of the lane, and had seen a woman throw the little boy down, and that she passed close to him, and went hurriedly away.   He said that he had no idea of the child having been killed at the time, but thought that the woman had chastised him for some offence or naughty trick.   He named a woman, and declared that he could swear to her.   Unluckily for him, the woman whom he designated had been very sick during the entire day, and confined to bed, to the positive knowledge of several friends and neighbours.   Some persons recognised Delahunt as having been with the boy, and amongst them was the woman from whom he had bought the cakes.   In a field adjoining the lane where the corpse was discovered, a knife was found, which was sworn to by his sister-in-law as having been sharpened by him, and subsequently missed.   She also identified the body of the child as that of the boy whom Delahunt had with him at her residence.   He was finally tried and convicted of the murder on the 14th January, 1842, and was executed on the 5th February.   He made a full confession of his guilt, and acknowledged that he had falsely accused Cooney the tinker of murdering the Italian, and that his evidence against the coal-porters was totally unfounded.   He disclaimed all malice or illwill against the poor child, Maguire. He declared that he only wanted to be rewarded for convicting some person of murder, and that he could not originate such a charge without the preliminary procurement of a corpse.   In a volume of Dickens's periodical, *All the Year Round,* and under the title of "Old Stories re-told," there is a full narration of murders committed by Burke, Bishop, and Hare, for the purpose of selling the bodies of their victims to anatomical schools.   Each distinct case of crime perpetrated by those miscreants was of less aggravated turpitude than the offence for which Delahunt was hanged, for they contemplated the destruction of the sufferer as the consummation of a design, but Delahunt deprived one individual of life on the speculation that he would thereby be enabled to obtain a reward, perhaps a trifling one, by consigning another fellow-creature to the precincts of a gaol, and ultimately to the ignominious horrors of a public execution, for a crime committed by himself, and imputed, by his deliberate perjury, to an innocent being, whose hand was unstained and whose heart was untainted.   For a considerable time after his execution, he was reputed, especially amongst the humbler classes, to have been a police spy, and to have been in receipt of frequent subsidies from the detective office.   He was never produced in any court as a witness at the instance of the police.   In the case of the coal-porters, he applied to me for funds to enable him to remain in Dublin until the trial was held and I refused his application.   He repeatedly offered superintendents and inspectors to swear to cases of illicit or irregular traffic in liquors, but they never believed his statements, nor would they, in any instance, avail themselves of his proffered testimony.   No villainy could be more unprofitable than Delahunt's systematic attempts to support himself by false accusations of others. I feel perfectly satisfied that, instead of deriving the wages of an informer or spy from the metropolitan police or from the constabulary, he never cost the public one penny beyond what sufficed for his maintenance in gaol whilst under committal for his diabolical offence, and to provide the halter which he most thoroughly merited.

The contemplation of such a character may not be

unproductive of some salutary results. Whilst we acknowledge and admire the blessed tendencies of the most elevated virtues, a wholesome and very instructive lesson may be derived from the contrast exhibited and the eventual disgrace and destruction almost invariably incident to a complete lapse into utter depravity.

CHAPTER XVIII.

MURDER OF MR. LITTLE——DETECTIVE INEFFICIENCY
——INDIVIDUAL EFFICIENCY——A FALSE ACCUSA-
TION EXPOSED——EXTRAORDINARY GRATITUDE——
A SALUTARY REFORMATION——A CHARGE OF FE-
LONY——POOR PUSS, WHO SHOT HER?——BAXTER
AND BARNES.

I SHALL now advert to a most atrocious murder which
was committed in the Metropolitan Police District in
1856. It occurred in the Northern division, and I was
requested by the present learned and worthy Chief Magistrate, Mr. J. W. O'Donnell, to assist in its investigation.
Mr. George Little, the Cashier of the Midland Great
Western Railway, had not returned to his residence on
the evening of the 14th November, and on the following
morning, his relatives enquired for him at the office in the
station. The office door was broken open, and he was
found lying on his face in a pool of blood, his throat
having been cut from ear to ear. At first the impression
was that he had committed suicide, for a considerable sum
of money was on his desk. However, it was ascertained
by an examination of the body, that many very severe
injuries had been inflicted, and that the scull had been
fractured by blows from a heavy blunt instrument. A

coroner's inquest returned a verdict of "Wilful murder by some person or persons unknown," and a large reward was advertised for the discovery and conviction of the perpetrator. No arrest was made on suspicion until the 21st of December, when a person was brought before the Northern Police Court, but was very speedily discharged. I refrain from mentioning the name, because there is no doubt that the charge was unfounded. It was rumoured that an experienced London detective had been specially engaged to afford his assistance in the furtherance of justice, but nothing of importance transpired until the 26th June, 1857, when a woman, named Spollen, informed a superintendent of police that her husband, James Spollen, was the murderer, and that he had concealed the bank-notes which he took from Mr. Little's office in a certain place immediately adjoining a small house which he occupied on the railway premises, he being in the Company's employment as a painter and cleanser. The superintendent immediately arrested Spollen, but kept him in his own custody from ten o'clock in the morning until nearly ten o'clock at night, when he brought him to a police station-house and gave him in charge for the murder, producing the wife of the accused as the charging party. The place indicated by the woman was immediately searched, and a considerable sum in bank-notes was discovered concealed in an ashpit, and packed in a small firkin, which had previously contained white paint. Some money in silver was also found in a canvas bag deposited in a cistern, and the utmost publicity was given to the searches, the results, and the source from whence the information concerning them was derived. His wife's evidence against Spollen was properly rejected by the magistrates; and although the case was sent for trial on other grounds, the result was an acquittal. During the magisterial investigation, I suggested that a portion of the Royal Canal close to the railway premises should be drained and searched, as I considered it very probable that some of the implements used in the murder had been thrown into the water. When the search commenced, the superintendent announced that whoever found the razor should receive a guinea. A razor was accordingly found in the mud almost immediately, but it was manifest that it had not been there until the search was directed, for it was perfectly free from rust or corrosion. However, another razor was found, and the name of " Spollen " was on the handle. A fitter's hammer was also taken out of the canal, and it was more than probable that the razor and hammer had been in fatal proximity to the throat and head of the unfortunate George Little. After the trial, some of the London papers commented in the strongest terms on the ignorance and stupidity evinced in the preliminary proceedings of the police officer to whom the case had been assigned. The bungling, blundering incompetency which characterised the transaction was described as truly Irish. They also complained that the English detectives who had been sent to Dublin were thwarted and impeded in all their efforts by the members of the Dublin force. I fully admit that the case was thoroughly mismanaged, but I must add that the person most prominently engaged, the superintendent, was an Englishman, and I deny that English detectives had to encounter Irish jealousy, as no person of the description was sent to Dublin in reference to that crime, or indeed in any instance within my recollection, without meeting a cordial, perhaps I might venture to say, a fraternal, reception from the Dublin Police. I may add that whenever our constables were sent to the English metropolitan district they invariably returned with a grateful recollection of the kindness manifested towards them.

In the case to which I have last adverted, and in some others which came under my observation, I attribute the failure of justice to the ignorance and consequent incapacity of members of the police force or of the constabulary engaged. However, I consider it only just to remark on the paucity of instruction afforded to constables for detective purposes. Activity of body, corporeal strength, general mental intelligence, and moderate educational acquirements, are considered sufficient qualifications for the discharge of detective duties, and further teaching is left to be acquired by future experience. In several continental states, reports of important criminal trials are arranged for the use of the police by an *archiviste,* and instruction is thereby afforded as to the means by which guilt was established, or, perhaps, to the mistakes or rash precipitancy by which justice was defeated, or innocence accused. The essential difference between our police and that which I have observed in France, Belgium, and Rhenish Prussia, is exhibited in the speedy arrests of suspected persons here, compared with the tardiness of apprehension in the latter countries, unless the prisoner is actually caught *in flagrante delicto.* The moment that a suspicion is entertained in Ireland, the supposed delinquent is seized, and thereby all chance of obtaining evidence by his subsequent acts is completely lost. The foreign system is to watch him night and day. This frequently eventuates in detecting him concealing property, weapons, or blood-stained clothes, or suddenly quitting his abode without any previous intimation, and perhaps under an assumed name. If we are to have an efficient police, we will find it indispensably necessary to keep well-informed, shrewd, patient, watchful detectives. I have known many who contended that a constable should adopt no disguise, but that, in the uniform of the force to which he belongs, he should perambulate the streets, suppress disorders, apprehend offenders, and when directed to execute warrants, he should go in search of the culprit openly and avowedly. To such I would suggest, that if in the organization of a police there is anything unconstitutional, it is rather to be found in the adoption of a uniform than in the attire of "plain clothes." The old common-law constable had no uniform; he went, and came, and mixed amongst other men, without a number on his collar or a crown on his buttons, and still his office and its functions were not denounced as unconstitutional. A policeman in uniform may patrol our streets, suppress riots, restrain indecency, and apprehend the pickpocket or drunkard; but it is not by such that the progress of the swindler is to be traced and stopped, the haunts of the burglar ascertained, or that the minute circumstances, trifling to the casual observer, but amounting, in the aggregate, to perfect conviction, are to be discovered and concatenated to establish the fearful guilt of the murderer.

Having remarked the inefficiency manifested by the officer to whom the management of the murder case at the railway was assigned, I think it fair to state, that amongst some other members of our detective division I have known instances in which great sagacity and promptitude were evinced. Shortly after my appointment to the magistracy, an old man died in a lodging-house in Bishop Street. The place in which he had lived for nine or ten years was a small room without the slightest indication of comfort or even of cleanliness. Nevertheless, he was

N

reputed to have been possessed of a considerable sum of money, which was supposed to be hoarded in some part of his humble habitation. Two of his relatives made oath that they believed him to have accumulated some hundreds of pounds; that they suspected and believed that the cash had been purloined; and they demanded that the house should be strictly searched. I gave a search-warrant to a detective named James Brennan, who proceeded to the house, and stated his function to the landlady. She declared that the man had been miserably poor, that he died in complete destitution, and that they had to bury him in a parish coffin. Brennan searched the premises most rigidly, but the expected treasure was not forthcoming. Some of the landlady's female neighbours expressed great indignation at " any honest woman's place being ransacked after such a manner." One of the garrulous sympathizers declared that " so far was the landlady from having a lot of money, that she was hard set to live, and that the very night the old man died, the poor woman had to pledge her best feather bed, at Booth's the pawnbroker's, for a few shillings." Brennan took his leave, and immediately went to the pawn-office. He had the bed produced, and observed that the stitching on one seam was fresher in appearance than on the others. He ripped the seam, and in the middle of the feathers he found seven notes, each of a £100, and two of £20. The affair eventuated in the money being divided amongst the kindred of the deceased. The landlady denied all knowledge of the money, and insisted that the old man must have concealed it himself. She was not prosecuted, but Brennan's intelligence was rewarded with one of the £20 notes.

The residence of the late Dr. Graves in Merrion Square

was robbed several years ago, by the thief's entrance at the windows of the front drawing-room, which had been left unfastened. The balcony did not appear accessible by ordinary means, but was easily attained from that of the adjoining house. Brennan was sent to examine the premises, and he at once perceived the traces left by a soiled foot in climbing by the pillars of the hall-door next to Dr. Graves's; he then walked over to the rails of the square, and found marks which satisfied him that some person had recently crossed; amongst the bushes there were a few heaps of twigs, the parings or prunings of the shrubs; and beneath one of them he discovered an excavation or *cache*, in which was a quantity of the stolen property. At night he lay down at a little distance from the place, and was not long there before a person approached and proceeded to take up the property. At the rails he was giving it to an associate, when, on a signal from Brennan, some other constables came forward, and the burglars were secured. They were subsequently convicted and transported.

A FALSE ACCUSATION EXPOSED.

I have known several instances in which innocence has derived complete protection, even from the inconvenience of any arrest or personal interference, from the tact and intelligence of members of that force, to which a most greedy appetite for convictions is freely attributed.

About ten years before I became a magistrate, a considerable portion of the County of Cork was a scene of disturbances, which might be fairly termed insurrectionary. Amongst other outrages which were then perpetrated, was the murder of a clergyman, the Rev. Mr. Hewson, who was shot on the high road, and in the open day, in the vicinity of Bandon. No clue was obtained whereby the guilty parties could be discovered, and the offence has never been punished. In the year 1842, a soldier in a regiment stationed at Fredericton, New Brunswick, stated to his officer that he had been concerned in the crime, and he named two persons as his accomplices; the man was sent home and brought up before me for examination. A detective informed me that he had been, at the period of the murder, orderly to the constabulary officer at Bandon; that he had been at the scene of the offence very soon after its commission, and that he wished to be present at the examination of the self-accused prisoner. To this I acceded, and the soldier detailed that on the day and at the hour when the clergyman was murdered, he and two men, whom he named, met the unfortunate gentleman on his way home, that one of them seized his horse, and the other shot him with a blunderbuss; that they immediately fled, and he made a statement of where and how they spent the remainder of the day. The detective, whose name, if I recollect rightly, was Benson, by my permission asked him, "Which of you backed the horse, and over-turned the gig into the ditch at the road-side?" to which the reply was, "I did." He then asked, "Which of you cut the traces?" The response was, "L—— did." He proceeded, "Which of you struck the poor woman who saw the murder, for screaming?" He was answered, "P—— did." The interrogator then declared to me that the fellow was telling a tissue of falsehoods, for the horse had not been backed into the grip, and the vehicle was not a gig, but an outside jaunting-car; that the traces had not been cut, neither was any woman near the place assaulted by the murderers. Subsequent inquiries established the fact, that one of the persons accused in the soldier's confession was, at the period of the murder, apprentice to a cabinet-maker in Cork, a reference to whom and to whose books showed that the party sought to be implicated had been in his master's concerns during the day of the assassination, and for a considerable time previous to and after the transaction ; and it appeared that the statement had been made for the mere purpose of its fabricator being sent home from service in a regiment with which he was discontented, and in which he had acquired a most disreputable character.

EXTRAORDINARY GRATITUDE.

The discharge of magisterial duties with firmness and impartiality occasionally evokes expressions of approbation from those by whom proceedings may have been instituted or closely observed, and may even elicit a complimentary notice from an editorial pen. A deep sense of *gratitude* for the exercise of magisterial functions is not so frequently avowed or ascribed. I am therefore disposed to bring before the reader the circumstances which, in a very public place, produced a compliance with a request of mine, accompanied by the expression, " Anything that I could do for you, Mr. Porter, if it was even to put my hands under your feet, should be a duty and a pleasure, for I can never be too grateful to such a worthy magistrate as you." This was said by a station-master of the Great Southern and Western Railway named Duffy, in 1851, in reply to an application for a coupée carriage for a friend of mine who was going to Cork with his wife and daughter. The guard of the train was directed by Mr. Duffy to be most attentive to the party. My friend subsequently remarked to the guard that the station-master evinced a great anxiety to please me. " So he ought," was the reply; "the poor fellow is married to a real incarnate devil, and Mr. Porter sends her to gaol whenever she is brought before him." Habitual intemperance, with concomitant violence, occasioned the frequent incarcerations for which the delinquent's husband felt so grateful.

A SALUTARY REFORMATION.

About the time to which the last anecdote refers, I was applied to, on a Monday afternoon, by a gentleman who asked and obtained a private interview. He was in a high social position, and possessed an ample fortune. He stated that his wife had lapsed into habits of intemperance which rendered his life wretched, and estranged him from association with his friends, to whom he could not bear to have her deplorable tendencies exposed. When inebriated she was excessively violent, and did not hesitate to assault the domestics, and that on the preceding evening she had assaulted, in his presence, a female servant, with a poker. I told him to have her summoned by the servant for the following Thursday, and I had three o'clock mentioned as the hour for hearing the complaint. The lady did not attend, and on proof of the service of the summons and a sworn information of the assault, I issued a warrant for her apprehension. She was brought before me after all the other business of the next day had been finished, and I required her to give bail in two sureties to keep the peace, and in default of such, to be imprisoned for three months. At Grangegorman, she was not compelled to associate with the other prisoners, and the matron's attention was invited to the case. At the termination of the second month, her husband, who had received frequent letters from her, felt confident that she had become reformed, and I discharged her at his instance and on his surety. I afterwards met them frequently in society. I have seen her at viceregal parties, and never observed the slightest appearance of, or tendency to, her former indulgence. I do not believe that she ever relapsed; but whilst I am happy to notice a complete reformation, my satisfaction is alloyed by the reflection that it was the only instance of such a change that I ever knew to occur.

A CHARGE OF FELONY.

I was frequently invited to the hospitable and joyous table of my cousin, the late Anthony Hawkins of Leopardstown, Stillorgan. On one occasion he entertained about a score of guests, of whom I was unquestionably the senior. Choice viands and generous wines sustained and stimulated the utmost hilarity; and when some of the company expressed apprehensions that further indulgence might bring them under the cognizance of the police, the host remarked that they would have a *friend in court*, for it could not be supposed that the jolly old magistrate would lean heavily in the morning on those who had been his boon companions of the preceding evening, and that each of them would get off for *a song*, which he would suggest to be given in advance. Two young fellows reminded me that they lived on Merchants' Quay, and as that was in my division, they entertained no fears. The company separated in time to avail themselves of the latest train to Dublin, and the two sparks travelled in the same carriage with me. Neither of them was in the slightest degree "the worse for liquor;" and when we parted at Harcourt Street Station we shook hands, and one said, "Good night, your worship, I hope you'll not be hard on us to-morrow." Next morning I was on duty at

Exchange Court, and when the charge sheets from Chancery Lane were laid before me, I was astonished beyond description to find my companions who had bespoken my leniency brought forward on an accusation of FELONY. A constable stated that he had seen one of the prisoners get on the shoulders of the other, and pull down a large gilt salmon, which formed the sign over the door of a fishing-tackle establishment on Essex Quay. On taking down the salmon, they were crossing over to the quay wall when he intercepted them, and with the aid of another policeman and a civilian, he captured and brought them to the station-house. Another witness proved that the prisoners stopped at the door over which the sign was suspended, and that one of them said, " Let us give the poor salmon a swim." This evidence induced me to believe that the transaction was not a deliberate theft, but a wanton, mischievous freak. The proprietor of the shop expressed the same opinion, and urged a summary adjudication. They offered to pay for the sign, as it had been broken by an accidental fall ; and the court was convulsed with laughter when the proprietor observed that the salmon had been taken " out of the lawful season." The spree cost the two delinquents the moderate sum of six pounds. The subsequent banterings which they had to endure amongst their festive associates completely deterred them from any further manifestation of fishing propensities.

POOR PUSS ! WHO SHOT HER ?

A friend to whose inspection I submitted the preceding pages suggested that as they detailed many mistakes and peccadillos of others, a reader might consider it an agreeable variety if I inserted a couple of errors peculiarly mine own. In accordance with his opinion I have to mention that shortly after I assumed magisterial duties at Kingstown, the proprietor of an extensive hotel in the immediate vicinity of the police-court received several letters threatening speedy and fatal violence to him and his family, unless certain demands on the part of his waiters, postillions, and carters, were complied with. He was justly incensed and alarmed at such threats, and submitted the obnoxious documents to the consideration of the authorities and to the detective agencies of the police force. His garden wall was close to the yard of the police-court, between which and the sea no building at that time intervened. It happened that an official, connected with the fiscal business of the county of Meath, had embezzled a considerable sum and attempted to abscond, but was captured on shipboard at Kingstown, and committed for further examination. The delinquent had provided himself with a most ample outfit for emigration and residence abroad ; and the articles found in his possession were deposited in a room adjoining the police-court and overlooking the hotel garden. Amongst them was a rifled air-gun of great power, and after the business of the court had been disposed of, I was, along with the chief clerk, Mr. Lees, indulging my curiosity by pumping and discharging the weapon. There was a bag of small bullets, of which we directed two or three at the wall of the yard. An unfortunate cat chanced to make her appearance in the hotel garden at a distance of fifty or sixty yards, and exclaiming that " I would give puss a start," I sent a bullet in her direction, without the slightest expectation that the shot would be fatal. The cat fell dead on the garden walk ; we closed the window, locked up the gun and bullets, and departed. Next morning, I was about to commence the charge-sheets, when the proprietor of the hotel applied

most earnestly for a private interview. He was greatly
agitated, and declared that he felt convinced of his life
being in danger from those who threatened to assassinate
him. "Your worship," he added, "they are manifestly
bent on mischief, for our poor cat was found dead in the
garden, and on examination she was found to have been
shot. The fellow who killed her, did so only to show that
I might expect the same treatment if an opportunity offered for shooting me." The poor man little knew that
the weapon which inflicted the injury was in the apartment where he was expressing his direful apprehensions,
and that he was seeking the sympathies and protection of
him who had done the mischief. I took means, through
a particular channel, to disabuse his mind of the feeling
that the cat's fate was intended to precede a similar termination to his own existence.

BAXTER AND BARNES.

The carriage complaints were usually disposed of at the
Head Police Office in a court upon the the ground floor.
The light was derived from windows opening on a yard,
and they were so near to the magisterial bench as to enable its occupant frequently to hear observations and conversations of an extraordinary nature. It was my custom
to remain after the carriage cases were heard, and when
the criminal charges or summonses were, in the upper
court, brought before some of my colleagues. I was thus
enabled, in comparative quietude, to prepare reports on
memorials referred by the executive or revenue authorities,
or perhaps, to enjoy an occasional leisure hour over a
magazine or newspaper. When the upper court was
crowded, persons would betake themselves to the yard and

frequently engage in conversation close to the windows, which in warm weather were generally open; but there was no indication to those outside of the presence inside of a listener to their communications. In the summer of 1854, I was sitting alone, and reading the latest news from the Crimea, when two women took their stand outside the open window, and one of them proceeded to impart her sorrows to her sympathizing friend. At the time to which I refer, recruiting was very rife in Dublin, and it was not uncommon for us to attest one hundred persons in a week. The utmost vigilance was exercised to prevent or detect desertion, and in the apprehension of deserters, a police sergeant named Barnes had particularly exerted himself, and had consequently received rewards to a considerable amount. This was the reason why his name was introduced into the narrative which I happened to overhear, and which I inscribed on a blank leaf of an interleaved statute. There is not one original idea of mine in the production, and I should not submit it to my readers if I did not consider it essential to the appreciation of the criticism subsequently pronounced by Mr. Barnes.

> Musha! Katey Doyle, do you know what?
>   Shure Jem has took the shilling,
> And off he 's gone to Aldershot,
>   It 's there he 'll get the drilling.
> The polis now along the Coombe*
>   No more will be resisted,
> And Fordham's Alley 's all in gloom
>   Since Jem has took and listed.
> So have you got a dhrop at all?
>   My sperrits is so sinking,
> I do not think I'd stop all
>   If wanst I take to drinking.

* A long thoroughfare in the Liberties of Dublin, supposed to have been originally called "The Come."

The night afore he wint to list
  I cribb'd his half week's wages,
And when the two 'r three hogs† he miss'd
  At wanst he wint outrageous.
Next mornin' to the Linen Hall
  He goes and takes the bounty ;
It would not be so bad at all
  If he had join'd the County ;
, For they 're not gone to foreign parts,
  And won't encounter dangers,
But, just as if to break our hearts,
  He join'd the Connaught Rangers.

The night afore he wint away
  He came to bid " good-bye" there.
I thought to get him for to stay,
  That thrick we couldn't try there,
For Barnes was watching, skulking round
  When Jem and I were parting—
That polisman would make a pound
  On any boy desarting.
I'm shure I'd like to take a quart
  Of Jameson's distillin',
To drink bad luck to all his sort—
  The tallow-faced ould villin.

So Jem is gone to Aldershot,
  Where 'tis I've no idea ;
Of coorse it is some desprate spot,
  Nigh-hand to the Crimea.
There 's some entrench'd upon a hill,
  Some hutted in a valley ;
I'm sure Jem would be better, still
  At home in Fordham's Alley.
For the Cossacks now he'll have to stob,
  Or shoot 'em holus bolus ;
I'm shure 'twould be an easier job
  At home to face the polis.

† A term used for English shillings, which previous to the change of currency, in 1825, passed in Ireland for thirteen pence each.

In a week or ten days after I had perpetrated this production, I was sitting in the upper court, when I was informed by the usher that Sergeant Barnes was most anxious to speak to me at my convenience and leisure. I directed that he should be admitted, and he proceeded to request that Mr. Baxter, one of the junior clerks, should be restrained from singing a song which he had picked up somewhere, and occasionally lilted to the other clerks when unemployed, as it was most disrespectful, and even termed him, Sergeant Barnes, " a tallow-faced old villain." I told the complainant that I should certainly prohibit Baxter from continuing his vocal pastime, as it was calculated to annoy an active and meritorious member of the police force. Barnes expressed his gratitude, and added, " I knew that your worship would never tolerate any of the clerks in abusing or ridiculing us. I readily acknowledge that I have received nearly £30 for detecting and taking deserters, but I would spend every farthing of the amount if I could only discover the author of Mr. Baxter's song, and I'd punish him to the utmost severity of the law for writing such a rigmarole about me." In about ten minutes after the interview, the song was torn out of the interleaved statute by the hand that had inscribed it. The sergeant soon after retired from the force on a pension, and was, for several years, in a confidential situation at the premises from which the whisky was considered so desirable to " drink bad luck to all his sort," namely, Jamieson's distillery.

CHAPTER XIX.

A RUN TO CONNAUGHT——A PRESENT——A PUZZLE——
MOLL RAFFLE——A LUCKY ACCUSATION——CROWN
WITNESSES——WHO BLEW UP KING WILLIAM ?——
SURGICAL ASSISTANCE——A REJECTED SUITOR——
GEORGE ROBINS——THE GREEK COUNT : THE
RATS——THE CHILD OF THE ALLEY——THE LUCKY
SHOT.

In the year 1842, I indulged in an excursion to the County
of Mayo, and enjoyed a sojourn of a fortnight at the
house of a most hospitable friend near Crossmolina. On
leaving Dublin, I travelled by rail to Mullingar, and from
thence proceeded by the mail-coach to my destination. I
may mention here that a few months previous, a transaction had occurred in the vicinity of Strokestown which was
of a most unusual, perhaps I might say an exceptional,
character in Connaught——namely, the murder of a landlord. I was the sole occupant of the inside of the vehicle,
and as the journey was nocturnal, I had several hours of
sound and refreshing sleep. The stoppage of the coach
in Strokestown to change horses awakened me, and I
lowered the window in order to alight. The door was at
once opened for me by a young fellow, who said, " Strokestown, sir." " Oh!" I replied, " this is where you shot

Major M——." " Troth it is," said he, " we are all rale docthors here, and when we can't cure, of coorse we kill." Such a jest, although prompt and witty, was not calculated to produce a favorable impression on the mind of a stranger; but during my visit to the West, I did not hear an angry word spoken, nor did I observe any tendency on the part of the humbler classes to treat those in higher positions with hostility or disrespect. I was perfectly pleased with the country and the people, and my friend's hospitality afforded me social gratifications in which there was one novelty which I peculiarly relished. It was a liquor derived from no foreign vineyard, but was so peculiarly Irish as to induce one whom I am certainly not singular in believing to be the greatest lyric poet that ever existed, to make it the subject of a song, adapted to the joyous and spirit-stirring air of " Paddy O'Rafferty." I shall quote the lines of the immortal Moore as fully justifying the predilection which I have acknowledged for the potation he describes :—

" Drink of this cup—you 'll find there 's a spell in
   Its every drop 'gainst the ills of mortality;
Talk of the cordial that sparkled for Helen,
   Her cup was a fiction, but this is reality.
Would you forget the dark world we are in,
   Just taste of the bubble that gleams on the top of it;
But would you rise above earth, till akin
   To Immortals themselves, you must drain every drop of it.
Send round the cup—for oh ! there 's a spell in
   Its every drop 'gainst the ills of mortality;
Talk of the cordial that sparkled for Helen,
   Her cup was a fiction, but this is reality.

" Never was philter form'd with such power
   To charm and bewilder as this we are quaffing ;
Its magic began when, in Autumn's rich hour,
   A harvest of gold in the fields it stood laughing.

There having, by Nature's enchantment, been fill'd
  With the balm and the bloom of her kindliest weather,
This wonderful juice from its core was distill'd
  To enliven such hearts as are here brought together.
Then drink of the cup—you'll find there's a spell in
  It's every drop 'gainst the ills of mortality;
Talk of the cordial that sparkled for Helen,
  Her cup was a fiction, but this is reality.

" And though, perhaps—but breathe it to no one—
  Like liquor the witch brews at midnight so awful,
In secret this philter was first taught to flow on,
  Yet 'tisn't less potent for being unlawful.
And ev'n though it taste of the smoke of that flame,
  Which in silence extracted its virtue forbidden,
Fill up, there's a fire in some hearts I could name,
  Which may work too its charm though as lawless and hidden.
So drink of the cup— for oh ! there's a spell in
  Its every drop 'gainst the ills of mortality ;
Talk of the cordial that sparkled for Helen,
  Her cup was a fiction, but this is reality."

A PRESENT.

Amongst my convivial friends in Mayo, I expressed my
regret that the liquor which I enjoyed so much in their
festive society was almost unknown and unattainable in
Dublin.   In two or three weeks after my return home, I
received an anonymous note, stating that a box would be
delivered at the Head Police Office, directed to me, and
advising that I should not have it opened by any other
hands but my own. The box arrived, and was treated
according to the suggestion.   It contained two jars, each
holding two gallons of " the reality."   A flat bottle was
frequently filled, and conveyed, in my breast-pocket, " to
enliven such hearts as I wished to bring together;" but at
last I found that the jars were nearly empty.   About half
a pint remained, and it was never drank.   I was aware

that the next day was fixed for the hearing of a number of complaints preferred for the evasion or violation of excise laws. I directed the office-attendant to wash and thoroughly cleanse the inkstands, which were on the public table, for the use of parties prosecuting or defending, and to bring the glasses to me. I procured some ink powder, on which I put the remaining portion of the Mayo "philter,," and supplied the stands with excellent ink, well suited for transcribing a *strong* charge or a *spirited* defence. It was not inodorous, and I was greatly amused by hearing the excise officers frequently observing to their superior and to their solicitor, that "they smelt illicit spirits." Mr. Morewood and Mr. Stormont also recognised the peculiar smell, and formed various conjectures; but none of the persons engaged ever imagined that the ink in their pens was made upon potteen. Immediately after the termination of the excise cases, one of my colleagues had the inkstands emptied and replenished with the ordinary ink. He said that "it was a fair joke on the gaugers, but when they were gone he could not submit to be tantalised by *the smell* without any chance of enjoying *the taste.*"

MOLL RAFFLE.

I was sitting one day at the police-court in Dublin, along with another magistrate, when a gentleman entered and preferred a very urgent request that one of us would accompany him to Kingstown, to witness and certify the execution of a power of attorney by his mother, in reference to certain funds in the Bank of England. The applicant was reputed to be the natural son of a very distinguished nobleman who had discharged viceregal duties in Ireland, and also in very important and extensive oriental territories. I never heard what the original name of the

o

lady had been, but she was known by the rather inelegant *soubriquet* of Moll Raffle. She had followed her aristocratic paramour to Ireland, and he had relieved himself from her claims or importunities by providing her with a husband, and her son with an official appointment of respectable rank and emolument. I had never seen her, and I was influenced by personal curiosity to accede to her son's request. We proceeded to Kingstown, and on arriving at a commodious and genteel residence, he desired the servant to inform Mrs. —— that he had brought the magistrate for the business required. In a few minutes she appeared, and although no longer youthful, or even middle-aged, a second look was not necessary to convince me that she must have been exquisitely beautiful in her features, and of a tall and symmetrical figure. Her right arm was bandaged and in a sling, and she exclaimed to her son that she was deeply mortified at having given me the trouble of coming so far on an ineffectual mission, for that she had unfortunately sustained a severe fall, having trodden on a loose stair-rod just after he had started for Dublin, and her wrist and hand were so much bruised as to render her incapable of making her signature. I told her that if she took the pen in her left hand, I would, at her instance and request, guide it so as to write her name, and that I would explain the matter in a special magisterial attestation on the document. To this suggestion she readily acceded, and the power of attorney was promptly perfected. She insisted that I should take luncheon, after which I left. Not having to return to official duties, I sauntered through Kingstown until about four o'clock, when I went to the jetty, which was crowded, as a military band was playing there. I was not long on the jetty before I saw Mrs. —— with half-a-dozen companions, but the sling was gone, and her right hand seemed perfectly capable of managing her parasol. I subsequently ascertained that "Moll Raffle" had never been taught to write, and that she thought it more agreeable to pretend that her hand had been hurt than to acknowledge her educational deficiency.

A LUCKY ACCUSATION.

In the year 1846, the Ribbon association, or fraternity, prevailed very extensively in the city of Dublin, and in the counties of Dublin, Wicklow, Kildare, and Meath. I believe that religious opinions or political tendencies had very little influence on their deliberations or proceedings. All the information that I acquired in reference to them led me to the conclusion that their temporal interests actuated them throughout. Threats, menaces, and even murderous violence were used without hesitation to deter competition with a ribbon-man in affairs of tenancy, traffic, or employment. I notice these tendencies merely as being connected with a most extraordinary incident at the time. A man named Lacy held a small farm somewhere between Brittas and Blessington, and at an early hour, on a Saturday morning, he left home, bringing, with a horse and cart, various commodities for sale in Dublin. Having disposed of his goods, he was about to start for home in the evening. He stopped at a shop in Bride Street to purchase some groceries, and tendered in payment a crown-piece. It was a coin of George the Third's reign, was rather worn, and had acquired a dark and very questionable appearance. The proprietor of the shop pronounced the crown to be base, and used some expressions which irritated Lacy, who replied to them in vituperative terms. The grocer observed a constable passing, and having called upon him, charged Lacy with tendering a base coin.   The man was taken to the station-house in Chancery Lane, his horse and cart were sent to a livery stable, and he remained in custody until Monday morning, when the charge was laid before me.   Mr. Stuart, of Dame Street, a silversmith, was examined, and in my presence tested the crown.   He pronounced it to be perfectly genuine.   I accordingly directed the accused party to be discharged from custody, and I was not surprised at his expressions of indignation for having been detained and locked up amongst thieves and disorderly characters, and his horse and cart sent to livery, whilst his family could not but feel alarmed for his safety, when he failed to return at the expected time.   I directed his horse and cart to be given to him, and that the livery should be defrayed from the police funds.   Scarcely had I disposed of the case when Lacy's wife arrived in an indescribable state of joyful excitement.   She clasped him in her arms, exclaiming, " You 're safe, all is right, thanks to God."   She manifested no resentment towards the grocer, but wished him good luck and prosperity.   The cause of her delight may be briefly explained, but it is not the less extraordinary.   Her husband had incurred the resentment of the ribbon-men of his vicinity, by offering for land against one of the fraternity.   On the Saturday night an armed party entered his house for the purpose of killing him, but their diabolical design was thwarted by the circumstance of their intended victim being in custody of the Dublin Police, upon an unfounded, but certainly not an unfortunate accusation.   His family had communicated with the constabulary, lest the intended assassination might be perpetrated on his journey home, and early on Monday morning his wife started in search of him, with the result which has been stated.

CROWN WITNESSES.

For several years subsequent to my appointment to magisterial office, there were two houses in Great Ship Street, on the side now entirely occupied by the barrack, which were appropriated to the accommodation of crown witnesses. There was an internal communication between those houses, and the witnesses, of both sexes, were allowed to associate free from all supervision, except what served to keep them from leaving the premises, unless accompanied by an attendant, and examining letters received or despatched by them. Their meals were generally taken together; and for the amusement or employment of their evenings, they were left entirely to themselves. Amongst those witnesses almost every variety of character was to be found. A young man, whose name has lapsed from my recollection, was charged by a female with attempting to commit an offence which I need not particularise, and I was directed to investigate the affair at the premises, without imparting to it any avoidable publicity. The accused party denied the misconduct imputed to him, and attributed the charge to spite and resentment on the part of the complainant and another inmate of the place. A woman stated that " the girl was vexed by the questions put to her, and the faults found with her evidence every time that her case was tried." I was greatly surprised to find that the crown witnesses were accustomed to have their evidence rehearsed before an amateur judge, an improvised jury, and a couple of supposed counsel, one to prosecute and the other to defend. If a case failed, the witnesses were instructed as to their deficiencies, either in manner or matter; and they were drilled to avoid admissions of any nature calculated to weaken their testimony. I made such representations to the Executive as produced the suppression of the Ship Street establishments.

WHO BLEW UP KING WILLIAM?

Very soon after my appointment to the police magistracy, there was a person named Jones convicted of being deeply implicated in the Ribbon system. He was not committed for trial from the Head Office, and I was not officially connected with any of the proceedings in his case. After he had been sent to another hemisphere under sentence of transportation, I heard casually from a professional man, on whose statements I placed the utmost reliance, that Jones had acknowledged to him being the person by whom the statue of King William in College Green was blown up in 1836. There was no prosecution instituted as to that extraordinary affair, and I notice it only on account of the statements subsequently made, and an incident which may be considered of an amusing character. Two women of a disreputable class were standing at the corner of Church Lane in College Green just after midnight. A man, whom they had not previously observed, descended quickly from the statue, and having crossed the rails which then intervened between the pedestal and the thoroughfare, he ignited a fuse which had been previously connected with some explosive substance placed between the figures of the steed and the rider. The man rapidly decamped, the fuse burned quickly, and there was an explosion which was heard in almost every part of the city, and by which the figure of the monarch was completely separated from his horse, and thrown into the public carriage-way, several yards from the pedestal. It was reported that a respectable citizen residing in the immediate vicinity, who had been suffering for some time previous from disease of the heart, rose from his bed in hasty alarm, and almost immediately dropped lifeless. Jones, according to the statement of my informant, subsequently tried to cut the head off the prostrate figure, but was deterred by the approach of a party of police from College Street.   I believe that those who examined the figures of man and horse expressed a decided opinion that the explosion had not been effected by gunpowder, and the statements of the acknowledged delinquent denied that gunpowder had been used, but without his specifying what material had effected such an extraordinary result.

SURGICAL ASSISTANCE.

In the year 1836, Lord Mulgrave, afterwards Marquis of Normanby, was Lord Lieutenant of Ireland. He had an aid-de-camp, a Captain B——, who has since supplemented that name by another commencing with O. That gentleman then was, and has since continued to be, a most desirable addition to any social or convivial re-union in which wit and comic humor were appreciated. On the night of the explosion, Captain B—— was returning from some festive scene, and reached College Green, on his way to the Castle, a few minutes after the occurrence. He instantly ordered his driver to make for Merrion Square as quickly as possible, and to stop at the residence of Crampton, who was the first surgical practitioner of the time, and who was very generally considered to have a most persistent anxiety to establish acquaintance and even intimacies amongst the aristocracy. Captain B—— applied himself to the knocker and door-bell until he had completely roused every inmate of the house, and to the first, who enquired the reason for his urgent application, he replied, "To let Surgeon Crampton know that a very distinguished personage had fallen from his horse in College Green, and sustained serious injuries." The hoax was successful. Crampton proceeded with the utmost haste to the place designated, and subsequently he caused considerable surprise by becoming the frequent narrator of the trick to which he had been subjected.

A REJECTED SUITOR.

In offering to my readers an incident or anecdote, I have the advantage of being free from any necessity for a consecutive arrangement. My recollections may suggest occurrences anterior to some already narrated without precluding me from a description of them. About the time, however, to which I have last adverted, I was residing in Lower Fitzwilliam Street, and a young lady, a near relative of my wife, was a frequent visiter. She was decidedly handsome, and possessed other attractions of no inconsiderable value. Her admirers were numerous, and amongst them there was no more ardent suitor than a Mr. Richard S——. He was an accomplished gentleman, of handsome countenance and fine portly figure. He sang very well, and almost always adapted his voice to the music of his own guitar. His family was of high respectability in a southern county, but some banking speculations had seriously diminished their financial resources. His addresses were most ardently directed, but the fair lady was not to be won. She was informed that her admirer supported himself by some employments or agencies in the corn trade. He was refused, and almost immediately disappeared from Irish society. When I resigned the police magistracy in 1861, I was invited by my friend, the late Marcus Costello, to visit him at Gibraltar, at which place he held the office of Attorney-

General. In a few weeks after my arrival there, he told me that some Spanish officers of high distinction were to cross from Algesiras, to visit the fortress and see the extraordinary productions of nature and art which are there so abundantly displayed. I accompanied him and several other functionaries to the Governor's residence, at which, amidst the firing of salutes and other manifestations of respect, the Spanish officers were received. The principal personage amongst them was highly decorated. He had distinguished himself in the then recent warfare with the Moors, and was a general in the army, besides holding an important provincial office which, as well as I recollect, caused him to be designated " Intendente." To my great astonishment, Don Ricardo de S. advanced to me, proferred his hand, enquired about many of his old acquaintances, and enabled me to recognise the quondam guitar performer, whose personal qualities and capabilities had been better appreciated abroad than in his native land. I may, in some later pages, have occasion to refer to other recollections of Gibraltar.

GEORGE ROBINS.

About the time of my accession to magisterial office, a sale was advertised of two properties on the river Blackwater. The descriptions specified two fine mansions, with the adjuncts of extensive stabling, gardens, ornamental plantations, and such a number of acres suited for pasture or tillage as would fairly entitle each place to be considered. a demesne worthy of the attention of all who desired a residence fit for high rank and liberal expenditure. The advertisements stated the properties to be beautifully picturesque, and as affording ample means to the sportsman for the gratification of all his tastes or inclinations. But

public attention was peculiarly excited by the announcement that the sale by auction would be conducted at
Morrison's in Dawson Street, by the far-famed London
auctioneer, GEORGE ROBINS.   Not being the least curious
of the community, I betook myself to the place appointed,
and found the room crowded at the hour of one o'clock,
P.M.   George allowed fifteen or twenty minutes to elapse
before he appeared and offered an apology for his delay, as
having been occasioned by the breaking down of a vehicle.
He then proceeded to address his auditors in a tone of,
perhaps assumed, despondency and discontent, to the
following effect:—" Ladies and gentlemen, I feel deeply
mortified at having to submit for public competition these
properties, of which I have not the slightest personal
knowledge.   I regret having accepted the engagement,
which I am decidedly unable to discharge to my own
satisfaction.   It was my intention to have viewed the
houses and lands, so as to know what I could truly state ;
but I was unfortunately detained in London, until it
became impossible for me to run down to Mallow or
Youghal before the auction.   I think it very probable that
I shall take an early opportunity to see the places which I
am now about to sell.   My curiosity has been excited
greatly by two gentlemen who travelled in the coach with
me on my journey through Wales.   They knew me ; and
in the course of our conversation, I mentioned that I was
proceeding to Dublin to sell these two properties on the
Blackwater.   They stated that they knew the places perfectly well, and that I might expect a brisk competition.
As we passed through the lovely scenery of Llangollen,
Clwyd, and some other enchanting places, I expressed the
most unqualified admiration of landscapes uniting all the
beauties which hill and valley, wood and water, towering

rocks and verdant glens can present to the view of a delighted traveller. My companions did not join in my fervent appreciation of the Welsh scenery. They said that it was certainly agreeable to the eye, but when compared with that of some other localities, it did not surpass mediocrity. When I reiterated my opinion that I had never previously viewed such beautiful landscapes, they replied that *if I only took a glance at the places on the Blackwater, which I was going over to sell, they would monopolise my admiration, and convince me of the utter inferiority of the most picturesque portion of Wales.* I have consequently a very great desire to see the two splendid demesnes which I must now offer for your competition." I do not insist on my readers giving implicit credence to the tale about the travelling companions. Whoever disbelieves it will not be singular.

THE GREEK COUNT—THE RATS.

I had the pleasure of being intimately acquainted with the late Thomas Symes of Leinster Street. He was a solicitor of the highest respectability, and was an universal favorite in a very extensive circle. He had travelled much, especially in the southern parts of Europe ; and few foreigners from those localities, if of rank or consideration, came to Dublin without experiencing his attentions. Amongst those whom I met at his house, there was only one in whom I observed a tendency to make statements which were worthy of observation and productive of amusement from the total absence of any truthful ingredient. He was a Greek, and was also a Count, and not a Baron, so that he could not be mistaken for a personage of the latter dignity, whose name commenced with the same letter. Count M—— was not the veritable Baron Munchausen;

but he was decidedly his rival in demands on the credulity of those who heard his asseverations.　He never spoke to the disparagement of any human being except Otho, who was then King of Greece, and whom he occasionally expressed a wish to burn.　He spoke English and some other languages with wonderful fluency, and no matter what subjects appeared most agreeable to any company, the Count never failed to introduce and expatiate on the surprising intelligence of RATS, and he invariaby closed each anecdote with a declaration that "upon his sacred word of honor it was strictly true."

"I was obliged," said he "to leave Athens by the tyrannical persecution of Otho, and I betook myself to Zante, in which island I possessed extensive currant grounds and olive plantations.　In our oil cellar we had a large tun and a great number of jars and flasks, which were generally well filled.　We found, however, that the jars and bottles prepared for corking and sealing in the evening were lessened by some inches as to their contents in the morning. Having closely and quietly watched, we found that the rats took it in turn to let down their tails into the vessels, so as to enable the others to lick off the oil thus abstracted. The store tun appeared to be full to the bung-hole; but when the contents were drawn off for refining, we discovered that the rats had kept the oil up to the orifice by dropping pebbles into the vessel.　I pledge you my sacred word, &c.

"I was one day strolling through the currant grounds, and provided with an excellent fowling-piece, in the hope of meeting with quail.　I was near to a small stream, when I observed two rats approaching the water.　They were so close together that their sides appeared to be touching, and I killed both in one shot.　On going to the spot where they were lying, I immediately perceived that one rat was blind, and between them there was a little straw blade, of which each had held an end in his mouth. It was thus that the blindness of one was productive of sagacious care and attention in the other. I pledge you," &c.

I have lately observed that the Count is mentioned in The Life and Recollections of the Hon Granville Berkeley, but without any allusion to the extraordinary tendencies and dexterous expedients which, amongst us, he attributed to such hateful vermin.

THE CHILD OF THE ALLEY.

Amongst my personal recollections, there is one which I hope to narrate without ruffling or alarming the most sensitively delicate of my readers, although amongst the prominent characters of the scene about a dozen belonged to the most wretched and degraded portion of the female sex, and dwelt in a mean, loathsome, and disreputable locality named Cole Alley, which was, and perhaps still continues to be, occupied by denizens of a similar description. I shall apply to them the term adopted by Hood in his exquisite production of " The Bridge of Sighs," and designate them " unfortunates." I had been a magistrate for three or four years, when I was one day informed by the attendant of the police-court that a deputation of females from Cole Alley earnestly besought me to give them an audience. My colleagues were amused at the application, and ironically congratulated me on such an exclusive preference; but I determined to accede to the request, and directed them to be admitted. About twelve of them entered the court, and amidst the " unfortunates" I perceived a female child of ten or eleven years of age.

The spokeswoman of the party led this child forward, and addressed me to the following effect:—

" Yer worship, this poor little girl was born in the alley. She was not quite a year old when the collar (cholera) made a great sweep up there, and took off her mother, who was one of us. The child had no one to care her, so we agreed to do the best we could for her, and we gave her a bit of food, a rag or two to cover her, and she lived about among us, so that we used to call her our own child. But now, yer worship, we see that she is coming to a time of life when to stay in the alley would be her destruction. We are doatingly fond of her, and it would be a heartscald to us all to think of her ever falling into our course of life. We would beg of you to have her put into some school or institution where she will be reared in decency, and trained to earn honest bread."

I at once stated to "the deputation" that I should do my utmost to realize their wishes, and that they might leave the child to my care. They embraced her most affectionately, and with the warmest thanks for my compliance, they departed. The Poor Law Unions had not been organized at the time, and I sent the child on a remand committal to the worthy matron of Grangegorman Prison, Mrs. Rawlins, with a note explaining the circumstances, and requesting that the little girl should be kept apart from the juvenile delinquents. My wishes were strictly complied with. On the following day, I dined at Portrane with the worthy George Evans. I mentioned the transaction to him, and he communicated it to his sister, Mrs. Putland. That lady was an impersonation of charity, and at once offered to have the " child of the alley " placed in one of the many institutions which she contributed to support. I regret that I am unable to state any further results, having omitted to make ulterior inquiries, but I have always considered the earnest application, perhaps I might fairly term it the *supplication,* of the Cole Alley "unfortunates" as the strongest acknowledgment, offered sincerely and spontaneously, by VICE of the superiority of VIRTUE.

THE LUCKY SHOT.

A female of the class to which I have adverted was an inmate of one of the many disreputable houses which constituted almost the entire of a street on the south side of Dublin. It was called "French Street;" but the obnoxious establishments having been suppressed, it is now designated "Upper Mercer Street." An English commercial traveller betook himself to the house in which the "unfortunate" resided. He was in a fearful state of *delirium tremens;* and having been refused a further supply of liquor, he took out a pistol, and shot the "unfortunate," lodging two bullets in her body. He was seized, and the woman was conveyed to Mercer's Hospital, which was in the immediate vicinity. Her wounds did not prove mortal, the balls were extracted; but whilst her recovery was uncertain, I went several times to the hospital for the purpose of taking her informations. She never expressed any resentment against her assailant, and she refused to prosecute him. Some of his family and friends contributed about £20, which sum was paid to her a few days before she was discharged, and she appropriated it to defray the expenses of her emigration. I was informed by the attendants that she often spoke of *the lucky shot,* by which she was enabled to quit a course of sin and degradation, and to essay a new life in a new land. This occurred, I think, in the year 1843.

CHAPTER XX.

O'CONNELL—SMITH O'BRIEN AND MEAGHER—JOHN
MITCHEL—INFORMERS—THE CLOSE OF 1848—
THE MILITARY—A FRENCH VIEW OF POPULAR
COMMOTIONS.

IN 1844 there was the most intense excitement amongst
all classes, sects, and parties of the Irish community, arising from the prosecutions instituted by the Attorney-
General, Thomas Berry Cusack Smith against O'Connell
and several others for various alleged violations of the
laws in their meetings, publications, and other proceedings
adopted by them to promote a repeal of the Union. The
preliminary informations were sworn before a judge, and
none of the police magistrates were called upon to interfere, in any way whatever, from the commencement to the
conclusion of the affair. On the 30th of May, the accused
were sentenced to certain terms of imprisonments and
fines, and they were liberated on the reversal of the judgment by the House of Lords, on the 6th September. A
few days before the sentence was pronounced, I dined in
company with Mr. John O'Connell, when he stated that
they expected to be sent to Newgate or Kilmainham. I
advised him to have a special application made to the
court to order the imprisonment in the Richmond Bridewell, which was cleanly and spacious, and where they

might have access to two extensive gardens.   My suggestion was adopted, and the prisoners were sent by a cir-
cuitous route, avoiding the great thoroughfares of the city,
to the bridewell.   In the evening I was going home to
my residence in Rathmines, when I overheard a woman
loudly expressing to a number of sympathetic listeners,
her hearty detestation and curse upon all "who had any
hand in sending the Liberator to the same place as that to
which Porter sends *his blackguards.*"

Thomas Berry Cusack Smith, the Attorney-General,
had been nicknamed, "Alphabet Smith," from the multiplicity of his names, and when the judgment of the
Queen's Bench was reversed, a ballad appeared to the
tune of "The Shan van vocht."   A police inspector asked
my opinion as to the prevention of it being chanted by the
street vocalists, and I advised him against making it more
known and more relished by the multitude, as it would be
by his interference.   It is as follows :—

" Musha, Dan who let you out ?
        Says the T. B. C.
For you 're here beyant a doubt,
        Says the T. B. C.
Sure I thought I locked you in,
You contrariest of min,
And what brings you here agin,
        Says the T. B. C.

Through the chimney did you climb ?
        Says the T. B. C.
For you 're up to any crime,
        Says the T. B. C.
There were locks both great and small,
Did you dare to pick them all ?
Did you scale the prison wall ?
        Says the T. B. C.

P

No, I did 'nt scale the wall,
     Says the Dan van vocht,
Through the flues I did 'nt crawl,
     Says the Dan van vocht,
Not a weapon did I take,
And no lock I tried to break,
Such attempts I 'd scorn to make,
     Says the Dan van vocht.

But might is foiled by right,
     Says the Dan van vocht,
As the darkness by the light,
     Says the Dan van vocht,
My cause was on a rock,
'Twas the law that picked the lock,
And I 'm free, my bantam cock,
     Says the Dan van vocht.

Oh ! confusion to you Dan,
     Says the T. B. C.
You 're a divil of a man,
     Says the T. B. C.
And we 're in a precious plight,
By your means this very night,
For you 've bothered us outright,
     Says the T. B. C."

During the progress of the prosecution against the
repealers, Tom Steele, who was one of those indicted,
interrupted the proceedings several times, audibly contra-
dicting some expressions of the Attorney-general, and
annoying him by exclamations and gestures. Tom prided
himself on being considered the *fidus Achates* of O'Connell,
and was never so happy as when closely associated with
his political leader. It was said, and I believe it was
perfectly true, that Smith succeeded in quieting Tom, by
intimating that if he continued to exclaim and gesticulate,
his name should be struck out of the indictment, and his

chance of participating in the expected martyrdom thereby annihilated.

Whilst O'Connell and the other state prisoners were in the Richmond Bridewell, they received a continual supply of the choicest provisions and wine sent as presents by their political adherents. It would be very difficult to particularise any article suited to a luxurious repast, which was not tendered for their enjoyment. I was twice at the prison, on magisterial business, during their detention, and on each occasion I saw materials fit for princely banquets brought for their use. I was rather surprised at one contribution which very soon disappeared. It was half a ton of *ice*, and it did not preserve its consistency beyond a few hours. I heard from some of the prison officials that O'Connell's meals were generally simple in their material, but that his appetite was healthy and strong. When released from confinement, he did not appear to have been weakened by its infliction.

It would not be in accordance with the objects of my reminiscences to advocate or condemn the political opinions or proceedings of any portion of the community, unless they involved direct incitements to, or the actual adoption of, open violence. In noticing O'Connell as a remarkable public character, I may express my conviction that he had a decided repugnance, even in the hottest times of political excitement, to the application of actual force. It may be said that he could " speak daggers," but he was disposed to " use none."

Whenever I had an opportunity to hear him, whether on legal or political occasions, I availed myself of it, in the anticipation of being highly amused, and I was scarcely ever disappointed. I am tempted to detail two or three of my recollections, which have not been noticed by any of his biographers.   I am aware that my expressions must be far inferior to his diction, but my readers will not, I hope, be too severe in criticising my inefficiency.

I was present at the trial of a very beautiful young lady who, with her mother and two other persons, was indicted for conspiring to take away a minor from his parents, and have him married to the young lady in Scotland.   The prosecution was conducted with considerable acrimony, and the Gretna-Green bride was described as a person of very tarnished reputation, whose favorite paramour had been *a blacksmith*.   No proofs were adduced of the imputed immorality, and O'Connell, in a speech for the defence, denounced it as a fabrication "which had not even the merit of originality, but was borrowed from the mythological assignment of *Vulcan to Venus*."

At the commencement of the first viceroyalty of the Marquis Wellesley, a newspaper was started in Parliament Street by a Mr. Hayden.   It was called *The Morning Star*, and its editorial articles were almost exclusively devoted to the most disparaging and insulting productions in reference to the Lord Lieutenant or O'Connell.   The latter was never forgotten ; and every term of obloquy was put in requisition for his diurnal vilification.   Firebrand, Rebel, Arch-mendicant, Liar, Impostor, Schemer, were liberally appropriated to him, and even the shape of his hat, and the mode of carrying his umbrella, became subjects of offensive observation.   The attention of the Attorney-General was attracted to an article in *The Morning Star*, headed "The profligate Lord Wharton," the writer of which stated that the history of the Wharton viceroyalty had never been fully published, because a true description of such a character would be considered as an incredible exaggeration, but that it might now be produced without any apprehension of such an opinion prevailing, inasmuch as its worst details would be found fully equalled in Dublin Castle under the auspices of its present occupant. A criminal information was filed against Mr. Hayden for a libel on the Lord Lieutenant; and he became extremely apprehensive of a severe punishment, resulting from his very offensive comparison of Lord Wellesley with Lord Wharton. He immediately engaged William Ford as his attorney, and the next step was to retain O'Connell as his principal counsel. The latter agreed to act, but required that he should be left completely free to adopt whatever line of defence he preferred, and to manage the case at his own discretion. The trial was held in the King's Bench before Bushe, the Chief Justice, and the opening statement for the prosecution was delivered by the Attorney-General, Plunket. Sir Charles Vernon, who held the appointment of registrar of newspapers, was the first witness; and he produced the official copy of the paper containing the alleged libel, and it was read by him for the court and jury. O'Connell was then at the outer bar, and occupied a seat on its front row. He submitted to the judge, that when a document was given in evidence, either party could insist on the entire of it being read. To this proposition the Chief Justice acceded, expressing a hope, however, that his time would not be wasted in listening to irrelevant matter. O'Connell then required Sir Charles to read sundry portions of the paper in which "a person named O'Connell" was made the subject of the most defamatory animadversions. The entire auditory were convulsed with laughter, as he gravely proceeded to elicit ardent wishes for the speedy hanging or transportation of the arch-agitator, the apostle of mischief, the disseminator of disaffection, the mendicant patriot, the disgrace to his profession, and the curse of his country.   When the case for the prosecution closed, he proceeded to address the jury, and his speech was replete with the highest encomiums on the Marquis Wellesley, to whose Indian government and diplomatic services he referred as exhibiting all the qualities of perfect statesmanship.   He then expressed his surprise at the Attorney-General condescending to notice the publication of a mere newspaper squib, which could not possibly affect the illustrious viceroy.   In the paper produced there were several unwarrantable attacks upon some person named O'Connell, who had instituted no proceedings against their publisher, although, perhaps, he was very likely to be affected injuriously by them, especially if his livelihood depended upon his character and reputation.   Bitterly as he had been assailed, he had remained quiescent, and so regardless of the invectives directed against him, that it was very probable he had no desire whatever to mulct or incarcerate his assailant, but would rather aid in terminating his anxieties, and sending him *home to his wife and five children.*

At the conclusion of his speech O'Connell left the court.   I had been sitting very near him, and went out at the same time.   Ford was in the vestibule, and when they met, O'Connell said, " Ford, I hope that I did not make a wrong cast in my closing sentence *; is the fellow married ?"*

Hayden was not convicted, the jury disagreed, and the prosecution was not renewed.   The publication of " The Morning Star " was almost immediately discontinued.

In 1834, the question of Repeal of the Union was introduced by O'Connell to the House of Commons, and negatived by an overwhelming majority.   The principal opponent of the motion was Thomas Spring Rice (afterwards Lord Monteagle) who was then one of the members for Limerick city, and a very general opinion was immediately entertained that he would never be elected there on any future occasion. In the autumn of 1834, I was appointed a revising barrister in reference to tithes, and in that capacity I visited Limerick. I had finished my business, and was preparing for my departure, when about two o'clock in the afternoon, O'Connell arrived at the hotel, (which was, I think, Cruise's,) and the street was immediately thronged to excess by an enthusiastic multitude. He was on his way to Dublin; but whether he wished to address the people or not, it was manifest that a speech from the balcony was unavoidable. I got as near to him as the crowded state of the apartment permitted, and was enabled to hear his oration fully; but of course I cannot do more than give its general import, and endeavour to describe its effect. He commenced by stating that a report had been circulated that he intended to interfere with the people of Limerick, and to direct, and even *to dictate*, the choice of their Parliamentary representatives. This rumour he denounced as a scandalous, infamous *lie*. He had no wish to curb or trammel them in the exercise of their rights, and he was not such a fool as to attempt dictation to a community too independent and intelligent to yield to any influence except dispassionate arguments suggested by patriotism and conducive to the welfare of their beloved country. Frequent and rapturous cheers from listening thousands evinced their appreciation of his address, especially when he referred to the valorous defence of their city by their forefathers. At length he said that his topics were exhausted, and that he had nothing to add unless they wished him to tell them a *little story*. Shouts were immediately raised for " the story, the story," and he proceeded to narrate that about the beginning of the present century an opinion was very prevalent that the French intended to invade Ireland, and it was considered probable that their fleet would enter the Shannon, and land the troops on the left side of that splendid river, in the vicinity of Limerick. The French had exacted such heavy contributions from the continental states which they had occupied, that very great apprehensions were entertained that their invasion of Ireland would be attended with similar results, and that the industrial resources of the country and the savings of the people would be speedily spoliated. There then lived near Foynes a farmer named Maurice Sullivan, a man of excellent character, religious, sober, thrifty, industrious, and intelligent. He had a loved and loving wife, comely and amiable, who made his home happy by the observance of every domestic duty, On a Sunday morning, they were returning from Mass, and were chatting as to the probability of the French coming over. He said that they would ruin thousands who were then comfortable and contented, and that they would help themselves to everything they fancied. " I have now," he added, " to tell you, my dear Jenny, that I have more money than you knew of. I have had good crops, and the cattle and sheep have thriven well and fetched high prices, and I have laid by close on eight hundred pounds. If a Frenchman came across my savings, he would not ask leave or licence, but plunder me at once."

" Maurice," replied his wife, " I must acknowledge to you that I have put by more than one hundred pounds that I made from time to time by the poultry and eggs and early vegetables. Now that we have made a clear breast to each other, what course shall we take to keep the money safe ? "

"Well," said he, "I was down, a few evenings ago, in the old churchyard, and noticed a hole at the corner of the big monument belonging to the RICE family. I think if I got a strong canister or jar, and packed the money in it, and hid it under the monument, closing up the hole completely, nobody would ever think of ransacking such a place as that, or suppose that it contained anything valuable."

"Maurice," replied Jenny, "it was a cute notion of yours, and I am sure that no Frenchman would ever go to root out your canister, but still with my consent not even a farthing shall ever be put there."

"Why, what is your objection?" said her husband.

"My objection is very simple," answered Jenny; "do anything else that you please, but not that, for *I wouldn't trust a Rice, living or dead.*"

The "little story" was vehemently cheered, and its concluding words became a political maxim amongst the repealers of Limerick. Rice had no longer a chance of election there, but he was returned at the next dissolution for an English borough, I believe for Cambridge. The "little story" appeared to me rather an extraordinary sequel to the disavowal of any desire to interfere, to direct, or to dictate.

In some recent publications I have seen it stated that O'Connell achieved a complete triumph over an inveterate termagant named Biddy Moriarty, whose quickness and copiousness of abusive diction deterred all others from engaging her in any wordy warfare. His success was ascribed to the application of mathematical terms to his vituperative antagonist, who became completely bewildered at finding herself designated a detested parallelogram, a notorious hypothenuse, an octagonal diagram, of rectan-

gular habits and rhomboidal practices. I do not believe
that he ever came in collision with the redoubtable Biddy,
for the tale of her discomfiture was very rife before
O'Connell had attained to great eminence, either politically
or professionally, and I have heard it told in the year 1817
in the presence of Curran, who was mentioned as her
successful antagonist, and complimented on the effective
means he adopted to overcome the incorrigible scold ; and
I recollect hearing him state that the encounter took place
at Rathcormack, in the County Cork. He added, that
having declared, towards the conclusion of the verbose
strife, that he could never condescend again to notice such
" an individual," the exasperated woman replied that he
had a power of impudence to say the like, for that she was
no more an *andyvidjal* than he was himself.

In reference to O'Connell, I have a very distinct recollection that in 1837-38 he took a prominent part in
opposing combinations amongst the working tradesmen
of Dublin. He attended public meetings, and spoke of
the evils arising from combinations or trade-strikes in the
strongest terms.   Hostility, amounting to threats of
personal violence, was displayed towards him by some of
those to whose opinions and proceedings he was adverse.
I have heard Joseph Denis Mullen state that he suggested
to O'Connell that the course adopted by him might
endanger his popularity, to which he replied :—

"When my popularity depends on the surrender or
compromise of my conscientious convictions, I shall not
seek to retain it."   It was in reference to his conduct at
that time that the late Lord Charlemont, when presiding
at a public banquet to the metropolitan members, of whom
O'Connell was one, and proposing the toast of the evening,

applied a very appropriate quotation, derived from classic
knowledge and suggested by classic taste—

> " Justum, et tenacem propositi virum
> *Non civium ardor prava jubentium ;*
> Non vultus instantis tyranni
> Mente quatit solida. "—*

In April, 1835, I had occasion to visit London, and,
during a sojourn of about three weeks, I spent several
evenings in the gallery of the House of Commons. There
had been a recent change of ministry, and the Melbourne
cabinet was formed. In the preceding Government Lord
Ashley had been a Lord of the Admiralty, and at the time
to which I refer, a sergeant-at-law, named Spankey, had
been returned, on the liberal interest, for a metropolitan
constituency, I believe Finsbury. I happened to be in
the gallery one evening when there was not a member of
the administration present, and the opposition benches
were also unoccupied by any of the leading conservatives.
There was no probability of any interesting discussion
arising, and the secretary of the admiralty was engaged in
moving the navy estimates to which he did not appear to
apprehend any objection, as they had been framed at a
considerable reduction of the preceding amounts. I was
about to retire from the gallery, when Lord Ashley arose,
and denounced the proposed votes as having originated in
a spirit of parsimony, and as tending to impair the most
important element of our national strength. Having
delivered a speech, in which the greatest ignorance of their
duties, and a most culpable neglect of our naval require-

---

* The man of firm and righteous will,
  No rabble clamorous for the wrong,
  No tyrant's brow, whose frown may kill,
  Can shake the strength that makes him strong.

ments were imputed to the Government; he was followed by Sergeant Spankey, who manifested the utmost hostility to the administration, and declared it to be unworthy of public confidence or respect. To the surprise of all present, O'Connell arose and expressed his opinion that the estimates had been judiciously framed, and that the government had evinced a laudable desire to economize the national expenses. He proceeded to say that he was not astonished at the hostility of the noble lord towards an administration by which he had been deprived of power and the sweets concomitant to power; but he was unable to comprehend the motives, or even to imagine the reasons, for the asperity and unmitigated hostility of the honorable and learned member, from whom the Government had not taken any power or official advantages, and to whom, it was believed, that they had offered *his full value.*

"Sir," exclaimed Spankey, "They offered me nothing."

"Mr. Speaker," said O'Connell, "That is exactly what I surmised."

Laughter, loud and of long continuance, followed this uncomplimentary explanation of the Sergeant's worth, and I believe that "Spankey's price" was for some time adapted as a term to signify a total deficiency of value.

Having detailed these few personal recollections, which I hope may not be considered too discursive, I have to approach the incidents of 1848, when the "Young Ireland" or "Confederate" movement occurred. It is not my intention to laud or censure those engaged in its furtherance or its repression, my only object being to state such facts as came under my personal observations, or of which I had official cognizance, leaving to the reader to derive amusement from some circumstances and useful information from others. I think it was on the 21st day of March that the crown-solicitor preferred charges of sedition against Smith O'Brien and Meagher, and required me to make them amenable. When the informations were sworn, I asked him if he had any objection to an intimation from me to the accused, that such proceedings had been instituted, in order that they might appear and give bail to stand their trial without subjecting them to the indignity of arrest. To this course Mr. Kemmis at once acceded; and I called on Smith O'Brien at his lodgings in Westland Row that evening, and found Meagher and several other persons along with him. When I stated the object of my visit, one of the company exclaimed, "Give no promise or undertaking to appear. Accept no courtesy from your prosecutors, but let the Government incur the odium of arresting you." Both of them, however, declined to follow such advice, and assured me that they would attend at the Head Office, at noon, on the next day. They thanked me for the inclination I had exhibited to save them, as much as possible, from personal annoyance; and as I was leaving, O'Brien laughingly exclaimed, "Your urbanity, Mr. Porter, shall not be forgotten; and when the government of Ireland comes into our hands, your official position shall not be disturbed." At the appointed time they gave the required bail, and I returned the informations for trial. They were indicted for sedition, and, unfortunately for themselves, were acquitted. I say "unfortunately," because if they had then been convicted, and imprisoned for three or four months, they would have been unable to engage in the proceedings which eventuated in their conviction for high treason, at Clonmel, in the following September. I think it worth remarking, that when they had utterly failed in their insurrectionary designs, and had been banished to a distant region, I occasionally heard

great culpability and folly imputed to them ; but in reference to their conduct, the most severe censures were
uttered by the lips of him who had urged them to reject
the slight courtesy and the forbearance of arrest, to which
I have alluded above.

In all the cases of treason-felony which were tried in
Dublin, the informations were sworn before me. I had
also to issue warrants for the apprehension of the principal organizers of Confederate clubs, and search-warrants
for concealed arms. Such transactions were numerous,
and the period was one of very fervid excitement. I am
therefore proud of being able to declare that no imputation of partiality, precipitance, or undue severity was preferred or suggested in reference to my magisterial conduct.
There were several instances in which I refrained from
issuing warrants on the evidence of constables or of private
informers ; but in all such cases the higher authorities
were made acquainted with the peculiar circumstances
under which further proceedings appeared to be unnecessary or inadvisable, and approved of the forbearance. If
a person was known to have joined a Confederate club, or
to have made seditious speeches, or to have subscribed
to a fund for the purchase of arms, or to have attended
meetings for drilling and training ; and if it was also
known that he had relinquished such associations and
practices, and especially if he was desirous of leaving the
country, there was no anxiety to prosecute him or delay
his departure.

JOHN MITCHEL.

The most important case tried in Dublin was that of
John Mitchel, for treason-felony, grounded on his publications in *The United Irishman* newspaper. He had been

committed by me, and on the 27th May he was convicted and sentenced to transportation for fourteen years. The only relic of the period in my possession is his "pattern pike," which was found in his house when the police seized the premises. On the day of his condemnation, I was passing along Capel Street on an outside hackney jaunting-car. At Mary's Abbey corner I was recognized by a crowd of roughs, and saluted with a volley of stones. Not one of the missiles struck me, but the carman received a blow on the point of his left elbow which caused intense pain and elicited copious maledictions. Police were close at hand, and protected me from further aggression. I suggested to the driver that the stone was not intended for him, to which he replied—"It hurt me all the same. Them vagabones should'nt throw stones without knowing who they'd hit."

INFORMERS.

No more offensive epithet can be applied in this country, in the warmest spirit of invective, than that of an "informer." I have repeatedly heard it asserted as a popular maxim, that all informers should be shot. I can truly and deliberately declare it to be my firm conviction, that if all the informers of 1848 were so disposed of, the Confederate clubs and revolutionary associations of Dublin would have been decimated. There were in one great commercial establishment *forty* Confederates, of whom *ten* were in communication with the police. I resided at Roundtown, and I would often have preferred walking into town or strolling homeward, when I had to take a seat on a hackney car or in an omnibus to avoid a request to step into Blackberry Lane or turn up the Barrack Avenue, and listen to details of proceedings of which it is highly probable I had been already fully apprised.

A smith, in a town between thirty and forty miles from Dublin, was engaged to manufacture pikes. He made two hundred and eighty pike-heads, and brought them, according to directions which he had received, to a place, the designation of which was peculiarly appropriate for the reception of such articles, for it was the *slaughter-house of a butcher*. They were of the best quality, in respect of materials and workmanship. The industrious tradesman delivered the "goods" to his customer, and was paid fully and promptly. He then made me acquainted with the transaction, and I referred him to the Commissioners of Police. They entrusted its management, or perhaps I might more correctly say its mismanagement, to a superintendent who, instead of having the premises closely watched, proceeded precipitately to seize the weapons. They were packed in strong deal cases, of the contents of which the butcher and his assistants declared that they had no knowledge. Before the Executive came to any conclusion as to what course should be adopted, the hopes of the revolutionists had been extinguished at Ballingarry. No prosecution was instituted, and the pike-heads were sent to England where, I believe, they were transferred to the naval department.

THE CLOSE OF 1848.

On the 18th July, 1848, Dublin was proclaimed under the Crime and Outrage Act, and a bill was introduced about the same time for suspending the Habeas Corpus Act. When the government adopted these measures, several of the clubs came to the conclusion that it would be advisable to dissolve. In almost every instance the police authorities were fully informed of such proceedings, and some of the persons, to whom the books and transactions were entrusted, made us acquainted with their contents. The government was extremely anxious to prevent the formation of revolutionary associations in the provinces; but as soon as the insurrectionary attempt of Smith O'Brien collapsed, the executive became less desirous of exercising severity. It was considered necessary to offer £500 reward for the apprehension of O'Brien, and £300 for the capture of each of his principal associates; but *I know* that the news of their arrival in a foreign land would have been more welcome in Dublin Castle than the intelligence of their arrest.

The authorities were aware that at a certain place in Sandymount, a suburb of Dublin, nightly meetings were held by some young men who had been engaged in the Confederate movement, for the purpose of consulting on the most feasible mode of leaving the country, and providing the requisite expenses for their departure. There was not the slightest inclination to balk their wishes or impede their progress. Some of them have attained wealthy and important positions in distant lands, and some have returned home, where they may spend their remaining days, undisturbed and undisturbing.

During the first six or seven months of 1848, the superior officers of regiments in Dublin made frequent communications respecting the assiduous exertions of the disaffected to sap the loyalty of the soldiery, and effect an introduction of the military element to their fraternity. Much time and money were applied to this purpose; but, although the sobriety of the soldier was frequently impaired, his loyalty remained intact, and his usual apology for an unsteady step, or for returning late to his quarters, ascribed the fault to "the bloody rebels." They had made him drink a great lot of bad toasts, and he wouldn't have done so for them, if the whisky had not been very good."

Q

The only instance of disaffection found to exist in a military body was amongst the Royal Artillery at Portobello barrack. An Irishman who had enlisted in London, in 1846, under a false name, induced thirteen of his comrades to join him in forming a Confederate association. Their usual place of meeting was very near to my residence at Roundtown; and the first information which I received concerning them arose from the resentment of a woman. I had some communication with Colonel Gordon, the Adjutant-general of the Ordnance, and we were both inclined to disbelieve the statement which I had received. Eventually, however, we became satisfied of its truth, and acquired such additional evidence as to render the case sufficiently strong to procure a conviction of all the delinquents by a court-martial. I earnestly advised Colonel Gordon to leave them unprosecuted, but to disperse them. He adopted my views, and in a few days not one of the fourteen was in Ireland, neither were any two sent to the same station. In 1861, I saw the principal offender at Gibraltar. He was then a sergeant.

The abortive attempt at revolution in 1848 was decidedly obstructive to the progress of all the industrial pursuits which conduce to the prosperity of a country and the comforts of a community. It also involved the expenditure of vast sums in maintaining military forces, augmented police and constabulary, and defraying the expenses of special commissions. There is only one agreeable recollection afforded by it. Neither side shed blood. Popular violence inflicted no mortal injury, and no victim was demanded by the ultimate restoration of Law and Order. I am now disposed to lay before my readers a short extract from a French author, (Le Comte de Melun,) in reference to insurrectionary movements. It is from his

" Life of Sister Rosalie, the Superioress of the Order of Charity." A work crowned by the French Academy.

" In the ranks of society against which they appear to be more specially directed, insurrections and revolutions suspend profit, diminish revenue, compel a restriction of outlay, and introduce inquietude and torment where security and abundance previously prevailed. But their consequences are far more afflicting and grievous upon those who live with great difficulty upon the labor of each day. The least commotion in the street stops the work, and of course the wages. It changes the difficulties of life into the deepest misery.

" Whatever may be the issue of the movements for which their aid is bespoken, the people are always the dupes and victims of these sanguinary comedies. Whilst many of those who speak in their name, who push them on to the conflict, who breathe into their ears the sentiments of revolution, conceal themselves during the combat, escape the consequences of defeat, and are always foremost to adjudge to themselves the advantages of success ; the wretched people are exposed to blows on the field of battle, to prison or exile in case of defeat, to the diminution of employment, and thereby to an abridgment of their resources if they are conquerors—for it requires much time, after a successful revolution, to restore security to capital, activity to commerce, its proper balance to society ; and the workman has not, as an inducement to patience, like the heads of parties, portfolios, important situations, and a share in the budget. Then, after having suffered much, and waited long for the day of compensation, the mere individual does not see it arrive, and remains as he was previously—a workman, when he does not become a pauper."

CHAPTER XXI.

CHOLERA : AN IMPATIENT PATIENT ; GOOD NEWS !
ONLY TYPHUS FEVER——ROYAL VISITS——SCOTCH
SUPERIORITY STRONGLY ASSERTED——A POLICE
BILL STIGMATISED——LEAVE OF ABSENCE——THE
RHINE——THE RHINELAND.

LEAVING to my readers, without any comment from myself, the consideration of the statements and sentiments
contained in the extracts from the French author, I pass
to the year 1849, which certainly afforded a most agreeable
contrast to its immediate predecessor in the almost total
cessation of political agitations and asperities. The only
regrettable circumstance to which my recollections of the
latter year can revert being the appearance of cholera in
Dublin, early in April, and its continuance, with intermit-
ting violence, until October. It was far less prevalent
than it had been in 1832, and, in almost every instance,
the disease was ascribed to the use of fish, fruit, acid
drinks, or habitual intemperance. In the great majority
of cases ardent spirits were administered ; and the police
were frequently complained to by officers of health and
other sanitary officials who had been called on to relieve
pretended sufferings, in the expectation of brandy or
whisky being promptly afforded. Occasionally, on being

refused the coveted dram, the mock sufferer became at once invigorated, and addressed abusive language and threats of personal violence to "the cholera fellow." Some instances of opprobrious and menacing expressions were brought by summons under my cognizance, and for such I prescribed a month's sojourn in the Richmond Bridewell, unless the delinquent found two good and substantial sureties for his good behaviour. One of these summonses was reported, I believe by Mr. Dunphy, in the *Freeman's Journal.* It was described as " an affair in which a patient became impatient, because he was not *stimulated* when he *simulated.*"

My residence at Roundtown was not far from a range of small cottages occupied by the laboring class. One of our female servants alarmed my family by stating that the cholera was very nigh, for that she had seen five poor people taken off to hospital from the cottages near the quarry. I mentioned her statement to a police sergeant, and requested him to inquire if it was correct. In about half an hour, he returned and said, " Your worship, I have good news for you. The cholera has not come near you : it is only the typhus fever."

ROYAL VISITS.

In 1849, Dublin had the honour of a Royal visit, which was regarded by all classes as a most gratifying event. On the 5th of August, her Majesty Queen Victoria arrived in Kingstown Harbour, accompanied by Prince Albert, the Prince of Wales, the Princess Royal, Prince Alfred, and the Princess Alice. The *Victoria and Albert* yacht was escorted by ten war steamers, and the squadron anchored about eight o'clock in the evening. The Queen made a public entry into Dublin on the following day,

and remained in Ireland until the 10th.   Having a perfect
recollection of George the Fourth's visit in 1821, I presume to say that the reception of Victoria was most
respectful and cordial, and did not indicate the slightest
approach to sycophantic adulation.   I would not apply
the same terms in describing the popular demonstrations
which her uncle's visit produced ; for if ever a community
manifested unanimous servility and insane enthusiasm, it
was when his Irish subjects accorded to George the Fourth
a homage almost idolatrous.   Both visits occurred in the
same month, but with an interval of twenty-eight years.
I hope that I shall not be deemed too discursive in mentioning that the King was received by the municipal authorities, with the usual ceremonies, at the northern end of
Upper Sackville Street, where a gate had been constructed
for his admission ; and over the external side there appeared a very conspicuous inscription, derived from the
sixth book of Virgil's Æneid—

> " Hic vir, hic est, tibi quem promitti sæpius audis,
>   Augustus." *

The meaning of this quotation did not seem a difficult
attainment, even to those who had never previously seen a
Latin word.   It was generally construed by such persons,
" Here he is ; it is all right ; he has come, as he promised,
in August."

It was during the King's sojourn at the Viceregal Lodge
in the Phœnix Park, that an anecdote became current of a
question having been addressed by him to an Irish foot-
man as to whether there was any person in the establishment who understood German ? to which the interrogated
domestic replied, " Please your Majesty, I don't know

---

* Here is the man ; here you may now behold
    Augustus, promised oft, and long foretold.

anyone who spakes Jarman, but I have a brother who plays the Jarman flute."

In 1849, when it became known that Queen Victoria would visit Dublin, a great influx of the nobility and gentry was reasonably expected. The city became also very attractive to persons of a different and objectionable description. Great numbers of mendicants arrived, and the increase of beggars on our streets became most disagreeably apparent. The Commissioners of Police immediately told off constables in plain clothes on the special duty of repressing the nuisance, and so vigilant and active were they, that our thoroughfares were less infested by beggars during the Royal visit than I ever knew them to be at any other period. The committals were generally for ten or fourteen days; and many of the vagrants were by no means slow in attributing their confinement to special orders from the Queen herself to have the beggars locked up while she was in Dublin. A woman, who was committed by me for a fortnight on a conviction for mendicancy, exclaimed, as she was leaving the police-court, " Mr. Porter is sending us to jail in hopes of getting himself made Sir Frank."

During the Queen's progress through the city on the 6th of August, the whole line of the procession was densely crowded, the windows were occupied, and banners, emblematic of respect and welcome, abundantly displayed; and she was universally hailed with enthusiastic shouts of applause. In the evening there was a general and most brilliant illumination. The whole day passed without the slightest tumult or accident, until about eleven o'clock at night, when the vast crowds were dispersed by the heaviest rain that I ever witnessed in Ireland. The shower lasted about an hour. During the succeeding four days,

Her Majesty visited the principal public institutions, and held a levee in Dublin Castle, the most numerous and influential that had ever been assembled there, and a drawing-room which exhibited an unprecedented display of rank, fashion, and beauty. On the 10th of August, she embarked at Kingstown, amidst the acclamations of assembled thousands, and sailed for England. She afforded signal acknowledgments of her appreciation of the reception she had experienced from her Irish subjects, for on leaving the pier at Kingstown, she ordered the Royal standard to be lowered and raised again on board the Royal yacht, a mark of honor never before employed except for a Royal personage. In a short time after her visit of 1849, she created her eldest son Earl of Dublin.

SCOTCH SUPERIORITY STRONGLY ASSERTED.

Several months elapsed after the exciting and gratifying demonstrations to which I have last adverted, during which time we had profound quietude, and a total cessation of political turmoils. I cannot recollect any incident, public or official, which I would consider worth a reader's notice. I shall mention, however, that there was then here an individual character with whom I had occasional communication, and from whom I derived considerable amusement almost every time we met. He was a man of high military rank, holding an important garrison appointment. Kind, courteous, and affable, he had, nevertheless, some extraordinary prejudices, which I took every opportunity to induce him to express. He was a Scotchman, who insisted that his country and its people were superior to every other region and race, and who did not hesitate to disparage any attempt to assign even an equality with the Scotch to the natives of any other kingdom. His greatest explosions of indignation seemed specially reserved for a comparison, if at all favorable, of the Irish with the Scotch. Consequently, I boldly ascribed a manifest superiority to my countrymen over his in intelligence, integrity, diligence, neatness, promptitude of action, and all other estimable qualities which could be evinced in either peaceful or martial avocations ; so that I was sure to produce a denial of all my statements, and a suggestion that I should never repeat them without blushing. Still I persevered, and enjoyed the excitement which my expressions elicited. A few days before he left Dublin we had a conference, and, as usual, I boasted of Burke, Grattan, Curran, Goldsmith, Moore, Sheridan, Wellington, Gough, &c. He insisted that Scotland could produce equal or perhaps superior characters, if she had the opportunity. I remarked that even when Irishmen engaged in nefarious criminal pursuits, they evinced superior dexterity, and that our thieves were peculiarly knowing and adroit. "Your thieves!" he exclaimed, " I'll be d——d if we haven't thieves in Edinburgh or Glasgow that your Dublin fellows couldn't hold a candle to."

A POLICE BILL STIGMATISED.

In the session of Parliament of 1850, a bill was brought in by the Government for the revision and consolidation of the acts regulating the Dublin Metropolitan Police. It was printed, and a considerable number of copies were circulated in Dublin. We regarded it as a most desirable measure, for it would, if passed, have substituted a simplified code for an involved and complicated hotch-potch of seven statutes containing about four hundred sections. The police authorities were extremely anxious for the success of the proposed bill, but it was objected to by others, delayed, and ultimately, at the close of the session, became one of the sufferers in the "Massacre of the Innocents." Whilst it was pending, an alderman made it the subject, at a meeting of the Corporation, of a most condemnatory speech. He stigmatised it as unconstitutional and tyrannical, and dwelt at considerable length on a section which would impart power to a divisional magistrate, in case dealers in certain commodities neglected or refused to comply with a notice to produce any article in their possession, alleged to have been stolen, to inflict on the person so neglecting or refusing, a penalty of *twenty pounds*, and in default of payment of such penalty, to commit the offender for *two months*. He indignantly demanded from what region of despotism had such a tyrannical proposition been imported, and declared that it would disgrace any legislature to enact, or any executive to enforce, such unconstitutional severity. He was spared the mortification of seeing such power imparted to a police magistrate. The obnoxious bill was not passed, and the law remained unaltered. By it the tyrannical penalty is only *fifty pounds*, with an alternative imprisonment of merely *six months*. I do not believe, however, that there has ever been an instance of such a penalty being exacted or such imprisonment inflicted.

LEAVE OF ABSENCE.

In the year 1851 my magisterial duties, which did not indeed afford any incident worthy of being particularized, were interrupted by a severe attack of gastric fever; on my recovery from which, I was directed by my medical attendant to proceed to Wiesbaden, and take such baths and drink such mineral waters as should be prescribed by a certain English physician residing there, Dr. Lewis. I waited on the Chief Secretary, Sir William Somerville, who subsequently became Lord Athlumney, and requested leave of absence for a month or six weeks. He took a printed form of reply, directed it to me, and signed it. By this document I was granted " leave of absence for ———." On remarking to him that he had not specified the duration of the indulgence, the worthy gentleman was pleased to compliment me by saying, " I have left a blank for the time. Go, and stay until your health and strength are completely renovated, and fill up the blank at your return. You are deserving of the most favorable treatment." I record with gratitude and pride such an acknowledgment of my anxious endeavours to discharge my official duties with efficiency ; but I must also say that kindness and benignity were amongst his prominent characteristics. I left Dublin at the latter end of May, and proceeded through London to Ostend, and from thence by railway to Bonn, where I commenced ascending " the wide and winding Rhine." Whilst waiting at the wharf for the steamer, and contemplating " The castled crag of Drachenfels," I thought of Byron's lines, in which he describes the scenery which appeared so enchanting to Childe Harold, and also how

> " Peasant girls with deep blue eyes,
> And hands which offer early flowers,
> Walk smiling o'er this paradise ; "

and I felt that the landscape before me transcended even his description. I had, however, the greatest contrast offered to my view so far as regarded eyes, hands, or smiles. Four females approached with flowers, which they desired to sell. They were all old women, and they constituted, in their features and figures, the most complete realization of hideous ugliness. It is not my intention to attempt any description of the scenes which successively astonished and delighted me whilst proceeding up the Rhine from Bonn to Mentz. I would fully adopt the unexaggerated truth contained in four short lines—

> " The river nobly foams and flows,
>   The charm of this enchanted ground,
> And all its thousand turns disclose
>   Some fresher beauty varying round."

I found the steamer extremely convenient and most agreeable, especially for a person debilitated by severe and recent indisposition. I do not recollect the charges for conveyance or refreshments, but I considered them moderate, and relished my repasts greatly, whether as regarded their materials, culinary preparation, or table attendance. The few hotels at which I stopped were very comfortable in every respect. At the Giant Hotel, Coblentz, I observed that the delicious wine, sparkling Moselle, was given for a Rhenish florin and a half, (two shillings and sixpence,) per bottle, and that Guinness's Dublin Porter was precisely the same price there. I have heard some Germans, who understood English, remark on the designation almost universally given to the Rhenish wines by us. The vineyards are nearly all on places considerably elevated, and the names of the wines have generally the prefix of " High." The German word is " Hoch," and they give it a guttural pronunciation which the Irish and Scotch can utter perfectly, but which an Englishman cannot accomplish. He hardens " hoch " into " hock," and adopts the prefix alone as the name of the exhilarating fluid, and we follow his example. The mistake, however, is perfectly harmless, for the abbreviation has not lessened the production, or deteriorated the flavor of the liquor.

At Coblentz, I saw in a square before a church, the name of which I do not remember, a monument with two inscriptions, the first of which I considered indicative of silly and premature pride, whilst the second formed an instance of a complete junction of wit and wisdom. In 1812, when the French had occupied Moscow, the prefect of Coblentz erected the monument and inscribed it thus—

AN. MDCCCXII.

MEMORABLE PAR LA CAMPAGNE

CONTRE LES RUSSES,

SOUS LA PREFECTURE DE JULES DOAZAN.*

In 1814 the fortunes of war had necessitated the retreat of the French before the allied forces, and Coblentz was occupied by the Russians. Instead of demolishing the memorable record of the previous campaign, the Russian commander of the force, by which the town was captured, caused a supplementary statement to be added, which clearly showed the complete change of affairs. The addition was as follows :—

VU ET APPROUVÉ PAR NOUS, COMMANDANT RUSSE DE LA VILLE DE COBLENTZ. 1 JAN. 1814.†

The people of Coblentz appeared to enjoy drawing a stranger's notice to these inscriptions, and it was easy to perceive that they considered the annexation of the Rhenish provinces to France, by the first Napoleon, as

---

* The year 1812. Memorable by the campaign against the Russians, during the prefecture of Jules Doazan.

† Seen and approved by me, the Russian commander of Coblentz, 1st Jan. 1814.

not merely objectionable, but detestable and insufferable.
I believe that the same sentiments pervaded every part of
Germany, which had been under the rule or in the occupation of the French.　As far as my sojourn in Germany
enabled me to form an opinion, I thought that the people
liked the English very much, and thoroughly disliked the
French.　I found them most friendly, and on several
occasions when I have wished to procure fruit, and produced money, pointing at the same time to apple, pear, or
plum trees, in the *unfenced* gardens and orchards near
Wiesbaden, the tree would be shaken, and signs made to
me to pick up the fallen fruits, and money would be declined.　This kindness was accorded to me because I was
deemed an Englishman.　I do not believe that an apple
would have been gratuitously tendered to a Frenchman.　In
the places of public amusement, I repeatedly heard a
certain lively tune played.　It seemed to be decidedly
popular, and I was informed that it owed its popularity to
the fact of having been the quick-step to which the
Prussians advanced upon the flank of the French army at
the close of the battle of Waterloo.

In the preceding paragraph, I have mentioned unfenced
gardens and orchards.　I have passed along roads in the
Rhenish land where, for five or six miles, there were no
fences whatever between the highway and grounds appropriated to the culture of choice fruits and vegetables, and
where no hedge, wall, or ditch intervened to distinguish or
separate one holding from another.　The bounds were
marked by poles, on the tops of which bits of straw or
dried rushes were plaited ; but even such marks were not
considered necessary at the edges of the public thoroughfare.　Of course, in those districts grazing was impracti-
cable.　No sheep or goats were to be seen, no horses,

unless such as were yoked or saddled; and the food for the cows was usually conveyed, in the morning and evening, from the place of its production, in a cart drawn by one of themselves. The summer feeding for the cattle consisted of clover, Italian rye-grass, Lucern, American cow-grass, or vetches. I observed that the fodder was cut and left lying sufficiently long to become flagged before it was given to the animals. The tillage in those districts presented a great contrast to the generality of Irish crops. Neatness and cleanliness characterized the German culture, and the weeds were excluded from the partnership which is so liberally accorded to them here. Near Wiesbaden, I saw a very flourishing crop, which occupied, in my opinion, about two acres, and I was informed by Dr. Greiss, that the elevation of the place above sea-level was 2400 ft. The growth was tobacco, for the production of which our soil and climate are as well suited as those in which the Germans cultivate it. There it is taxed, or, as I believe, taken by the Government at a valuation, and made an Imperial monopoly. Here it is prohibited, to form, perhaps, a very apt and forcible illustration of the principle of Free Trade.

The springs at Wiesbaden are not numerous, but they constitute great natural curiosities. There is one which, if I remember rightly, is called the Kochbrunnen. It is intensely hot; and I was told that even in winter, the water is used for scalding the hair off slaughtered pigs. It gushes up profusely; and yet, within fifty yards of it, there is a spring extremely cold and effervescent, precisely similar to the Seltzer water. Whilst the Roman empire continued, almost all the Rhineland was appurtenant to it, and Wiesbaden was then designated " Mattiacæ aquæ." It is believed that Nero visited it for the benefit of his health; and there is a locality close to the town, where he is said to have sojourned, and which is named Nerothal, (Nero's valley.) Some ancient edifices have Latin inscriptions denoting their former use or the names of their pristine occupants. The Germans take special care of such antique remains; and instead of destroying relics of heathenism, they show them as indicating a state of darkness and degradation to which Christianity offers the greatest and most glorious contrast. In reference to the gratitude of their votaries to Pagan deities for benefits attributed to the exercise of their peculiar powers, I only recollect one mythological inscription, which I was prevented from forgetting by a ludicrous comment on it, made by a Manchester visitant at Wiesbaden. In the Ræmerbad, (Roman bath,) there was a mural tablet in perfect preservation, every letter on the stone being as distinct as when cut many centuries ago. It was as follows:—

" ÆSCULAPIO SANATORI, MILITES QUATUORDECIMÆ LEGIONIS, OB
VALETUDINEM RESTAURATAM, HANC TABULAM VOTIVAM.
D. D. D."

The Manchester gent and I had become acquainted at the *table d' hôte* of the "Four Seasons," and we happened to stroll into the Ræmerbad at the same time. Pointing to the mural tablet, he said—

"Mr. Porter, they say that is Latin."

"Yes," I replied, "you have been rightly informed."

"Could you untwist it, and tell us what it is about?"

"I shall try. To Æsculapius the healer, the soldiers of the fourteenth legion, in consequence of their health being restored, give, inscribe, and dedicate this votive tablet."

"Good heavens!" he exclaimed, "those chaps were wide awake; and they knew how to pay a nice compliment, for of course this Skewlaypius *was their regimental doctor.*"

I regretted that there was not another tablet extant declaratory of their veneration and devotion to Mars, for it would have elicited the interesting suggestion that his military rank was, at least, that of a colonel.

I recollect seeing on an ancient tower of octagonal form, near Andernach, an inscription, in reference to which I heard many conjectures, and some of them extremely absurd. It was as follows :—

" SISTE PAULULUM, AMBULA PAULULUM, SEDERE VETITUM EST, ET DORMIRE EST MORI."*

The conclusion at which I arrived was, that immediately beneath this direction a sentinel's station had been established, and that whether he stood, or walked "his lonely round," he was to bear in mind that to slumber on his post was inexcusable, and subjected him to the forfeiture of life.

One day I sat, in the large dining-room of the Four Seasons, near a noble lord who, with his lady, had been there for some weeks. She was a native of Germany, and he was an Irishman who possessed extensive estates in a southern county. I heard him say to a gentleman, who was recommending him to visit Frankfort-on-the-Maine, that he could not adopt his suggestion, as he was obliged to start for home on the next day but one. That evening I was speaking to the landlord, and mentioned that I had heard my noble countryman tell his friend that he was about to leave. The landlord replied, " I am delighted to hear that they are going, for *her other husband* is to be here next week, and their meeting would be rather unpleasant, especially as he is bringing *his other wife.*

* Stand awhile, walk awhile, to sit down is forbidden, and to sleep is to die."

R

At a short distance from Wiesbaden, the road to Schlangenbad (the serpent's bath) passes through a portion of a very extensive forest. In one of my rambles, I left the highway, and walked into the dense wood, and when I thought that I had gone far enough, and that it was time to return, I became suddenly aware that I had lost my way. In a state of extreme uneasiness I walked for more than an hour, frequently shouting, but without hearing any responsive voice. Dismal ideas arose in my mind as to the probability of having to meet dangers and privations beyond my power of resistance or endurance. At length I found that there was a hill before me, on which the trees were rather sparse; and having attained the elevation, I was relieved from my apprehensions by a glimpse of the Rhine, and immediately directed my steps towards the river, and soon emerged from the forest. If any of my readers should contemplate a visit to any place in the vicinity of extensive woods, they will avoid all liability to such annoyance as I suffered, by refraining from solitary forest rambles, and by taking such excursions with a guide, or with companions acquainted with the localities. Before I left Wiesbaden, a young gentleman named Vernon was found dead in the Taunus forest. His death was attributed to the bite of an adder or viper.

In the Kursahl, at Wiesbaden, there was a *Roulette* table, and also one for *Rouge et Noir*. The gambling was not considered at all comparable to the play at Baden-Baden; nevertheless, I have seen many instances of serious, perhaps of ruinous losses. On one occasion I observed an Englishman who sat down at the *Rouge et Noir* table. He had a large leathern purse full of gold, and certainly more than one thousand pounds in Bank of England notes of fifty pounds each. In less than an hour, all his money was absorbed, and some exclamations, garnished with imprecations, as he retired, impressed me with the opinion that he was reduced to destitution. Whilst I express the warmest approval of the abolition of those gambling establishments, and their recent suppression in the German towns, I must admit having tried my luck occasionally to the extent of four florins (about six shillings and eightpence.) In almost every instance the remorseless rake added my stake to the accumulations of " the bank." On the last evening that I was at the Kursahl, I went in a party of nine persons, of whom six were ladies. One of my fair companions proposed that each of us should contribute four florins, and stake the amount on red. This was acceded to, and I stepped forward and placed the money on the colour. The bystanders were numerous, and when it was announced that the red had won, I picked up the seventy-two florins, but whilst doing so, I heard an exclamation from one of the crowd—" That would be a nice story to tell at the Dublin police-office."

During my stay at Wiesbaden, I visited Mentz, or Mayence, several times. On the first occasion, I was crossing the bridge from the right bank of the Rhine, and met a young officer in Austrian uniform. At that period Mentz was termed a Confederate town, and its garrison was composed of an equal number of Prussian and Austrian troops. I had seen enough of them at Wiesbaden to satisfy me that an inquiry on the part of a stranger would receive a kind and polite reply. I consequently accosted the gentleman in French, being quite destitute of German beyond the name of the place to which I wished to go, which was the Music Garden. To my surprise and great gratification, he said, " If it is the same thing to you, Mr. Porter, to speak English, I shall give you any information in my power." I told him that I wanted a direction to the Music Garden, and he replied, " I have to leave an order with the officer on guard at the Cassel end of the bridge, and then I shall return to my quarters, and the Music Garden is on the way, I shall show it to you in a few minutes." During our walk, I asked him how he knew my name, and was informed that he remembered seeing me at the assizes of Nenagh ; that he was a " Tipperary boy," born and reared within sight of the Devil's Bit Mountain, and his name was Scully. He was a captain in an infantry regiment, and appeared to be perfectly contented with his position and its attendant prospects. We thoroughly fraternized, and I never again went to Mentz without calling at his quarters. He expressed an intention of visiting Ireland, and promised to favor me with a renewal of our friendly intercourse in Dublin ; but my hopes of seeing him have not been realized, and I fear that he has not escaped all the disastrous combats in which, since 1851, the Austrian forces have been engaged.

Nothing tends more to render a sojourn in the Rhineland agreeable, than the great number of persons connected with hotels, railways, steamers, and other public establishments, who understand English. Indeed I may extend the observation to Belgium also. A foreigner in Dublin, if he is unacquainted with our language, has to encounter more difficulties than we would have to contend with in the places to which I have referred. This is to be regretted ; for exquisitely beautiful as Rhenish, Swiss, or Italian scenery may be justly considered, still Ireland can present to a foreign tourist, views numerous and extensive, which cannot be surpassed in picturesque beauty. I have never met a foreigner who had seen the principal places of attraction in our country, who was not most enthusiastic in his expressions of admiration. Our insular position is no longer a serious obstacle to the traveller who may wish to visit even the most remote districts ; and it is to be hoped that at no distant time Ireland shall be far better known by strangers. They should be encouraged by the most respectful and attentive treatment ; and when we find that in the Mechanics' Institute of Dublin, a member will be instructed in French, German, or Italian, at the very moderate charge of six shillings per quarter, it is not creditable to our trading and operative classes that they should not attain to educational acquirements equal to those possessed by a considerable number of the same classes in several continental countries. Although I am a Dublin man, I regret that I must admit the superiority of Cork as regards the means of satisfactory communication with foreigners, understanding them and being understood.

Before I close my observations on the very interesting portion of Germany in which I had so agreeable a sojourn, I shall relate a couple of incidents from which my readers may form an idea as to the honest tendencies of the people. I spent an evening, along with some of my Wiesbaden associates, at the Music Garden of Mentz, and the weather being rather close and sultry, I took off a waterproof overcoat, and laid it on a rockery just beside our refreshment table. When the musical performances and other amusements had terminated, I departed without recollecting the garment, and arrived at Wiesbaden before I became aware of my forgetfulness. Next morning I set off to Mentz to try my chance of recovering the vestment, but with very slight hopes of succeeding. At the garden, a person connected with the establishment, on being

informed of my business, said, in English, " Come to the
place where you threw off your overcoat, and you will
most probably find it." Accordingly, when we reached
the rockery, I saw the coat lying where I placed it, and
having possessed myself of it, observed to my conductor
that I was extremely lucky, for unquestionably more than
one thousand persons must have passed the spot on the
previous evening. " Oh, yes," replied the German; " the
garden was crowded, but there was not a man here who
saw your coat lying there, *without knowing that it was not
his.*"

At Biebrich, the office of the steamers plying on the
Rhine is in a house on the quay. It faces the south, but
abuts the public thoroughfare without any rails or other
fence. On the front wall there were two vines, on which
there was an abundant crop of grapes; and on the day of
my departure, whilst waiting for the steamer, I remarked
to the agent that his fruit was almost ripe, and that it
appeared to be of first-rate quality. He said that another
week would suffice to ripen them perfectly, and that they
were of very fine flavor. I observed that there was a
strong temptation for his neighbours, and even for the
casual passengers who walked the quay, to assume a partnership in such desirable productions. He seemed surprised at my observation, and told me that no person
would interfere with his vines, adding, " The grapes will
be all left for me to gather. They have never been taken
by anyone else, for *they are grown on my wall, and are
mine.*" I do not think that in any part of the United
Kingdom there would be the slightest chance of fruit
grown in a similar public situation, and unprotected by a
strong fence, being left to the enjoyment of its owner, or
even allowed to ripen.

CHAPTER XXII.

BRUSSELS——ROYAL CHILDREN——THE GREAT EXHI-
BITION IN LONDON——HOME AGAIN : A PREACHER
——UNLUCKY RIOTERS——VISIT TO PARIS——MICHEL
PERRIN.

ON my way home from the Rhineland, I stopped for two
days in Brussels, the second of which happened to be the
day on which the anniversary of the attainment of Belgian
independence was celebrated. I recollect seeing a monument which had been erected to the memory of those who
had been killed in the ranks of the Belgian revolutionists,
and amongst the names inscribed on it I observed " Corcoran, Irlandais," so that the Emerald Isle was not totally
unrepresented on the occasion. Brussels was very full
at the time of the fête, and in its crowded streets and
squares a tolerable idea might be obtained of the confusion
of tongues incident to the abortive attempt to erect the
Tower of Babel. German, French, Flemish, English,
Italian, Spanish, and the various languages of the more
northern countries were abundantly ventilated, and with
an effect which I thought extremely amusing. The city
presented a very martial appearance, for not only the
regular troops but the national guards also of the kingdom
were made available for a grand review by their sovereign,

Leopold the First.   Each regiment had its *"vivandieres,"* and I was informed that those of the national guards were women of the same social rank as the members of the regiment to which they were attached.   Their costume was as much assimilated to the uniforms of their respective regiments as female attire would permit.   The grenadiers had *vivandieres* of a height proportionally tall; the other regiments were accompanied by women, perhaps I should say ladies, of lesser stature, but all of them were, in my opinion, unexceptionally beautiful, and of most graceful and decorous demeanor.

At the time to which I refer, 1851, I was impressed with the conviction that no people could be more attached to a sovereign than the Belgians were to Leopold and to his family.   I did not form that opinion from the loud and spontaneous acclamations which greeted him and his children in the streets and at the review, but from the joyous expression which irradiated the countenances of all ranks and conditions, and impressed me with the belief that their loyalty was not merely respectful, but thoroughly sincere and affectionate.   Regal splendor may dazzle its beholders, and popular demonstrations may excite and perhaps enlist many of those who witness their display; but I venture to assert that human nature can produce no spectacle more worthy of being admired and remembered than the cordial and enthusiastic reception of a benign and beloved monarch, by contented, happy, and loyal subjects.

ROYAL CHILDREN.

On the occasion to which I have last referred, one of the royal carriages contained three children, two boys and a girl, with their tutor and governess.   The girl was Leopold's only daughter, and her name was identical with that of his first wife, Charlotte. The little Belgian princess was then eleven years of age, and was exceedingly pretty. She was delicately fair, blue-eyed, and flaxen-haired, and appeared to appreciate highly the popular acclamations which were frequently announced as specially intended for her. The joyous countenance, irradiated by the excitement incident to demonstrations of enthusiastic approbation, seemed inaccessible to the wrinkles of care, and exempt from the lachrymal effects of sorrow. Nevertheless, that royal child has furnished a most piteous instance of the mutability of fortune, of accumulated miseries substituted for the apparent approach of transcendent happiness. To her have been allotted

" The hopes that but allure to fly,
　The joys that vanish while we sip ;
Like Dead-Sea fruits that tempt the eye,
　But turn to ashes on the lip !"

In about six years after the time to which my reminiscence refers, she became the consort of Ferdinand Maximilian, eldest brother of the Emperor of Austria, who subsequently, at the instance of Napoleon the Third, assumed the title of Emperor of Mexico, but having utterly failed in his efforts to establish the Imperial authority to which he aspired, was shot as a culprit, by order of the President Juarez, in 1867, leaving his bereaved widow in such affliction as to produce a state of insanity from which she is not expected to recover.

THE GREAT EXHIBITION IN LONDON.

On my return from the Continent, I spent a few days in London, and had a most gratifying opportunity of seeing the Great Exhibition in Hyde Park, which, apart from its own attractions and merits, afforded an example to the civilized nations of the world, stimulating their pursuits of the industrial arts, awakening dormant energies, and evoking amicable competitions and peaceful rivalries. I happened to express to the Commissioner of Police, a wish to be admitted to the building at night, and he gave me a note to the Superintendent in charge there, directing him to conduct me through it. The structure was lighted sufficiently to afford means to the police on duty to keep it safe from the designs of marauders and from accidental injury. Profound silence was only interrupted by the chiming of the clocks, and the announcement at certain intervals of " All 's well." The solitude, the subdued light, the banners of all nations, statues and other works of art, of which I was the only spectator in that splendid and extensive edifice, suggested contemplative feelings which I am not adequate to express; but I can safely assert that my midnight visit to the great Crystal Palace of 1851, afforded me greater gratification than I ever derived from any public spectacle however gorgeous or crowded.

HOME AGAIN: A PREACHER.

When I returned to Dublin, I found that one of the magistrates of the northern division was only waiting for my appearance before making an application for leave of absence; and his request having been acceded to, it was arranged that I was to do duty in the northern court on two days in each week, namely, Tuesdays and Thursdays. I was sitting in my own court on a Wednesday, when a constable preferred a charge against a man named Dowling, for collecting a crowd, causing a very great obstruction in Parliament Street, and refusing to move on when required. He was a street-preacher, who appeared to be extremely fanatical, insisting that he had a special mission to announce the glad tidings of salvation to the benighted people of Dublin. On hearing the evidence, I stated that his conduct was a nuisance, and that I should send the case for trial, unless the constable withdrew the complaint on the express promise of the accused party that the offence should not be repeated. To this the prosecutor agreed, and the preacher said "he would shake the dust off his shoes as a testimony against me, but that I should never again have to investigate such a complaint against him." He was discharged ; but on the following day, I had to dispose of a similar charge against him in the northern court. He manifested very little displeasure against his prosecutor, but seemed to reserve all his indignation for me ; and when I reminded him of the promise he had made on the previous day, he replied that he had made himself acquainted with the bounds of my division in the south of the district, and did not intend ever to raise his voice there again, but that I was not satisfied to get rid of him, *but had followed him* to the northern division, to continue an unworthy persecution of a zealous but humble laborer in the vineyard of salvation. I was highly amused, as were many of the persons present, at the tendency attributed to me to pursue the street-preacher ; and when he declared that he would leave Dublin, I suggested to the police constable the withdrawal of his charge, to which he readily acceded, and the accused party was discharged. In about six weeks after this incident I went to Liverpool with a near relative who was about to proceed to Australia, and having gone into the police-courts there when the morning business was about to commence, one of the clerks told the magistrate (Mr. Rushton) that I was present, and he most courteously offered me a seat on the bench. The first charge on the sheet was for obstructing the thoroughfare, by collecting a crowd, and refusing to desist from preaching there; and Dowling was the delinquent. He did not wait for the constable to be sworn or the charge stated, but at once exclaimed that he despaired of obtaining any justice, when they had *imported me from Dublin* to sit in judgment on him there. His excitement and indignation produced great merriment, especially when Mr. Rushton told him that I was not there in any official capacity, but as a private individual who had not interfered, directly or indirectly, in any matter coming before the court. He was discharged with a caution. I have never seen him since; and I mention the case of this street-preacher only to show how accidental circumstances may produce, in some minds, the most unfounded conclusions.

UNLUCKY RIOTERS.

On my resumption of duty in Dublin, I had very few cases of importance or peculiar interest to dispose of. I may mention one in which two men were charged with being actively engaged in a riotous tumult in Dean Street, and assaulting the police. They had been extremely violent, and one of the constables had been so severely injured as to be incapacitated for duty during several days. In almost all such cases the prosecutors prefer a summary decision; and in the one to which my present remarks apply, I stated that I considered the prisoners, Foley and Magrath, deserved the utmost punishment which I was empowered to award, namely, two months' imprisonment with hard labor. The culprits loudly exclaimed against such a judgment, and vociferated that they should get a full and fair trial by a jury. I acceded to their demand, and returned the informations to the next commission of *Oyer et Terminer* for the city of Dublin. There never was a more complete exemplification of an escape from the frying-pan by a fall into the fire. They were tried and convicted before Baron Richards, and he sentenced them to be imprisoned for twelve months, and kept to hard labor each alternate month. Their repugnance to a summary conviction had received great publicity; and the increased punishment to which they were subjected had the effect of reconciling the delinquents who were subsequently brought to the police-court to the fullest exercise, by the magistrates, of their summary jurisdiction.

VISIT TO PARIS.

In 1853 a prosecution was instituted by a lady, named Kelly, against a Mr. Birch, whom she accused of embezzling or stealing a very considerable sum of money. Her informations were sworn before my colleague, Mr. Magee, and he issued a warrant for the apprehension of Birch, which was delivered to a very intelligent and active officer, who subsequently was promoted to be the chief superintendent. The accused party was supposed to be in France, whither it was intended to send Mr. Ryan with the warrant. I had nothing whatever to do with the case, and I chanced to be sitting beside Mr. Magee when an application was made to him that he should go to France, having his expenses fully paid, and taking with him all the documents relating to the charge, for the information and satisfaction of the French authorities. Mr. Magee at once refused the request, alleging that his health would not admit of rapid travelling, but suggesting that Mr. Porter might undertake the journey, and fetch all the papers likely to induce the French functionaries to consent to the extradition of Birch, in the event of Ryan being able to find him.   I consented to this arrangement, and set off for Paris, where I remained for a fortnight without any arrest having been effected of the accused party by the officer holding the warrant.   I was never called on to produce the informations, and had no warrant in my possession, nor did I feel the slightest anxiety on the subject.   Ryan was proceeding to France, when he ascertained that Birch was in Southampton, and there the capture was effected,   A rumor was circulated in Dublin that I had gone to Paris to make a search, personally, for the alleged offender, when, in fact, I had neither the power nor the inclination to interfere beyond producing the informations which had been sworn before my colleague, and to authenticate them if required.   My expenses were fully paid, and I found, on returning to Dublin, that the prosecution was abandoned.   My short sojourn in the French capital was extremely pleasant ; and having made myself known, as a Dublin police-magistrate, by the production of my passport at the prefecture, I experienced very kind and agreeable attentions.   A man who spoke English was directed to attend me when visiting the public institutions, and I received a tricolored card, which procured me admission to all the theatres.   I am tempted to mention one performance which I saw in a small theatre on the Boulevard near the large barracks, (La Caserne de Prince Eugene.)   I do not recollect the title of the piece, but it exhibited the most extraordinary adaptation of machinery that I ever beheld, and the stage-tricks transcended all that I had previously seen or supposed possible.   A scene represented a railway terminus, and on the arrival of a train, the engine exploded, and the carriage next to it was torn asunder. One passenger was supposed to have had his head knocked off, his arms separated from his shoulders, and his lower extremities from his hips, and the body, head, and limbs were seen, as the vapor cleared off, lying on the roof of a shed. Ladders were instantly applied, and the passenger was taken down piecemeal. A bench was pushed forward on the platform, it seemed covered with dark cushions, and the trunk of the victim was placed on it, the head was affixed and the lower extremities were attached, an arm was added on the left side, when a poodle dog joined in the performance by seizing the other arm and taking it off the stage. Instantly the man arose, apparently with only one arm, and pursued the dog, exclaiming that the cursed poodle should not have his arm for supper. He returned, bringing the arm, and resumed his place on the bench, where the apparent reunion of his frame was completed. A surgeon was supposed to have been sent for, and he came too late to claim any share in the restoration of life and vigor to the dismembered patient. On proceeding to feel the pulse, he was rewarded by a slap on the check, accompanied with the contemptuous intimation of " *Voici votre honoraire.*" (Here's your fee.) I may remark that there did not appear to be any dripping of blood on the shed, neither did the platform or bench show any gory stains; and the performers who represented railway officials of the various grades, and passengers, male and female, to the number of twenty at least, intervened four or five times between the bench and the audience, as if actuated by the deepest anxiety for the supposed sufferer. I was not much surprised at the apparent deficiency of the right arm, for I had several times seen the late Pat Brophy, of Dawson Street, Dublin, representing Nelson in a *tableau vivant,* and he managed on those occasions to appear as if he had lost an arm. The incidents which I have attempted to describe we.. only stage-tricks, but they were most perfectly accomplished.

A gentleman, who appeared to me to fill the office of secretary or chief clerk at the prefecture, availed himself of several opportunities for having conversations with me in English. I related to him some of the anecdotes and circumstances which I have included in the preceding pages, and he reciprocated by affording me much information and amusement. At our last interview, M. Hubert gave me six volumes, containing memoirs derived from the archives of the Parisian police, from the time of Cardinal Richelieu's administration down to the accession of Louis Philip. I cannot offer many extracts from these volumes to the reader, but I shall notice two narratives which I was assured were, in their main circumstances, *strictly true.* One was subsequently shown to me in a collection of tales, and I considered it so amusing that I shall translate it in these pages. The other will, I hope, be deemed a striking instance of mere fact being far stranger than fiction. The former was entitled " Michel Perrin," and it is as follows :—

MICHEL PERRIN.

" I must go; I must depart as soon as possible. I plainly perceive that she has sold her watch without informing me. She has to work hard from morning to night ; the needle of a woman cannot provide for the requirements of two persons. Ah! I ought to have left long before this ! But where to go ? without money, without family influence, without friends ! How to get on in a world where I have never as yet lived, of the habits

and customs of which I am as uninformed as an infant
child! Nevertheless, I shall go, were I to beg on the
highway; were I to die of hunger, I shall go."

This soliloquy is referred to the eighth year of the Republic, in a very humble apartment, which perhaps still
exists at Dijon, and which was then inhabited by a former
pastor of a small village in the department of the Cote-
d'Or. Michel Perrin, who had lived up to that time in
performing acts of charity, praying to his Creator, and
cultivating the garden of his manse, had found himself
torn from the asylum in which twenty-two years of his
tranquil existence had been spent. Deprived of the slender
stipend attached to his functions, persecuted by some
agents of the Republican Government, and suspected by
all, the poor priest had rambled for a considerable time
from village to village, sometimes to avoid captivity, sometimes to avail himself of the friendship of the many kind
hearts whose gratitude he had earned in happier times.
Lastly, for a year he had lived at Dijon. There he had
rejoined his sister, Madeleine Perrin, the supreme mistress
of his establishment, and also his sole support in the
world.

Madeleine, on leaving the manse, had betaken herself
direct to Dijon, where she hoped to renew some old friend-
ships, and to support herself by needlework. She had
fully succeeded in utilising her talents for sewing to the
extent of providing for her own wants; but when the good
pastor, yielding to her earnest entreaties, had come to occupy one of the two little garret-rooms which constituted
her residence, Madeleine soon became aware that a man,
still in vigorous health and of good appetite, is more difficult to be fed than to be lodged.

She nevertheless completely refrained from discovering

s

to her dear Michel the slightest shadow of her uneasiness regarding the future of them both. Anyone who heard her singing whilst plying her needle, or who had witnessed how, after having placed upon the table a savory repast, she cried, "Michel, your dinner is ready," would pronounce her to be a happy lass. However, at night, Madeleine was no sooner on her bed, and aware, by his loud snoring, that her brother was soundly sleeping, than a crowd of sad thoughts would arise to besiege her mind. When a delay in the payment of her earnings produced some difficulties, eight days of sickness brought a fearful aggravation of her misery. Moreover, she was becoming aged, being only two years younger than Michel, who was entering on his fiftieth year. Already her sight was weakened, and soon she might be unable to sew, even with the aid of glasses. In vain did poor Madeleine strive to dispel thoughts so dark, so afflicting. More than once did the rising sun irradiate her chamber, and recall her to work without her eyes having been closed by sleep.

On his part, Michel Perrin, notwithstanding the efforts of his sister to conceal the result of his residence with her, was not slow in discovering the sad truth. From that time he had not ceased to form plans to effect the earning on his own part of even a few pence; but Madeleine repelled every suggestion which appeared to her as tending to lessen the dignity of the reverend pastor. Only one project had received her assent. She agreed to see her brother, whose studies had been refined and extensive, giving lessons in Greek and Latin, so that no person could have a son or nephew without being besought by her to make the boy learn the dead languages, and to choose Michel Perrin as his master; but whether the people of Dijon made little of those old acquirements, or that the learning of a village pastor did not inspire them with sufficient confidence, Madeleine addressed herself in vain to her friends or employers to give the smallest pupil to her brother, at even the smallest price. " He is still very clever," the poor woman would say, when she tried one of her vain efforts ; " I wish you would come and see us. He never reads anything but Latin or Greek, except when he is at his breviary. If that does not convince you of his capability, I can say no more." She derived from all her applications only deep sighs without even shallow hopes.

It was true that the worthy pastor had no other amusement whatsoever than repeated perusals of Homer and Tacitus, which he had managed to save from the wreck of his scanty chattels. They constituted his whole library. Leading a life completely retired, when the weather precluded him from taking a solitary ramble, he passed his time in reading, praying, or chatting with his sister, whose voice was almost the only one by which he had been accosted during the past twelve months ; consequently, although his affection for Madeleine had been always very great, it had become so intense as to make him regard another separation from her as the most deplorable of all his misfortunes. It was therefore in a miserable state of mind that he awaited Madeleine's return, each time that she left home in a renewed hope of procuring him pupils. For a considerable time he had refrained from asking her the question too often followed by the reply of disappointment. It was enough for her to give him a silent embrace, and that after she had thrown her shawl upon the bed, she betook herself at once to her work, for him to form the determination of leaving ; and the sale of her watch, to which she attached peculiar value, confirmed his resolution.

He had decided on the following week as the time for a separation too afflicting, when one morning Madeleine returned, her countenance indicating that her mind was engrossed by some recent and unusual subject. Michel Perrin, absorbed in his reflections, did not at first observe her serious features. She was seated and working near the window, whilst the pastor, with an open book lying on his knees, was racking his mind as to how he could obtain the means of sustaining life when he would quit his sole remaining asylum.

"What a misfortune that Paris is so far off," said Madeleine several times, without perceiving perhaps that she was speaking aloud.

At the fourth or fifth repetition of this expression, Michel raised his head—"Why so, my dear sister?" said he; "wherefore do you wish Paris to be nearer?"

"Ah! wherefore? It would take too much of your time to listen to me, my dear brother, and you are reading your breviary, I believe."

"Tell me fully the reasons for your wish," replied the pastor, laying his book upon the table.

"It is because I have chanced to hear a matter so astonishing, so surprising. It must be admitted that some people are extremely lucky."

"We cannot be considered so," said Michel, as he breathed a heavy sigh.

"No; but your old class-fellow, Eugene Camus. Are you aware that he went to Paris in quest of employment? Well, he has come back for a few days, after having obtained a situation of two thousand francs a-year in the consolidated taxes."

"A place of two thousand francs!" exclaimed the good pastor. "You are right in saying that some are very lucky, Madeleine, for I would adduce this poor Eugene Camus as the most thorough blockhead and dunce that ever came from the college of Juilly."

"Well, he was dying of hunger at Paris for nearly two years; but his good fortune brought it about that another pupil of the Oratorians, Joseph Fouché, of whom you have frequently spoken to me———"

"Oh! Joseph Fouché should be a very different kind of man. I am very glad to hear that he is still living. A cunning fellow without any doubt, and always amongst the first. He and I acted together, as they said in the college; he helped me in my tasks, and in return I fought for him; for I was a stout, healthy youth, and Joseph Fouché was by no means strong."

"That has not hindered him from getting forward in the world, I must say that for him. He is minister— minister of, what shall I term it? It is all the same; it appears that when one becomes minister he may do whatever he wishes, and as his greatest pleasure consists in making the fortunes of his old class-fellows———"

"If I was sure of that," interrupted the poor pastor, with great emotion.

"I think he gave you a sufficient proof in placing Camus as I have described," replied Madeleine; "but Camus, being in Paris, could see him, could speak to him."

"And why should not I go to Paris, Madeleine?" exclaimed Michel Perrin, with an air of determination. "I shall go, sister; I shall see Fouché; I shall speak with him; since he has recognised Camus, who was not more than two years at Juilly, I am certain that he will recognise me also."

"Would you wish to undertake so long a journey,

Michel ?" said the kind sister, in great dismay ; "no, no, my dear brother."

" Hear me, Madeleine," replied the pastor, moving his seat close to her, " whether I go to Paris or elsewhere, I shall leave this place."

" You are going away !   You wish to leave me !"

" Your earnings are merely sufficient for your own support, my dear Madeleine.   I do not wish any longer to eat the half of them ; and all that you can say to induce me to remain will only annoy me, without making me abandon my resolution.   Departing from this place, is it not the better course for me to go to Paris than any other place, inasmuch as you give me the hope of finding a friend there ?"

" But Paris is so far," said Madeleine, bursting into tears.

" Bah ! sixty or eighty leagues, what is that distance to a good walker?   What annoys me the most, is having to take from you two or three crowns to support me on the road and at the commencement of my sojourn.   Can you make out so much ?"

" I shall not let you depart for Paris with two or three crowns, Michel, you may be assured of that," said poor Madeleine, sobbing.

" That would be beyond my requirements, sister. Something tells that once I arrive there, I shall find resources, and that my first letter from Paris will bring you good news."

The poor clergyman appeared so full of hope from the success of his journey, that he finished by imparting it to Madeleine.   Without being fully consoled, she smiled sometimes at the agreeable perspective which her brother offered to her imagination.   He perhaps did not indulge in very sanguine expectations, but having decided on being no longer a burden to her, he felt that he could act as a messenger or woodcutter when the good Madeleine was not at hand to prevent him.

The preparations for such a journey not being of a nature to delay it, in two days after that of which we have been speaking, Madeleine carefully made up a bundle for her beloved brother, which he was to carry on the end of a stick, and gave him a sealed rouleau in which, she said, there were forty francs; and when the brother and sister had embraced each other again and again, in tearful affliction, they separated.

The pastor accomplished ten leagues in his first day's journey, impelled by the double anxiety for a speedy arrival, and an avoidance of expense on the road. He was far richer than he supposed; for on the second day, his purse being empty, although he had lived on bread and cheese, he opened the rouleau, and his surprise equalled his grateful affection when he found three pieces of gold besides the forty francs. Feeling certain that Madeleine had not been able to provide such a sum without contracting debts, he resolved not to spend this gold, and to send it back by the first opportunity; but he was not the less thankful for her sisterly love.

As soon as he had taken up his abode at the most moderately furnished hotel of the capital, he did not lose a moment in acquiring information on various subjects which he considered conducive to his chances of obtaining an industrial livelihood. From his landlord he learned that Joseph Fouché was the minister of the general police, and that all the ministers gave a public audience once in each week, but that in order to obtain a special interview, it was necessary to request it by letter.   Accordingly he penned the following note :—

"Citizen Minister,
        " Michel Perrin implores his former class-fellow, Joseph Fouché, to receive him as soon as possible.   He is lodging at the hotel *du Soleil*, rue Mouffetard."
                        " *Vale et me ama.*"
                        " Health and respect."

Michel supposed that prefixing a Latin adieu to "Health and Respect," would remind Joseph of the time when, seated on the same bench, they were studying Cicero.   Almost an entire week elapsed without any reply from the minister; and when Michel asked his landlord if it ever happened that such notes were left unanswered, the latter mentioned about fifty instances of such neglect, almost without drawing breath.

His hopes were thus completely annihilated; and already he was only thinking of earning his bread by the sweat of his brow, when one evening the porter brought him a letter.   After breaking the seal with a trembling hand, he read these words which seemed to him to be written in letters of gold :—

" The minister of the general police will receive the citizen, Michel Perrin, on Thursday the 24th inst., at one o'clock."

A person should, like our hero, have returned after having, in a state of utter despondency, traversed the streets of Paris, those streets so populous, but in which he would seek in vain for even an individual inclined to extend the hand of succour, to be able to form an idea of his joyful hope that he had at last found a protector—a powerful protector.   Accordingly, he wrote, before retiring to rest, to Madeleine, *that he was to be with the minister of the general police on the ensuing Thursday.*

On the appointed day, Michel Perrin was in the ante-chamber of the minister before noon. Seated on the edge of a bench, he endeavoured to banish the timidity natural to those who have continuously lived apart from the world, and which the sight of a mansion in which everything indicated power and opulence tended to augment. To embolden himself, he recurred to his college days, and he was repeating for perhaps the hundredth time that Joseph Fouché had been his class-fellow, when he was called in.

Fouché was alone in his cabinet, seated before a desk covered with papers. He had hardly raised his head and fixed his small reddish eyes on the person entering, than assuming a cheerful manner—"There was no necessity," he said, "to announce you, for on my faith, I could not have met you in the street without recognising you."*

At this friendly reception the poor pastor fully resumed his courage.

"And you too, citizen minister," he answered, "cordially grasping the hand which Fouché extended to him, you have so slightly changed that I believe myself recurring to the time when old Vieil allotted us our tasks."

The figure of the minister assumed an appearance of cheerfulness which was by no means habitual. Perhaps the sight of an old college comrade served to relieve him of some disagreeable reflections, perhaps it recalled to a deputy of the convention the recollection of the time when his life was simple and innocent.

"Sit down there," he said in a gay tone, "and tell me

* I was informed by M. Turpin that Fouché frequently related the incidents of this narrative which were subsequent to the interview, but without naming his old class-fellow.

F. T. P.

how you have got on in this world, since we lost sight of each other."

" I have lived for many years as happily as possible," replied Michel with a sigh ; " for shortly after my ordination, I obtained a living in the most agreeable village of Burgundy."

" A poor position at present, that of a pastor must be!" replied the minister, shaking his head.

" So poor in fact that after having been thrust out of the door of my manse, ruined, persecuted, I have lived during the last seven years on the benefactions of some charitable, kind souls."

" And why the devil did you not try to get out of your difficulties ?   You should bestir yourself."

" Bestir, bestir !   That is easy said.   At first I was obliged to hide myself in the farms, in the cottages, because I was suspected, or they pretended so ; and I would ask you of what should I be suspected ?   But in short, matters proceeded thus in the department of the Cote-d'Or."

" And in many other departments," said Fouché ; " but when you no longer feared for your head, you should have thought of your purse."

" If thinking of it would have filled it, it would never have become empty," replied Michel with a sorrowful smile.   " I believe more ideas pass through the mind of a poor fellow who is trying to gain a crown, than passed through the mind of Homer when making the Iliad or Odyssey."

" And that did not lead you to any decided course ?"

" To nothing but to come to Paris."   Michel paused, but not without directing on his college friend a look more expressive than any words.

Fouché smiled. "Did you know that I was minister?" said he.

"Certainly."

"And you have counted on me," replied Fouché, with a kindness inspired by the thorough frankness of this man.

"Counted on you so much," replied the poor pastor, "that after God you are my only hope. Employ me where you wish, at whatever you choose, my destitution has absorbed all other difficulties. I shall not recoil from any description of employment. I am resolved to do anything by which I can earn my subsistence."

"To do anything!" repeated Fouché, with some surprise, "then you would not refuse to be employed in my department."

"Oh! that is all that I ask!" cried Michel Perrin, his eyes sparkling with joy.

"Undoubtedly you would acquire more money than your parish ever produced."

"Is it possible?"

"Certainly; men who resemble you are rather scarce." And Fouché fixed his eyes on the becoming figure of the pastor. "I know that you are very intelligent, and you can express yourself clearly and explicitly."

"It is certainly advantageous to have received a classical education," said Michel, with a modest air, although he was in fact highly gratified by the compliment.

"Besides, I can put complete confidence in you, whilst with the generality"——

The door of the cabinet opened, and an usher informed the minister that the first consul required his presence at the Tuileries immediately.

Fouché bundled a number of papers into a portfolio with all the haste of a man who fears to lose a minute.

" As to me, as to me ?" said the poor pastor, who with terror beheld him preparing to leave without any definite promise.

" Hold," said the minister, writing hastily two lines on a scrap of paper, " take this to Desmarest, chief of division." He then hurried to his carriage and drove away.

The pastor had barely read these words, " *Desmarest is to employ Michel Perrin, and to pay him liberally,*" when in the utmost delight, he proceeded to the office of the functionary mentioned, and the order which he brought procured his immediate admission.

The citizen Desmarest, who appeared to him to assume more importance than the minister himself, inasmuch as he had not been his class-fellow, took the paper, read it, and without offering him a seat, asked him if he was the person named Michel Perrin.

" The same, citizen."

" You have just left the minister ? "

" Only this moment ; for we had chatted together a full half hour, as two good friends would do who had not met for a considerable time."

" Be seated, Citizen Perrin. Is it the minister's intention that you are to correspond directly with him or with me ?"

" It would seem that in referring me to you, citizen."

" As he has said nothing positive in this respect, it is with me you will have to do."

" And when shall I commence ?"

" Without delay ; for the minister, in directing me to pay you liberally, undoubtedly believed that there was need of your ability and zeal."

" For my zeal I can fully answer," replied Michel. " I hope that, with some little experience in the discharge of actual duty, my ability shall equal it."

"I have no doubt of it, no doubt whatever. You have been sent to me by a man who is never mistaken in his estimate of individual capability. I shall enter your name on the list of those employed here. You shall have twenty francs per day, and your payment shall commence from this morning."

At these words, the poor pastor had great difficulty in restraining an enthusiastic expression of gratitude for such treatment. He said that he longed to render himself sufficiently useful to justify the good opinion entertained of him, and he asked the chief of the division to designate at once the duty he was eager to commence.

"For to-day, I have no particular directions to give you; but you will come to me in two or three days. Meanwhile, go through the city, traverse the promenades and other public places, dine in the restaurateurs, especially in the good restaurateurs."

"Ah! as for the prime restaurateurs," said Michel, smiling, "they shall not see me at all. I believe them to be far too costly for my purse."

"I understand," replied Desmarest; "perhaps, you are short of cash; but I am going to pay you a fortnight in advance. Will that suffice?"

"For a long time, I assure you," answered the good pastor, full of gratitude, "although I have really a scruple, not having done any duty yet."

"Bah! it is almost always the usage here; the intentions of the minister were certainly not to have you sent to the mean eating-houses."

"What good angel has led me to these worthy people?" said Michel Perrin to himself; and whilst he was expressing reiterated thanks, the chief of division, having no time to lose, wrote an order for the cashier, and handed it to him, telling him to go and get his payment, and not to return before the following Monday, unless he had something pressing to say.

If the first thought of the pastor, when he found himself the possessor of three hundred francs, tended towards God, the second was for Madeleine, and he could not dream of dining before he had written four pages to that good sister, and made his letter the bearer of half his treasure to Dijon. Then, with light heart and mind at ease, he resolved to follow the advice of the Citizen Desmarest, and to enjoy a little portion of the Parisian pleasures. " I have four good days before me up to Monday," he said, " and indeed I shall take some amusement."

In consequence, he betook himself to walk about the city. Paris, which up to this time had appeared sad, muddy, smoky, took all at once a cheerful appearance in his eyes, for a man whose mind is at ease, sees matters very differently from the aspect they present to an afflicted person. He was not fatigued by visiting the beautiful monuments, public buildings, bridges, gardens, and parks, and he imagined himself transported to fairyland. The Boulevards soon became his favorite promenade. Owing to the variety of amusements which he found there, the good pastor could pass his entire day without experiencing one moment of ennui. The shops, equipages, puppet-shows attracting and occupying his attention; not until night did he direct his steps to the Rue Mouffetard, delighted with the sights of the day, and greatly pleased at having been able to provide himself with two plentiful meals, an indulgence which he had for a long time previous been unable to procure.

When Monday arrived, Michel Perrin presented himself at the ministry of police, rather anxious to ascertain whether the employment about to be assigned to him might not be beyond his capacity.

"Ah! 'tis you," said Desmarest, who appeared busily searching for a paper which he could not find on his desk. "Well! where the devil have I thrust it? What have you done these four days past?"

"I have run about the city as if I was only twenty years old," replied the pastor gaily.

"Something infernal must have happened it," said the chief of division, opening a drawer that he had not tried before. "All was quiet, I suppose."

"Ah! perfectly quiet! Every one I saw appeared, like myself, to be bent on amusements."

"The malcontents are not giving up their designs for all that. (Could I have taken it home with me by mistake?)"

"Yes; the discontented people. That is what a poor fellow told me yesterday in a chat which we had at the Boulevard du Temple, and, in faith, I think he was one of them himself."

The pastor stopped speaking for a few moments after these words.

"Speak on; go on," said Desmarest, who continued to rummage his papers; "I am listening to you whilst I am looking for this cursed letter. What sort of man was this fellow?"

"He is a former garde du corps of the Comte d'Artois."

"Is he young? (This is enough to set one mad!)"

"About my age."

"(Ah! I have found it at last.) Well, your former garde du corps?"

"He told me his entire history."

"What a confiding man! Well?"

"It was a simple, plain story, and indeed I told him that I was a clergyman, that——"

"You told him that you had been a clergyman?" exclaimed Desmarest, laughing immoderately.

"Undoubtedly," replied Michel, rather disconcerted.

"All right, all right," said the chief of division in a tone of approval. "What makes me laugh is, that if you had told me the same thing when you first came here, you would not have surprised me, and I should have believed you at once: I observe in you so much of the air of a man who has worn a priestly habit."

"I have never been able to divest myself of that air, although it has often proved almost fatal to me," said Michel, with a sigh.

"At present, on the contrary, it is most favorable; your figure, your entire appearance inspires confidence."

The pastor bowed to express his thanks.

"And without doubt," continued Desmarest, "the good Royalist of the Boulevard is living on hope like all his friends. He has some lively expectations of a happy change of his circumstances."

"He has indeed, many."

"What do they depend on?"

"Ah! I do not know. The first time that he saw me this man could not tell me all his affairs."

"That is very natural," said the chief of division. "Have you arranged to see him again?"

"We have settled to have a game of chess one of these days, provided I may be free to return to the Café Turc."

"And what prevents you?"

"If the business which you will appoint for me to-day requires my entire time."

".I have no business to appoint for you," answered Desmarest, " but as I am greatly burdened myself at present, you may return to this matter or to any other until Thursday; come to me on that day."

Michel Perrin, not wishing to be troublesome, hastened to salute his chief and to leave the office, but not without being greatly surprised that they paid him so liberally for doing nothing. Nevertheless, feeling certain that ultimately he would be set to work, he laughed as he walked on the quay. "Three more holidays," he said, "and in faith we'll enjoy them!" And he resumed the life of a Parisian cockney.*

The following Thursday, after having waited near two hours in the antechamber with some men of very sinister aspect, the pastor was admitted to citizen Desmarest, who smiled graciously, saying—

" Well, what news ? "

" News!" exclaimed Michel quite astonished.

" Yes; when you come here undoubtedly you must have something to tell me."

" In fact, citizen, as this is Thursday, I have come to know if it is to-day that you desire to commence employing me."

" No, a hundred times no! I have already told you to take your own course, to go through Paris like a man who thinks only of amusing himself and seeing everything."

" I do nothing else through the length of the day," said the pastor laughing.

" Well, that is the minister's intention and mine ; have you settled your game of chess? Have you again met your garde du corps ? "

" No."

* The word in the original is " badaud."

T

" The devil ! " said Desmarest, who at that time was specially looking after the Royalists ; " but at least you know his name ? "

" He never told it to me."

The chief of division shrugged his shoulders, smiling.

" You have let him see that you were too knowing for him."

" Quite the contrary," replied Michel, " for I told him at once that my ideas were very simple."

" I am beginning to think so too," muttered Desmarest; then to terminate the interview, he bowed and added, " let me see you on Monday."

" Certainly," said the pastor to himself, as he took the direction of the Palais-Royal with the intention of dining at the café de Foi ; " certainly if this continues I can congratulate myself on having obtained a most agreeable position. As long as my business consists in waiting on my chief twice in the week, I run no risk of losing my employment through incapacity."

When he entered on the following Monday, he had waited a very long time until a number of persons passed, who stated that they were ordered to attend.

" The usher says that you have been waiting for six or seven hours," said the citizen Desmarest. " I had some important business to transact, or you should have been admitted sooner ; for I suppose that you have something pressing to tell me."

" Nothing whatever, citizen," quietly replied the pastor, " I always come very early, that you may have me at hand, if you wish to have me called."

" It is certain that you are admirably punctual, citizen Perrin ; I said so yesterday to the minister."

" I hope that in this respect you shall never have to reproach me," replied the pastor, bowing.

" You pass your days in your chamber," said Desmarest.

" Me! I run like a mountaineer; yesterday I did more than two leagues on the flagways of Paris."

" And you have seen nothing, heard nothing worthy of your attention and mine ? "

" Ah ! " said the pastor laughing; " it requires so little to attract my attention and to enable me to pass the time, that you would not wish to lose your time listening to such trifles."

" Well ! be it so," said the citizen Desmarest, whose astonishment had reached its acme; " Good day, return to-morrow, I request of you."

Michel Perrin had scarcely closed the door of the cabinet, when the chief of division rang and obtained the immediate attendance of one of the *mouchards* or detectives who were in the antechamber.

" Follow the man in the brown great-coat who has just left me," said he; " follow him throughout the day, and come to report to me to-morrow morning."

Until late in the evening the poor pastor could not move a foot or hand, or speak a word without a note being made of it by the clever spy who had become his shadow ; so that on the next day, when he received the order to enter the cabinet of Desmarest, the latter knew better than he did himself all that he had said or done the preceding evening.

" Now," thought the chief of division, " unless he is deaf, blind, or dumb, he will not be silent this morning;" and desiring him to be seated—" Come," said he, " you are about, I hope, to give me an account of yesterday's business."

The good pastor was always somewhat surprised at the interest which his chief seemed to take in his actions or movements; he replied, with an air of astonishment—

"My business of yesterday! I passed my time, since our last interview, in nearly the same manner as I passed all the other days since our first meeting. In the morning I walked to the Tuileries; in the evening I strolled on the Boulevards."

"I am not asking about your acts or movements," interrupted Desmarest, "but about what you were able to observe."

"Oh! nothing new," replied Michel Perrin; "I am beginning to know all these places as well as I do my own pocket."

"This man cannot be of a sane mind," said Desmarest to himself. Then taking patience—

"Do me the favor of telling me where you dined yesterday, citizen Perrin."

"At a restaurateur's in the Palais-Royal," replied the pastor, whom this kind of interrogatory surprised to the utmost.

"And afterwards?"

"I went to take my coffee at the café du Caveau."

"And whilst you were taking your coffee, what passed there? I beg of you to tell me."

"Oh! nothing that I know."

"What! did you not remark three young fellows who were talking just beside you, whose table was next to yours?"

"Stay, stay; I recollect now that there were indeed, just beside me, some gentlemen; I cannot say whether three or four, but I know they had a bowl of punch."

"And they used most horrible language regarding the

First Consul," added the chief of division with anger; "they even went so far as to threaten his life !"

" As for that, I am completely uninformed on the subject, inasmuch as, having observed two or three times that these gentlemen lowered their voices when I turned my head towards them, I moved off to a table farther from them. I did not wish to have even the appearance of listening to them, you understand."

" By my faith, this is too bad !" exclaimed Desmarest. " What occupation do you think that you have at the ministry of police ? "

" Ah !" said the pastor, quickly, " that is exactly what I have been desiring to know during the last fifteen days."

" Eh, zounds! you are a spy for the police !"

" A mouchard ? "

" A mouchard ! "

The pastor bounded from his seat, his cheeks flushed, his lips quivering. " Monsieur !—But it is not to you that I have to speak," said he, hastily rushing from the apartment.

He ran to the door of the minister, and wished to have it opened.

" The minister has gone out," answered one of the ushers, laughing in his face.

" I shall wait for him; I shall wait the whole day if it be necessary."

" Wait for him, then, in the street," said the usher, " for you cannot remain here."

" Be it so," replied the poor pastor, resolved to place himself before the gate of the hotel, but he had barely crossed the courtyard, when Fouché, on his return, alighted from his carriage.

Michel Perrin did not hesitate to rush towards the door.

"I beg of you to hear me for a minute, citizen minister," said he, in an altered tone.

Fouché, although somewhat surprised at the sight of this excited applicant, recognised Michel Perrin, and permitted him to follow him.

"Well! what now?" asked he, when they were alone. "Have you discovered some conspiracy, to be thus almost beside yourself?"

"I have discovered that you have made a jest of the friend of your youth," replied the good pastor, with a courage derived from resentment. "Poor as I am, and powerful as you are, I would never wish to have been subjected to such treatment."

"May I die if I know what you are speaking about," replied Fouché, looking closely at him to ascertain if he was in his right senses.

"Have you not issued your orders to your citizen Desmarest?"

"Undoubtedly; he has even told me," added Fouché, laughing, "that you earned your money very badly."

"Ah! my deepest regret is having received that sum of money, for unfortunately I am unable to return it: I have sent the half to my poor sister Madeleine. I have remaining at most only——"

"Eh! who says a word about your returning money, you fool? As long as I choose to employ you, what has Desmarest to say about it?"

"To employ me! to employ me as a spy!" cried Michel, reddening with indignation.

"Methinks your scruples arise rather late, when you

have been attached to the police for fifteen days," replied Fouché.

" It was only on this day that I discovered it," cried the poor pastor.

" What! did you not know it? Was it only to-day you ascertained your function?" said the minister, as, struck by the comic tendency of the matter, he indulged in great laughter.

" I should never have supposed it," answered Michel Perrin, proudly; "your man told me of it."

" It was a fortunate thing that he afforded you such an interesting disclosure," said Fouché, who vainly endeavoured to resume his gravity; "but, in fact, Michel, did you not come to me, stating that you were dying of hunger, and that you were resolved to do anything to provide the means of supporting life?"

" Certainly; I would have agreed to sweep your apartments, to carry the fuel for your stoves, to do everything that might be done without forfeiting reputation and losing self-respect." And, in saying these words, the poor pastor raised his fine head, which fretting and privation had already covered with snowy locks.

Honor exercises an influence even upon those who have tampered with their own. Fouché discontinued his laughter, and approaching his class-fellow—

" There has been a misunderstanding, Michel," said he, taking his hand; "let us forget this, and continue good friends, especially," he added, "as I have most delightful news for you: it is that they are about to restore your parish to you."

" Another hoax," said Michel Perrin, shrugging his shoulders, with an air of incredulity.

" No ; on my faith. Public worship is re-established. You know, or perhaps you do not know, that Cardinal Gonsalvi was here for a considerable time, to arrange the basis of a concordat with the Pope. This concordat is signed ; the First Consul communicated it yesterday to his Council of State."

" Ah ! if I again saw my good peasants ! If I returned to my manse with Madeleine !" cried the good pastor, his eyes sparkling with joy ; " but," added he, " perhaps the parish will be given to another ?"

" I shall take special care that it shall not," replied the minister. " Your parish was in Burgundy, I believe ?"

" Just beside Dijon. I had it for a year."

" You shall receive news from me very soon ; but, in the meantime, I advise you to return to your sister. Paris is full of people too crafty for you ; and as you must live," continued Fouche, " take this rouleau of twenty-five louis."

" No, no ; I shall take no more money," said the good pastor, pushing aside the hand of the minister.

" You must take it. You do not imagine, I hope, that this would be a recompense for the services you have rendered," said Fouché, laughing heartily. " It is given to you by me for yourself, for your sister."

" Well, be it so," replied Michel, greatly softened. " I cannot reject the gift of an honest man."

Fouché stifled a sigh. " Adieu," said he ; " return to Dijon."

The following year, Michel Perrin had resumed his clerical functions ; and Madeleine again became the lady and mistress of the manse. The peace, the comfort, the security for the future which they enjoyed, seemed to be enhanced by the recollection of past sufferings.

If Madeleine, in whom there was a little vanity, remarked to her brother, when returning from church, that all the peasants took off their hats—

"Yes, yes," the pastor answered in a low voice, and with a smile, "THE WORTHY FELLOWS ARE NOT AT ALL AWARE THAT FOR FIFTEEN DAYS I WAS A POLICE SPY."

CHAPTER XXIII.

THE COUNT OR CONVICT, WHICH ?——THE FAWN'S ESCAPE.

I now proceed to the narration of the other case which I received from M. Hubert, the facts of which are far more extraordinary than any of the exuberant fictions presented in the pages of romance.

In the early part of May, 1818, the Place Vendome was occupied by detachments from the garrison of Paris, for the purpose of effecting certain military requirements and arrangements. They were under the command of the Comte de Pontis de Sainte-Helene, colonel of the 72nd Legion. Amidst a brilliant cortege, he appeared, bearing on his breast the insignia of officer of the Legion of Honor, Chevalier de Saint-Louis, and also the Spanish orders of Alcantara and Saint-Wladimir. One of the spectators, meanly attired, and of rather sinister appearance, attempted to approach the distinguished officer, but he was unceremoniously repelled by those to whom the duty of keeping the ground had been assigned. He found no difficulty, however, in ascertaining that the residence of the Comte was in the Rue Basse-Saint-Denis ; and when the military duties of the day had been fulfilled, and the gallant nobleman returned to his house, he was apprised that a stranger was waiting in the antechamber on some affairs which he declared to be of paramount importance. The Count proceeded to the apartment, and was there accosted in rather familiar terms.

" You must remember me ; I am Darios, your former comrade of the chain. I bear you no illwill, and do not wish to take any advantage of you, but you are rich and I am miserably destitute. Give me your succour, relieve my necessities, and you may depend on my prudence and gratitude."

The Comte de Pontis de Sainte-Helene affected to treat this intruder as an impostor or madman. He summoned his attendants, and had Darios at once expelled from the premises. The latter, in the highest state of exasperation at such treatment, betook himself to the office of the Minister of the Interior, and having eventually succeeded in obtaining an audience of the Duc Decazes, declared to the minister that the Comte de Pontis de Sainte-Helene was no other than Pierre Coignard, who, on the 18th October, 1800, had been condemned by the criminal tribunal of the department of the Seine to fourteen years of hard labor, for various robberies committed by nocturnal housebreaking, and also by means of false keys. That in about five years he had managed to elude the vigilance of the prison authorities of Toulon, and had escaped from the Bagne. The Duc Decazes was completely amazed at this statement, and inasmuch as it was made by one who acknowledged himself to be a convicted criminal, he at first considered it to be false and malicious. Other reasons, of a political nature, made him determine to avoid any personal participation in an inquiry resulting from such averments; and as the imputations were directed against a person in a high military position, he referred the matter to General Despinoy, who commanded the division of the army to which the accused belonged. The co-operation of the police was obtained, and the celebrated Vidocq was brought into requisition. It was fully ascertained that Coignard, after escaping from Toulon, had made his way to Catalonia, in Spain, where he formed an intimate acquaintance with a young female, named Maria Rosa. She constituted the entire domestic establishment of the veritable Comte de Pontis de Sainte-Helene, who was a French emigrant, and of an ancient family belonging to Soissons. He had been in the Spanish service, and had distinguished himself in South America. Having returned to Europe in broken health, he was reduced to great poverty by the inability of the Spanish government to meet the claims of their dependants, or even to make any effectual resistance against the French invasion, which was then in very active progress. Death relieved him from his privations, and Coignard induced Maria Rosa to become his accomplice in assuming the designation of the deceased nobleman. The family papers and pedigree were made available by the spurious Comte and Comtesse, and Coignard proceeded to join the irregular troops or guerilla bands, which were under the orders of Mina, to whom he introduced himself as a French nobleman, exiled as a legitimist, and anxious to combat to the utmost the upstart who had usurped the throne of his country. He either received, or subsequently pretended that he received, the orders of Alcantara and Saint-Wladimir during his time of service under Mina, but he did not remain long in the Spanish ranks, and alleged that ill health rendered his retirement unavoidable. In a short time, however, he presented himself to Soult, and implored to be received into the army of his native country. He continued in a military capacity, fortunate in escaping the casualties of war, and in gradually attaining higher rank, until the departure of Napoleon for Elba, and then, free from all suspicions of his false pretensions, he professed to belong to the *ancienne noblesse,* and to regard the restoration of the Bourbon dynasty as the vindication of a right and the realization of a blessing. When Napoleon returned, Louis the Eighteenth betook himself to Ghent, and the Comte de Pontis de Sainte-Helene conciliated his confidence and esteem by becoming a participator of his short exile. He was basking in courtly favor, when his former "comrade of the chain" recognised him in the Place Vendome, and when his prudence, nay, even his instinctive caution so completely deserted him that he affected to treat a statement which he knew to be perfectly true, as the threats of an impostor or the ravings of a lunatic. It is highly probable that a small pension, paid weekly or monthly, to Darios would have ensured his silence.

But in reference to this most extraordinary culprit, it remains to be mentioned that the police discovered and proved before the *Cour d'assises de la Seine,* on the 10th July, 1819, that Coignard, even after he had attained to rank and opulence, was in communication with several of the most accomplished robbers of Paris, and that he aided them by using the opportunities derived from his intimacy with persons of wealth and proprietors of costly mansions, to ascertain where their money and plate were kept, and at what time the property might be pillaged with the least risk of interruption or detection. When he found the proofs of his past and of his continued delinquencies accumulated beyond any possibility of resisting an adverse judgment, he attempted to escape, and on being arrested, he discharged several pistol shots at the police officers, by

which two of them were dangerously wounded and permanently disabled.   Amongst the associates of his aristocratic career, there was far less indignation expressed at his
robberies or dishonest proclivities, than at his audacious
assumption of exalted rank, and his intrusion amongst a
class, the members of which would evince greater lenity to
the opening of a banker's coffers by means of false keys,
than to the attainment of admission to a courtly circle by
a pretended title of nobility.   Conclusive evidence having
been adduced of the identity of Coignard as an escaped
convict, and also of his subsequent complicity in several
criminal transactions, he was remitted to Toulon, there to
be imprisoned for life and kept to hard labor.   When he
left the Bicetre, on the 24th July, 1819, on the galley
chain, an enormous crowd assembled to witness his
departure, and his demeanour was remarked as indicating
neither despondency nor contrition.   In the towns through
which he passed, he excited the utmost curiosity.   The
false Comtesse, Maria Rosa, proceeded to Toulon, and
subsisting on whatever she had been able to save from
the wreck of her previous fortunes, she continued firmly
attached to the wretched Coignard.   She visited him
whenever permitted, and afforded him every attention that
the rules of the prison allowed.   She died in 1829, and he
survived her only until the succeeding spring.

I think that in laying before my readers the details of
this romantic reality, I have given to them an instance of
fact being far more extraordinary than fiction.   The materials in the narrative last related are not suitable for being
woven into one piece in the loom of fiction.   Those who
would make a Count the hero or principal character of an
imaginative production, would shrink from choosing him
amongst the galley slaves of Toulon.   Those who would

make a convict a prominent actor in any ideal drama, would consider it too ridiculous to dignify him with a title immediately after his escape from penal servitude.

As to the memoirs derived from the archives of the Police of Paris, a person disposed to make selections would have two difficulties to encounter; namely, where to commence and where to conclude his extracts. I may mention that there are some which certainly should not be presented for public perusal, and which I would totally abstain from translating; for although I might have no intention of publishing them, I would not leave their details in manuscript. They might vitiate, but could not improve. I could not, in these pages, insert all that I consider amusing or instructive, although perfectly unobjectionable, without extending this publication to an unusual amplitude, and causing the result of my Parisian visit, comparatively to monopolise it. I have translated every incident in the memoirs which I felt confident of being free from impropriety, and perhaps, at a future period, I shall venture to submit them to public consideration. At present I shall content myself by submitting two narratives to my readers, and then, with a few remarks on some of the novels of Alexandre Dumas, and with one or two of my personal recollections, I shall leave Paris for Dublin, until an interval of ten years has elapsed, when my acquaintance with the French capital shall be renewed as satisfactorily, I hope, to my readers as it was to myself.

THE FAWN'S ESCAPE.

The tale on which I am entering is designated in the memoirs, "The Fawn's Escape" and the applicability of that title will appear when the reader arrives at the Deer Park, (Parc-aux-Cerfs.) The preliminary observations were certainly not written on any previous edition to that of 1838, when the Orleans branch of the Bourbon family was in the ascendency.

Philippe Auguste de Sainte-Foix, chevalier d'Arc, was the grandson of Louis the Fourteenth. The career of this person, during the succeeding reign, powerfully illustrates the fearful state into which society had merged, and proves that when the door is opened for the entry of one vice, several others are likely to gain admission. It is worthy of notice that the profligacy of the higher classes during the reign of the depraved Louis the Fifteenth, was fully equal to the ferocity that overthrew the throne of his successor, and, on the ruins of all civil and religious insti tutions, established a reign of Terror. The people witnessed all the precepts of divine or moral authority not only violated, but openly ridiculed ; and we cannot feel much surprise at the utter disregard of all the claims put forward by the higher classes, when we recollect that they had long ceased to possess the slightest self-respect. The robes of nobility were not torn to rags by the wild and furious passions of a fierce democracy, until long after they had been trailed in the mire by their aristocratic owners. But we are not proceeding to write political considerations on the causes or effects of revolutions ; we only invite attention to the peculiar state of society at the period to which our tale refers, and leaving the reader to reflect for himself upon its consequences. We return to the chevalier d'Arc.

An illustrious though illegitimate origin might be expected to elevate his mind, render him susceptible of high feelings, and capable of noble deeds ; but in him it only inspired a ridiculous vanity and unmeasured impudence. Perverted in his youth by the vicious philosophy of the time, he followed its abominable maxims to the letter, and speedily compelled all who had any respect for themselves, to repulse his approaches and repudiate his intimacy. He consequently soon became admissible only to those haunts which were open to any person who had a title to disgrace and a sword to carry.

On reaching manhood, he entered into possession of an estate in the vicinity of St. Cloud, which had been bequeathed to him by his father, the Comte de Toulouse, one of the sons of Madame de Montespan. Being of a handsome person, and of insinuating though frivolous manners, he attracted the notice of a young widow, who had been, soon after her marriage, bereaved of a very old and very wealthy husband, for whose death she was prevented from becoming utterly inconsolable by the acquisition of a very ample fortune. The chevalier perceived that to the fair widow he was not an indifferent object, and, without the slightest intention of ultimate matrimony, he professed the most boundless love. He was warmly received, vows were interchanged, and to encourage his advances, the widow occasionally spoke of her extensive possessions in different parts of the kingdom; but far from insinuating that she wished to reserve any portion of her property from her future husband, she generally managed to introduce a favorite maxim—"That between two united hearts there should be a community of interests."

The chevalier dined at the widow's mansion; the entertainment was superb, and the table was covered with plate, with the exception of the soups, which were served in porcelain. Affecting the familiarity of a lover, the chevalier insisted that his fair hostess should permit him to supply this deficiency, and on the following day two

u

splendid soup tureens were sent to Madame, with a *billet doux*, to which the dear, fond creature attached more value than to the handsome present it accompanied.

In about a fortnight after, the chevalier took an opportunity of mentioning that he was unpleasantly circumstanced through the oversight of his house steward, who had neglected to have his plate brought from a chateau in Picardy, where he had passed the previous autumn. "Dear friend," he added, "I am to entertain to-morrow the Comte Ecouy and the Duc de Rohan, and owing to this fatality I find myself unable to make an appearance even respectable. Will you lend me whatever you can spare, and thus save my credit with my guests?"

Charmed at an opportunity of obliging her well-beloved, the widow reserved not even a spoon, all was sent with alacrity ; but in two days she received a letter enclosing the duplicates of her plate, and containing the assurance, that he should never have made it available for his necessities but for the recollection of her own sentiment, "That between two united hearts there should be a community of interests."

Impoverished by his profligacy, he petitioned the King. Louis the Fifteenth recollected him as a playmate of his youth, and sent him a draft on the treasurer of his household for eight thousand livres. As the amount was specified in figures, the chevalier added a cipher, which augmented the royal generosity to an unreasonable amount. The King was urged to compel the restitution of the sum thus obtained, and his majesty replied, " In my situation I cannot pay too dearly for a useful lesson. It will teach me, for the future, to economise less the letters of the alphabet."

Afterwards the Chevalier d'Arc became one of the most

indefatigable purveyors for the Parc-aux-Cerfs; and in reference to this part of his life, we have to notice the following, which is romantic in the extreme, and is also free from any details of an immoral tendency, rather a rare feature in any adventure connected with the Parc-aux-Cerfs.

The chevalier being admitted, by reason of the reputation of his father and his consanguinity to the Duc de Penthievre, to an intimacy with some respectable gentlemen of Querci sojourning at Paris, whither they had come to solicit official employment, or seek royal favor, was not long in remarking the exquisite beauty of the only daughter of one of them. Mademoiselle de Pal——* was beloved by a young officer of musketeers, of honorable family and high character, every way worthy of her hand, and they deferred the marriage only until the realization of their hopes from courtly favor would leave the family in more easy circumstances.

But a demon entered their residence when they admitted the Chevalier d'Arc. He applied himself to stimulate the soul of the Comte de Pal——, father of Mademoiselle Helene, with suggestions of guilty ambition, until the foolish but obstinate old man determined to effect the admission of his daughter into the Parc-aux-Cerfs. But how to procure the concurrence of the two brothers of the old gentleman, one Lieutenant-Colonel the Baron de M——, the other an abbé, and grand vicar of the Bishop of Tulle. These gentlemen, high in their sense of honor, and proud in their family recollections, would scorn to see fortune coming through so vile an avenue. How to

---

* This abbreviation, strictly copied from the memoirs, appears to be intended to conceal the complete designation of the young lady and her family.

reconcile a virtuous girl to her own degradation.	Above all, how to dispose of her lover.

To make an open attack was impossible.	Meanwhile, the old dotard of a count, infatuated by the suggestions which the Chevalier d'Arc continually whispered, fancied himself a minister of state, destined to save France from every peril by the guidance of his sage advice; moreover, he saw in his brother the baron, a marshal of France, and in his younger brother, an archbishop or cardinal.	This picture enchanted him, and instead of kicking his infamous tempter out of doors, he listened to no other counsel but his. The virtue of his daughter became a chimera and a trifle compared with the advantages which must result to the entire community from an influence acquired over the yielding mind of a libertine monarch.

The chevalier, on his part, had committed himself in the affair beyond retreat.	The King had heard something of it.	His valet, Lebel, and the portly lady, the directress of the Parc-aux-Cerfs, were impatiently awaiting the appearance of this eighth wonder of the world.	They worried the intermeddling chevalier, and he soon concluded that the palladium of the royal protection should be secured as soon as possible, and by all possible means.	He and the father of the young lady had recourse to stratagem.	They lived in Paris in the Rue des Moulins.	One morning, under the pretext of preferring a request to M. de Choiseul, lately installed minister, the Comte de Pal——, his daughter, and the Chevalier d'Arc proceeded to Versailles.	On their arrival, they enquired the hour at which the minister received public applicants, and finding that there was some time to spare, the chevalier proposed a promenade through the town.	The suggestion was approved by the father, and the daughter acquiesced.

They take their way through a lonely lane. The long wall, by which it is bounded on one side, is pierced by a door which happens to be open, and discloses a view of a beautiful garden. They ask of a domestic who is passing if they can be permitted to walk in this delightful place. The reply is affirmative, and they enter; and at the end of a shady avenue, they meet a lady.

"Oh! it is the Marchioness d'Allinvilliers."

"Oh! the much-esteemed Chevalier d'Arc!—what a pleasure!"

"I am enchanted, madame, at this instance of good fortune in meeting you. I presume to present to you the Comte de Pal——, my most intimate friend, and Mademoiselle, his daughter."

High compliments are reciprocated. The Marchioness, so luckily encountered, assumes the guidance of the party. They admire the beauty and magnificence of the place. At last they arrive at a kiosque, erected in the purest oriental style, and there they find a repast of the choicest pastry, fruits, liqueurs, wines, and iced water. Mademoiselle Helene de Pal—— is pressed to eat and drink. She complies; and after having taken refreshment, a sudden stupor overcomes her, and she yields to a somnolency totally irresistible.

On awaking, she is astonished to find herself in a sumptuous bed. She is informed of all that has passed by the Marchioness d'Allinvilliers, whom she recognizes, and by whom she is affectionately embraced. A letter is placed in her hands from her father, in which she is informed that he has not been able to refuse to so kind a lady, the care of his daughter during the period of his stay in the capital. He will see her at every visit to Versailles, and Mademoiselle de Pal—— will be more comfortably and respectably circumstanced than she could be in furnished lodgings with him.

This had a great semblance of truth; and although certain precautions and restraints appeared extraordinary, the young lady was so perfectly innocent as to entertain no suspicion of the infamous nature of the mansion in which she was placed. She had not acquired a knowledge of the character of the Chevalier d'Arc, which was very different from that of provincial gentlemen, and she had not the most remote idea of the functions which he exercised at court. In the evening, she was induced to enter the saloon. There, to her utter surprise, she recognized the King, in a gentleman who stood with his back to the chimney.

A conversation ensued, in which his Majesty used much gallant and polite language, and in which he stated that he came there without any ceremony, as the Marchioness was his foster-sister. On his retiring, they surrounded the young lady, and exclaimed that she should be proud of the distinguished attentions of the King. In short, every allurement which can be addressed to vanity was tried on one whose mind was guided by sentiments of a higher nature. Helene, far from acquiescing in the views of the depraved creatures, of both sexes, with whom she was associated, regarded all their suggestions with undisguised repugnance. The same evening, a royal page brought her a porcelain vase, containing a bouquet of natural flowers, upon which appeared a butterfly formed of sparkling gems. Upon the handles were fastened two diamond ornaments, shaped like pears, of very large dimensions and surpassing brilliancy. These were accompanied by necklaces composed of precious stones, remarkable for splendor, purity, and magnitude.

Ecstasy seemed to pervade the circle. Mademoiselle de Pal——, in a firm and deliberate tone, apprised the Marchioness, that, at an early hour on the succeeding day, she wished to return to her paternal home. Her uncle, the abbé, would undertake to have the present returned. There was an outcry—

"You darling, to quit me! Ah! you wicked one! what ingratitude! Moreover, how could I expose you, lonely and unprotected? I would not entrust you to anyone; my responsibility is pledged. You will remain until the next visit of your father, the Comte."

Constrained to yield to this specious resistance, Mademoiselle de Pal—— retired to her chamber, and there wrote to her father an account of all that had passed, and urged the imperative necessity of immediately flying from the gallantry of the King. The poor child comforted herself in the expectation of a prompt succour from her father. What would have been her feelings if she had witnessed the transports of joy in which the old gentleman indulged at the apparent certainty of accomplishing his designs? It was a complete delirium! Repeatedly he embraced the Chevalier d'Arc, whose pockets he replenished with money. Then taking his pen, he hastened to reply that it appeared premature to impute evil designs to any person; that the King could have no bad intentions. Finally, they owed his Majesty so much love and respect, that all other feelings should be absorbed in reference to him.

The conclusion of this letter plunged the virtuous girl in despair. After two more days, she received a second visit from the King, and was offered homage of a more marked character—the most costly stuffs, and various other articles of such enormous value as could not be authorized by simple gallantry or innocent admiration.

Mademoiselle de Pal——, distracted, overwhelmed, saw herself abandoned by those on whom the very feelings of nature should have imposed the duty of protecting her innocence. She did not accuse her father directly, but her mind was beset with frightful suspicions.

One morning, at an early hour, the Marchioness not having left her bed-chamber, a girl, who filled some very subordinate station in the establishment, came into the apartment of Mademoiselle, in the absence of the *femme-de-chambre* who had been assigned to her. This damsel, entering cautiously, informed Helene that a handsome lad, in her father's livery, had brought a letter which he would deliver only to herself in person.

Too much tormented not to distinguish any favorable circumstance in her unhappy situation—knowing, moreover, that her father had not permitted his two old servants to bring his family livery to Paris—she was only too ready to take advantage of the opportunity afforded by the early hour; consequently, she consented to receive the envoy.

An exclamation of surprise and delight escaped her. It was her lover, the Vicomte de Benavent Rhodès, a gentleman of very high extraction, quite ready to believe that his fathers constituted a younger and distant branch of the sovereign counts of Rhodès. He was a black musketeer, young, brave, and thoroughly daring. The Comte de Pal——, a man without prudence or reserve, had permitted his brother to discover his secret, and even to become acquainted with the letter of his daughter. This worthy ecclesiastic, indignant at the projects of his brother, lost not a moment before informing the person most interested in defeating the base plots of the royal seraglio. The family was distracted, but the circumstances required delicate management. They had to deal

with the difficulty of struggling against the proceedings of
an obstinate old man, who found historic sanctions for
his conduct in the innumerable pollutions of the Court.
The great evil consisted in the abuse of an acknowledged
power, the authority of a parent. Besides, where were
they to find Helene? He kept the secret as soon as he
found his family in revolt against his projects. The em-
barrassment was great, but the Vicomte de Benavent,
better informed than the respectable abbé, at once surmised all that passed; how, owing to the villainy of the
Chevalier d'Arc, the fair Helene was already in the infamous precincts of the Parc-aux-Cerfs. He wished to go
himself, and warn his mistress of the dangers by which
she was surrounded.

Certain that he could never penetrate into this place if
he went in his ordinary attire, for habitual watchfulness
interdicted the entry of the *gardes-du-corps*, the *officiers-
aux-gardes*, and the musketeers, grey or black, as persons
of suspicious reputation amongst those who had the guar-
dianship of youth and beauty, the lover flattered himself
that he would deceive the " Argus " by assuming a livery,
and presenting himself at an early hour.

He was not wrong in his conjectures; and by choosing
the early hour he gained the assistance of the poor female drudge who introduced him. Once in presence of
Mademoiselle de Pal——, he kissed her hand, and placed
in it a letter from the abbé in the following terms:—

" My dearest Niece,
" I write to you in all the affliction of a broken heart. Your poor
father has been scandalously led astray by a knave, a swindler, a man
without an honorable idea, and destitute of faith and morals. Dear
niece, are you aware that you are now in the Parc-aux-Cerfs? Who
detains you there? The abominable directress of that polluted mansion.
Your ruin is resolved on. I trust that God will not abandon you, and

that this affair may terminate without crime or scandal. Consult with the Vicomte (M. de Benavent.)   He is regarded by me as my future nephew. If your plans should not succeed, then God will guide the steps of one of His ministers, and should I find it necessary to approach the King, I shall not recoil from my duty.   Adieu, let us invoke the Virgin, the saints, your holy patroness, and above all, the Three Persons of the all-powerful and all-merciful Trinity."

The musketeer at once arranged with the young lady that precisely at midnight she should descend from her chamber, and he furnished her, for that purpose, with a silken ladder wrapped in a handkerchief.   She was to make for a part of the wall over which a white plume would be displayed, and having arrived there, she was to clap her hands three times, and her liberators would appear.

These matters having been arranged, prudence required the lovers to separate ; but the Vicomte, who at first had been more timid than the object of his affection, protracted his adieu until Mademoiselle Justine, an artful spy over the youthful inmates, arrived.   At sight of her, the musketeer took his leave in the style of a valet.   This was in vain ; she was not to be deceived, and her practised eye detected the man of quality.   The provincial livery could not conceal true grace and courtly bearing beneath its gaudy laces.   At once she proceeded to make her report to *Madame*.   Alarm spread through the camp, and they took immediate measures to defeat the plans of the young couple.   Helene passed the rest of the day almost alone.   *Madame* having sought admission, a violent headache was alleged as a justification for declining an interview.   She soon returned, and being admitted by Justine, she openly divulged the purposes which she entertained.   Helene gave full vent to her scorn and unqualified disdain.   This was indiscreet, but the error arose not more from her youthful inexperience than from the noble sincerity and purity of her mind. Flattery was tried, and she was addressed in terms of the highest exaggeration as to the brilliant position to which the royal favor would necessarily exalt her. This produced a declaration from her that love unsanctioned by marriage commenced with infamy and terminated in perdition. This language excited a perfect tempest of invective, her scruples were derided, and to the most galling sneers were added direct threats of ruin to all her kindred, and also to the family of her lover.

Tears were her reply, but her determination was unchanged. She expressed a wish to retire early. In this she was indulged; and as midnight sounded she attached the silken cord to the window, and abandoning herself to Providence, she rapidly descended. Having reached the ground in safety, she knelt and offered her thanks to Heaven for this successful commencement. Then, approaching the exterior wall, she perceived the white plume raised above it upon a pole. She clapped her hands, and immediately heard all the indications of a violent contest. Murmurs, imprecations, the clash of weapons, and several pistol shots were almost simultaneous. The uproar increased; a struggle, hand to hand, seemed to terminate in the departure of the combatants, and although the signal continued displayed, profound silence ensued.

The poor girl was overwhelmed with terror, her conjectures were tortures thoroughly agonizing; but just as the external tumult ceased, *Madame* issued from the mansion, attended by six male servants bearing torches.

"Indeed, Mademoiselle," said this debased woman, "you cannot expect us to indulge your wishes for midnight promenades in an inclement season. The air is sharp, and your health is delicate. Please to re-enter the mansion. The physician will hold us responsible for the results of such indiscretion; and our tenderness for you compels us to guard against your caprices. Until you become more reasonable, you must occupy an apartment from which you shall not find it so easy to issue."

Mademoiselle de Pal—— did not condescend to reply to this cool impertinence, but she understood that in such a contest her adversaries were unscrupulous as to the means they employed. Alone, almost lifeless with terror, and abandoned by her father, she apprehended the most sinister designs, and her undisguised disgust excited an implacable hostility amongst those to whom the superiority of virtue was odious. " In fact," murmured the mistress of the mansion, " we are far more foolish than she is herself, to labour for her exaltation; the insulting creature will only detest us the more for our exertions."

They placed her on the ground floor, and assigned her some apartments furnished in the most luxurious manner; but the windows were carefully fitted with iron bars. When Justine had a second time undressed her mistress, *Madame* betook herself to rest.

Mademoiselle de Pal—— spent the night in tears, for she understood too well what had occurred. Men previously posted had been waiting for her lover. Perhaps he had paid, even with his life, for his generous intervention. She implored God to protect the young musketeer, and to avert the crushing resentment of the King.

In the morning she requested an audience of *Madame,* which was immediately granted, and she earnestly implored of her not to report what had passed to his Majesty. " I know not what I might do on another occasion," was the reply, " but in the present case I have only to express my regret that the King is already fully informed upon the subject."

" It will be upon me then," promptly observed Helene, " that his wrath must fall, since my generous defender is dead."

" Dead! the Vicomte de Benavent-Rhodès! You are pleased to think so," remarked this depraved woman, in a bantering tone. " Certainly it is not owing to him and his associates that some of the King's servants did not perish. Happily, there has been more noise than actual injury ; but this gentleman and four other musketeers are in the custody of the grand-prevot, and they must answer to justice for an armed attack, at midnight, on a royal residence. The laws of France attach capital punishment to such an outrage."

Mademoiselle de Pal—— uttered a piercing shriek, and fell into violent convulsions, which excited great alarm in the mind of *Madame,* lest the death, or even the severe indisposition, of the young beauty, should be imputed to her indiscretion. She sought to assuage her sufferings, and when restoratives had produced relief, strongly advised her to apply to his Majesty, who was of a merciful disposition, and would not refuse pardon to the musketeers at her intercession.

The dread of the price which would be demanded for this favor contributed to diminish the pleasure which the hope of clemency excited. Nevertheless she resolved to meet the peril, trusting to overcome it, and to conquer culpable intentions by purity of heart and the innate power of virtue. When she ascertained that Louis XV. had arrived, she proceeded to the saloon. The conversation was gay, brilliant, and varied. Mademoiselle displayed the intrepidity which is so frequently the attendant of innocence, and although her face was suffused with blushes, her voice was distinct and unfaltering, as she gracefully and respectfully besought the King to pardon the five prisoners. Louis reverted to his feelings towards herself, and observed that it lay in her power to induce him to interfere in a matter which involved a direct offence against his personal safety and his rights. He indulged in the chivalrous levity which has so often characterised the Bourbons, remarking that he was her slave, but that even a slave should not be exasperated. Finally, he gave her distinctly to understand that the fate of the prisoners depended on her compliance.

She demanded four days' interval, which the king acceded to, adding that she could not follow a better example than that of Jephtha's daughter.

Two days had elapsed, the king was going to mass, when a priest placed himself in front of the cortege.

"Monsieur l'Abbé," said the Duc de Richelieu, "stand aside, you impede his Majesty's passage."

"Sire," exclaimed the priest, "Sire!" and he raised his voice, notwithstanding the repeated admonitions of the Duc de Richelieu that silence should be observed, and that the King was not to be accosted then or there.

"Sire, in the name of God, and appealing to the pious traditions of your race, I implore an audience. Reflect that a moment's delay may endanger your hopes of Paradise."

The firmness and dignified demeanor of the ecclesiastic produced an extraordinary effect upon his Majesty. He stopped, reflected an instant, and then replied—

"Be it so, Monsieur; after mass you may come to my closet, I shall hear you there."

This strange incident perplexed the court. The Comte

and the Baron de Pal——were well known amongst the courtiers; but their brother, pious and unpresuming, passed unnoticed in a place where no one appeared important unless by the favor they received, or by the influence they possessed. Impelled by curiosity, a crowd surrounded the abbé, and were lost in various conjectures. Mass being over, the door of the royal closet opened, and the captain of the guard advanced and enquired for the abbé to whom the King had promised an audience. The abbé presented himself and was admitted. He addressed the King in terms of profound respect, but protested against the detention of his niece, and also pleaded the cause of the young musketeer and his companions. In speaking of the young lady and her lover, his language was pathetic and persuasive; but he did not hesitate to remind the monarch of the enormity of deliberate, premeditated sin, and of the awful consequences before that tribunal of eternal justice where monarchs would be judged without reference to earthly power, save as to how far they had abused it. He was urging his arguments, when the official entered and presented a letter which the King immediately perused, and raised his eyes and hands in great perturbation. "Ah! Monsieur l'Abbé," he exclaimed, "do not proceed any further. The danger is imminent. Go, invested with plenary authority, at once to the Parc-aux-Cerfs."

"Me, sire!"

"Yes, you; I want not your indignant looks. Lose not a moment, run, demand Mademoiselle de Pal——."

"My niece!"

"The same; prevent the accomplishment of her fatal resolution. Let her know that I renounce—but no, she is destroyed; it is all over. Take and read that. My God, how obstinate and self-willed these little girls are!"

The abbé, astonished at this event, hastily perused the letter.

> " Sire," wrote the young lady, " I am apprised that it is by my dishonor the life of the Vicomte de Benavent can be saved. I prefer saving his life by the sacrifice of mine own. If you do not wish to be answerable for my fate before an Almighty judge, do not punish a lover whom you have rendered sufficiently miserable already by my untimely death. I shall have ceased to live when this letter meets your eyes."

" But go, Monsieur," the King exclaimed again. " These priests are effective only in the pulpit ; they can advise well, but cannot act with energy."

The horror of that note imparted speed to the abbé ; he ran to the Parc-aux-Cerfs, preceded by the Marquis de Pontecoulant, who was sent specially by the King. The mansion was in an indescribable state, its inmates filled with consternation at the desperate course adopted by the hapless Helene. Several physicians were present, and various antidotes had been tried, but without any satisfactory results, At sight of the abbé, the bedside was left free for his approach.

" Oh ! my niece," said the priest, in a voice almost choked with grief, " how could you presume to dispose of your life ?"

" I preferred death to infamy."

" My niece, your honor is respected, and the King concedes your requests. The Vicomte de Benavent and his comrades are at liberty."

" Then I go to my grave consoled and contented."

" Dearest Helene ! live to make a husband happy ; live to impart joy to your family."

" It is too late."

The abbé cast imploring looks on the medical men, whose countenances mutely indicated their conviction of the hopelessness of the case. The sad sacrifice appeared nearly consummated. How she had obtained the poison none could tell. Dissolution seemed imminent, when a man of lofty stature, whose features, though extremely swarthy, expressed great intelligence, entered the room. In one hand he bore a small glass, and in the other a phial, containing a liquid of the deepest green color, and perfectly clear. " I come by the King's command," he exclaimed ; and passing, through the yielding crowd, to the bedside, he half filled the glass with water, into which he dropped a portion of the green elixir. Directing Justine to raise the drooping head of the apparently expiring girl, he succeeded in getting her to swallow the medicine. Immediately a fierce spasm convulsed her frame ; she raised herself with surprising energy, but instantly fell back on the pillow.

" She is dead !" exclaimed many of those present.

" She is saved," replied the tall, swarthy man, in a tone of perfect confidence. He was the celebrated Comte de Saint-Germain, whose influence with Louis XV. appeared mysterious to the courtiers, but really arose from his extensive information and research. In theory and practice his scientific attainments were of a very high order, and appeared still more surprising when contrasted with the ignorance and imbecility of the aristocracy of that period.

Mademoiselle de Pal—— recovered so speedily as to be capable of removing, under her uncle's care, in about a week. On leaving the Parc-aux-Cerfs, THE ESCAPED FAWN received, by order of the King, a splendid note-case, in which there was a draft on the Controller-General for five hundred thousand francs (£20,000.) On the previous evening the King said to the Vicomte de Benavent :

" Monsieur, on this occasion I am endowing virtue."

x

Then he added, with a laugh, " One swallow does not make a summer."*

On the day that Mademoiselle left the Parc-aux-Cerfs, her worthless father was banished from court, and enjoined to live on his estate at Vivarais. The chevalier d'Arc had the effrontery to present himself at court as if nothing to his discredit had occurred. The King remarked to him, that in affairs of gallantry, the consent of the young lady was more necessary than that of her father ; and suggested that he should in future avoid appearing in Paris or Versailles, and fix his residence at Tulle. He accordingly retired to that place, where he died in 1779.

* The original phrase is " Une fois n'est pas coutume."

CHAPTER XXIV.

THE COUNT DE COUCY—DUMAS—A THREATENED SUICIDE.

It is probable that these pages will be perused by some who recollect a recent attempt to substitute a child procured in an English workhouse for the veritable heir to an Irish earldom. It is extremely improbable that, in any part of the world, they may be read by any person unacquainted with the main circumstances of the lengthened investigations which terminated in the conviction of a spurious aspirant to an English baronetcy. I shall now offer my second selection from the French memoirs. It relates to a claim to a title of nobility, and, looking to the source from which the statements have been derived, I think they may fairly be designated a true account of a falsehood.

The Marquis de Coucy sent his son to be nursed at Gonesse, where he was left during three years, as was usual at that period (the reign of Louis XIV.) The young Count was then brought back to his paternal home, and became the idolized darling of his parents, who had no other child. When the proper time arrived to commence his education, the first masters were engaged. His progress was most rapid, and at sixteen, having completed his preliminary studies, he was entered at the Military Academy.

One day, whilst he was amusing himself along with some of the Rohans, the Tremouilles, a Duguesclin or two, and several of the young Rochefoucaults, a decrepit female, hideously ugly, excessively dirty, although not badly clad, proposed to this party of high-born lads to .tell their fortunes. Some haughtily rejected the old impostor, others eagerly embraced her offer, and amongst them the young Coucy. She took the hands of four or five in succession, told them her idle stories, and pocketed their money.

All, through a motive of amusement, even those who were not desirous of making a personal experience of her imaginative power, surrounded the fortune-teller. When it came to the turn of the young Count de Coucy to extend his palm, he offered it. The old hag examined his hand for a much longer time than she had devoted to the inspection of the preceding ones, and suddenly rejecting it with every indication of disdain, she exclaimed—"Back, fellow! Begone, clown! I am here to speak only to gentle-folk, and not to tell the future destiny of a peasant's son."

At these words there was a universal laugh : some ridiculing the old woman on her divining power, others venting a good-humoured raillery upon their companion. He knew not whether to be jocular or angry. They informed the old woman of the name and title of the illustrious youth whom she had designated the son of a peasant, but she continued to swear by all the saints that the young Coucy was nothing else. The uproar occasioned by this denunciation continued to such a pitch, that the captain of cavalry, the commandant of the academy, interfered, and calling a groom, directed him to turn out that woman.

"That a woman!" exclaimed the groom; "I would wager that it is a man."

Another groom declared that he had seen an individual, in the habit of a peasant, enter a neighbouring tavern, from whence, in about a quarter of an hour, he had issued disguised as a female; and he averred that the fortune-teller whom they had just expelled was the same person. The young Count de Coucy heard these statements with indifference; but as they referred to a creature who had seemed to take pleasure in insulting him, they did not entirely lapse from his recollection.

Six months passed. One morning the Marquis de Coucy, being in his room, was discussing with the Marchioness a project of marriage for the young Count; they were anxious to marry him to a princess of the house of Lorraine. In the midst of their deliberations, a valet-de-chambre appeared. He was the brother of the young Count's foster-father, and the servant to whom the Marquis manifested the greatest liking and confidence. He apologised for disturbing their conversation, and stated that a young man, of a most elegant demeanor and prepossessing manner, and whose appearance seemed almost familiar to him, requested to be admitted.

"Let him come in," said the Marquis. The stranger is introduced. He is youthful, and appears not to have passed his seventeenth year; his figure slight and symmetrical; his aspect expressive and bland; his carriage is good, he has a sweet smile, and his salute is agreeable. Still his deportment does not suggest that noble blood is coursing through his veins. He has not the aristocratic air which a courtly life imparts, or the polished manner derived from elevated society.

The young man appears under the influence of some strong emotions; he produces a letter, and presents it to the Marquis. It is received, and the youthful stranger sinks upon his knees, and covers his face with his hands, as if about to implore pardon for some great transgression. Here is the letter :—

"MONSEIGNEUR,—Sixteen years have this day elapsed since, yielding to the pernicious suggestions of my wife, I committed a horrible crime, of which I now accuse myself, and for which I must endeavor to make all possible reparation, by a full acknowledgment of my offence. This luckless day saw your legitimate heir taken from his cradle, and my poor son substituted for the noble child. The imposture still continues, and it is the son of Maurice Lesourd and Madeleine Ledaille that, in your princely mansion, occupies the position due to your legitimate offspring, whose youth has been condemned to the weary labours of a rustic life. Whilst my wife lived, I reluctantly concealed this scandalous transaction, but her death, this very day, terminates my guilty silence; and as I do not involve her in the punishment due to my offence, I feel the less repugnance in submitting to the justice of the violated laws. I send you, monseigneur, your son; he will deliver this letter, and it is for you to place him in his rightful position. I shall receive, in return, the unfortunate creature from whom a brilliant career of life is thus withdrawn. Can my utmost tenderness ever repay him for the loss incident to this disclosure?

"I am ready to maintain, before any tribunal, the integrity of this statement; and I cherish the hope, that I may still enjoy some portion of your distinguished protection. I have the honor to be, Monseigneur, your most humble, most respectful servant,—

"MAURICE LESOURD."

The Marquis could not believe his eyes. The Marchioness fell lifeless at the reading of this startling communication; but presently, yielding to a natural impulse, raising the young man from his humble posture, they pressed him to their hearts, and mingled their tears whilst recognising his title to their affections.

One thing surprised the Marquis, the style of the letter. The young man declared that it was written by the brother-in-law of Lesourd, the chief clerk of a Parisian notary. " He it was," added the youth, " that stimulated Lesourd to this act of justice ; he is an excellent man, worthy of the patronage of Monseigneur——"

" Say your father's patronage," replied the Marquis ; " but his noble conduct shall not lack acknowledgment and recompense ; from this day he shall be my confidential agent. My present agent wishes to retire, being aged and infirm."

Meanwhile, the Marchioness, recovering from her excitement, recollecting the virtues and high endowments of him whom she was no longer to term her son, began to consider that to deprive him of the rights with which he had been so long vested, would require something more than the mere will, or even the conclusive determination, of the Marquis. Her husband found himself meshed in the most embarrassing manner ; and the new aspirant, who is already invested with the title of Count de Coucy, perceives that he has to encounter an obstacle of which he had not calculated the strength and magnitude, namely, the adverse possession by his rival for upwards of fourteen years of the position in which he now sought to supersede him. How was he to deprive him of title, rank, fortune ? How was he to banish him from a family of which he had so long been a cherished member ? There was nothing in his deportment denoting the inferiority of his birth. He bore no resemblance, indeed, to either the Marquis or Marchioness de Coucy, but his likeness to the father of the latter had frequently been remarked.

He now enters the apartment. His air is noble, and with respectful affection he embraces the parents of his love. Their fondness for him of whom they had been so proud, and by whom their anxieties and hopes had been engrossed, is irrepressible. They are plunged into heart-breaking perplexity. They cannot allow the awful storm suddenly to burst upon him. Neither the Marquis nor his lady could summon courage for an explanation, which, nevertheless, it was impossible long to defer. The new claimant is withdrawn for the time, a large sum is given for his use, and both of the parents, to whom he has so lately presented himself as their offspring, assure him that a speedy and rigid investigation shall be insti-tuted.

Persons of the highest discretion and of the greatest sagacity are put in requisition. Experienced magistrates, profound lawyers, are consulted. They mostly declare that the confession of the foster-father is insufficient; but some incline to a different opinion. The matter could not be concealed; in a few days it becomes publicly known. The partisans of the new claimant make loud comments on the insulting and disdainful manner with which a fortune-teller at the academy had repelled the Count, telling him that he was a plebeian. The gentlemen who were present attested this fact, to which immense import-ance was attached.

The unfortunate Count trembled with rage at these attacks. He tenderly loved his parents, and was deeply shocked at the bare possibility of losing their affections. M. de la Rochefoucault, his most intimate friend, an-nounced to him the damaging effect of the scene with the gypsy. For a long time the Count had forgotten this event; but when it was mentioned by his friend, all the circumstances recurred to his mind, and amongst them the expressions of the two grooms. They are sent for.

One repeats that he believed the person referred to was a man disguised as a female; the other declared that he had seen a peasant enter the tavern known as *de la Bonne-Foi, rue du Petit-Lion-Saint-Sauveur,* and that the same person soon after issued forth in female attire.

The Count and his advisers betook themselves to this tavern. They did not find it easy to enlighten the proprietor, or bring him to appreciate the importance of their inquiries; but when he had sufficiently collected his ideas, he declared that a peasant of Gonesse, with whom he was personally acquainted, one Lesourd, had asked to be accommodated with a room in which he could disguise himself, and, he added, that Lesourd stated his motive for the trick to be, that he was employed by the parents of a young man to watch his conduct at the academy, and that the disguise thus adopted afforded him the best means of making his observations.

This was an important discovery. Lesourd encountered it by declaring that the better to punish himself for his substitution of the false heir, and to prepare a triumph for the cause of truth, he had made this preliminary denunciation of his son. This reason appeared unsatisfactory; such conduct was not straightforward or candid. Truth abhors disguises. Still the mystery was undiscovered, and all remained involved in doubt. The most conflicting opinions continued to be entertained, and the best society in Paris sought no other topic for conversation than the merits of the respective claimants to the honors of the illustrious house of Coucy.

We have to recollect that, on the recommendation of the new candidate, the brother-in-law of Lesourd had been appointed agent to the Marquis de Coucy. He had quitted the notarial office in which he had been previously

employed, and for several weeks had discharged the duties
of his new and important function.   He had laboured
with great zeal to establish the claims of the recent
comer, and omitted no opportunity of furthering his cause.
This man, Romain Ladaille, possessed a spaniel, an extremely sagacious and gentle animal.   The Marchioness
became fond of the dog, and allowed it into the apartments of the mansion, where it became a complete pet.
One morning Romain was engaged with the Marquis on
some business of importance.   A manuscript was wanting.
After a slight delay the agent found it, and laying it before
the Marquis, he casually observed, " If I had not found
the paper, Fidele would have relieved us of the difficulty;
he is so intelligent a dog, he finds anything that is lost."
Upon this he paces round the chamber, conceals his portfolio beneath the cushions of a sofa, and then returning
to his seat, calls the dog, pretends to lament the loss of
something valuable, and makes a gesture to Fidele to
search for the missing article.   The animal at once be-
takes himself to the task, as if he fully comprehended a
glance of his master ; he smells about the apartment, and
presently drags the portfolio from its place of concealment.

The Marquis was highly amused ; he called the dog,
and disengaging the portfolio from his teeth, a letter drops
from it.   The superscription is his own name.   He opens
it, and as he reads an indescribable agitation pervades his
frame ; his hand trembles, the blood forsakes his cheeks,
and his strength scarcely suffices to ring the bell.   A
servant appears, and receives an order.   In a few moments
an exempt of the Police enters, and respectfully requires
to know for what purpose he has been summoned.

" To arrest this villain," cries the Marquis, pointing to

his agent; "and to affix your signature to the margin of this letter, which I have just received from his portfolio, and which I must request you to peruse."

The Marchioness having been apprised of some extraordinary discovery having been made, hastens to her husband. "Ah, beloved ¡wife," he says to her, "God has had pity on our misery; the imposture is unveiled. Listen, it is Heaven itself that succours us." And he reads—

" MONSEIGNEUR,

" I am on my death-bed, and at this awful moment, truth is a duty which I owe to you. You have been my benefactor ; I have been reared in your household ; you were bountiful to me on my marriage, and by you I was chosen to nurse your only child. Three years have passed since my husband, induced by some pernicious temptation, besought me to pass our son Pierrot as yours, but I have always refused to commit this crime. Nevertheless, I fear that after my death this guilty design will be persevered in. I therefore apprise you of the sure means of its detection. In his childhood Pierrot fell into the fire, and the accident has left visible marks on his legs and left arm. These scars will serve to show which is your son and which the impostor, in case they should attempt to deceive you on the subject. Your son has not the slightest mark of a burn on any part of his frame. All our neighbours are aware of the accident having occurred to my child. I confide this letter to Romain, my brother, and have enjoined him to deliver it to you. On receiving it, send for my husband, read it to him, and he will renounce his evil project. But for the love of God, and in the requital of the service I now render, pardon my unfortunate husband, and do not abandon my poor Pierrot, my own wretched son.

" I have the honor to be, &c., &c.

" MADELEINE LADAILLE *femme* LESOURD."

Gonesse, May 22nd, 1712.

Beyond this letter there was nothing required to prove the fraud of Lesourd and his brother-in-law. The latter fell on his knees before the Marquis, beseeching mercy, and throwing on his brother-in-law all the odium of the infamous design in which, he said, the threats of Lesourd had compelled him to participate. Lesourd, when brought forward, wished to exculpate himself by attributing to Romain the entire plan and subsequent furtherance of the iniquitous affair. Thus, these two scoundrels aggravated still more their detestable guilt. They finished by declaring that the youthful Pierrot was their willing accomplice.

The police, by some inquiries, succeeded in demonstrating that the two brothers-in-law were equally willing to promote their nefarious scheme. Justice had some vindication. Lesourd and Romain were sent to the galleys, but the Marchioness interceded for Pierrot. Some money was given to him, and he went to America. There, this detestable fellow continued to call himself the Count de Coucy.

The spaniel Fidele became the cherished pet of the true count; Romain never could account how the letter of his sister, which he treasured carefully as the means of domineering over his nephew in case his attempt on the title of de Coucy should prove successful, had been taken from a casket in which he had placed it, as a most important possession ; how it was transferred to the portfolio he could never conjecture. But the police received, in the course of their investigations, some statements from which they were led to believe that Romain was occasionally a somnambulist.

DUMAS.

Dumas, in the construction of the plots of some of his novels, seems to have availed himself of facts derived from the Police Memoirs, over which, however, he spreads a very ample drapery of fiction. In "The Three Musketeers" he ascribes to a Gascon gentleman, d'Artagnan, a clearness of perception, a promptitude of action, and a personal intrepidity which were really exhibited by one who was born much nearer to the Shannon than to the Garonne, and who was a confidential attendant in the household of the Duke of Buckingham, and is mentioned by Bois-Robert, one of Richelieu's spies, in the following terms :—

" I shall first state to his Eminence, that chance having enabled me again to meet an Irishman whom I had known in Paris, when he was pursuing his studies ; I then rendered him some service, and he, from that moment, manifested to me the most ardent gratitude. On leaving Paris, he proceeded to England, where, very luckily, he became the valet-de-chambre of his grace the Duke of Buckingham. Although the emoluments of that situation must be considerable, Patrick O'Reilly (which is the name of this Irishman) is always without a halfpenny. In this respect he imitates his noble master. I have received him kindly whenever he came to see me ; and such is my zeal in the service of Monseigneur, that I have submitted to associate with this valet, hoping to obtain some useful information respecting his master. It was also for this purpose that I advanced him some money."

Dumas does not entirely ignore the name of Patrick O'Reilly, but he gives it to a jeweller, whom he mentions as the wealthiest and most skilful of all then following that trade in London. In his novel of the Count of Monte Cristo, he introduces the hero as the chief officer of a fine merchant ship. It would have been more true, though perhaps rather vulgar, to have presented to his readers, a shoemaker, of the description called chamber masters, whose name was François Picaud, and who, through motives of jealousy or envy, was represented to Savary, duc de Rovigo, as an agent or spy for the English and the royalists of La Vendee.   He was imprisoned, his intended marriage having been prevented by his arrest, and continued incarcerated at Fenestrelle from 1807 to 1814.   In the prison he was appropriated as a personal attendant to a Milanese ecclesiastic, of high rank, who died in January, 1814, having confided to Picaud full information as to his immense property, and the places where the documents necessary to it were to be found. He also gave him a brief testamentary grant of all he possessed or was entitled to.   There was a very great value accruing to the legatee in diamonds and hidden coin, but that treasure was in the vicinity of Milan, and the statements respecting the Chateau d'If, and the island of Monte Cristo, were complete fictions.

As to the last novel to which I have adverted, I am tempted into finding very great fault with one of its incidents, which appears most unnatural, and therefore most improbable.   I refer to the scene between the ruined merchant and his son, in which a father acknowledges his intention to commit suicide, and ultimately persuades his son to acquiesce in such a crime ; nay, even to use to his parent, with the pistols lying before him prepared for the catastrophe, the expression, " Die in peace, my father, I will live."   This is, I repeat, unnatural and improbable. The English are said to be a suicidal people, amongst whom a November day produces throat-cutting, pistoling, and poisoning ; but in England was there ever an instance of suicide being the subject of consultation between parent and child ?   Oh ! never ; nor do we believe that such could appear to our continental neighbours more consistent with the state and feelings of society amongst them than it is amongst ourselves.

A THREATENED SUICIDE.

I may mention, in reference to suicidal attempts, that I witnessed what I at first considered a dreadful attempt on the part of a Frenchman to terminate his existence before some hundreds of spectators, and in the immediate presence of a handsome young woman, whose frigid indifference to his ardent passion for her he loudly declared had rendered his life insupportable. It was during my visit to Paris in 1853, and occurred on a Sunday, in the grounds adjoining the palace of St. Cloud, where there were numerous tables occupied fully by parties enjoying the viands and wine, beer, or coffee, procured from two restaurants, which were also well supplied with the choicest confections. The demented lover, who was very well-looking, and seemed to be about five and twenty years of age, declared, unless Mademoiselle would agree to marry him in the ensuing week, he was determined to die there, and shed his blood at her feet. She appeared worse than indifferent to his entreaties and to the fatal intentions which he expressed, for she laughed most heartlessly at his expressions of hopeless despair. Leaving the table, he threw an overcoat across his arm, and hurried to one of the restaurants, from which he very quickly returned, and made a final demand that Mademoiselle should decide his fate. She continued inexorable, and I felt great surprise that none of those who heard him interfered either by expostulation or actual restraint. With frantic gesticulations he drew a pocket-pistol from under the folds of his overcoat, and thrust it into his mouth. It produced, however, no explosion. The pistol gave way between his closing teeth, and the barrel was soon lodged in his stomach. The apparently deadly weapon was made of chocolate, of which the obdurate damsel, still laughing, insisted on getting a portion.

CHAPTER XXV.

DARGAN'S EXHIBITION—A BELL AND KNOCKER—
LORD GOUGH—FATHER PECHERINE'S CASE—
ASSAULTS AND THEFTS—THE CITY MILITIA—
A SCALD QUICKLY CURED—SAILORS LEAVING
THEIR SHIP.

I RETURNED to Dublin in 1853, on the 10th of May, and
had the pleasure of witnessing the opening of the Great
Industrial Exhibition in Merrion Square on the 12th. It
was a great success, and caused a very considerable influx
of visiters to Dublin, not merely from other parts of the
United Kingdom, but also from the continent of Europe,
and even more distant regions. It is unnecessary to dilate
on the beneficial tendency of such displays to awaken
tastes and excite emulation in reference to artistic productions of beauty or utility, for it is almost universally
acknowledged; but I am convinced that they produce
very salutary effects by bringing each class of society into
the view and under the observation of the others, approxi-
mating without confounding them, requiring no relinquish-
ment of rank or undue familiarity. The building in which
the exhibition was held was erected at the personal expense of William Dargan, and cost £26,000. A statue, on
the pedestal of which " Dargan " is inscribed, now stands

Y

upon the scene of his patriotic liberality. No other inscription is requisite to have his generosity acknowledged and his memory revered by his countrymen. Previous to the opening in 1853, it was suggested in the public press and at the sittings of the committee, that as the inauguration of the English exhibition in 1851 had been accompanied by a prayer for the occasion, offered by a prelate of the highest rank, a similar course should be observed in Dublin. However, the opening here was not attended by any ecclesiastical demonstration, and some few of the spectators considered the omission culpable. At the close of the ceremony, three or four young men passed out at the same time that my brother magistrate, James Magee, and I were leaving. There was no indication as to the religious denomination to which they belonged, but we were greatly amused at the zealous and fervent piety of one who designated the omission of prayer, on such an occasion, as "a d——d shame."

The Dublin Exhibition of 1853 continued open until the end of October, and during that time there was only one charge brought for magisterial investigation from within its limits, and it was preferred before me. There was a portion of the building termed the "Medieval Court," and a man was accused of stealing, in that place, a coat belonging to a person employed on the premises. He confessed his guilt, and I awarded him two months' imprisonment with hard labor for the unlawful possession of the article. This solitary offence would, perhaps, have lapsed from my memory but for the total ignorance of the term "medieval" evinced by the parties concerned, for they all spoke of the transaction as having occurred in the "*middle-evil court.*"

It may appear almost incredible to some of my readers

that, during the erection of the Exhibition building, and
for upwards of five months in which it was resorted to
by thousands, and I may add the comparatively short time
subsequently occupied in taking down the structure and
removing the materials, there was no other infraction of
the law brought under magisterial cognizance than the
petty larceny case which I have mentioned. I hope that
I shall not be considered too discursive if I introduce here
an extraordinary and very gratifying statement of an anterior date. The Great Southern and Western Railway
of Ireland was opened to Carlow in 1846. The splendid
terminus at the King's Bridge and several miles of the
line are in the Dublin Metropolitan Police district. The
works on that portion included very extensive buildings
and deep excavations, and I have been credibly informed
that they cost upwards of fifty thousand pounds. A vast
number of persons were employed, comprising the various
artisans, laborers, (commonly called navvies,) and drivers.
I was in office during the entire time of their operations,
and there was not even one complaint or charge preferred
as arising amongst any class or between individuals.
Mr. Dargan, the contractor, at a festive meeting jocularly
congratulated me "on having a sinecure, as far as regarded
the people at the King's Bridge, where there were no prosecutions required, except the prosecution of the works."
I regret that at the present time such very gratifying
qualities could not be expected to a similar extent in
similar undertakings. Intemperance has become too prevalent, especially amongst the operative portion of the
community, to admit of large numbers being brought
together daily, without occasional, or perhaps frequent
quarrels.

A BELL AND KNOCKER.

There had been in 1852 a contested election for the city of Dublin, and the defeated party, as is usual on such occasions, attributed their failure to the use, on the part of their adversaries, of every unfair stratagem and corrupt inducement.   At the commencement of the Session of Parliament in 1853, it was rumoured that a petition would be lodged to invalidate the return, especially on the grounds of extensive bribery amongst the freemen.   It was alleged that a certain alderman was the confidential treasurer of the funds appropriated for the venal voters, and that a person named BELL had been employed to procure the men and dispense the money.   The alderman was one of my most intimate friends, and I frequently enjoyed his hospitality.   I was also acquainted with several of the other party who were loud in their denunciations of the corruption of which Bell was alleged to have been the instrument.   When I heard them speaking of the sums distributed amongst the freemen, I contented myself by affecting to lament the injustice to which I was individually subjected, that I was a freeman of my native city, and that I might have participated in the distribution to which they referred, were it not for an odious statutable enactment which prohibited a Dublin Police magistrate from exercising the franchise, and realizing its incidental advantages, whilst the English Metropolitan Magistrates were subjected to no such disqualification.   One of my friends who happened to be the editor of a newspaper, remarked that I seemed disposed to treat the recent bribery with levity, and to regard it as mere fun, and I replied that he was not far wrong in his conjecture, and that I would advise him to adopt a similar course.   He asked me to commit my ideas to writing and transmit them to him. I acceded to his request, and he published my communication; but I feel confident that neither publicly nor privately did he divulge the name of its author. No parliamentary petition was presented; and the bountiful treatment of the freemen was only noticed publicly in my poor production of—

THE MAGIC BELL.

My retrospection of that election
    Accords perfection to the magic " Bell,"
Whose notes so soothing were felt each booth in
    Where freemen voted so prompt and well.
That Bell so cheering, our hopes uprearing,
    As Green Street nearing we came to poll,
With *notes* persuasive, soft and adhesive,
    And touch evasive of law's control.

There are joy-bells swinging, and sweetly ringing,
    Their blithe sounds flinging from Christ Church high,
And Father Yore has erected more
    On the Liffey's shore to the Four Courts nigh.
But more sublime than their varied chime
    Of a festal time or a funeral knell,
Was the Bell so soothing, felt every booth in
    Where freemen voted so prompt and well.

From the gifted Prout, we derive no doubt,
    Sweet strains about days of infancy,
When " The bells of Shandon did sound so grand on
    The pleasant waters of the River Lee."
We may search in vain, we'll ne'er meet again
    With a sweeter strain than Moore's " Evening Bell;"
But a Bell more soothing was felt each booth in
    Where freemen voted so prompt and well.

The hermit lowly, whose thoughts are solely
    On subjects holy, delights to hear,
When morn is shining or eve declining,
    Sweet peals combining, his soul to cheer.
From far or near to his raptured ear
    No sound so dear ever reach'd his cell,
Like the Bell so soothing, felt every booth in
    Where freemen voted so prompt and well.

In a few days after the publication of the foregoing lines, I dined at his residence near Salthill, with my friend the alderman, and in the course of the evening he mentioned that Bell was greatly annoyed by such a production, and that he considered it libellous. I asked how could he show that it applied to him. My worthy host said that it could not apply to any other person, and I then remarked that it was not malicious or of an injurious tendency, and that it had been written merely as an attempt at harmless fun. This elicited the question of how I knew in what spirit it had been written, to which I replied, that I had written it myself, intending to be jocose; and that if my verses were not considered worthy of laurel, they certainly did not deserve the application of birch. To this expression I received a contradiction unanimous but good-humored; and it was agreed that if the public whipping of a police magistrate could be effected, it would be an interesting novelty and a general gratification. There were two other aldermen present besides our host, and they repeatedly assured me, even when shaking hands at the conclusion of the entertainment, that they would provide some punishment for my transgression. On the following evening I was at the house of a friend on Merchants' Quay, and when I returned home, after midnight, I found that the knocker of my hall-door had disappeared. My servant stated that two gentlemen had called, one of whom expressed a wish to see me, and on being informed that I was not at home, said that he would write a note in my study and leave it for me. Whilst he was so employed, the other remained in the hall. At their departure the servant did not perceive that the knocker had been abstracted; but at my return I at once observed the loss, and on opening the note, which was written in a hand manifestly disguised, I read the following communication :—

" Mr. Porter is so expert in the fabrication of a Bell, that he may confine himself to ringing without knocking."

Although I felt considerable annoyance at such an unwarrantable trespass, whereby I lost a very handsome and expensive brass knocker, I did not indulge in resentful expressions or state the suspicions which I entertained. The door remained without a knocker, as if I intended to acquiesce in the suggestion of only using a bell. The door had not been injured or defaced, for the knocker had not been wrenched away, but had been unscrewed by the person who remained in the hall whilst the other was penning the note to me. I was repeatedly quizzed, and subjected to mock condolence, but I treated the matter as a practical joke, and ascribed the disappearance of my knocker to aldermanic influence. In about a fortnight I was invited to another dinner at Salthill, and met there the same parties who had been at the previous entertainment. Amongst the various pleasantries of the evening, my knocker was not forgotten, and my health was drank, accompanied by what I considered a bantering wish for the restitution of the brazen appendage to my hall-door. On my return home I was surprised to find the door furnished with a knocker, which I soon recognized as my own. It appeared that almost immediately after I had left home, a man came to my house, stating that I had ordered the article at Bryan's ironmongery warehouse in Bride Street, and he proceeded to fix it on. I have never since that time meddled with any " Bell," and my door has not been interfered with in any disagreeable manner.

LORD GOUGH.

About the end of 1853, I was for a few weeks engaged in magisterial duties at Kingstown, and on one occasion I observed the late Viscount Gough entering the police-court, and taking a seat in the part to which the public were indiscriminately admitted. There was some case pending, at the hearing of which he wished to be present, and I immediately requested his Lordship to honor me by occupying a seat beside me, adding that I could not consent to a person of his high rank and illustrious character remaining in any position inferior to my own. He declined my proposal, but consented to take a chair between the bench and the right-hand side of the court. His chair was rather close to the grate, which was full of fuel, only a few minutes previously kindled. The court was crowded, and soon became very warm, but his Lordship's proximity to the grate almost immediately compelled him to change his position. Apologizing for the interruption, he asked me to direct the office constable to remove his chair to the left side of the court, and to place it near a window. Acceding at once to the request of the noble, illustrious, and worthy old warrior, I ordered his seat to be moved to the place which he preferred, adding, that I hoped the gentlemen of the press would report the remarkable fact, that Lord Gough retreated from the fire of the police, although he never had shrank from any other fire, however hot it might have been. A member of his family told me, in a few days after, that his Lordship considered my observation as most complimentary and gratifying.

FATHER PECHERINE'S CASE.

In the discharge of my magisterial duties at Kingstown, I had to dispose of a charge against a Roman Catholic clergyman named Pecherine, for publicly burning a copy of the Bible. The accused party was a foreigner, who had become a member of the order of Redemptorists, and joined a number of that community in holding "a mission" at Kingstown, in November, 1855.

He preached very frequently to numerous congregations, and excited great admiration and even surprise by the fluency of his language and correctness of diction. Finding that many books and tracts had been distributed, in Kingstown and its vincinity, containing doctrines or controversial arguments of which he and his religious associates disapproved, he exhorted his hearers to bring all such publications to him, and having received a considerable quantity, he burned them in a large fire lighted within the precincts of the church where the mission was held, and between the building and the exterior railing. It was alleged that amongst the articles thus consumed, there was a copy of the Scriptures. A prosecution was instituted before me, which was met by a denial that any perfect copy of the Bible had been burned; and that if even a portion of one had been thus destroyed, it was by mere mischance, and without his knowledge, intention, or approval. The proceedings before me produced intense excitement, and a great manifestation, especially amongst the humbler classes, of the asperities usually incident to indications of religious differences. I sent the case to trial at the ensuing commission of *Oyer et Terminer* for the County of Dublin, and the result was an acquittal; but I refer to the occasion as having produced some very striking instances of the most inconsiderate and rash violence, committed without any provocation whatever on the part of those assailed, and in the supposition that they had been concerned in a proceeding with which they were totally unconnected.

ASSAULTS AND THEFTS.

Previous to the investigation of the complaints preferred on summons and information, the custody cases were, as usual, disposed of, and I had nine prisoners brought before me for having been drunk on the public thoroughfare. Some had been quiet and submissive, and they were fined one shilling each. Others who had been noisy or disorderly had fines of half-a-crown or a crown inflicted. Amongst the former was a newsboy, of about nineteen years of age, who had only one hand. Having paid his fine, he was liberated, and passed out into George's Street, where a crowd had collected to get the earliest intelligence as to the progress and result of Father Pecherine's case. When the newsboy appeared a girl in the crowd exclaimed, " There's the horrid villain that is just after swearing against the priest." Immediately he was seized, violently beaten, and dashed through a large plate-glass window in the front of a shop. Some police constables were close at hand, and saw the sudden attack on the poor lad. They rushed forward and arrested four men who had been prominent in assaulting the newsboy, and one of them was fully identified as the person who had first laid hands on him and incited the others. I do not recollect the names of the delinquents, nor is it material to the narrative that I should, but when I asked if they had any defence, or if they wished to make any statement, the ringleader addressed me to the following effect—

" I thought, your worship, that he was after swearing against the priest, or I wouldn't have laid a finger on him. It was all a mistake, and we never intended to break the shop window. Indeed he broke that himself trying to get away. Moreover, if what was done was wrong, I have been well punished for it already."

I immediately designated the excuse alleged by the prisoner as an aggravation of his offence, for if the person attacked had been a witness, the violence used towards him tended to defeat public justice, and to substitute might for right, making anarchy predominant. I added that I did not understand the allegation of the prisoner, that he had been already punished for his gross misconduct, and I wished him to explain.

" Your worship," he replied, " I am a carpenter, and I was going to buy some timber for repairs to a house at Sandycove. I had two sovereigns and a half in a little leather purse in my waistcoat pocket. As soon as I was brought into the police-station, I missed the money, and I have no doubt but my pockets were picked in the crowd, and during the confusion."

Wishing to take a short interval for considering whether I should adjudicate summarily, or send the case for trial at the Quarter Sessions, I postponed it for a week, urging the police to detect, if possible, the girl who had caused the tumult and assault, and I allowed the prisoners to be discharged from custody on giving ample bail for their re-appearance, and proceeded to take the evidence adduced on the summons against the priest. When the business of the day was nearly concluded, two women were brought in, having been taken in the fact of assaulting a young woman at the market, which, at the time, was rather crowded. The violence inflicted was very severe, and it appeared that as the injured party was approaching the place where the others were standing, a girl, described as being about twenty years of age, exclaimed, "Here she comes, the ———— ———— that has been swearing Father Pecherine's life away." Immediately a scene similar to the one in the morning was acted by female performers, the foremost being a large powerful woman, the wife of a publican in a neighbouring village. The supposed witness had been struck, kicked, and scratched; her hair pulled, and her clothes torn, and the similarity of the two zealous manifestations was fully evinced by the publican's wife, declaring that "she thought" the suffering party had been swearing against the priest, and she bitterly deplored the loss of three pounds of which her pocket had been picked in the "scrimmage." Two other women were subsequently arrested who *thought* too hastily and acted too violently, but the inciter had managed to elude detection, and it was believed that immediately after her second exploit, she had hurried off to the railway and gone up to Dublin with her booty. I dealt summarily with the female prisoners, as the young woman whom they attacked was obliged to leave immediately for Manchester, where she had procured some engagement as a domestic. I inflicted the very trifling penalty of sixpence on each delinquent for the assault, but I supplemented each conviction with two pounds costs to the party assailed. This decision, in reference to the costs, was extremely repugnant to the feelings of those against whom it was awarded. It was at once pronounced to be hard, and they declared their total inability to pay so much for a "little mistake," and their disapproval of my judgment was greatly augmented by the alternative which was left to their option of two months' imprisonment with hard labor.

The fines and costs were almost immediately paid, and I believe they were defrayed by a subscription. On the newsboy's case being resumed, he declined all further prosecution, and declared that he had been sufficiently remunerated. The girl who had incited the attacks was detected in the act of picking a pocket in a place of worship at Kingstown, about a fortnight after the occurrence which I have detailed. She was not brought before me, but having been committed for trial by Mr. Wyse, her delinquencies procured her "a complete retirement from business" for seven years. She was not an unthrifty thief, for it appeared at her trial that a savings' bank book was found on searching her lodgings, in which £37 were entered to her credit. It occurs to me that the name of this culprit was Catherine Gaffney. Dishonesty is very seldom associated with frugality. I have heard, during my magisterial experience, of only two instances of the union of such tendencies. I have already mentioned one. The other was a man named John Donohoe, a shop porter in the employment of the late Alderman Butler, in Christ Church Place. He was convicted, in February, 1853, of five distinct larcenies on his master's premises; and whilst he was robbing on every possible opportunity, he had £64 in a savings' bank.

THE CITY MILITIA.

At the commencement of the Crimean War, the militia regiments of the United Kingdom were embodied. The City of Dublin Light Infantry and Artillery and the County regiment were almost entirely raised in the metropolitan district. Recruiting for the line was also very briskly pursued here, and I can safely and deliberately state, that the military enrolments relieved our district of a great number of loose characters, whose abstraction was very salutary to our community. When the city militia became sufficiently strong for active service, they were embarked at Kingstown for Liverpool in a large steamer. I was on the jetty, and I do not think the English language could supply any opprobrious term that was not loudly ventilated in reference to me. The copious application of every variety of invective was really amusing to me, and it was only noticed by a frequent smile or an occasional laugh. It was remarked by one, that "if the d——l didn't take owld Porter, we might as well be without a d——l at all;" but another expressed his opinion, "that the d——l was in no hurry to grip the owld rascal, as he was certain to get him at last." I am sure, however, that if another police magistrate had been also present, he would have been considered fully entitled to participate equally in the compliments which I monopolized, and which I only notice in the hope that some remarks which I intend to submit to my readers in a subsequent page may be considered interesting, and perhaps, I may add, important.

A SCALD QUICKLY CURED.

An infantry regiment of the line was embarked at Kingstown, in a very capacious steamer, I believe the Medusa, for Gibraltar or Malta. There was a large quantity of baggage which the men were actively engaged in conveying on board and stowing away. I was sauntering on the jetty when, at one o'clock, they were directed " to knock off for dinner." The meal was served on deck, and consisted of soup, bread, and meat, and the recipients availed themselves of every position in which they could speedily enjoy their repast. The circular seat around the window on the quarter-deck was fully occupied. The soup was brought up in large tin basins, and the bread was amply supplied, ready cut, from wicker baskets. One of the men who occupied the circular seat, seeing a basket of bread placed almost within his reach, stood up, advanced about a yard, and having procured what he required, stepped backward to resume his place. Meanwhile, one of the attendants had placed a large vessel of soup on the portion of the bench apparently vacant, and the soldier sat down in it. With a loud scream, indicative of acute pain, he rushed to the tafferel, and plunged into the sea. He was immediately rescued from the risk of drowning, and having been brought on board, was sent below for medical treatment, and to get his wet clothes changed. I saw him on deck in the course of the afternoon, and he stated that he was suffering very little, and that he would be " all right" very soon. Unless the temperature of the soup was below scalding heat, the instantaneous application of the cold water, although of a saline character, must have been extremely efficacious.

SAILORS LEAVING THEIR SHIP.

A large ship was quartered to convey the head-quarters of the 11th hussars from Kingstown to Balaklava. A considerable number of horses were embarked, and there were slings fastened to the roof and passing under each animal's body, which supported him whilst sleeping, but without allowing him to lie down. All arrangements for sailing had been completed. A steamer was provided to tow the vessel to the outside of the Kish Bank, and the wind was as favorable as possible for proceeding down the Channel. The captain announced, about ten o'clock, a.m., that he would leave at noon, whereupon three of his crew asked him to defer his departure until the next day, and to allow them to spend the intermediate time ashore. On his refusal, they required him to hoist a signal, which, to the best of my recollection, was *a blue shirt*, at the fore-top, and he complied with their demand, inasmuch as, according to his statement to me, his refusal would subject him to most severe penal consequences. The signal denoted that there were persons on board willing to serve in the Royal Navy; and as soon as it was displayed, a lieutenant who was stationed at Kingstown, on the duty of naval recruiting, went on board, and was informed by the three sailors that they were desirous of joining his service. He acceded to their application, and the captain found himself unable to put to sea for want of sufficient hands, and without any expectation of being able to supply the deficiency for some days. In this emergency, he applied to me to have the men treated as wilful absconders, and to send them back to the ship. I had a communication with the lieutenant, whose name, I think, was Henderson; and whilst he fully admitted the hardship of which the captain complained, he declared that his orders were so stringently imperative that he could exercise no discretion, and had no alternative course to adopt. I observed that by retaining the men there would be a serious injury inflicted by one department of the public service on another, and that it amounted to military exertion being paralyzed by naval interference. He agreed with me as to the injurious effect of having the ship detained, but declared that he was unable to prevent it. I said that under the circumstances, I was inclined to have the men taken and sent back to the vessel from which they had virtually absconded. To this he replied, that he would offer no resistance to the execution of any warrant or order that I might issue, but that he would report the proceeding to the Admiralty. Thereupon, I suggested to the captain to have the ship taken from alongside the jetty to the centre of the harbour, and to stop any further communication with the shore. This was immediately done, and I then sent a warrant for the seamen, and had them conveyed on board, having previously advised them to go of their own accord, which they declined doing, with the intimation that if they ever returned to Ireland, they would smash every bone in my body, even if they were to be hanged the next minute for killing such a d——d old scoundrel. When they arrived at the ship, they told the captain that they would not do any duty, to which he replied that, whilst they refused to work, they need not expect to get any rations. The rest of the crew disapproved of their conduct, and I believe that they soon became reconciled to a resumption of duty. The lieutenant informed me, in a few days after the transaction, that he had fully reported the circumstances to the Admiralty, and that they approved of the course I had adopted, and exonerated him from any censure. I was subsequently informed by him, that on the arrival of the ship at Balaklava, she was boarded by a party from the flag-ship, and the officer in command produced the documents incident to the enlistment of the three men at Kingstown, and claimed them as belonging to the naval service. They had, however, the advantage of being allowed their pay, as seamen in the Queen's service, from the date of their enrolment at Kingstown, and they also had their wages from the vessel in which they had been employed during the voyage to the Crimea.

z

None of them have returned as yet to realize their fearful intention on him whom they designated "a d——d old scoundrel;" and he never entertained the slightest apprehensions of any violent commentary on the course he adopted towards them.

CHAPTER XXVI.

EFFECTS OF ENLISTMENT——MARTIAL TENDENCIES——
THE SHE BARRACKS——THE DUBLIN GARRISON——
AN ARTILLERY AMAZON——A COLONEL OF DRA-
GOONS——DONNYBROOK FAIR——THE LIQUOR
TRAFFIC.

IN one of the preceding pages I stated that "the military enrolments relieved our district of a great number of loose characters, whose abstraction was very salutary to our community." I subsequently expressed an intention to submit to my readers "some remarks that might be considered interesting, and perhaps important."

It is unnecessary to particularise the numerous varieties of objectionable tendencies and habits, any of which will be considered sufficient to constitute the person exhibiting them "an undoubted scamp." In Dublin and its suburban districts, society has never been free from the evils incident to the existence of such disreputable characters; but I fully believe that we are not more tainted by them than any other part of the United Kingdom of equal extent and population. The three regiments of militia embodied at the commencement of the Crimean war relieved us of some hundreds of loose, disorderly, or dishonest fellows, the riddance of whom produced a very desirable decrease in the custody cases of our police-courts. However, at the termination of the war, those regiments were brought back, and disembodied in the locality where they had been raised; and many persons might reasonably expect very disagreeable and injurious results from the return of those whose departure was regarded as a happy riddance by the community from which they had been abstracted. But very few instances occurred of the discharged militia-men relapsing into disreputable habits and criminal practices. Military service had produced a great and most desirable reformatory effect. Supervision, strict without unnecessary severity, with the adjuncts of regular and wholesome diet, comfortable clothing and personal cleanliness, emulation in the efficient discharge of duty, and the incitements arising from the preference accorded in various minor appointments and employments to the well-conducted soldier—all these, together with a change from the scene of previous improprieties and disreputable associations, strongly tended to generate a desire for improvement, and the acquisition of a new character. Similar results were observable in reference to the last enrolment and subsequent disembodiment of those regiments consequent on the outbreak and suppression of the Indian mutiny. I wrote to the late Lord Herbert of Lea, then Mr. Sydney Herbert, and Secretary of State for War, in reference to the reformatory results, which I attributed to military influence. He read my letter in the House of Commons when moving the army estimates, and excited much laughter by stating that he did not think it expedient to mention the name of the writer or the regiments to which the communication referred.

My eldest son was a lieutenant in the County of Dublin Militia, which, soon after being embodied, was stationed at Waterford. One morning he was crossing the barrack yard from his quarters, to serve on a regimental court-martial, before which some disorderly or insubordinate characters were to be brought, when he was accosted by the wife of one of the delinquents. She earnestly besought him not to be very severe on "poor Larry," and that it would be a hardship if he got worse treatment in Waterford than he'd get in Dublin for a little spree. She added, "The owld gentleman, your father, long life to him, never put the poor fellow up for more than a week at a time."

MARTIAL TENDENCIES.

During the period of my magisterial duty, I almost invariably discharged the afternoon business, by an arrangement with my colleagues, which tended to their convenience and mine. The attestations of recruits were very seldom taken in the morning, and consequently they were generally made before me. At the commencement of the Crimean war, recruiting was very rife, and I was frequently appealed to by the recruit as to the particular place in which the regiment for which he was enlisted was stationed, inasmuch as he had bargained to be sent "where the fighting was going on." This desire could not be attributed to any excitement arising from sudden caprice or whim, or from indulgence in liquor, for the attestation was never administered until twenty-four hours had elapsed after enlisting, and unless the recruit appeared perfectly sober, and aware of the responsibility which, with his own free will, he was required to assume.

There was a man named Roger Tobin, who lived somewhere about the classic locality of Stoneybatter. He appeared to be about twenty-five years of age, tall, strong, intelligent, healthy, and handsome. There were at least a dozen public-houses which the recruiting sergeants frequently visited at the time of the Crimean campaign, being then in quest of the martial spirits to whom pay, booty, promotion, and military glory were promised as certain acquisitions, all considerations of danger or death being left unmentioned and ignored as improbable or impossible. Roger would enter one of these houses, having previously ascertained that the sergeant had not yet arrived, and he would locate himself in a chair or on a bench close to a table, and order some moderate refreshment. He manifested an intense anxiety as to the most recent news from the seat of war, and generally succeeded in making the proceedings of our army the subject of conversation amongst the persons present. When the collector of future heroes appeared, he was sure to be greeted by Roger with the warmest wishes for his success in providing gallant hearts and strong hands to repel the encroachments of Russia. The poor Poles would be commiserated, and our brave French allies eulogized. Every topic calculated to excite martial feelings would be adverted to by the enthusiastic Roger. Such expressions would naturally lead the sergeant to conclude that he might calculate on one recruit accompanying him back to barracks, and his request or suggestion of immediate enlistment met with a ready acquiescence. The magic shilling having been paid, the new recruit would spend it in an additional libation, and address an earnest exhortation to any young fellows then present to follow his example. The sergeant would not be slow in giving a further advance, the application of which to convivial purposes might procure him two or three additional adherents. Ten shillings, or perhaps more, having been joyously spent, Roger was informed that he was to accompany the sergeant, and any others who had joined, and receive accommodation in the barrack, from whence he would be brought next day to the police-court for attestation. Promptly acceding to this direction, and raising his fine manly figure, he left the table, and enabled the disgusted sergeant to perceive that his recruit was club-footed, and totally incapable of ever being put in marching order. How the expenses incurred were afterwards liquidated, whether the sergeant was the loser, or the liability devolved on the recruiting department, I am unable to state, but I fully believe that Roger repeated the same trick on many occasions. It would seem that each serjeant did not wish to be the last victim, and consequently none of them disclosed the deception to the new comers, or to those in other parts of the metropolitan district. Roger's game was spoiled by a warning communicated to the recruiting stations from the police.

THE SHE BARRACKS.

When the Richmond Barracks were built at Golden Bridge, they were intended to afford ample accommodation for more than an entire regiment. There were also barracks at Island Bridge, and the distance between both was about half a mile. The former were generally occupied by infantry, and the latter by artillery. A person in the vicinity had a large building constructed through a speculative motive of a very extraordinary kind. He was aware that soldiers marrying without leave, or whose wives were dishonest, turbulent, quarrelsome, slovenly, or habitually intemperate, were not allowed to bring such objectionable characters into the regimental quarters. He consequently calculated that he would find no difficulty in having his premises occupied by tenants, to whose habits and morals he attached no importance, provided they paid the rent, and his expectations were not disappointed. His apartments were no sooner vacated by the incorrigible termagants of one regiment, than a succession of vixens was supplied from another to fill the unedifying edifice. The proprietor had not appropriated any particular name to the building, but it became speedily known in the district under the designation of "The She Barracks." In the southern division of the police district, there were five extensive military barracks, and I can unhesitatingly declare, that the cases supplied for police intervention or magisterial decision from them all, were completely outnumbered by those derived from the compartively diminutive limits of the structure designed for the use and associated with the name of the softer sex. The details of the various charges and summonses in which inmates of these premises were compromised, would neither be instructive nor amusing, but I cannot ever forget a case in which two women, the wives of artillerymen, appeared, on summons and cross-summons, to swear against each other to the greatest extent of culpability. Each of them imputed to her adversary the inclination and avowed intention to commit every offence of a violent or malicious description, and neither came unprovided with witnesses ready to surmount the most elevated pinnacles of exaggeration. Whilst this auction of swearing was in progress, the husbands of the two inmates of the She Barracks were seated together, quietly listening to the proceedings, apparently on very friendly terms with each other, and not evincing any anxiety for the success of their respective consorts. At the close, I directed the informations of the parties to be engrossed, and stated that I would commit both for a month, unless they respectively found a surety in five pounds for their future good behaviour. I added, that as they were strangers, I did not suppose they could easily find bail amongst their neighbours, and that I was satisfied to take the husband of each as a surety for his wife. Immediately I was addressed by one of the artillerymen to the following purport :—

" May it please your honor, I'm only a private soldier, and where would I get five pounds in a day or two, when they begin again. Besides, if I was a fit bail, I would sooner be bound for his wife's behaviour than for my own wife's. 'Tis best to let them go." Then turning to his comrade, he added, " Come, Sam, we're likely to have a quiet month while they're both up."

Nevertheless, he was disappointed, for the two viragoes, acting on the suggestion of an attorney who had been engaged in the case, came almost immediately to terms, and neither of them would make an information. They were consequently liberated, and instead of having a quiet month, I am sure that the artillerymen had, during that time, to undergo some heavy domestic bombardments.

THE DUBLIN GARRISON.

The regular military establishments in our district produced very few cases for decision by the civil authorities. I am not able to state the exact strength of the Dublin garrison, but I believe that it is the largest in the United Kingdom, and that the seven barracks never contain less than five thousand men of all ranks and arms. Since the commencement of the present century, this city has had quartered within its limits or immediate suburbs every regular regiment in the service, and large bodies of militia. In 1813, a private dragoon named Tuite deserted, and on a Sunday morning stopped a gentleman named Goulding on South Circular Road, near Portobello, for the purpose of robbing him. The offence had a fatal conclusion, for Goulding was shot through the heart, and the murderer was apprehended and executed. After his conviction he acknowledged his guilt, but declared that he intended only to rob, and that the discharge of the pistol was occasioned by his trepidation. In 1818, a corporal named Alliard was indicted for murdering a woman named Flood, in a cellar in Thomas Street, and he was acquitted. These two cases constituted all the capital charges preferred against soldiers before civil tribunals in our district from 1800 to the present time. During my magistrature of upwards of twenty years' duration, I had to send two private soldiers for trial on a charge of passing base coin, and one of them was convicted. I had no cognizance or knowledge of offences purely military as to their nature or number. Whenever a soldier was found on a public thoroughfare in a state of intoxication, he was taken by the police, and when sober, sent by magisterial order to the officer commanding at his quarters; but the number of such captures was very inconsiderable. Indeed if the entire population of the district had been strictly similar to the military in their habits and conduct, my office would have been almost a sinecure.

AN ARTILLERY AMAZON.

There was an affair brought under my cognizance about seven years previous to my retirement, of which I have a perfect recollection, and in which, I am free to confess, I busied myself beyond my magisterial duties for mere amusement. An artillery soldier strolled into town from his barracks at Portobello, and having indulged freely in liquor, betook himself to a house in Bow Lane, off Mercer

Street, about ten o'clock at night. He was unable to return to his quarters, and having been undressed, was placed in bed to sleep off his intoxication. The inmates of the house were by no means of a reputable description, and amongst them was a female unusually tall in stature, and with proportional amplitude of figure. In a sudden whim, she arrayed herself in the uniform of the sleeping soldier, and set out on a nocturnal promenade, to the infinite amusement of her associates, by some of whom she was accompanied. Their obstreperous merriment attracted the attention of the police, and eventuated in the arrest of the amazon. On my arrival at the police-court on the following morning, I was apprised of the extraordinary charge which awaited my investigation; and I immediately communicated with a gentleman with whom I was personally acquainted, and who was in a high position connected with the Ordnance Office. He came to me, and we arranged that I should not dispose of the case in the police-court until the circumstances were made known to the military authorities at Portobello. When the woman was brought before me, I directed a sergeant of police to take her in a covered vehicle to the barrack, and, in the meantime, the artillery man was captured in Bow Lane by a party sent from the barracks; and as his own attire was not forthcoming, he was brought away in a cab, and with habiliments not altogether suitable to his sex or his station. The heroine was submitted to some of the women, who divested her of the martial appearance she had assumed, and transferred the garments to two non-commissioned officers, who gave in return the clothes or improvised vestments that covered the soldier during his return to barracks. I did not inflict any further punishment on the woman, and I believe that the artillery man was not severely treated; but I was informed by some of his officers that he was made the object of the most persistent banter and ridicule amongst his comrades, who accorded him the soubriquet of "Mary Anne." I believe, indeed, that severe corporal punishment inflicted on his delinquency would not have deterred the other soldiers from the commission of a similar error so effectually as the jests and sarcasms supplied from amongst themselves, and suggested by the appearance of one who had returned from his roving so very unsuitably.

A COLONEL OF DRAGOONS.

Before I pass from the recollections and favorable impressions produced by the almost uniform good conduct of the gallant members of our garrison, I am disposed to give my readers a short narrative, without any other comment than the expression of an opinion that it is one of the many instances in which fact appears stranger than fiction. A lady, the widow of a medical officer, having presented a memorial soliciting a commission for her son, received a reply appointing him to a regiment in one of our most distant colonies, and involving the necessity of his speedy departure from this country. At her request I interested myself to procure for him an outfit, promptly supplied, of excellent quality and of very reasonable price. It was furnished by Buckmaster, Malyn, and Co., of Dawson Street, who have also an extensive establishment in London. I had occasion to call two or three times during the execution of the order, and I was making one of those visits when two officers entered. On seeing them, Mr. Malyn said to me, " This colonel is a most extraordinary man; when he is gone I shall tell you why I say so." The officers were in the uniform of a heavy dragoon regiment; one was the lieutenant-colonel, the other was the adjutant. The former was in face and figure such a man as I would consider that no painter or statuary would decline to accept as a faultless model for a splendid artistic production. His communication was very brief, but he appeared to be intelligent and courteous. When he departed, Mr. Malyn told me that he remembered him working on their shopboard, as a tailor, at their house in New Burlington Street, London; that he knew his business perfectly, being skilful, sober, and industrious. Nevertheless, he disliked such a sedentary occupation, and being fond of equestrian exercise, enlisted in the dragoons. Having entered the service, his conduct was such as gained the approbation of his superiors, and he soon attained the rank of sergeant. In active service he evinced patience, promptitude, and courage; and the adjutancy having become vacant he was appointed to it, with a concomitant commission. Being thus entitled to be received in society as an officer and a gentleman, he gained respect and esteem in his new position, and also succeeded in marrying a lady possessed of a very ample fortune, by which he was enabled to expedite promotion whenever it could be acquired by purchase. His success would seem to have resulted from persistent good conduct, winning and retaining the favorable opinions of all who could materially aid his advancement. The most imaginative of our romance writers would certainly shrink from presenting for our perusal the ideal descent of a field-officer's epaulets upon the shoulders of a journeyman tailor.

DONNYBROOK FAIR.

I have to notice an event which occurred in 1855, and was productive of most salutary results, not merely to the suburb in which it was effected, but to the entire city and county of Dublin; I mean the abolition or suppression of Donnybrook Fair. This excellent proceeding was effected at the instance and mainly by the exertions of Alderman Joseph Boyce, who was Lord Mayor of Dublin in the last-mentioned year. It would be almost impossible to describe the scenes of drunkenness, violence, gambling, and gross indecency that characterized an entire week in the month of August, every year whilst " The Brook " afforded its immoral attractions, causing our prisons to be immediately crowded with loose, disorderly, or dishonest characters, so as to resemble hospitals in a locality suddenly visited by an epidemic or contagious distemper. I do not believe that, for many years previous to its suppression, Donny-brook Fair was ever held without being the direct or indirect cause of a life or lives being lost. It lasted for a week ; and the greatest intemperance and violence seemed to be specially displayed on the day known as " the Walk-ing Sunday." I visited the fair on several occasions in my days of boyhood, and I can recollect some sad accidents in which lives were lost or limbs fractured by vehicles having been driven furiously by drunken " jarveys." I have seen the body of a female taken out of a mill-race close to the fair green, into which she had fallen in a state of intoxica-tion. I witnessed a very furious encounter on the bridge between coal-porters and some other class of combatants, in which a man was thrown over the battlement and killed by the fall; but the worst experience that I had of Donnybrook was in 1820, when an amiable and most inoffensive young gentleman, named James Rogerson, was walking beside me through the main street of the village, about eight o'clock in the evening, and was struck in the head by a large stone thrown at another person. He was felled by the blow, and was raised in a state of insensibility. After he had revived a little, I took him in a covered car to his father's residence in William Street, where he died in a few days from the effects of the injury, and the perpetrator of the fatal assault was never made amenable for the offence. From the time when I attained the police magistracy in 1841 until 1855, I had to deal with an ample share of the charges and summonses arising from the annual nuisance of Donnybrook Fair; and I fully agreed with my colleagues in considering such duties as "moral scavenging;" and just as pedestrians might apologise for mud-covered feet or bespattered garments being unavoidable in filthy thoroughfares, so the delinquencies arising from the various evil excitements abundantly offered in the locality where they occurred, were almost invariably imputed to the offender having unfortunately gone to "The Brook." I must admit that in disposing of drunken or disorderly cases, I was often influenced by the consideration that when such an annual abomination was tolerated in a civilized community, it was a ground for slightly mitigating the punishments incurred by yielding to its abundant temptations.

In the early pages of these reminiscences I mentioned that a Lord Lieutenant of Ireland had dined in a tent at Donnybrook Fair. I have heard doubts expressed as to the correctness of such a statement. I now reiterate it, adding that it occurred in 1808, in the viceroyalty of the Duke of Richmond. It was noticed in several newspapers of the time, but not with the slightest expression of disapproval. It was almost an established custom for the Lord Mayor and Sheriffs, with many of the aldermen and common council, to dine at the fair, but their festivities were enjoyed in a house. The place was then in the ·city of Dublin, but it has since, along with a large adjoining district, been added to the county of Dublin as regards any civil or criminal jurisdiction, but the parliamentary franchises are available in the city, although the district forms no portion of it, and possesses no municipal privileges whatever. This arrangement, or perhaps it might be termed "derangement," occurred in 1832. I shall not digress into any remarks on local changes of a political nature, but resume my recollections of the fair now so properly abolished.

Almost every tent displayed the proprietor's name, and generally the place of his residence, to induce visiters, from the same direction, to give him a preference. Colored signs were frequently exhibited, which at night became transparencies by a lamp being placed behind each. On one might be seen the representation of a fellow apparently dancing with a young female, whilst underneath was inscribed—

> " Here Paddy comes to have a swig,
>   A better one he never took ;
> And now he 'll dance an irish jig
>   With Dolly Dunne of Donnybrook."

I recollect another sign representing a bee-hive, for the exhibition of which no reason of an industrial nature was adduced. It displayed the following invitation :—

> " In this hive we 're all alive,
>   Good whisky makes us funny ;
> So don 't pass by, but stop and try
>   The sweetness of our honey."

Such were some instances of the allurements to participate in dissipations then not merely permitted, but encouraged, but which have happily been prevented from continuing their periodical infractions of public peace, and their interruptions of quietude and industry. I shall conclude my observations on the subject by quoting a verse of one of Ned Lysaght's songs, which tends strongly to prove that drunken violence was not merely tolerated, but made the occasion of a laudatory strain—

> " Whoe'er had the luck to see Donnybrook fair,
>   An Irishman, all in his glory, was there,
>   With his sprig of shillelagh and shamrock so green.
>   His clothes spic and span new, without e'er a speck,
>   A neat Barcelona* entwined on his neck ;
>   He goes into a tent and he spends half-a-crown,
>   He comes out, *meets a friend, and for love knocks him down*,
>   With his sprig of shillelagh and shamrock so green."

I sincerely hope that the " glory " derived from Donnybrook Fair has been for ever quenched, and that future indications of love for a friend will not require to be illustrated by the application of a shillelagh. Some of my readers may not be aware that this designation of a cudgel is derived from a barony named Shillelagh, in the County of Wicklow, which has been celebrated for its oak woods from a very remote period. I believe at present they are the property of Earl Fitzwilliam ; and I have frequently heard that the timber contained in the roof of Westminster Hall was supplied from them. I am not aware, however, that the propinquity of such material has produced any quarrelsome or combative tendencies amongst the senators or legal practitioners who frequent the locality.

THE LIQUOR TRAFFIC.

I am disposed to offer here a few observations in reference to the liquor traffic, and the effect of the laws by

* A showy description of silk handkerchief, supposed to be derived from a Spanish city, and associated with its name.

which it is regulated. I have heard the commission of every offence in which violence was a principal ingredient, attributed to the demoralising and infuriating indulgence in strong drinks. I am convinced, by my official experience, that hundreds of crimes unattended with actual violence, have also originated in the debasing craving for stimulating liquors. Frauds and thefts have been abundantly committed from such an incentive; and even affection has been extinguished by its loathsome power so completely, as to make the criminality and degrading infamy of a son or daughter subsidiary to the gratification of intemperate habits; and the result of recent legislation has certainly neither remedied, nor in my humble opinion mitigated, the prevalence of drunkenness and its multifarious concomitant evils. We are informed that a strict observance of the statute prohibiting the opening of public-houses on Sunday before two o'clock, p.m., has been enforced, and notwithstanding that regulation, we see numerous cases of intoxication in our thoroughfares two or three hours before the publicans open. On a Sunday in the present year, a servant-man left my house between ten and eleven o'clock, in the forenoon, and returned, or rather was brought back, in less than two hours completely intoxicated. In such a case the law is only operative in restraining the regular licensed trader. To deal with those infractions of the law and of public decency, the visitorial powers of the police and constabulary should be greatly extended; and the penalties incident to a conviction for the illicit traffic should be augmented to at least fourfold the amount now authorised, with the alternative, in case of non-payment, of three or four months' imprisonment with hard labor. In the preceding pages I have mentioned a conviction for smuggling tobacco, on which a penalty of one hundred pounds or six months' imprisonment was awarded. I recollect a detection of an illicit still in a house on Haddington Road, in reference to which the Excise authorities required that every adult found on the premises should be subjected to very severe penalties, or imprisonment for some months; and when I declined to convict a young woman who was washing clothes in the dwelling-house, and who was not a resident, but merely employed there occasionally, the professional gentlemen engaged in the prosecution were very dissatisfied with my decision. Offences against the Customs or Excise, which tend to withhold or lessen the revenue, even in the slightest degree, are made legally liable to penal consequences, compared with which the infractions of laws intended to protect the community from the innumerable evils generated by intemperance, may be regarded as trifling indiscretions, undeserving of strict and severe repression. If a trader sends forth from his premises one hundred drunken customers, to exhibit every phase of violent or indecent behaviour, his conduct is not visited with one-tenth of the punishment incurred by selling a glass of potteen whisky.

CHAPTER XXVII.

THE COLLEGE ROW—THE COOK STREET PRINTER——A QUESTION AND ANSWER—A BARRISTER—AN ATTORNEY—GIBRALTAR.

THE latter portion of my period of magisterial service was very scanty in the production of events worthy of being recorded.   On the 12th of March, 1858, the Earl of Eglinton arrived in Dublin to assume the Lord Lieutenancy, as successor to the Earl of Carlisle, who had left on the 8th of that month, in consequence of the dissolution of the Palmerston Ministry.   I believe that in the respective selections of Lords Carlisle and Eglinton, the Liberal and Conservative administrations succeeded in giving to the Irish community functionaries deservedly popular with all ranks and conditions.   I therefore consider it a subject of great regret that the entry of the latter nobleman, on the day above mentioned, should have been attended with a riot in College Green, in which the police and the students of the University came into collision.   The place of the occurrence was not within the limits of the police division to which I was attached, but I happened to be in a house very close to the scene, and had the fullest opportunity of witnessing the entire affair.   It commenced by the throwing of squibs and crackers from within the rails in front of the College, which rendered the horses of the mounted police and of a few dragoons very unquiet, and irritated some of the riders. I believe that amongst the persons engaged in annoying the police there were many who were not students. An attempt to repress forcibly the throwing of the squibs and crackers produced the addition of some stones to the missiles, and the affair eventuated in the reading of the Riot Act by Colonel Browne, the Commissioner of Police, and the clearing of the space between the building and the front railing by an attack of the police, in which some severe blows were inflicted. Happily, none of them resulted in fatal or permanent injury. A very lengthened investigation supervened, during which animosity and irritation almost entirely subsided, and were replaced by feelings of mutual kindness. I think that an extract from the proceedings, dated the 10th of April, may afford to my readers a most creditable and praiseworthy manifestation by the police and the students. I may mention that Mr. M‘Donough, Q.C., was engaged in the inquiry on the part of the collegians, when Colonel Browne expressed himself as follows :—

" I am sure Mr. M‘Donough will not be displeased with me if I say that I thought the police, whom I consider a fine body of young men, had been ill-treated for an hour or two by a number of young gentlemen. They were on unpleasant duty, not of their own will ; and I was more annoyed to see them so treated than if there had been fifty dozen stones showered on myself. They, too, were irritated at seeing stones thrown at me. All I now wish to say is this, I take the entire responsibility of all that occurred on myself. (Sensation.) I gave the order, and ought to be accountable for everything that happened. It is not because two or three of the men have, and no doubt did, act intemperately, that the others should be punished. The whole concern should be thrown on me ; and I hope the collegians will cast it on me, and forgive me.   I have a great regard for the collegians, and have always had, and to the last moment of my life I shall remember the kindness with which they have treated me.   I thought that a good feeling existed between my men and them, and I think there did. I feel regret for what has occurred—regret that will go down with me to my grave, and I say none but myself alone ought to bear the consequences of what has occurred."

Mr. M'Donough—" After that expression of regret, Colonel Browne, I, as a gentleman, shall not ask you another question." (Loud expression of approbation from the students and others present.)

Mr. M'Dermott, (Police Magistrate)—" I hope the language of Colonel Browne will be received in the spirit in which it is offered.   It is as creditable to him as the ebullition of feeling which we have just heard, and at which I do not wonder, is creditable to the students of Trinity College."

Mr. M'Donough—" And I am proud and happy that my young friends have shown how they can feel."

The applause was continued for some time longer. Colonel Browne, who seemed to be altogether overcome by emotion, retired amidst warm demonstrations of regard. No ulterior proceedings were adopted, and thus terminated the only collision or misunderstanding between the civil authorities and the students of the University that occurred from the commencement of my magisterial duties in 1841 to the present time.   Colonel Browne retired from office in 1858, upon a pension of £800 per annum.   He has also the half-pay of a lieutenant-colonel, and is a

Companion of the Bath. He is decorated with the Peninsular medal for military service in the army under Wellington in his early Spanish campaigns. He was succeeded as Commissioner of Police by Colonel Lake, whose services have been highly and deservedly appreciated, especially in the defence of Kars, when besieged by the Russians.

Almost immediately after the collision between the police and the collegians, a song was composed, in reference to the affair, by a gentleman who has acquired by it and several other productions of a comic character, a reputation which obtains for him a most enthusiastic reception in the choicest convivial reunions. He introduces the most extravagant fictions, and enunciates them with such apparent seriousness, as suffices completely to dissolve the gravity of his hearers. His song on the " College Row" imputes the " doleful tragedy" to the resentment of the Duchess of Sutherland, Lord Carlisle's sister, consequent on his loss of the Lord Lieutenancy, and the appointment of Lord Eglinton. She communicates by telegrams with the Commissioners of Police, and remits five hundred pounds to supply their force with ardent spirits, closing the communication with an injunction, that in case of any enthusiasm being manifested by the students on the public entry of Eglinton, they should be at once subjected to the most unsparing application of swords, batons, and bayonets. The ballad describes the carnage provoked by the explosion of a few crackers and squibs, as being fully equal to the worst excesses of our Indian sepoys in their mutinous massacres. I have heard it sung in the presence of Colonel Browne and of other police functionaries; and from all who heard its fearful but fictitious details, it elicited the utmost merriment. I have been informed that in his subsequent viceroyalty, Lord Carlisle and his Chief Secretary had it frequently sung by the author, who is now connected with the Dublin police in an important professional capacity.

THE COOK STREET PRINTER.

Shortly after the affair between the collegians and the police, a complaint preferred by the Crown solicitor was brought under my personal cognizance, and subsequently became the subject of a lyric production, in which it was almost impossible to determine whether exaggeration or fiction predominated. There was a printer in Cook Street remarkable for bodily deformity and mental acerbity. His trade almost entirely consisted in the publication of ballads, which were bought by itinerant vocalists, who came each evening to replenish their stocks of amatory, political, or comic productions. In proportion to the number of customers who crowded his shop and contended for a speedy supply, the publisher varied and multiplied his maledictions, and most impartially cursed and abused them all alike. His habitual vituperations were disregarded or laughed at, and were generally ascribed to mental infirmity; but he embarked in a speculation which brought him under the serious notice of the authorities as being intolerably offensive. He published an almanac, the marginal notes and memoranda of which were replete with sedition, and in which the public functionaries were grossly stigmatised. It happened that the corporation had effected a contract with the proprietor of a quarry in Wales for the the supply of stone of a quality considered best adapted for the repair of the streets of Dublin, and the day on which the contract had been accepted by the civic body was noted in the almanac as the date of an infamous preference of foreign production, and an exclusion of Irish industry and material through corrupt and debasing motives. This statement, however, constituted no portion whatever of the charges preferred before me, which consisted almost entirely of references to former attempts of a rebellious character, with expressions of deep regret for their failure, and hopes that the patriotic energies of the Irish nation would, in the next encounter, prove more effective in crushing Saxon despotism than had been the efforts of the glorious Sarsfield, the noble Lord Edward, the martyred Emmett, or the more recent champions of Hibernian freedom—O'Brien, Meagher, and Mitchell. Colonel Browne was not even aware of the proceedings before me having been instituted; and Mr. Whiteside, the present Chief Justice, was never concerned in any case before me during my tenure of magisterial office. The printer of the almanac appeared on a summons to show cause why informations should not be taken against him, and returned for trial on numerous and deliberate seditious statements published by him. The late Mr. John Adye Curran appeared as his counsel, and proposed to give sureties for his client's appearance to meet the charges preferred, if the Crown solicitor deemed it necessary to continue the prosecution, offering also to give up all copies of the almanac remaining in stock, and to abandon its future publication. The Crown solicitor, Mr. Kemmis, at once acceded to this proposal, and, on the sureties having been produced, I allowed the accused party to leave, and entered in the summons-book that the complaint was "dismissed without prejudice." I did not manifest the slightest sympathy for the delinquent, but informed him that he owed his escape from severe punishment entirely to the lenity of the Crown solicitor, and not to any disinclination on my part to have him made seriously and severely responsible for his misconduct.   In a few days he became the subject of a lyric panegyric, in which his prosecution was attributed to Colonel Browne and Mr. Whiteside, and the stoppage of the proceedings was ascribed *to me* and to Mr. Curran ; the course adopted by the latter gentleman being the only thread of truth interwoven in a web of fiction, and sung to an old Irish air, which I am not able to particularise.   It has been entitled by an additional fiction—

THE LOWER CASTLE YARD.

You gallant-hearted Irishmen,
 Come listen to my lay,
The melancholy muse I woo,
 She comes in tears to-day.
Oh Wirra ! Wirrasthrue, says she,
 Sure Dublin's noblest bard
Is took before his tyrants
 In the Lower Castle Yard.

In Cook Street was our Printer born,
 In Cook Street he was bred,
The legends of Hibernia's land
 His young ideas fed,
How Brian Boru and Granyah too,
 Did Saxons disregard.
And the flag of green once waved serene
 In the Upper Castle Yard.

His first animadversions
 Were on the paving stones,
Why should you send your cash to Wales,
 To Taffy or to Jones ?
Why not lay down, throughout the town,
 Your Irish granite hard ?
And macadamize the dirty spies
 In the Lower Castle Yard ?

Colonel Browne, he being a Welshman,
  Swore by St. David's bones
He 'd prosecute the Irishman
  Who dare oppose their stones.
He order'd Whiteside to indict
  And carcerate the Bard ;
Let him try, says he, Geology,
  In the Lower Castle Yard.

But good luck to Frank Thorpe Porter,
  That expounder of the laws,
Likewise to Adye Curran,
  Who was counsel in the cause.
They tann'd the hide of long Whiteside,
  And did him disregard,
And freed our Printer from his fangs,
  In the Lower Castle Yard.

A QUESTION AND ANSWER.

I was occasionally sent for by the Chief Secretary of the Lord Lieutenant in reference to matters of a local nature on which it was desirable to obtain prompt and confidential information. I cannot say that any of those functionaries ever applied to me on a subject which I considered very important, and I was never informed what was the ultimate object of the inquiry. I believe that in several instances the wish was to acquire some topics or materials for replies to deputations. It was intimated to me, in 1853, one day about two o'clock, that the Chief Secretary desired to see me immediately, and I accordingly proceeded to his office. He said that he wished to know whether the trade and commerce of Dublin was in a state of healthy progress, or of retrogression as compared with the two previous years. I told him that the files of the Dublin Gazette would enable him fully to ascertain the increase or decrease of bankruptcies within the city in the last year compared with any recent period, and that the Imports and Exports published under the sanction of the Customs authorities could be easily procured and examined. He declined to adopt the course I suggested as being complex, and requiring too much time to ascertain its results; and he then said that he wished me to come on the next day and tell him whether I believed that the general trade and commerce of Dublin were in a better or worse state during the past twelve months than they had been for the two previous years. I attended at the time appointed, and expressed a most decided opinion that the trading community had been far more prosperous in the latter period, and that I believed their business was one half greater than it had been during the terms with which it was to be compared. The Right Honorable functionary asked me when I had arrived at such a conclusion; to which I simply answered that my opinion had been formed since our last interview. I was then interrogated as to what documents I had examined, or what class of traders I had consulted, to which I replied that I had read nothing on the subject, and had spoken to a few traders merely as to certain commodities in which I was aware that they dealt. I was asked what commodities I meant, and the Secretary seemed rather surprised when I mentioned coarse papers and packing cordage, in which articles I was informed that they were doing an increased and increasing traffic. I added that when there was a brisk demand for such materials it denoted that the sale of shop goods must be also brisk, just as extensive purchases of seeds, manures, or tillage implements, would indicate greater activity in agricultural or horticultural pursuits. A young gentleman, who acted as private or confidential secretary to the Chief Secretary, was present when I expressed such opinions and my reason for their adoption, and when his principal indulged in a laugh which was, perhaps, somewhat derisive of the importance I ascribed to wrapping papers and twine, he amply participated in the merriment. I then said that I might possibly augment their amusement by imparting the result of another inquiry which I had made, and which tended to confirm my previous statements. I had been informed, in almost all the pre-eminent musical establishments, that there had been a considerable increase in the sale of pianofortes, and I felt perfectly convinced that a pianoforte was very rarely purchased by a person in embarrassed circumstances, whilst it was almost invariably considered a desirable addition to the domestic recreation of a comfortable and solvent family. This statement produced more laughter, and as the interview was not of a secret nature, my references to wrapping-paper, twine, and pianofortes, became sufficiently known to obtain for me a considerable amount of banter. The Secretary subsequently told me that several other persons whom he consulted gave him opinions similar to mine on the commercial state of Dublin, although their calculations and inferences were derived from very different sources. I still entertain the impression that the grounds on which I formed my conclusion were by no means unworthy of consideration.

A BARRISTER.

In some of the preceding pages I have mentioned several attorneys whose professional avocations were extensively connected with the police-courts, and whose conduct and character entitled them to our esteem and respect. Whilst they would endeavour to induce the magistrates to adopt the construction of a statute or by-law in the sense most favorable to their clients, they sedulously avoided the

suppression or exaggeration of facts when seeking a mitigation of punishment, or applying for the acceptance of
bail. There were, however, two or three professional men
who occasionally subjected us to the very disagreeable, perhaps I may say the disgusting, duty of listening to statements subsequently ascertained to be totally false, and which
they were undoubtedly aware of being unfounded. One
gentleman, who was a member of my own profession, had
a wonderful aptitude for citing cases purporting to have
been decided in the English courts, and in complete
accordance with the course which he was desirous we
should pursue. We soon found that many of those cases
were suppositious, and many others distorted and misre-
presented. Our chief clerk, Mr. Cox, having assisted on
a particular occasion in detecting several misquotations,
observed, that if the learned counsel ever attained to the
peerage, his most appropriate title would be Lord Phibs-
borough.*

AN ATTORNEY.

There was another practitioner, an attorney, who was
known by the nickname of "Bluebottle," inasmuch as
his tendency was to taint whatever he touched, and to
evince a preference for garbage. He happened to be present on one occasion, when a man and woman were
charged before me "for creating a disturbance in Dame
Street, and using abusive, insulting, and threatening language on the public thoroughfare." The woman stated
that the man was her husband; that he was in comfortable
circumstances, but left her in destitution, and refused to
contribute to her support. She produced a marriage certificate and various other documents in support of her

---

* A suburb of Dublin, pronounced *fibs*borough.

allegation, and I discharged the parties, with a caution against ventilating their domestic wrongs or differences in the public streets, suggesting to the female, that if she obtained admission to the South Union Workhouse as a destitute pauper, the guardians would make her husband responsible for deserting her, and rendering her a charge upon the rates. As her excitement and volubility appeared likely to create more disturbance, if she and her husband went forth together, I directed her to leave at once, and suggested, on her departure, that the man might remain until she had left the court and its vicinity. When she went out, she was followed by Bluebottle, who accosted her at the foot of the stairs, and told her that he would take immediate steps to compel her husband to afford her a suitable maintenance. Affecting to sympathise deeply with a destitute and friendless female, he induced her to give him all her documents, and also a small photographic picture, in which she and her husband appeared holding each other by the right hand. He then desired her to go away, promising to meet her at the Lord Mayor's court on the following day. This conversation and arrangement occurred very close to the door of the custody-room, and was fully overheard by the constable in charge, of whose proximity the ardent vindicator of the poor woman's wrongs had no knowledge or suspicion. When she departed, Bluebottle stepped up to the court, and beckoned to the husband, whom he brought to the precise spot where the previous conference had occurred. He then told him that he had obtained all the woman's papers, the certificate, and the picture, and that he was willing to give him a great bargain of the entire for one pound. The man declared that all the cash in his possession amounted only to twelve shillings and sixpence, which he was will-

ing to pay for the articles.   Bluebottle agreed to take the
latter sum, and received it, but before he delivered the picture
and documents, the constable emerged from the vestibule
of the custody-room and arrested him.   He was brought
immediately before me in his genuine name of Richard
Walsh, and I had to decide whether the certificate, picture, and letters he was about to dispose of, brought him
under a culpable liability.   The 53rd section of the 5th
Vic., sess. 2, chap. 24, enacts—

" That every person who shall be brought before any of the divisional
justices, charged with having in his possession, or on his premises, with his
knowledge, or conveying in any manner anything which may be reasonably
suspected to be stolen or unlawfully obtained, and who shall not give an
account to the satisfaction of such justice how he came by the same, shall
be deemed guilty of a misdemeanor, and on conviction thereof before such
justice or justices, shall be liable to a penalty not more than five pounds,
or in the discretion of the justice, may be imprisoned in any gaol or house
of correction within the police district, with or without hard labour, for
any time not exceeding two calendar months."

On the facts as proved before me, I made the picture
and the certificate the subjects of a conviction for unlawful
possession, and sent Mr. Walsh for two months to the
Richmond Bridewell, to be kept during that time at hard
labor.   I declined to make any order for returning the
twelve shillings and sixpence to the man from whom it
had been received, whose name, as well as I can recollect,
was Crozier ; but his wife was put in possession of the
articles which she had entrusted to the treacherous
attorney.   I believe that he was the only member of his
profession on whom, since the commencement of the present century, a criminal conviction inflicted a disgraceful
punishment in the metropolitan district.   He was inclined
to corpulence, and had a very plethoric appearance.   In a

few days after his committal, I received a note from the governor of the prison in the following terms :—

"SIR,

"In reference to the case of Richard Walsh, committed by you for two months, with hard labour, I beg leave to report that the medical officers of the prison think it would be dangerous to work a person of his age and full habit of body on the treadmill. I believe, however, that I can make him perfectly available as an oakum-picker. I have the honor, &c., &c."

This communication was entered in the official letter-book of the police-court, and consequently became generally known. The delinquent was a person of extreme effrontery, and the members of his profession considered him to be habitually supercilious and offensive. When the term of his punishment was completed, he had the almost incredible audacity to attempt to resume practice in the criminal courts. None of the other attorneys would act or associate with him, and his presence always produced complaints against the " very disagreeable smell of oakum." He died, as I have been informed, uncommiserated and unaided, in extreme indigence. From the incidents which I have narrated, a lesson may be derived to the effect, that the man who disgraces a profession will soon render his pursuit of it thoroughly unprofitable.

GIBRALTAR.

My official reminiscences are nearly terminated. The latter years of my magistracy were not marked by any important public events or political excitement. In 1861 my health became seriously impaired, and a medical commission of six members reported in favor of my superannuation. My dear friend, Marcus Costello, the attorney-general of Gibraltar, having been apprised that I had been greatly debilitated by bronchitis and pleurisy, sent me a brief note to go out at once, and to say by return of post when he might expect me. In compliance with his invitation, I sailed from Southampton on the 27th of April, in the Peninsular and Oriental Company's steamer, "Delta," and on the 29th we were crossing the Bay of Biscay. My memory reverted to a ballad which I had heard sung by Incledon, descriptive of the fearfully tempestuous state in which that bay is generally found. One of his verses is, I believe, as follows :—

> " Loud roar'd the dreadful thunder,
>   The rain a deluge show'rs,
> The clouds were rent asunder
>   By lightning's vivid pow'rs.
> The night all drear and dark,
> Closed round our wretched bark,
> As she lay, on that day,
>   In the Bay of Biscay, O !"

I presume to attempt a description of what I observed in crossing this estuary; and I can truly affirm, that whatever may be the defects of my composition, it does not contain the slightest exaggeration—

> " The light-blue sky is o'er us,
>   The dark-blue sea beneath,
> The wave scarce moves before us,
>   As zephyrs gently breathe.
> The great unfathom'd deep,
> Calm as an infant's sleep,
> Cheers our way, on this day,
>   Through the Bay of Biscay, O !
>
> " The mighty steam-ship cleaving
>   The tide, displays her pow'r,
> The wondrous feat achieving
>   Of fifteen knots an hour;
> We speedily shall gain
> A sight of sunny Spain.
> No delay checks our way
>   Through the Bay of Biscay, O !"

When we did attain sight of the Spanish coast, it afforded a very marked contrast to the picturesque views presented by the shores of Ireland and England. There were no towering and precipitous cliffs or verdant slopes to be seen, and almost the only indications of the country being inhabited were some watch-towers from which in former days warning signals were exhibited to denote the approach of hostile or predatory vessels from Algiers or Barbary. Being totally unacquainted with Transatlantic and Mediterranean scenery, I can exercise a very limited judgment, but of all the marine views I have seen I consider the most beautiful to be the bay of Dublin, and the ugliest to be the far-famed Trafalgar.

I landed at Gibraltar on the 2nd of May, and was not inclined, at my arrival, to form a very favorable opinion of the climate, for I never had previously seen such heavy rain as fell on that day and continued until midnight. Mr. Costello's man-servant, hearing me remark the unpleasant state of the weather, said, "that it was the last rain of the season, and that we should have no more until the middle of September." I did not attach much credence to his statement, but, although my visit lasted for four months, I never saw another drop of rain there. He was a native of the place, and spoke from experience.

My friend's residence was not far from the southern extremity of Gibraltar, which is also supposed to be the southern extremity of Europe, and there were three roads leading from it to the main body of the city which is near the north front. They were constructed, I suppose, for the purpose of affording the most ample means of communication along the sloping face of the mountain, and between the batteries which defiantly bristle all through the territory. On the second day of my arrival, I set out

to walk to the town, and, for the sake of the view which
it commanded, I took the most elevated road.   There
were no dwellings on it, and it went through an exhausted
quarry, to which the drummers and bugle boys were
brought for instruction.   A squad of them were about to
commence their practice just as I passed their front,
whereupon one of them lowered his instrument, and exclaimed to a comrade, "Oh! Fitzpatrick, there's ould Porter
from Dublin."   On reaching the city I was recognised by
some officers of the 7th Fusileers.   Indeed I am disposed
to believe that a considerable number of the private soldiers
of the garrison had been attested by me in the Dublin
police-court, for I received frequent salutes whenever I
sauntered past the barracks or guard stations.

My health rapidly improved, and in a few days I
attained renovated strength.   There was no lack of varied
amusement or social enjoyment, and until the intense heat
of July and August precluded any movement outside the
house, between morning and evening, I never passed a
tedious or tiresome minute.   Even in the hot time,
especially if the wind is westerly, an evening saunter along
the low road and through the Alameda is very agreeable.
The people, especially those of the Spanish race, rise about
four or five o'clock in the morning during the sultry
months.   They go to market and attend to their commercial arrangements and domestic affairs until nine or
ten o'clock, then, having breakfasted, they betake themselves to bed and enjoy a "Siesta."   I adopted the same
course as far as the retirement to bed was concerned, and
found it extremely pleasant.   I went to sleep almost
immediately after lying down, and seldom awoke until
four or five o'clock.   Then walking slowly down to the
bay I took a plunge in the salt water, and generally

returned endowed with an appetite for a hearty dinner and a liberal supplement of sherry and ice, after which a stroll to the Alaméda and a seat under the cool shade of an acacia or bella sombra tree, with a military band playing on an adjoining bastion, enabled me and my friend to pass the evening in good humour with the world and with each other.

CHAPTER XXVIII.

GIBRALTAR.—*Continued.*

THE road by which Gibraltar is approached from Spain is, for a considerable distance, completely level. The connecting isthmus is flanked by the bay and the Mediterranean, and the latter has been admitted, in the English territory, into extensive and deep excavations, which confine the means of access to a very narrow breadth. The face of the fortress on this side displays a stupendous and precipitous formation, in which galleries have been constructed, from the embrasures of which a fire of heavy artillery can be directed, sufficient, as I was informed by an officer of engineers, not only to annihilate a hostile force, but to destroy the avenue itself, whilst the occupants of those batteries would be almost completely exempt from retaliatory casualities. On entering the gate on the north front, a battery of about forty guns is passed, and it is known by the unpalatable designation of "The Devil's Tongue." Close to it, and forming part of the city, are two districts, of which one is named Portuguese town and the other, Irish town. I endeavoured to ascertain the origin of the Hibernian term for the latter locality, but my inquiries failed to elicit any information, beyond the fact of the name having existed for the place previous to the capture of the fortress by the British in 1704. The residence of the Governor was in former times occupied by a religious community, and it retains the appellation of " The Convent." A stranger is occasionally surprised by hearing that the Governor's lady has given a splendid ball, or that his Excellency has entertained a number of distinguished persons *at the Convent*. The gardens command a delightful view of the bay, and are remarkable for large bushes of myrtles and roses, beautiful fuchsias, and geraniums, whilst the finest grapes, figs, pomegranates, peaches, apricots, and melons are profusely produced without requiring artificial heat or the protection of glass. The climate is too hot for the growth of apples, pears, gooseberries, currants, or raspberries. Oranges are very abundant, but are not palatable when gathered from the tree, as they are all of the Seville or bitter kind, and are used for making marmalade, which is highly valued in the sultry months when butter is unattainable.

Although this interesting and impregnable possession is so generally termed The *Rock* of Gibraltar, there is a considerable portion of its surface highly capable of cultivation. The most prevalent weeds are the nasturtium, snapdragon, and convolvulus; and there is an indigenous pea, the blossom of which is exquisitely beautiful in appearance, but completely scentless. At the termination of the rainy season, a plant springs up in great profusion in the ravines and watercourses. It is about a foot in height, and the blossoms are very pretty, some of the plants bearing white flowers, some red, and others blue. The Spaniards call it " Don Pedro," and the English have named it " Four o'clock." The petals open about that hour in the afternoon, and the blossoms continue expanded, and diffusing a delightful fragrance until day-break, when they invariably close up. The Spanish name is derived from a fable, which describes Don Pedro to have been a confirmed rake, who slept all the day and spent the night in revelling, until an indignant fairy transformed him into a plant, which retains his habit.

The east side of Gibraltar is washed by the Mediterranean, and there are very few guns mounted along that line, of which four-fifths are totally inaccessible. The signal station is at the summit of the mountain, and from the parapet wall, beside the flagstaff, a pebble can be dropped into the water with a direct fall of fourteen hundred and ninety-four feet. The rock formation on the entire territory is exclusively limestone, and I broke off some of it at the station, and found it a complete mass of concrete shells, whereby it is manifestly proved that the mountain must have been originally in a submarine position. The strait between it and Barbary is more than fourteen miles in breadth, and I was informed that the depth of water midway was three thousand six hundred feet.

Snakes and lizards are frequently seen in the Alameda, in private enclosures, and in the cemeteries. I was assured, however, that none of the former were of a venomous character, and I caught several with the utmost impunity. The lizards are almost all of a bright green color, and do not exceed a foot in length. The shape is precisely the same as that of an alligator. Monkeys were formerly rather numerous, but they have become almost extinct. Some of the oldest residents told me that they had never seen one. During my sojourn, the place was twice visited by flights of quail from Africa, suddenly coming in myriads, and as suddenly departing.

There is a cemetery just outside the city at a place called

the " Ragged Staff." I could not ascertain how that name originated, but the cemetery is remarkable for a considerable number of tombstones placed over the remains of persons who died at Gibraltar from the effects of wounds received at Trafalgar. Each inscription commences with " Sacred to the memory of ———," and it then proceeds to enumerate the virtues, personal merits, and intrepid deeds of the deceased. I remarked one stone placed upon the grave of James Dudley, by the direction and at the expense of his shipmates, who valued him highly for his kind and generous disposition, and for his undaunted courage in the closest and fiercest conflicts, as he always evinced great skill and *deep penetration*. It then states that he died of wounds received in the battle off Cape Trafalgar, where he acted as master gunner of His Majesty's ship, Colossus. I thought on reading this inscription, that " deep penetration" was a very natural attribute for the gunner of a line-of-battle ship.

In the beginning of July, 1861, a brig from America, bound for Gibraltar, and laden with ice, got ashore in a fog near Cape Spartell, on the Barbary coast, and just at the entrance of the straits. A Moorish boat brought speedy news of this disaster, and the Redpole steamer was ordered to proceed to the assistance of the stranded vessel. I requested the naval superintendent, the late Admiral Warden, to allow me to go over to the place in the " Redpole," to enjoy the novelty of the trip, and see the intended operations. He most kindly complied, and the officer in command provided me with a comfortable berth, and treated me with great hospitality. We found the brig aground, but uninjured ; and when a few tons of her cargo were removed she floated, and was towed by the steamer to her destination. Several Moors came on board, and assisted in lightening the vessel for a trifling remuneration ; and they afforded very great amusement by their gestures and exclamations, their expressions being interpreted by a Tangierine lad, who was employed in the steamer. They had never seen ice previously, and were inclined to believe it a supernatural or magical production. They were astonished at the coldness and hardness of the glassy blocks, and at their rapid dissolution when exposed to the rays of a Mauritanian sun ; but they were very soon reconciled to the magical material, and seemed to appreciate highly the introduction of it to some sherbet and lemonade with which they were regaled, steadfastly declining any stronger potations.

During my visit to Gibraltar, I went to see bull-fights at Algesiras, San Roque, and Malaga. They are certainly national institutions, which I firmly believe could not be abolished or avowedly discouraged in Spain by any government, although their tendency is most undeniably debasing and brutalising. At the time to which my narrative refers, the bulls throughout nearly the whole province of Andalusia were procured from the domains of a very wealthy widow, whose name has escaped my memory. She generally attended the exhibitions in which the wild ferocity of her animals was considered a most desirable quality, and always received an enthusiastic welcome, even the most exalted and fairest of her own sex joining in the exclamation of " Viva la Viuda." (Long live the widow.)

At Algesiras I saw a bull in the *Circo* that evinced no fierceness or combative inclination. The poor brute tried to avoid his assailants, and to push back the door through which he had entered. His quietude excited the utmost indignation, and even the females joined in the cry of

" Fuego !" (Fire.) Accordingly, darts were thrown at the animal, in each of which, close to the barbed point, there was a charge of gunpowder, connected in the interior of the weapon with a lighted fuse. When some of these charges exploded in his flesh, he became completely maddened, to the great gratification of the spectators, by whom, I have no doubt, the death of even a human victim occasionally, would be regarded as an exciting and interesting addition to their amusement.

The attire of the mounted combatants at the bull-fights appeared to me to be far more gaudy than graceful. Their limbs, below the hips, were so thickly padded as to look as large as the upper portions of their persons ; and in their encounters they did not ride rapidly forward, but merely opposed the lance to the onset of the bull. In each of eighteen collisions which I witnessed, the horse was frightfully gored and destroyed, his rider being saved by the matadores throwing their scarlet cloaks over the eyes of the bull, and plunging their swords to the hilt in his neck, so as to reach the spine. I am now tempted to quote a few lines from the first canto of " Childe Harold's Pilgrimage," to which I shall subjoin an observation, from which it will appear that what I saw differed vastly in one respect from the glowing description extracted from Byron's romantic production—

" Hush'd is the din of tongues—*on gallant steeds,*
　　With milk-white crest, gold spurs, and light-poised lance,
　Four cavaliers prepare for venturous deeds,
　　And lowly bending, to the lists advance ;
　Rich are their scarfs, *their chargers featly prance:*
　　If in the dangerous game they shine to-day,
　The crowd's loud shout and ladies' lovely glance,
　　Best prize of better acts, they bear away,
　　And all that kings or chiefs e'er gain their toils repay."

Of the eighteen "gallant steeds" which I saw at the bull-fights, there was not one to which I would attach the value of five pounds. None of them essayed to "prance," and unquestionably if a horse equal to the best of them appeared on the streets of Dublin between the shafts of a hackney vehicle, his owner would incur the suspension of his license for plying a horse totally unfit for public accommodation.

The most picturesque assemblage that I ever beheld was the public market at Gibraltar on Sunday morning. Persons of the lower class in the parts of Spain which I visited, are, during the week-days, as poorly attired as any that can be found in a corresponding position in the towns of Ireland, but they are invariably provided with a suit specially reserved for Sundays and two or three festivals. The men have conical hats, round which rows of showy ribbons are twined; and their coats, waistcoats, and small clothes, of whatever colors they fancy, are profusely furnished with globular little buttons of bright metal. Sandals, shoes, or buskins display gilt or silvered fastenings. Gay neckties, and a brooch or chain, complete the holiday costume. I am not competent to describe the female attire, but it comprises a head-dress of lace, fastened with glittering clasps or buckles; boots or shoes gaily ornamented; and a gown of rich material, almost invariably encircled at the waist by a girdle of metallic tissue. Ornaments of gold and jewels, or their semblance, appear in abundance. From a thousand to fifteen hundred such persons may be seen at the market on Sundays, between five and six o'clock in the morning. Females of various ranks, wives or daughters of persons in the garrison, appear arrayed in their best attire. Boats from Tangier and Oran land their produce, to be disposed of by dealers wearing Moorish or

Arabic costumes. Sailors from the ships of war and artillerymen mingle their blue uniforms amongst the scarlet-clad regimental soldiers. A similar scene cannot be exhibited in any part of the United Kingdom ; and the diversity of attire is fully equalled by the diversity of language which is there to be heard.

Towards the end of May, 1861, the assizes for the city and territory of Gibraltar were held, and at their conclusion, the judge, Sir James Cochrane, asked leave of absence for two months, and I was appointed as his *locum tenens* for that time. I received several official documents incident to the position, and amongst them was the commission of a Justice of the Peace, which was not a temporary authority, and it is still in my possession. I am, perhaps, the only person in Ireland whose designation of J.P. is unconnected with any locality in the United Kingdom. My judicial duties consisted in hearing a few petitions from insolvents seeking discharges from imprisonment, and granting two or three fiats under an Admiralty jurisdiction, in reference to alleged collisions between vessels in the bay. Although my authority was of very brief duration, it imparted, during its continuance, rank next to that of the Governor. It devolved on me, accompanied by his Excellency's principal aid-de-camp, to wait on the present Empress of Austria, who arrived at Gibraltar in the royal yacht, " Victoria and Albert," on her way home from Madeira, where she had been staying for some time to renovate her health. I never beheld a woman of more prepossessing appearance, and I considered her deportment perfectly dignified, but also extremely courteous. She accepted the Governor's invitation to a dejeuner at the convent, but premised, that as she was returning to her family, happily free from any indisposition, she was desirous of first visiting the Catholic cathedral, to return thanks to the Almighty for the merciful manifestation which she had experienced. Accordingly, the streets were lined by the troops, and royal salutes from the principal batteries greeted her landing, and attended her return to the steamer, after the coaling and other preparations for continuing the voyage to Trieste had been accomplished.

On one of many occasions that I had the honor and pleasure of enjoying the hospitality of the Governor, Sir William Coddrington, I sat next to the officer who commanded a Portuguese frigate, "The Braganza," that anchored for a few days at the New Mole. He was one of the Royal family of Portugal, and bore the title of Duke of Oporto. His Royal Highness spoke English tolerably well; and having heard me mention Dublin as my native place, asked me numerous questions respecting Ireland and the Irish. I suggested to him that he might induce his Government to let him have a cruise to our shores, that some of our bays were very beautiful, and that a run from Cork to Killarney would not require much time to accomplish, whilst it would assuredly afford him great gratification. At the close of our conversation, he said, " Sir, if you should at any time visit Lisbon, if I shall be there, I hope that you will call on me : I shall be happy to see you, and to endeavour to make the place agreeable to you." I expressed my warm thanks for his courteous expression, but I have not availed myself of his kindness, nor have I any intention to do so. He is now King of Portugal; but at the time when I had the honor of sitting beside him, there were, I believe, three members of his family whose respective claims to the throne were prior to his.

On a Saturday afternoon, in the beginning of July, 1861,

I was passing through the hall at the Governor's residence, on my way to the garden to which I was allowed the fullest access. The windows were all open; and groups of persons, including the Governor and some members of his family, were sitting beneath the trees, but within hearing of any expressions uttered in an ordinary tone in the hall. A naval captain, in full uniform, hastily entered from the street, and said to the servants in attendance, " Let the Governor be immediately informed that *Captain Jones has brought The Scourge for him.*" On hearing this announcement, I exclaimed, " Good heavens! What has he done to deserve that ? " This occasioned some laughter, in which, I believe, his Excellency participated. The Scourge was not unexpected, and its arrival was very satisfactory. On the 25th of the previous month, the present Sultan of the Ottoman Empire had commenced his reign ; and Sir William Coddrington, having been the Commander-in-Chief of our army at the conclusion of the Crimean war, was very judiciously selected to proceed in the Scourge steamer to Constantinople, for the purpose of presenting Queen Victoria's letter of congratulation on his accession, to the Turkish monarch. His Excellency left Gibraltar on his mission in two or three hours after Captain Jones' arrival, and a Lieutenant-Governor, Colonel Stehelin, of the Engineers, was sworn into office by me on the following Wednesday; but in the interim, my position, as acting judge, gave me precedence of all other functionaries, civil or military, in the territory. If I had been told, before leaving home, that such an elevation, even for a few hours, would occur, I should have deemed it incredible.

About the beginning of August, 1861, two vessels of the Russian Imperial navy, a frigate and a corvette, both steamers, came into Gibraltar, and anchored for the purpose of coaling. A considerable portion of their crews were indulged by their commanding officers with leave to come ashore; and certainly they could not have landed at any place more likely to excite surprise and gratify curiosity during a ramble of a few hours through it. However, they did not evince any anxiety for a close inspection of the fortress, or how its natural formation and elaborate constructions imparted unrivalled strength. Potency of a far different description engrossed their attention. They proceeded to some taverns or public-houses near to the boat-wharf, and only a few entered the premises, whilst the others remained in groups under trees or shaded by the walls. In less than an hour they were all drunk, and many of them were lying on the thoroughfare in the most helpless state of complete intoxication. The scene of their unrestrained indulgence was about one hundred yards from the residence of my friend, and the windows of his drawing-room, from which I had a full view of them, were all open. If I had been only half as far from them, without having them in sight, I should never have noticed their total lapse from sobriety, for there was no shouting, or singing, or quarrelling; in fact, their intoxication was a silent enjoyment, and formed a most thorough contrast to that of every liquor-loving group that ever came under my observation on any other occasions. They were taken down to their boats by parties of their shipmates who were on duty, and consequently constrained to keep sober.

I believe that the population of Gibraltar, in 1861, was about 16,000 persons, exclusive of the officials and military. The Christian portion consisted of Roman Catholics, Protestants, and Presbyterians. There was a considerable number of Jews, amongst whom several were reputed to be extremely wealthy, and there were some resident Mahometans. It might be supposed that in such a mixed community, religious bickering and polemical acerbity would be sometimes manifested, but my own observation, and the deliberate statements of all those with whom I associated or communicated, enable me to express my decided conviction that the place was as free from religious animosity or controversial skirmishing as Ireland is from toads or snakes. I have seen the funerals of persons belonging respectively to the various religious denominations; and although the covering of the hearse or bier, the presence of priestly functionaries in sacerdotal costume, or the direction in which the procession was moving, indicated the religion which the deceased had professed, all those who met it on the way to the cemetery, stood with uncovered heads as the corpse passed them, and offered to those engaged in the mournful ceremony a courteous but tacit mark of sympathy and respect.

Although Gibraltar has been deliberately recognised and acknowledged to be British territory by the Spanish government, prominent members of political parties have repeatedly advocated a demand for its restoration to Spain, and there have been some Englishmen who expressed opinions of a similar tendency. Alfonso, who has recently been elevated to regal dignity in Madrid, introduced the subject in his address on assuming the sovereignty; and we may expect, if his realm becomes completely subject to his rule, and ceases to be the theatre of sanguinary intestine encounters, that a claim will be addressed to the British government for the cession of a fortress which was tremendously strong when it was captured, and has been, by consummate skill, and a profuse expenditure, rendered completely impregnable. A prompt and direct refusal will, I have no doubt, be the reply to all demands or requests for the transfer of this important possession; but I feel perfectly convinced that a British minister might safely refer the application to the decision of the inhabitants, the great majority of whom have been born in the place, and are, to all intents and purposes, British subjects. I do not think it possible for a population to be more attached to any government than they are to our rule; and if Spanish agents were permitted to canvass them, and proceeded to solicit their adhesion, they would find their mission replete with danger. In 1861, being one day in the shop of a bootmaker, named Finochio, I amused myself by pretending to argue with my friend, Dr. Williams, in the presence of some native residents, that the territory was really Spanish, and that it should be relinquished by England. I was greatly surprised, and in some degree alarmed, at the effect produced by my observations on the hearers. Finochio rushed impetuously to the door of his shop, which commanded a view of the signal-station, on which the British flag was displayed, and pointing to it he exclaimed, " I would rather endure to be bombarded or famished—I would rather see the whole town burned to ashes, than have that flag changed for any other. Let me tell you, sir, that if you talk to the people here about England giving them up to Spain, some of them will lose temper and insult you." The others approved fully of Finochio's observations. However, it is not difficult to ascertain the grounds and reasons for such attachment on the part of the native population. Their tenements are almost entirely held directly from the Crown; and although the leases are not in general granted for a longer period than twenty-one years, the rents are very seldom raised, or a renewal refused at the expiration of the term, if the tenant has been punctual and improving. Taverns and hotels are subjected to considerable licence duties, and there is some charge incident to the importation of spirits. These are the only taxes which, I believe, are levied in the territory. Wine, tea, sugar, coffee, tobacco, wearing apparel, and furniture, or materials for the two latter are freely admitted. The streets and roads are constructed by the military, and cleansed by convict labor. The places of worship are exempt from rents to the Crown, and the legal institutions are highly appreciated by the people, who regard the administration of justice, and especially the trial by jury, according to the laws of England, as forming a most favorable contrast to the proceedings before the Spanish tribunals in the cities and towns of Andalusia. I may add, that in 1861 there was a very extensive trade in English manufactures and many other productions, especially tobacco, carried on by smuggling vessels conveying contraband cargoes to Spain, Portugal, Italy, and the Balearic Islands. I believe, that in no part of the world are there more devoted, although not disinterested, supporters of English authority than were to be found navigating their picturesque latteen craft, laden with articles derived from the factories of Manchester, Leeds, Nottingham, or Sheffield.

I have already mentioned several Spanish towns which I visited for the purpose of seeing bull-fights. I was also at some fairs ; and although there are some points in the Spanish character and habitudes which I am far from admiring, I must, in justice to the people who came under my observation, state that I never saw one of them intoxicated, although wine and spirits are, in their country, to be had for less than half what they cost here. Some gentlemen at Gibraltar, who had travelled through Spain, told me that they believed there was more drunkenness in our small possession than in the entire kingdom. I never saw a Spanish person of respectable appearance, drink a glass of undiluted sherry. The addition of cold water in equal quantity seemed indispensable. I have seen muleteers setting out on a journey requiring an entire day for its completion, and they carried no animal food. Each man had a bottle containing a little more than a pint of a red wine called Priorato, a couple of onions, and a large roll of bread made of two-thirds of maize, ground fine, and one-third of wheaten flour. They consider onions and bread, sliced and eaten together, as very nutritive diet, and their strong and healthful appearance justifies their opinion. The Priorato wine has a taste somewhat resembling Port, but I was forbidden by medical authority to take it at all, and I was told that the berries of the elder tree were plentifully added to the grapes in its manufacture.

Spaniards of the humbler class and of either sex, who bring edible commodities for sale in Gibraltar, demand a much higher price from any person whom they believe to have just arrived, and not to have acquired a knowledge of the marketable value of the articles, than they ask of those whose faces are familiar, or with whom they have had previous dealings. Nevertheless, they do not manifest any surprise or indignation at being offered, or any laxity in accepting, a mere fractional portion of the sum first mentioned. A milkman demanded two shillings and two pence for about three pints of goat's milk, which he left with me on being offered sixpence. A woman sold me muscatel grapes for a shilling, after having named eight shillings and eight pence for them. I had an opportunity of sending home to Dublin some Murcian melons, and proposed to purchase six which had been brought to market in a limber kind of basket or net-work neatly made of rushes. The vendor did not speak English, and I reciprocated his ignorance of my language by being equally unacquainted with his vernacular. He managed, mostly by signs, to apprise me that he required six dollars for his fruit. I regarded this demand, amounting to twenty-six shillings, as utterly unreasonable, and relinquished all expectation of acquiring a gratifying treat for my people, when Dr. Williams happened to approach, and on being informed of my disappointment, became an interpreter and negotiator between the Spaniard and me. His interference eventuated in rendering me the owner of the fruit and the basket, in which the melons could be very conveniently transmitted, at the very reasonable price of seven shillings. He told me that he had expostulated with the seller on his attempt to obtain from a purchaser more than three-fold the fair value of the articles ; but the Spaniard considered himself fully justified in the course he had adopted previous to my friend's arrival, inasmuch as he believed me to be a complete stranger, ignorant of the language, and of the usual prices demanded for fruits, but that in any future dealings with me I should not be overcharged, although he was quite convinced that, like all other English gentlemen, I was very rich and well able to pay.

The mention of my friend's name reminds me that in Gibraltar there is no scarcity of surgeons and physicians possessing high professional qualifications. The more respectable classes of society avail themselves, in their ailments, of the aid which skill and experience can fully impart. The lower classes seem insensible or indifferent to the character or capability of those to whom they have

recourse, and there are in the territory some practitioners
who profess to repair human hurts or maladies, and also
the injuries of certain inanimate articles.   There is an
inscription on the front of a small shop, that I venture
to transcribe, even at the risk of mistaking the exact
spelling of the Spanish words, and I subjoin an English
translation :—

"BARBERO, SANGUEDOR Y SACAMUELAS,
SE REPAREN ABANICOS PARAGUAS Y PARASOLES."

"BARBER, BLEEDER, AND TOOTH-DRAWER,
FANS, UMBRELLAS, AND PARASOLS REPAIRED."

CHAPTER XXIX.

GIBRALTAR (CONTINUED)—DEPARTURE FOR HOME
——CHARITY, REAL CHARITY——A DEATH AND FU-
NERAL——THE BAY OF BISCAY AGAIN——AT HOME:
LEISURE NO PLEASURE——A REVIEW.

TOWARDS the conclusion of my visit to Gibraltar, a marriage was solemnized between an officer commanding a
frigate lying off the New Mole and a young lady of very
prepossessing appearance who came from England, accompanied by her mother and some other relatives. The ceremony was performed at the Protestant Church about
eleven o'clock in the forenoon, and an arrangement had
been made that the wedding dejeuner should take place
on board the vessel, after which the happy couple were to
proceed by boat to Algesiras to spend the honeymoon.
The frigate was directly in view of Mr. Costello's residence, and with the help of a binocular glass I could see
persons on deck as plainly as if I stood amongst them.
As soon as the bridegroom came ashore to proceed to the
church, several boats came from the stairs at the Ragged
Staff, conveying a profuse supply of evergreens and flowers.
These were quickly taken aloft by the crew who swarmed
up, and in a few minutes the masts, yards, and rigging
were festooned with floral decorations, amongst which the

peculiarly appropriate nuptial ornament, " a wreath of orange blossoms," was conspicuously displayed on each bow and quarter. The other ships were dressed in the usual manner, but the frigate appeared pre-eminently beautiful. The reception of the bride and bridegroom and their cortege was most enthusiastic. I was assured by several naval officers that the display, which excited the unqualified admiration of all who witnessed it, was a spontaneous manifestation on the part of the crew of their respect and affection for their captain. I regret that I do not recollect his name, but the feeling evinced towards him was not the only instance that came under my observation indicative of great attachment on the part of British sailors for their commanders.

To the respectable residents of Gibraltar, whether official or commercial, the place affords many advantages. The comforts attainable in the cities of the United Kingdom can be there procured on terms in many respects more moderate, and in none, as far as I could learn, seriously greater, whilst many articles of domestic requirement are vastly cheaper, owing to their importation not being subjected to Customs' duties. The prices of shoes, boots, and hats appeared to me to be lower than those I should have to pay in Dublin for a similar description and quality of goods. Woollen, linen, and cotton fabrics are somewhat dearer than here, and tables, chairs, and bedsteads, unless made of very old and well-seasoned wood, shrink and shrivel in the sultry time, and require repairs involving some outlay. The expenses incident to soft goods and furniture are not much complained of, and do not appear to be considered serious inconveniences.

Respectable residents or visiters can have, at a cost of twenty shillings yearly, access to a library, from which useful information and amusement may be extensively derived. The building is of elegant structure, of extensive dimensions, and its furniture unites beauty of appearance with utility and comfort. It is supplied with the principal newspapers and periodical publications of the civilized world, and its shelves contain about twenty thousand volumes, most conveniently arranged, and comprising the choicest specimens of ancient and modern literature. No person should visit Gibraltar, even during the time required for coaling a steamer, without taking a glance or two at the library and from its windows, for some of them command a splendid view of the bay and of a considerable portion of the fortress, whilst many others are immediately over parterres of the choicest and most luxuriant floral productions.

Having enumerated almost every agreeable or advantageous circumstance that I can recollect respecting the time I spent in Gibraltar, I shall proceed to notice the only alloys to the varied pleasures which I experienced there. From the middle of June to the beginning of September the heat is extremely oppressive, and when the wind is easterly, as it frequently was during my sojourn, its effect is extremely debilitating to the body and depressing to the mind. During the sultry months no rain ever falls, and, nevertheless, the wind coming from the Levant is surcharged with moisture. Clothes hung out to dry under a scorching sun continue as damp as when first exposed, or perhaps become more so. Fish or flesh meat killed in the morning will not be eatable in seven or eight hours. Wine bottled, marmalade or jams made, turn acid very soon. The slightest exertion becomes a labour, and persons are less censurable for inattention to the comforts of others as they lapse into indifference to their own requirements. A long continuance of an east wind would probably prove disastrously unhealthy, but it seldom lasts long, and generally, after a couple of days or a few hours, it is succeeded by a westerly breeze from the broad Atlantic, cool, dry, and invigorating.

This impregnable fortress, which may defy all human efforts for its forcible reduction, is not proof against the invasion of countless small but most sanguinary creatures that, if they could audibly express their universal craving, would make an unvaried and continuous demand of blood. The mosquitoes appear early in June, and are a most persistent nuisance during the sultry months. It is no slight advantage to Great Britain and Ireland to be free from their annoyance. I suffered greatly from their envenomed bites, and although sex or age appears to be utterly disregarded in their insatiate and incessant attacks, they are reputed to accord a preference to the blood of a stranger. The slightest aperture in the curtains of my bed resulted in numerous punctures being made in the skin of my face and hands. My friend Costello slept in an uncurtained bed, and was not attacked by the mosquitoes. He told me that, after he had resided in Gibraltar for a couple of years, they ceased to annoy him. Dr. Williams described them as " the most affectionate little creatures in the world, for if you killed one, some hundreds would come to his funeral."

During the months of May and June in 1861, I heard more cannon shots than ever reached my ears in the rest of my existence. The artillery were practising daily for several hours at floating targets in the bay, and the noise was certainly far from agreeable to me. In the expression of a wish for more quietude, I met no sympathy from those who had resided in Gibraltar for a year or two, and who had become accustomed to the firing, and perhaps, if I spent a few months more in the fortress my nerves would have become more obtuse. The convict depot, outside the line wall, was very near to the battery principally used for practice, and I have seen the premises occupied by the superintendent completely clouded with smoke, whilst his walls reverberated the repeated discharges of heavy cannon. He directed my attention to the domestic fowl, of which he had a considerable number, and to the poultry of various kinds having become quite accustomed and apparently reconciled to the appalling sounds, and to the fire and smoke copiously emitted in their proximity.

I was told, in casual conversations with artillery officers, that one-third of the ammunition contained in the magazines of Gibraltar was expended yearly, and that the deficiency was supplied by an equal quantity from home. I was informed that gunpowder becomes deteriorated if kept beyond three years, and that the most advantageous use of the old stock was to expend it in artillery practice. Some of the floating targets were stated to be eight hundred yards, and others six hundred from the battery. I saw shells used very frequently, and was informed that the practice was not efficient or satisfactory if at least one-third of the shells did not explode directly over the target. The bay is occasionally visited by large shoals of porpoises, and in calm weather they frolic in great numbers on the surface of the water. On a day in June, 1861, they were extremely abundant, and no where more so than close to the floating targets. Every shell discharged, killed or disabled some of them without frightening the others or dissolving their "aggregate meeting." Some tons of porpoises were collected after the firing ceased, and subjected, I believe, to some process for the extraction of oil. I was a spectator, for about two hours, of the scene I have endeavoured to describe, and it impressed me with an awful appreciation of our artillery as applicable to actual warfare.

DEPARTURE FOR HOME.

Early in the month of September I mentioned, in a conversation with the naval superintendent, my intention to leave Gibraltar for England by the first homeward-bound steamer of the Peninsular and Oriental Company that arrived. He observed that the " St. Jean d'Acre," the flag-ship of Admiral Elliot, was to sail for Plymouth on the 8th or 9th, and that if I chose to go in her he would ask the Admiral to give me a passage. To this most friendly proposal I thankfully acceded, and received, through Captain Warden, an invitation from the Admiral, and an intimation that a cot should be slung up for me in his saloon. At the appointed time, I went on board, and met with a most gratifying reception from the Admiral and the other officers. I was apprised that the ship was to call at Tangier, and also at Cadiz, which might cause a delay of some hours at each place. We went very quickly to Tangier, where a communication was received for the British ambassador at Madrid, to be transmitted to him from Cadiz. On arriving off the latter place, the Admiral landed and came back in about an hour to have his personal luggage packed up, to put his sailing captain in full command of the vessel, and then to proceed himself to Madrid as speedily as possible, in accordance with a telegraphic message from our ambassador. All requisite arrangements were very quickly completed ; but before he eft the ship he addressed the officers and crew, expressing briefly but strongly his regret at parting from those who had evinced, whilst under his command, the greatest efficiency in the discharge of their duties, accompanied by numerous manifestations of respect and attachment, of which he felt extremely proud, and should never be forgetful. As soon as his barge pulled off, the crew, of their own accord, rapidly manned the yards, and cheered him most enthusiastically until he entered the port and was no longer in sight. It was a most affectionate farewell, and must have been thoroughly disinterested, for the ship was going home to be paid off, and, consequently, her officers and crew would be dispersed amongst the general body of the naval service. Immediately after we left Cadiz, the midshipmen came into the saloon to receive lessons from the naval instructor; and as each of them entered he saluted me with a semblance of the utmost respect and humility, as " Admiral Porter." When I disclaimed the rank and authority ascribed to me by the middies, one of them replied, that when the Admiral had gone away, leaving me in full possession of his cabin, they had agreed to make me an admiral, at all events until we reached Plymouth; and he begged leave to suggest that the first exercise of my authority ought to be an order to the instructor to give them a holiday or two. I laughed heartily at the young scamp's suggestion, and the lessons commenced. The instructor reprimanded one of his pupils for not having previously studied some pages assigned to him to learn, saying, " You will never attain rank in the navy if you continue so ignorant of Navigation." The middy replied, pointing to me, " The admiral who is sitting there is of very high rank, and I could safely swear that I know as much about navigation as he does."

CHARITY; REAL CHARITY.

A woman and two children had been sent on board the "St. Jean d'Acre" at Gibraltar to be taken to England. Her name was Crompton, and she was the widow of a carpenter who had been accidentally killed at the New Mole two or three months previous to our departure. Of the children, both boys, one was still unweaned, and the poor mother and her offspring appeared to be miserably destitute. Their scanty clothing was squalid and ragged, and her health had been seriously impaired. She said that her native place was in Durham, and that on arriving at Plymouth she should apply to be transmitted home by the parochial authorities. We were not forty-eight hours at sea before she and her infants were comfortably and neatly clad, the outer garments being made of blue serge, and the others of checkered stuff. She and her elder boy were furnished with hats and boots, fitting perfectly, the uppers of the latter being made of canvas darkly varnished. I was greatly surprised at the skill displayed in attiring the poor creatures, for the needlework was faultless. The younger child was made the favorite plaything of the crew, who seemed delighted to pet and nurse him. When our voyage was completed, a subscription amongst the officers, seamen, and marines provided her with twenty-two pounds, to which I added half a sovereign. The boatswain was the principal collector for the poor widow, whom he described, in nautical phraseology, to be " at dead low water."

A DEATH AND FUNERAL.

The progress of the "St. Jean d'Acre" did not appear to me to be very speedy after our departure from Cadiz until we arrived off Cape St. Vincent. The vessel was propelled solely by the steam-screw. She was large and heavy, and the weather was quite calm, so that sails were useless. I did not regret the delay, for I could not be in more agreeable society, and I never experienced any tendency whatever to sea-sickness. However, just as we sighted St. Vincent, a strong and very favorable breeze sprung up, and the sails were ordered to be set. Whilst all hands were engaged aloft, I was sitting on the quarter-deck, enjoying the novelty of the scene before me, and admiring the celerity with which the work was accomplished. The men were beginning to descend, when a poor fellow named Parkes dropped from a great height. I think he fell from what is termed the mizen-topsail-yard, and he came down very close to me. I instantly took him under the armpits and drew him lengthways on his back. He muttered, "Too much tobacco," and died instantly. It appeared that he had been cautioned by the medical officers against the excessive chewing of tobacco, but his neglect of the warning, and a persistent indulgence in the unwholesome mastication, produced a very fatal fall. In the evening of the following day, his body was committed to the deep. It was sewn in his hammock, in which a large cannon ball was also enclosed. The band played some mournful music whilst the corpse was conveyed to a grating, on which it was laid, covered with the British flag. The officers were in full uniform, and all the men not actually engaged in navigating the ship came on deck. The chaplain read the Burial Service of the Church of England, substituting "the deep" for "the ground," and the grating and flag were then released from their horizontal position, and the body, slipping from between them, sank into the ocean. The ceremony was extremely solemn and respectful ;

but as soon as it concluded, the band went down between decks and commenced playing very lively tunes, and the crew betook themselves to dancing and other pastimes incident to an hour of merry "sky-larking." I believe that in the navy and army it is deemed desirable to discourage the continuance, after discharging the last duties to the deceased sailor or soldier, of gloomy thoughts or dismal recollections.

THE BAY OF BISCAY AGAIN.

When we arrived in the Bay of Biscay, it was in a state very unlike that which I endeavoured to describe in reference to my passage through it on my voyage to Gibraltar. It then fully realised the Byronic line—

> " And ocean slumber'd like an unwean'd child ;"

but when I viewed it from the deck of the homeward-bound war-steamer, its surface was free from foam, and perfectly glassy, but the smooth, unbroken water exhibited stupendous undulations. We had a steady breeze on our quarter, filling every sail, and directing the roll of the sea completely with us, and our decks were quite dry. From the summit of a mountain wave, we slided noiselessly down, and were immediately raised again to a great but transient elevation. In my former passage across the bay, I was charmed by its unusual placidity, and on my return I was struck with admiration of its grand appearance, and highly gratified by the safe and very quick run that we accomplished.

We anchored in Plymouth harbour late in the evening of the 16th of September, and I landed on the following morning, and remained at a hotel for two days, awaiting the arrival of the steamer on her way from London to Dublin. During my short stay, I was able to go through Plymouth, Devonport, and their environs, which, whilst they display natural beauties of no ordinary character, afford to a stranger, in their public establishments, many objects which cannot fail to excite admiration. Eventually, I reached Dublin on the 21st, and received the affectionate congratulations of my family on my return to them in perfect health. On the day after my arrival, my youngest child designated me " the sweetest papa in the world." The appellation was undoubtedly suggested by the circumstance, that I had brought home 100 lbs. of orange marmalade, 70 lbs. of preserved nectarines, 70 lbs. of apricot jam, and six large Murcian melons. The excellence of my sweets was fully proved by the rapidity of their consumption. I fetched from Gibraltar a snake and a green lizard, which I sent to the Zoological Gardens ; but I believe they did not long survive their transportation from the South of Spain to our cold and humid climate.

AT HOME—LEISURE NO PLEASURE.

After my return from Gibraltar, I found the tenor of my life in Dublin forming the greatest contrast to the twenty years during which I had been engaged in magisterial duties of a multifarious nature, extending from the cognizance of lapses from sobriety or neglect of sweeping a footway, to authorising a search for concealed pikes or firearms, or taking informations and issuing warrants for treason-felony. I regarded my release from any further attendance at the place in Exchange-court, dignified by the appellation of the Head-Office, as a most agreeable and healthful change ; but I often regretted the cessation of my functions at the branch-court in Kingstown, where I enjoyed the ventilation of a pure atmosphere through cleanly and elevated premises, whilst the bench which I occupied commanded a view of almost the entire Bay of Dublin. I also derived from my official position a free passage, by first-class carriage, on the Dublin and Kingstown Railway, and occasionally received passes on the Great Southern and Western Line, enabling me to visit Cork or Killarney. All these advantages terminated on my retirement. Persons sometimes came to my house, supposing that I still had sufficient authority to take declarations or attest signatures ; and when informed that my functions had ceased, expressed their disappointment at finding that I was " no longer of any use." My next-door neighbour was a Rev. Dr. Browne ; and a gentleman who had some business with him, but did not exactly know his residence, pointed out my door to a cabman, and desired him to " try there." Cabby replied, " No, sir, that is where Porter, the *decayed magistrate,* lives." I do not believe, however, that in the use of such an expression any wilful disrespect was intended. I have often heard owners and drivers of public vehicles declare that they regretted my retirement.

The Italians have a very current phrase,* which attaches delight to the total absence of employment. I never could appreciate idleness as pleasurable ; and I believe that numerous instances of mental abberration have originated in the want of occupation. I am disposed to insert in these pages a few productions of my first year of unrelished leisure. If their

* Dolce far niente.

perusal is pleasing to a reader, they require no apology; and if they are considered unworthy of attention, they may serve as a warning to others against being induced to waste their time in similar attempts.

A REVIEW.

A gentleman of literary tendencies, and for whom I had a great personal regard, mentioned to a small party of friends his intention to publish a semi-monthly periodical in Dublin, under the title of "The Irish Review." I stated that whilst wishing the utmost success to his undertaking, my hopes were extremely slender, and adduced what I considered cogent reasons for the opinion expressed. None of the others coincided with me, and one of them jocularly remarked that a penance should be imposed on me by requiring me to write the preface. With this proposition the others fully agreed, and although I steadfastly declined to comply with their requisition, I expressed a willingness to attempt a contribution of a prefatory nature, the topics and composition being completely left to my own discretion, or perhaps I should say, indiscretion. The production was sent and published, and although the periodical was not ultimately successful, a better result may possibly attend the next attempt to establish an enlightened and impartial organ of literary criticism in the Irish metropolis. My contribution was headed—

AN IRISH REVIEW.

WHEN Albion, proud Albion, heard threats of invasion,
Her spirit and energy met the occasion;
She call'd on her sons, and they readily back'd her,
And perhaps for that reason, no foes have attack'd her.

Of Ireland, it seems, there were doubtings and fears ;
From us they declined to demand volunteers;
They thought that if bay'nets and muskets we got,
We 'd exchange with each other a thrust or a shot.

They thought Tipperary could ne'er meet Tyrone,
And part in whole skin without any sore bone,
That lads from old Galway or Southern Tralee ;
With Derry's apprentices might disagree.

We 've no volunteers, and we 'll not have a fight,
Our colors are peaceful, they 're plain black and white ;
But without volunteers in green, scarlet, or blue,
We 're determined on having AN IRISH REVIEW.

A review—where a mere moral force we demand,
A review—at which Intellect takes the command,
A review—where each Science delights to combine,
A review—where Wit's facings appear in the line.

A review—where a *press* procures *willing* recruits,
A review—where at Folly the satirist shoots ;
At poor *Private* Folly no aim is directed,
But *General* Folly 's the mark that 's selected.

To *Gen'ral* Goodhumor the duty 's assign'd
Of keeping the ground, and the public shall find
He 'll drive away Rancor and Prejudice, too,
Till *Gen'ral* Applause greets THE IRISH REVIEW.

LINES IN AN ALBUM.

I wrote at the request of my beloved and truly lamented
son, Austin Duggan Porter, the following lines in his
Album :—

My youthful years have pass'd away,
My step hath lost its lightness,
And scanty locks, once brown, then gray,
Now show unvaried whiteness.
My failing eyes can see but few
Of early friends remaining,
Yet have I many reasons true
To keep me from complaining.

To be a blessing to mine age,
  I see mine offspring striving;
And even in this little page
  My boyhood seems reviving.
I feel that they who bear my name
  My early tastes inherit,
And their pursuits are just the same
  As pleased my youthful spirit.

CHAPTER XXX.

A DUBLIN DENTIST.

SEVERAL friends have suggested that, even at the risk of being considered discursive or irregular in the arrangement of my Gleanings and Reminiscences, I should not conclude without narrating a few of the incidents which my intimacy with the late Patrick Brophy, of Dawson Street, the State Dentist, enabled me to witness or to hear described by him.

He had commenced industrial avocations as an apprentice to a jeweller in Skinner Row, and became singularly skilful in the execution of articles in the precious metals, especially in the making of necklaces or setting of gems. He subsequently obtained employment from a German dentist who lived in Golden Lane; and from him he acquired a practical knowledge of the operative means necessary for the relief of personal suffering by stuffing or extracting teeth. The German returned to his native country in 1815, and Brophy immediately succeeded to his Dublin business. When I became acquainted with him, he was living in Dawson Street, and reputed to be in the most extensive practice of a profession for which he had not received any special preliminary instruction. He was extremely convivial, but far more willing to give than to receive invitations; and although his table was most profusely supplied with the choicest wines and spirits, I never perceived in him the slightest indication of intemperance. Amongst his intimates the most intimate was a gentleman who resided in the town of Galway, and whose person was so very bulky as to obtain for him the *soubriquet* of " The Great Western." He required no invitations to Brophy's table, for whenever he visited Dublin, he became a daily dinner guest during his stay; and certainly his host did not hesitate to make him the subject of tricks or bantering. At one time, Brophy had just returned from a Parisian trip, and brought home two or three shawl or scarf-pins made of polished steel, and having large mother-of-pearl heads. The " Great Western " was in town, and was in his usual place at dinner time, on a day when I happened to be a guest. Pat had a dark scarf on his neck, and it was fastened with one of the Parisian pins which I afterwards heard had cost about tenpence. His bulky friend had a finger ring, on which there was one diamond, and soon after dinner, he took it off, and handed it to Brophy, saying—

" Pat, you are considered a very competent judge of diamonds : what would you value that ring at ? "

Brophy examined the article, and replied, " I think it is worth about thirty pounds."

" Well," said the other, " I bought it this morning at West's in Capel Street, for thirty guineas."

" I do not think you should be dissatisfied with your bargain. It is a nice, clear stone, and has been very neatly set." was the observation of our host; but the proprietor of the ring very soon observed that Pat was sporting a beautiful pearl pin, and asked him where he had procured it.

"This pin," said Brophy, taking it out of his scarf, and holding it up to the view of his interrogator, "should be in some national museum or institution where the relics of departed heroism and the memorials of glorious achievements would excite the curiosity and admiration of future generations. I have neither the time nor the ability necessary to the description of its formation or value. I almost wish that I never became its possessor."

The "Great Western" took the pin, and expressed his admiration at the neatness of its formation, and the clearness and smoothness of the beautiful pearl, of which he implored his dear friend Pat to disclose the entire history. Pat consented, and proceeded as follows :—

"I was for several years on terms of the closest intimacy with the late Dr. Auchmuty, who had a dispensary at Rathfarnham. In his latter years his teeth had completely decayed, and I made him a set, with which he was highly pleased, and for which I declined to accept of any remuneration. I kept them in order by occasional repairs and cleaning, and frequently visited the old doctor, for whom I had the highest esteem, and whose conversation was extremely interesting, for he had been a naval surgeon, and served on board the "Victory" at the battle of Trafalgar. At length he found his health declining very rapidly, and felt that his end was approaching; and he said to me, a short time before his death, that he wished to leave me a token of his gratitude for my attentions, and begged me to accept this pin, which he assured me was formed from a nail drawn from the timbers of the "Victory," steeled and highly polished, and then mounted with the pearl, *which he had taken from Nelson's eye.* Such is the simple history of this extraordinary relic."

"Oh! what a treasure you obtained from your old

friend!" exclaimed the "Great Western," "exquisitely beautiful in appearance, and also surpassingly interesting in reference to its materials and origin."

"Its intrinsic value," said Brophy, "is not half, or perhaps a quarter, of what your ring cost."

"I would give two such rings for that pin," was the reply.

"Suppose I let you have it for one."

"I would close the bargain at once."

"Then close it," said Pat, handing the pin to the Great Western, from whom he received in return the thirty-guinea ring.

Within forty-eight hours all the very numerous friends and acquaintances of the dentist became fully informed respecting the substitution of the Parisian shawl-pin for the pearl off Nelson's eye. The former owner of the ring became the object of cajolery and mock condolence wheresoever he appeared, and no one quizzed or bantered him more than his friend Pat, who advised him to get up a raffle for the pin, and offered to take three tickets, provided each chance of obtaining the Trafalgar relic did not exceed four-pence. He retained the ring ; but, certainly, the "Great Western" could console himself in the enjoyment of very frequent repasts, which he appeared fully to appreciate.

When Prince Napoleon, some years since, went round Great Britain and Ireland in the Imperial yacht, "La Reine Hortense," he was detained at Galway by the weather becoming extremely boisterous. Having landed and arranged to remain for a few days at the railway hotel, he was waited on by the "Great Western," who then happened to be the High Sheriff, and who, accompanied by some of the principal gentry, welcomed the

Prince, and expressed an anxiety to give him a cordial reception and to render his sojourn agreeable. The sheriff addressed him in French, but was immediately requested to speak English, with which language the Prince stated that he was perfectly acquainted. In a short time after, I was dining at Brophy's, and the Galway functionary commenced a narration of the interview, but was immediately interrupted by Pat, who told him that we knew all about the affair already.

"How can you know anything about it?" said the sheriff; "there was nothing published beyond the fact of our having called to pay our respects."

"Oh!" replied Pat, "one of your companions was here very soon after, and gave me the particulars fully, and I mentioned them to a great many of my friends. He said that you told those who were going with you that you would address Napoleon in French, and when you and the others were admitted, you began to speak, but was immediately stopped by the Prince, who said, 'Mr. Sheriff, you will greatly oblige me by speaking English, for I assure you and the other Galway gentlemen that I do not understand the *Irish* language.'"

The laughter excited by Brophy's imaginative statement that the sheriff's French had been mistaken for Irish was renewed and increased by the earnest declaration of the latter that the Prince had not uttered a word about the Irish language, nor imputed any imperfection to his French. By his energetic denials of the fiction he rendered it extremely amusing.

Along with great hospitality, Brophy afforded his guests frequent and varied amusements. He had a considerable number of costumes, which enabled him to impart a grotesque and motley appearance to the occupants of his dinner-table, or to produce a *tableau vivant* in his drawing-room. There was a young barrister whose stature exceeded six feet, and he was generally wigged, robed, and placed on an elevated seat, to be styled "The Lord High Chancellor." I was usually equipped to personate a Lord Mayor; but whenever his favorite tableau of the death of Nelson was produced, I was in the garb of a sailor, and had to catch the falling hero as soon as one who sang, with a splendid voice and great musical taste, the recitative and air descriptive of the casualty, came to the lines announcing—

> " At length the fatal wound,
> Which spread dismay around,
> The hero's breast received."

The vocalist was not in view; he was in a side wing, where he was accompanied by pianoforte music, and the shot was simulated by a blow on a drum. Brophy's Nelson was a perfect make-up. He wore an admiral's uniform, presenting an armless sleeve and various decorations, and the green shade over *the pearl* on the sightless eye was not forgotten. I recollect one representation, when he fell more against my shoulder than across my arm and knee, but he immediately stood up and exclaimed, "D——n it, that wont do; I must die again."

He was very fond of music, and played the violin frequently, but confined his performances to jigs, reels, and lively Irish tunes. I called one evening, when I was told that he was not at home, but as I was leaving, the servant followed me, and I was informed that he wished me to go down to the lower room of " the return," where he had " a couple of fiddlers." When I entered the apartment, he said that he was glad I came, as I had two legs, and could increase the number amongst them to half-a-dozen.

Each of his companions was minus a leg, but their hands were in perfect order, and their music was extremely pleasing.

The late Lord Rossmore was very intimate with Brophy, who was certainly not singular in admiring the many amiable and agreeable qualities invariably evinced by his noble friend. On one occasion Pat had engaged a first-rate player on the Irish pipes named Conolly or Coneely, to enliven upwards of a dozen guests by his very delectable music. He was totally blind, and was placed on a chair in a corner of the parlour, where he played whilst we were dining, but he had been previously supplied with a plentiful repast. In the course of the evening, Brophy had a small table placed before the piper, and said that he had afforded us very great pleasure, but he should take a little rest, unyoke the pipes, and have a tumbler of punch, which was made by Brophy and put just at his hand. Almost immediately after this arrangement had been effected, Captain Toosey Williams urged Lord Rossmore to take the pipes and favor us with a tune or two. We all joined in the request to " his lordship," and he acceded to our wishes, and played several pieces of exquisitely sweet music, interspersed with most extraordinary imitations. In one, which was named " The Hare in the Corn," he produced sounds very much resembling the cry of harriers, and other tones like the notes of a hunting horn, terminating with two or three simulated squeaks, supposed to indicate the capture of the hare. He then proceeded to play the beautiful Scotch air of " Ye banks and braes o' bonnie Doun," to which we were listening with great delight, when the blind piper rose from his seat, and exclaimed with furious indignation—

" I did not expect such treatment from any people

calling themselves gentlemen.   It was a most scandalous shame to bring me, a poor dark man, here to be humbugged as you are trying to do, calling on *my lord* to yoke my pipes and play for ye.   He is as much "a lord" as I am myself ; the d——l a lord ever played as he does, he's nothing but a rale piper.   It is not honest or decent to try and deceive me, but you can't do it."

Brophy succeeded in pacifying the enraged musician by admitting that the performer was a real piper, and we had two or three tunes more.   Conolly's indignation produced very great merriment amongst us, and no one enjoyed it more than the noble object of his censure.

There was a citizen of high commercial position, who was, I believe, justly reputed to be very wealthy.   He was a widower, and had become habituated to take a very copious allowance of grog immediately before retiring to rest. He had a son whose society Brophy highly relished, for he had been an amateur performer in every scene of warfare to which he could obtain access.   He had served in Portugal under the standard of Donna Maria, and subsequently joined the foreign legion embodied to contend against the claims of Don Carlos to the crown of Spain.   The contests in which he had participated, and the vicissitudes he had undergone, enabled him to relate many interesting occurrences.   He was a very agreeable companion, and was always welcome in Dawson Street.   Brophy had made a set of teeth for the old gentleman, and when doing some occasional repairs, was informed of the fact, that every night the teeth were placed in a vessel of cold water, where they remained until their owner restored them to his jaws in the morning.   One evening the young man was expressing great dissatisfaction at the dull, tame, and insipid life he was leading, without having any incentive or opportunity to exhibit energy or attempt enterprise; and he added, that although he was well lodged, clothed, and dieted, he was personally penniless, for his father never allowed him any pocket-money.

" I'll get you a little cash," said Brophy. " Slip into his bedchamber, and bring me his teeth; he puts them in a water-basin before he goes to bed." In a night or two the suggestion was adopted, and Brophy immediately made some slight alteration to prevent them exactly fitting their owner, who very soon arrived in a most disconsolate state, and was scarcely able to express articulately the inconvenience and annoyance to which he was subjected. He admitted that he had not been quite sober when he went to bed, but felt certain that he had left the teeth in the basin as usual.

Brophy sympathised with the toothless patient, and told him that he would lose no time in remedying the disaster. He measured the mouth, and then said that there was a set nearly ready for a person who had bespoken them, which, with a little alteration, might fit the present occasion. The teeth were tried, they were a little too tight in one place, and not close enough in another; but these faults were speedily redressed, and the old gentleman was enabled to express distinctly his perfect satisfaction, adding—

" It is all right, Pat. There could not be a better dentist found in the world; and only that they did not fit when you tried them at first, I would almost swear that *my own teeth were back again in my head.*"

Brophy received twenty pounds, which were immediately transferred to the young fellow, who subsequently went to Italy to fight for the Pope, but never returned.

Patrick Brophy was a widower when my acquaintance

with him commenced.   At his marriage he had received
from the bride's father one thousand pounds in cash,
and a bond for a thousand pounds, the interest on which
was to be paid half-yearly, and the principal to be liquidated
at the death of the obligor.   A sudden and very severe indisposition proved fatal to the bride in nine days after her
wedding, and in the evening after her interment her husband returned the cash and bond to her parent.   Although
such conduct was certainly disinterested, and might by
many be deemed even generous, he never relished any
allusion or reference to it.

I believe that about the commencement of his dentistry
pursuits, Brophy had some employment connected with
Doctor Steevens' Hospital.   I have heard that he used to
repair or clean some instruments for the use of the institution ; but I know that when he had attained to extensive
practice and the incident advantages, he frequently evinced
a great desire for the prosperity and advancement of it,
and he frequently visited the old hospital, to all the wards
of which he had full access.   There was a stringent pro-
hibition of the smoking of tobacco by any person whatever in the wards or passages, and a disobedience or
neglect of this order was punishable by immediate expulsion from the premises.   James Cusack, who, as a surgeon, was not to be surpassed, was the principal of the
professional authorities, and he entertained a peculiar
abhorrence of the slightest fume of tobacco being observed
on the premises.   On an afternoon stroll I accompanied
Brophy until we were within a few yards of the building,
when Cusack's carriage came rapidly up, and he alighted,
and entered as soon as possible the principal male ward,
in the most distant bed of which he saw a man in a sitting
posture and smoking a pipe.   The offender, perceiving

that he was detected, reclined back, and drew the bed-clothes about his shoulders. Cusack stepped rapidly to the bedside, and said—

" You have been smoking."

" No, sir."

" I saw you, you lying scoundrel."

" No, sir."

Cusack was standing close to the culprit, and turning round, he shouted for the attendants, who hurried to him; along with them Brophy and I entered the ward, when Cusack resumed—

" This man has been smoking tobacco ; the pipe was in his mouth when I came into the ward."

" No, sir."

" You have the pipe in the bed with you."

" No, sir."

" Lift this fellow to another bed, and see that he has nothing wrapped in his shirt."

The order was obeyed, and then the vacated bed was strictly searched, the bolster, quilt, blankets, sheets, and mattress separately examined, but no pipe was forth-coming. Cusack repeated his positive assertions, that he had seen the fellow smoking, but he could only elicit another " No, sir." He was retiring from the ward, not perplexed in his conviction of having witnessed the for-bidden indulgence, but disappointed and annoyed at the fruitless search. Returning to the offender, he said—

" I promise to forgive you fully, and leave you quite unpunished, if you now tell me where you put the pipe."

" Try your own pocket, sir."

Cusack put his hand in the back pocket of his overcoat, and there found the pipe, which the delinquent had slipped in as the other had turned about to call the attendants.

Great laughter supervened, in which the eminent and amiable James Cusack heartily joined. When we were leaving the hospital, Brophy went into the ward and gave the smoker half-a-crown, and on our way home he remarked that the fellow deserved a reward, as undoubtedly his trick upon Cusack was " as good as a play."

An intimate friend, whom I could also term a schoolfellow, named Vickers, was my companion on a Sunday walk in the summer of 1852, and we happened to direct our course to the Royal Hospital of Kilmainham, and finding that the door of the grounds so long used as a public cemetery was open, we entered, and seated ourselves in the centre of the inclosure, formerly known as " Bully's Acre," or the Hospital Fields, resting ourselves on the remains of an old monument, and enjoying the prospect presented by the varied and undulating surface of the Phœnix Park, and the rich country in its vicinity. My companion had been a medical student in his youth, and he related an adventure which the locality suggested to his recollection, and with the results of which Brophy was stated to have been unpleasantly and unprofitably connected. His narrative was as follows :—

" We had a very stirring row in that corner one night, when I was apprentice to old Aby Colles ; for at that time we had generally to provide our own *subjects*, or to purchase them, at a very high price, from men who followed the calling of " sack-em-ups ;" and as money was not always plenty, we used to form parties for the purpose of invading this and other burial-grounds, and exhuming the bodies. Brophy, the dentist, had a brother named Maurice, whom he was desirous of putting into the medical profession. He was a manly, generous fellow, and possessed a very strong inclination for anything that denoted enter-

2 E

prise, or promised excitement. Pat had taken a cottage and garden in Rathmines, and for his whim or amusement he went into a shop in Kennedy's lane and purchased a spade; and having given his address, the seller wrote the name and address on the handle of the implement. The spade was sent home, and upon the same day a party was organised, of which I constituted one, to visit this place and disinter two or three bodies that had been buried in the morning. I mentioned to Maurice the project we had formed, and he eagerly joined in the undertaking. All was arranged; and we drove out to this place, left our cars at a little distance, and entered the ground, determined to work silently and quickly. However, our volunteer friend had provided himself with his brother's spade, and certainly used it with great despatch, although not so noiselessly as might be wished. But we had been watched. We were seen entering the cemetery, and a body of men, armed with every rough weapon that they could procure, came suddenly upon us. We had to retreat, and made a running fight until we reached the wall, and there our associate was attacked by a man who, with fearful imprecations, declared he would have his life. Blows were quickly interchanged; the combatants closed; and a fierce struggle occurred, which was terminated by Maurice urging his antagonist to the wall, and very speedily pitching him over; the depth at the other side was at least ten feet, although where the encounter occurred was only a foot or two lower than the wall top. The man fell exclaiming that he was murdered. He groaned heavily; and we succeeded with great difficulty, and not without some severe blows from sticks and stones, in effecting an escape from a scene where we felt almost fully convinced that we had left a warm corpse in our attempt to obtain a cold one.

"On reaching Dublin, I accompanied Maurice to the house of his brother, who was greatly alarmed at our appearance, and still more at our narration of the adventure. When it was concluded, he eagerly asked where was the spade, and on being apprised that it had been left in the cemetery, he exclaimed that we would all be hung, or at best transported. 'I knew,' said he to his brother, 'that you would get yourself into an infernal scrape sooner or later; and now your only chance is to set off on foot, and make your way to Naas. I shall have an inside seat taken in the Limerick day-coach for a gentleman who will get in there; make your way to Limerick, and we will try and manage a passage for you from some southern port to get abroad.' Arrangements were made with brief despatch; our companion departed; and the dentist retired to an uneasy bed, perplexed by fears of coroner's inquest, wilful murder, hue and cry, apprehension, trial, conviction, and execution of his unlucky brother.

"Next morning he had scarcely finished his breakfast when he was informed that M'Donough, the peace-officer, required to see him. He admitted the unwelcome visitant, and was informed that his orders* were to bring Mr. Brophy immediately to the Head Police-Office, and to keep him from communicating with any other person before he arrived there. There was no further explanation; and Brophy thought it prudent to refrain from any question beyond asking if he might take a car. This was at once acceded to; and as the peace-officer and his *quasi* prisoner were getting on the vehicle, a woman rapidly approached

* Such orders were not unusual in former times.

and screamed forth the dentist's name. He ascribed this circumstance to the grief or resentment of a bereaved widow or sister, who thought that she beheld in him one of the murderous authors of her misery; but the car drove off rapidly, and the police-office was reached without any further incident or interruption.

"The office was crowded, and at the table was seated Mr. William Hall, an attorney. Brophy and he were well acquainted, and a salute passed between them as the dentist sat down near the other. The magistrates were in their private room, engaged in some conference or consultation. After the lapse of a few minutes, Brophy ventured a word to Mr. Hall—

"'This is a very unpleasant business, Billy.'

"'Very annoying, indeed,' replied the other, 'I have not met a more unpleasant case for some time.'

"'Billy, would a little money be of any avail?'

"'Why, my dear fellow, thirty pounds would put an end to it altogether.'

"'Thirty pounds! Don't say another word. Here's the money. I depend on you that all will be right.'

"The magistrates* entered, and Billy Hall immediately proceeded to express his great gratification that it would not be necessary, or indeed possible, to go any further with the charge then pending before them. 'In fact,' said he, 'it is impossible to continue the prosecution, for the respectable gentleman, whose name was alleged to have been forged, has paid the bill, and it is now my duty to have it handed over to him in your worship's presence.'

"A bill of exchange was delivered, in compliance with

---

* I have often heard Pemberton and Ross Cox describe this scene as fully remembered by them.

Hall's direction, to Patrick Brophy, who found his name written as drawer upon it, in a manner closely resembling his own signature. Evidently surprised, he exclaimed that he thought he had been sent for on another matter.

" ' What other matter, sir ? ' inquired Major Sirr.

" ' Oh, nothing, nothing, sir,' said the enraged but fearful Brophy, who felt that an explanation, which would relieve him from the loss just incurred, might involve his brother Maurice in an accusation of dreadful import. ' Perhaps,' said a peace-officer,' the gentleman knows something about a spade which we have below. We stopped a young vagabond pledging it on the Coombe, and it appears quite new. There was a name and direction on the handle, but the fellow scraped it almost entirely out. We have found, however, on inquiry in Kennedy's lane, that this gentleman bought such a spade at Bryan Murphy's yesterday.'

" ' That spade,' said Brophy, ' is gone from Dublin. It was bought for a friend, and is forty miles away by this time.'

" ' Then, what other business were you thinking of ? ' resumed the inquisitive Major.

" ' Perhaps,' suggested Alderman Darley, 'his anxiety refers to the young woman from Dolphin's Barn, who is charged with concealing the birth of her infant, and who so obstinately refuses to tell who is its father.'

" ' Alas ! for the depravity of man,' said the Major. ' Shall we never be free from vice and its consequences, sin and sorrow, crime and punishment ? '

" ' Why, Major,' said Brophy, taking courage, ' I don't think you'll be quite free of them in a hurry; but I'd like to find out the other parties concerned in this darling bill, for, by G——, I'll make some of them pay it if I can.'

" ' Fie, sir !' said the Major. ' It is plain that a mistaken lenity has led you to adopt a forgery ; and I only hope that there may be more of them in circulation ; for now having paid one, you cannot refuse the others ; and as it is, I have a strong inclination to fine you for blasphemous swearing.'

" ' Don't mind it, Major,' said Brophy, ' I won't *swear* any more; but when I get out of this, I think that I'll *curse* a little.'

" He departed, having paid thirty pounds for a forgery of his own name, and had no consolation beyond discovering, which he did very soon, that the fellow who had been thrown over the wall was not dead, nor even materially injured, and had taken his beating without making much noise about it, once it was over. The spade had been found by some poor vagrant, who sought quietly to dispose of it. Maurice was brought home again, and Pat was forced to acknowledge, amongst his bantering associates, that the *spade* had turned up ' a trump' for the forger."

CHAPTER XXXI.

A TRIP TO THE NORTH—METRICAL ATTEMPTS—
  CONTRASTS—PARIS: A FAIR—A REVIEW—
  NADAR'S BALLOON—SPORT, TURF, BOXING—
  LIQUOR VEHICLES—NO HODS—A HORSE, A DOG,
  RATS.

I took a run to Belfast in 1862, and from thence through
Carrickfergus, and along the coast-road to the Giant's
Causeway, where I spent two days most agreeably. At the
Causeway hotel I met several gentlemen, to one of whom I
was known, and by him was introduced to the others. Their
society was extremely pleasant; for although they differed
in their views and opinions on certain subjects, their conversation was completely free from acerbity. In referring
to the preference of certain colors by the inhabitants of
northern or southern districts, an anecdote was related of
a wrangle between two young fellows who had come from
very distant parts of Ireland, to be employed in one of the
great monetary establishments of Dublin, and who resided
at Sandymount. I have not introduced into my preceding
pages any expressions indicative of political or religious
preferences, and I think that the "wrangle" may be submitted to the perusal of all parties or sects without offend-
ing their feelings or exciting their prejudices. I thought it

curious and amusing, and it induced me to attempt to
narrate, in a versified form, the antagonistic tendencies
of—

GREEN AND ORANGE—ORANGE AND GREEN.

" THERE is a flow'r I dearly love, and which with pride I bear
Upon my head, or next my heart, none with it can compare ;
It is the Orange Lily, to which glorious memories cling,
Of Derry, Boyne, or Aughrim, 'twill the recollection bring.
Some roots I have procured to plant, and when their flow'rs appear,
I'll hail them as the emblems of the cause I hold most dear."
Thus spoke a sturdy Northern lad.　A Munster boy was nigh,
And heard the words which, he conceived, an insult did imply.
"I hate, I loathe your gaudy flow'r," disdainfully he cried ;
" It shall not grow, its tints to show, wherever I abide.
Your lily shall be trampled if it ever meets my sight."
The blood of both was thus aroused and eager for a fight ;
An aged man reproved them, bade their bitter taunts to cease,
And then suggested that his taste each might indulge in peace.
" My friend, I'll plant your lily, let its color glad your eyes,
No hateful green shall intervene to rival its rich dyes.
There's space enough throughout the land where those who love to see
The verdant hue may freely view the sod, the shrub, the tree."
The old man took the lily roots entrusted to his care,
With which the rival youths agreed no more to interfere.
In genial soil, of aspect warm, at once he planted them,
But as each primal leaf arose he nipp'd it from the stem.
He said the green must not appear the orange flow'r beside,
The blossom bright should meet the sight in undisputed pride.
But then the blossom, lone and bare, without the friendly aid
Of leaves to shield its rising stem soon wither'd and decay'd.
The abortive root unto the youths the old man then display'd.
" Both colors are essential to the perfect flow'r," he said.
" You cannot have the orange if the green you take away,
The plant affords a lesson—may it reach your hearts, I pray."

METRICAL ATTEMPTS.

I shall venture to offer two or three more productions
to the readers of these pages.　If my metrical attempts

are considered even below mediocrity, they will serve to make others more acceptable. The coarse, homely attire of the peasant is a foil tending strongly to enhance admiration for the courtly costumes of the upper classes; and the weeds that blossom in our hedgerows, or on the sides of our highways, render us unconsciously more appreciative of the floral beauties displayed in the gardens of aristocratic mansions. My own recollections enable me to compare much of the past with the present, and render me desirous of endeavouring to describe some of the changes which have occurred since—

LONG AGO.

YON tree whose massive timber
   The storms assail in vain,
I've seen a sapling limber
   A child might rend in twain;
And in the churchyard yonder,
   It's planter's lying low,
Whilst on its growth I ponder,
   And think of LONG AGO.

Yon brook that quickly courses
   To turn the busy mill,
Then spent its unclaim'd forces
   Adown the heath-clad hill.
The heather to plantation
   Has yielded, and below,
A bustling railway station
   Contrasts with LONG AGO.

The breeze is freshly blowing
   Full in yon harbour's face,
And yet some craft are going
   Their wat'ry way to trace.
The adverse wind unheeding,
   The waves aside they throw;
By steam their journey speeding—
   How changed from LONG AGO.

I meet a friend—he mentions
   That news of import grand,
O'er half the earth's dimensions
   Has reach'd the Irish land.
Th' events occurr'd this morning,
   And now each fact we know
By an electric warning,
   Undreamt of LONG AGO.

The village school is ending
   Its labors for the day,
Each child, released, is wending
   Its joyous homeward way.
Blithe be their youthful gambols,
   Uncheck'd by care or woe,
As were my boyhood's rambles,
   How long, how LONG AGO.

And as my tott'ring paces
   Proceed, there 's at my side
One whom for varied graces
   I gladly made my bride.
Her dark hair then contrasted
   With locks now tinged with snow,
But still our love has lasted
   The same as LONG AGO.

Thus let it be for ever—
   Let Youth enjoy its time;
Let Age, contented, never
   Regret its vanish'd prime.
Life's joys, life's hopes, life's duties,
   Each passing year will show,
And retrospective beauties
   Appear in LONG AGO.

Amongst the pictures which have, within my memory, been exhibited in Dublin, one painted by Paul Delaroche was regarded by me with surpassing admiration, in which feeling I was certainly not singular, for I found it equally appreciated by many others who viewed it at Le Sage's in Sackville Street. It was said to have originated in an extraordinary reverie of the artist, who, whilst suffering from fever, imagined that he beheld the corse of a young and beautiful female, whose hands and feet had been tightly bound, drifting along a deep and rapid river. On recovering from his malady, Delaroche delineated this vision, and then considered what title he should give the production. On searching the records of martyrdom he could not discover the name of any sainted victim of persecution who had perished in the manner indicated; but finding that the Emperor Diocletian had, about the year of our Lord 300, caused some hundreds of his Christian subjects to be drowned in the Tiber for refusing to abjure their faith, he named the picture "La Martyre Chretienne." It has been engraved, lithographed, and photographed so much, as to evince a general admiration of the conception and artistic power of the painter. I have written some lines on this subject, and have endeavoured to adopt the metre of Ariosto, which I consider not unsuitable to an incident connected with Italy and the ancient days of the Eternal City. The concluding stanza alludes to the lambent circle which, in the painting, appears above the head of—

THE CHRISTIAN MARTYR.

THE sedgy margin of his yellow stream
  Beholds old Tiber rolling to the main,
In eddies silver'd by the struggling beam,
  Wooing the ripples which it can't retain.
A mutual mockery, a vap'ry dream,
  Illusive, unsubstantial, cold, and vain
As human hopes, like ev'rything of earth,
Passing, unpausing, dying e'en in birth.

That river has beheld the glorious day
   When chaste Lucretia's wrongs awoke the ire
That freed her country from the Tarquin's sway;
   Upon that bank Virginia from her sire,
Loathing the brutal Appius to obey,
   When in his breast there raged a base desire,
In her pure heart received the fatal knife,
Preferring death to a dishonor'd life.

Upon that bank in youthful beauty stood
   The virgin Clœlia, when with high disdain
She scorn'd Porsenna's pow'r, and deem'd the flood
   Was easier to stem than tyrant's chain
Could be endured; and there the multitude
   Of foes on Cocles fiercely press'd in vain,
There, one 'gainst thousands, he maintain'd his post,
And foil'd the foremost of Etruria's host.

Upon that classic bank did Mutius stand,
   And in the midst of his astonish'd foes
Upon the altar there he placed his hand
   Unshrinking, round it whilst the flames arose,
To show th' invader of his native land
   How he could scorn the torture's fiercest throes,
And that no tyrant's power could be secure
Against a patriot's purpose, firm and pure.

All these were high and noble in their daring,
   In distant ages were their deeds achieved,
But they had earthly motives strongly bearing
   Them onward in their course, for they believed
That man would honor them. Nor scant nor sparing
   Has been the classic fame they have received,
And History still delights to gild her pages
With deeds like their's from Rome's incipient ages.

But still old Tiber's course hath onward sped,
   And other incidents of higher fame
Have on his banks a holy lustre shed.
   There Diocletian did his will proclaim——

That to the ancient stream there should be led
  His Christian subjects, and the sacred name
Of Christ should be abjured, or Tiber's wave
Should those engulf who own'd His pow'r to save.

In youthful innocence a beauteous maid
  Stands 'mongst the victims doom'd, with lips compress'd,
And eyes already closed—she hath essay'd
  To banish earthly thoughts. Upon her breast
Her hands are folded—she hath meekly pray'd,
  And He to whom her pray'r has been address'd,
To whom she clings all faithful, gives her pow'r
To meet the terrors of life's closing hour.

They bind her hands—she heeds not the infliction
  Of cords that sink into her tender limb;
She's thinking of her Saviour's crucifixion—
  Her soul hath flown to Calvary to Him.
She meekly hears each heathen malediction,
  Heav'n seems to ope as earth appears more dim;
Her fate severe for thrones she would not barter,
And now she sinks—a Christian Maiden Martyr!

Her form is slowly gliding to the sea,
  Her soul to Paradise its way is winging,
Upon her pallid face serenity
  Shows that to earth her heart was never clinging;
To all the elements her corse may be
  Abandoned, but the seraph choir is singing,
And chaplets fairer than the flow'rs of Eden
In Heav'n shall deck the martyr'd Christian maiden.

Still o'er her drifting form a circlet golden
  Upon the river sheds its lambent rays,
As though it would the lively hope embolden
  The martyr's truth shall shine in future days,
And when her bones have moulder'd deep and cold in
  Their ocean grave, men shall accord their praise
To him whose reverie or vision mystic
Her suff'rings shall depict with grace artistic.

The following lines were suggested by a visit to an extensive paper manufactory at Inchicore, which, I regret to say, is not working at present :—

I STRAY'D along a village street,
　And as in listless mood I wander'd,
The breeze had wafted to my feet
　Something on which awhile I ponder'd.

Was it a precious talisman,
　Whose magic tracings doth unfold
A right by which its bearer can
　Claim and obtain the treasured gold ?

Was it a flow'r with tints array'd
　Such as the vernal suns bestow,
Richer than monarch e'er display'd,
　Was it a fragrant flowret ?　No !

Was it a feather dropt away
　From some wild bird of varied hues ?
From moors whereon the plovers stray,
　Or groves wherein the ringdove coos ?

Was it the down the thistle yields,
　That sails through air like drifting snow ?
Or fairy flax from fenny fields,
　Or plume from warrior's helmet ?　No !

Or manhood's locks, or maiden's hair,
　Wafted by breeze through village street ?
Nor this, nor these—but lying there
　A filthy rag was at my feet.

With dirt begrimed, that remnant mean,
　Crush'd in the mire, I saw no more ;
But yet I mused on what had been
　Its various uses heretofore.

The great, the humble, grave or gay,
　Noble or base, whoe'er it clothed,
Reject it now, and cast away,
　'Tis only seen but to be loathed.

Such were my thoughts till slumber came,
  And then by fancy's vivid light
Methought that rag, the very same—
  Appear'd again before my sight.

No longer were its folds defiled,
  But pure and white it seem'd as snow,
And 'neath a roller whirling wild,
  I saw the worthless fragment go.

And bleach'd and clean, by that machine
  'Twas triturated fast ;
And when 'twas found completely ground,
  O'er wires its pulp was pass'd.

And on and on that rag hath gone,
  'Neath cylinders I traced it,
And there it roll'd through heat and cold,
  Whilst giant force embraced it.

And I could mark th' electric spark *
  Gleam like a fairy taper;
And fair and smooth as the brow of youth,
  That filthy rag was PAPER.

Material fit for Holy Writ
  And tidings of salvation—
Material grand for a struggling land
  When seeking liberation.

Material proud to warn aloud
  'Gainst slavery's subtle meshes—
Material true to teach the few
  The many's rights are precious.

Material meet for tidings sweet
  Of distant recollection—
Material best to purge each breast
  Of Bigotry's infection.

* The paper, when coiled upon the receiving roller, is very electrical, until it becomes perfectly cool. If the hand is held within five or six inches of it, sparks are elicited, and a lucifer match may be ignited without bringing it nearer to the " material."

Material bright to guide and light
    The onward march of Reason—
Oh ! that old rag has form'd a flag
    For man's best thoughts to blazon.

Then may its use each day produce,
    From pen and press united,
Each noble thought by which we ought
    To feel our souls excited.

May Honor grand, with Virtue bland,
    Inspire it and direct it,
Till wheresoe'er 'tis hoisted, there
    That flag shall be respected.

In the pages which I have yet to submit to the indulgent consideration of my readers, it is not my intention to continue the insertion of specimens of my metrical tendencies. The remainder of my reminiscences are chiefly derived from a residence of eighteen months in Paris in 1864-5. That city has been subjected to much suffering amongst her inhabitants, and to the destruction of magnificent palatial and municipal edifices since the time to which my visit refers; and the Imperial dynasty, that then seemed perfectly secure against Bourbon rivalry or republican designs, has experienced a complete extinction, without any apparent chance of its revival. Notwithstanding all the changes which have occurred within the last ten years, I feel convinced that there are many sights which the French capital can still present to the observation of a traveller from this country, and which will remain indelibly impressed on his memory, either through their intrinsic beauty or magnificence, or still more by the marked contrast they exhibit to objects similar in name here, but in which the name is the only resemblance. He who reflects on the presence of some objects and the absence of others, will be frequently more astonished at not seeing than in beholding. I think that this remark can be exemplified. There is a fair in Paris which is held, during the entire month of January, on the Boulevards, extending from the Madeleine to the Place de la Bastile, a distance of about three English miles. It is resorted to by the most respectable classes. There are wooden booths erected at both sides of the Boulevard, on the footways; and the articles offered for sale comprise "everything, and anything else you may wish for." Children have their toys and confections. Hats, lamps, shoes, boots, jewels, hosiery, glass, birds, mountebanks, newspapers, portable baths, guns, groceries, gloves, cutlery, false teeth, false beards, false eyes, false legs, tempt the adults. There are, however, no horses, cattle, sheep, or swine offered for sale, the live stock consisting only of poultry, rabbits, pigeons, and Guinea-pigs. To an Irishman it is a fair only in name. I visited it frequently, and saw it early and late, but I did not hear an altercation or see a fight, or any person intoxicated. Oh, Donnybrook! how different from your defunct glories! How could a Patlander recognise any resemblance in a scene of peaceable amusement, excited and busy, but without a reel or a blow, to the classic spot, where " batin' was chape as dirt " amongst

" Hearts soft with whisky, and heads soft with blows "?

A REVIEW.

I was at a review in honor of the Emperor's birth-day, or perhaps it should be termed the " Napoleon day," for it was held on the 15th of August, 1864, the real natal day of the third Napoleon being the 20th of April, and the other day being the anniversary of the first **Napoleon's** nativity in 1769. There were more than 100,000 troops on the ground, the Champ de Mars, but nearly the half were National Guards. The concourse of spectators was immense. When his Imperial Majesty arrived, there was not a hat raised, neither was there a shout uttered, nor a shot fired. The troops defiled before him in slow and and quick time, and then he departed. I must have been afflicted on that day with temporary deafness, for I saw it announced in several newspapers of the following morning, that his Majesty had been received with the loudest acclamations.

NADAR'S BALLOON.

Neither at the review to which I have adverted, nor at the ascent of Nadar's giant balloon, where a still greater multitude were assembled, did I see an intoxicated person, or witness any disturbance or altercation. I am far from averring that intoxication does not occur amongst the French, but I believe it to be very infrequent. On a summer's evening, in the Avenue de Neuilly, I observed three workmen, and they were inebriated. Each of them was insisting that the other two should carry him, and they successively tried the experiment, but it terminated always in the tumbling of the three. The spectators were laughing, and the fellows themselves seemed to enjoy the fun, without the slightest asperity towards those who indulged in merriment at their falls. I thought that in my own country there would have been a very prompt offer made, by any tipsy fellows who were laughed at, to supply the company present with an immediate assortment of darkened eyes and ensanguined noses.

SPORT, TURF, BOXING.

Some of our words have been pretty generally adopted by the Parisians. " *Sport* " is frequently used in reference to hunting and racing, but I never heard it applied to shooting or coursing ; and it is remarkable that the word, with the addition of an " e," also signifies the basket of a mendicant friar. Le *Turf* is, as a racing term, understood in the same sense as amongst ourselves ; and the monosyllable by which we express a pugilistic contest, is used to invite or describe an encounter between two combatants who are unprovided with weapons. Outside a wine-house, at Vaugirard, I witnessed a quarrel, and heard the invitation, " *Voulez vous box ?*" The affair commenced by the parties stripping off their blouses, and then, with raised arms and open hands, capering before each other, as if watching an opportunity to strike. I did not see a box given ; for, after a few feints, one combatant gave the other a fearful kick in the pit of the stomach, which stretched him in the greatest agony, and loud acclamations from amongst the bystanders greeted the conqueror. On another occasion, in the Rue de L'oratoire, after a similar challenge, the parties did not strike or kick, but had a wrestle, which terminated in one getting the other down ; he then seated himself on his prostrate antagonist, and proceeded to strike him violently on the head with a *sabot*, or wooden shoe, without any interference or disapproval on the part of the persons present. A *sergent de ville* having seen the crowd, came up, and required the victor to cease hammering his foe. He was instantly obeyed, the vanquished party arose and decamped, and the police-officer walked on without taking any further notice of the affair. A bystander expressed his sympathy with the conqueror, by remarking, that after having gone to the trouble of getting the fellow down, it was a pity that he was not allowed to punish him.

LIQOUR VEHICLES.

I did not at any time in Paris see two persons in attendance on any vehicle used in the conveyance of liquor. One man took charge of a long, narrow dray, on which a number of barrels were placed in two, or perhaps three, tiers; they were secured by ropes passing from rere to front, and there tightened by a kind of capstan, with bars and a catch-bolt. There was also a hinge between the shafts and the body, which allowed the front to be elevated and the rere to be lowered. One man managed this machinery, and could deliver the entire or any part of the load with safety and despatch. The adoption of similar vehicles in the liquor traffic of our country would be decidedly economical; but additional labour would be required to lower large casks into underground cellars, a description of store which is very uncommon in Paris.

NO HODS.

In one of the early productions of my schoolfellow and frequent playmate, Samuel Lover, he narrates an anecdote of two Dublin hodmen, one of whom expressed doubts as to the capability of the other to carry a hod, heavily laden, up a ladder to the roof of a high house. This produced on the part of the other, a wager of a gallon of porter, that he would carry the very man who had taunted him, in a hod, and deliver him over the parapet, five stories above the street. The bet was made, and one fellow seated himself in the hod, and was carried by the other safely to the roof; he then acknowledged that he had lost, but added, " When you were about five rungs of the ladder from the top, I thought you were getting a little weak, and that *I had a fine chance of winning the gallon.*" I do not think such a dangerous wager could arise in Paris, for although very extensive buildings were in progress during my sojourn, I never saw such an implement as a hod there. All the materials were hoisted up by ropes, pulleys, and windlasses. Horse labour was very much used, and small steam-engines were occasionally employed. The lives and limbs of the Parisian workmen were consequently safe from the risks incident to a false step or a rottten rung.

A HORSE, A DOG, RATS.

The French occasionally train animals to exhibit amu-sing tricks and tendencies ; and the surprise of a spectator is not excited so much by what he sees done, as by the conjectures he forms or hears expressed by others, as to the means adopted in bringing animals to the observance of extraordinary habits, or the habitual performance of prescribed duties. When the Messieurs Pereire were building the magnificent structures which form the Boulevard Malesherbes, a large black English horse was employed to raise materials by a rope and pulleys. He worked kindly at his laborious task ; but as soon as the bell rang for breakfast, dinner, or the termination of the day's work, he stopped, and would not resume until the usual time for feeding or rest had elapsed.

At the corner of the junction of the Rue de Castiglione with the Rue de Rivoli, a shoeblack plied his humble vocation, and derived great assistance in obtaining employment from a poodle dog, that had been trained to run, with paws purposely soiled, across the feet of persons coming towards his master's bench and brushes. The dog was, perhaps, the greatest curiosity in the locality, for he never attempted to renew his trespass on the boots or shoes of those who had spent two sous in having them polished by his proprietor. I have frequently seen him actively engaged; but he confined his attentions to the male sex; and I can add, as a circumstance very creditable to those on whom his avocation was exercised, that I never saw him kicked or struck. His daily duties were of a very extraordinary nature; but far more extraordinary must have been the training by which he was qualified for their performance.

On the Esplanade des Invalides I witnessed a most extraordinary exhibition. A very aged man appeared, drawing a small four-wheeled truck. He stopped and rang a handbell for some minutes. When a number of spectators had collected, he opened a slide on the top of the truck. and in the most endearing terms invited his pets, his darlings, to come forth. The darlings came at his call, and consisted of about three dozen rats, mostly of a white or cream color, with red eyes. They crept up his legs, crowded on his head and shoulders, nestled inside his vest, and eagerly fed on some fragments of cheese and some Indian corn, which he produced from a dirty old bag. He then took a tin box, in the lid of which there was a hole, sufficient to admit one rat at a time; and having given the word of command, the "darlings" proceeded to enter. It seemed too small to contain the entire number; but he insisted on their entrance, scolded them, and swore vehemently at their tardiness. At length all had disappeared. and I then perceived that the bottom of the box was fastened to the upper part by hooks, which the old man drew back, and raising the box he displayed a compact mass of rats, packed almost in a square. He gave the word and they separated, and having got some water, re-entered the truck, and the old fellow sent round the hat to collect a few copper from the spectators. I could not refuse a trifle for an exhibition which I considered very curious, but very disgusting. I looked with loathing upon the intimacy between the nasty vermin and their pauper master; and I should have seen, with great satisfaction, the entire school consigned to the attentions of half-a-dozen terriers.

CHAPTER XXXII.

CONTRASTS——FRENCH KITCHENS——SHOPS AND SIGNS
——THE SEINE——TREES AND FLOWERS——A PRETTY
THIEF——FRENCH WIT——FRENCH SILVER——THE
HOTEL DES INVALIDES.

In narrating the incidents that came under my personal
observation, and the impressions produced by many of
them on my mind, during a residence of eighteen months
in the French capital, I have to suffer the disadvantage of
a lapse of ten years, during which some tremendous visitations have produced very disastrous effects, which may
be attributed not only to the successful hostility of a
foreign enemy, but also to the unrestrained and sanguinary violence arising from domestic turbulence. These
unhappy events may have occasioned changes in the morals and habits of the Parisians which would prevent
recent travellers from deeming my descriptions correct
or my conclusions reasonable. Having premised the possibility of a considerable social alteration, I resume, and
shall advert to certain comparative qualities of persons in
this country and in Paris, belonging to similar classes,
presuming to recommend them to the consideration, not
only of those who may visit the French city, but to all
who are desirous of the improvement and civilized progress

of thousands around us. Let me put some unpleasant but truthful contrasts. If I walk, between the hours of nine and twelve at night, from Stephen's Green, by Grafton Street, Westmoreland Street, and Sackville Street, to the Rotundo, I shall see from two to three dozen intoxicated females, and hear many loathsome expressions. On Monday mornings, there have been frequently upwards of fifty females convicted before me for drunkenness; and it would appear, by the statistical tables of the Dublin police, that the numbers have not decreased since my retirement from office. Now, without stigmatizing my own native Dublin as a peculiar locality of public impropriety, I would fearlessly assert that the English Metropolitan district is as bad, that Liverpool is worse, and our own Cork not better. The contrast presented to the reader is, that during a residence of eighteen months in Paris, and in that time frequently passing at late hours through quarters in which much poverty is to be seen, and to which great immorality is generally ascribed, I never saw a female under the influence of liquor, and never heard an expression or witnessed a gesture of an indecent character.

I ascribe much of the intemperance of the operative classes in Ireland, aye, and in Great Britain also, to the absence in general of each sex from the potations of the other. I shall venture on a narrative, which the stenographic talent of Mr. Hughes enabled him to acquire whilst waiting in the yard or lobby of the police-court, and listening to a woman detailing the misfortunes of some of her friends :—

"Mrs. Rafferty had just run out to get a grain of tay and a quarther of shugger. Mrs. M'Mullen, the shoe-maker's wife, had a few half-pence left after paying for a pair of soles and some binding; and was it not quare that they should meet Jenny Riordan just round the corner at Cassidy's door ?   Cassidy always kept ' the best of sper-rits,' and Jenny Riordan stood for little Patsy M'Mullen only a fortnight before.   Mrs. M'Mullen insisted that half a glass a-piece would do them no harm, if they'd slip into Cassidy's.   Well, in they went ; and just as they were passing ' behind the tay chests,' that all the world mightn't see them, who should be there but Kitty Laffan and Betty Rooney.   Poor Betty had just left her sarvice, and had half a quarter's wages in her pocket ; and she wished to explain why she wouldn't stay in that place, as her mistress was too particular entirely.   They were all decent women, that never took more than ' half a glass' at a time.   But they were all very genteel, and had a proper spirit ; so each insisted on ' standing,' until each half glass had become half a pint.   Mrs. M'Mullen got home after losing the pair of soles on the way, and got terrible usage from her husband.   Mrs. Rafferty had a little difference with Betty Rooney, and as Betty felt her-self rather strong after the last little sup, she cut Mrs. Rafferty's head with a pewter quart that happened, un-luckily, to be 'convenient.'   Mrs. Rafferty put Betty's eyes into mourning for the next week ; and the big polis-man (I don't know his name, but they call him ' Coffin-foot,' because you might bury a child in his shoe) escorted the combatants to Chancery Lane."   Some more of the party were picked up on their way home, and taken to Newmarket, and were brought up to the Head Office next morning.   The husbands of these half-glass takers could not say much about the matter, for they had a little jolli-fication amongst themselves on the previous Monday, and two of them beat their respective wives very severely, for daring to go skulking and prying after them, and disturbing them, under the pretence of getting them home.

Such was not an exaggerated picture, nor did it deal with an unusual occurrence; but there was a vast difference between it and the indulgences of the corresponding class in Paris. There, if a married operative took himself to the fair of St. Cloud, to the Bois de Boulogne, or Vincennes, his wife almost invariably not only accompanied him, and if they had a family, brought one or two of the children with her, but she also assumed the direction of the humble festivity over which she presided. Then, as to the refreshments, no seclusion was sought: on the contrary, if the weather was fine, the open air was preferred. Their landlord, their employers, their neighbours might be passing, or perhaps occupying the next tables, whilst the Frenchman and his family were enjoying themselves. The woman shared the wine, beer, coffee, cakes, or whatever formed the repast. Their superiors were recognised, and saluted with grave respect. Their acquaintances were accosted with politeness and apparent cordiality, but were not invited to join. Wine was not much used; beer, of German or English manufacture, especially the latter, was the drink most desired. The man sat, chatted, and smoked; the woman occupied herself with the children, or perhaps with needle-work. The various incidents of a French metropolitan thoroughfare or pleasure-grounds amused and sometimes excited them. Intoxication and its concomitant indecencies and absurdities were ignored. A man could not but feel repugnance to excess in the presence of his wife, and with his children almost at his knees; and, moreover, publicity is an important auxiliary to the promotion and maintenance of decorum. In the British empire, the respectability of a neighbourhood is considered a valid reason against granting a licence for the sale of liquor to be consumed on the premises, in the vicinity. In Paris, there is *a restaurant* in the gardens of the Tuileries, another at the Luxembourg, and two within the palatial grounds of St. Cloud, unless recent events have caused their suppression, which there is no reason to suppose to have occurred. In every part of France that I visited, I felt convinced that the policy was to have liquors moderately supplied to sober customers, and to impart full publicity to the sale and consumption. Amongst us the classes of society are separated from the view, and consequently from the moral influences of each other; and licensed public-houses in all our populous localities are provided with places arranged for the reception and refreshment (?) of the lower orders, where they may meet "no one better than themselves "— where they may skulk in and reel out.

I turn to another topic which involved a great and very apparent difference between the operative and laboring classes who came under my observation in Paris and those of corresponding grades in my own country. In the French capital, works were in progress of a most extensive nature. Great eminences were to be levelled, and valleys filled up; old streets were to disappear, to be replaced by spacious Boulevards, lined with splendid mansions. I was informed that upwards of 200,000 laboring men were employed in daily toilsome work, but to avoid any imputation of an exaggerated statement, I shall suppose the number not to exceed one-half of the thousands mentioned by my informants. As to those whom I saw engaged in mere labor, one look at their wrists and ankles—one glance at their weather-bronzed features and high cheek bones would suffice to satisfy any observer of the unceasing exertions incident to their avocations. Their necks were open, and a hat or cap, a blouse, trousers, shoes, and stockings were the only garments to be seen. Their clothes in general appeared old and worn; a patched elbow, a patched knee was to be seen with the great majority : but amongst them I looked repeatedly, but invariably in vain, for even *one ragged man.* I may mention that the words *"une loque"* (a rag) was considered amongst the lower classes in Paris as expressive of the utmost contempt for the person, male or female, to whom it would be applied.

FRENCH KITCHENS.

To such of my readers as may visit Paris, I presume to suggest that they will be amused and perhaps surprised by examining two or three French kitchens. The space appropriated to culinary purposes, even in establishments containing numerous inmates, is in general less than one-half the size of the apartment used for similar purposes amongst us. The cooking is done by " a range," which usually occupies one-third of the room. Covers, stew-pans, saucepans, salad baskets, ladles, &c. appear on the shelves or hang thickly upon the walls. They are very cleanly in appearance. The French own Cayenne, but I never met a French cook who was acquainted with such a stimulant as Cayenne pepper, nor did I ever see it at table. Mushrooms are profusely used in a variety of ways, and by their extensive artificial cultivation, are procurable almost in all seasons, but catsup appears to be unknown, nor is there a specific word in the language by which it can be expressed. The French have been contemptuously designated " frog-eaters," but if you wish to indulge in a repast of frogs, you will have to pay as much for it as would procure you a far larger portion of turtle in

London or Liverpool.   The hind-quarters of the frog are the only parts used in French cookery.   Snails are highly esteemed, and enormous quantities are displayed for sale, in baskets or barrels, at certain houses, which exhibit inscriptions that they are celebrated for snails *(specialité pour escargots.)*   I tried a plate once, and must candidly admit that the stomach overcame the palate, or perhaps I should say that prejudice conquered judgment.   I have never seen them served up to table, unless in soup, and my plate contained at least a dozen.   I took one, thought it a delicious morsel, swallowed it, and essayed another. Nothing could be nicer, and down it went, but then my stomach suggested that I was eating snails.   In vain the palate pleaded ; I could go no further, and compromised with the stomach that if it retained the two, no more should be offered.   I do not consider myself an epicure, but can easily imagine that a lover of dainties might regret that he had not been trained in early life to take, without repugnance, *a mess of snails.*

If you fancy corned beef and the vulgar vegetable which is abundantly used, but never named at our tables by lips polite, let your thoughts revert to home, and postpone the repast until your return, for at a French table it is not to be seen.   If you get a nice slice of ham you are at liberty to wish for a little strong Irish mustard to give it a relish; the French mustard is made with vinegar and flavored with garlic, and is certainly a very unpleasant contrast to ours.   If you wish for pepper or salt, turn the haft of your silver or plated fork and help yourself with it.   I never saw a salt-spoon or pepper-castor at a French table.

SHOPS AND SIGNS.

The shops on the principal commercial thoroughfares of Paris are tastefully constructed, and their internal arrangements, in almost every instance, appear creditable to the proprietor and convenient to his customers. Still, I do not think that Grafton Street, College Green, Dame Street, Westmorland Street, or Sackville Street, would be disparaged by a comparison with the Parisian streets in which similar trades are pursued as those to which, in the above-mentioned places, the Dublin shops are appropriated. Perhaps I should not employ the term "shop" for it appears to have fallen greatly into disuse, and to have been supplanted by houses, temples, halls, emporiums, magazines, bazaars, institutions, and repositories. I like the old respectable, bread-winning word; and I cannot forget the expression attributed to the first Napoleon, that he overcame every difficulty until he had to encounter the hostility of "ships and shops." However, I fear I am digressing, and shall proceed to notice some differences which a tourist may observe between our shops and those of Paris. In my opinion, nothing proves the advance of education, although of a very limited nature, in Dublin more than the almost universal abandonment of signs and peculiar designations over our shops. In my early boyhood, few of the laboring class, or even of the domestic servants, could read. It was hazardous to send a messenger to Messrs. Worthington and Dawson, hardware merchants, 27 Thomas Street. Signs were absolutely necessary for those who could not read; so we had the "New Frying Pan," the "Golden Boot," the "Three Nuns," the "Plough," the "Raven," and hundreds of others displayed. Nicknames were sometimes advantageous to traders ; O'Brien of Christ Church yard would rather have his till plundered than be deprived of his designation of "Cheap John." "Squinting Dick's" was an unfailing direction to a rich trader's in Mary's Abbey, where he viewed both sides of the street at one glance. In France. I feel convinced that the education of the "million" has not advanced as it has with us, and consequently signs and peculiar titles for commercial establishments are extensively used. In Paris the number and variety is astonishing, and in some instances very irreverent. That name, at the mention of which every knee should bend, is over more than one shop. Saintly names and effigies designate many houses engaged in the sale of mere worldly wares or fashionable vanities. A picture of the first Napoleon is displayed on one house as "La Redingôte Grise," (the grey riding coat,) and on another he appears as "Le Petit Caporal" (the little corporal.) Some signs bespeak the patronage of the aristocratic legitimists, others refer to French progress in the arts, or prowess in the battle-field. Some of the shops amuse by ludicrous propinquities. In the Rue de Rivoli one house, over the door of which Cupid appears persistently stationary, is inscribed with an announcement of marriage outfits; next door to it is an extensive establishment of baby linen. On one of the Boulevards, St. Michael the archangel is only a door removed from—the prophet Mahomet.

I have to enunciate a deliberate opinion, which to those who have not visited the French capital will undoubtedly appear extraordinary, and perhaps be by them considered exaggerated. It is to the effect that if I had to select the Parisian shop most worthy of a prize for comparative cleanliness, beauty of internal arrangement, quality and variety of productions incident to the trade, I should feel

bound to award the preference to some one of the many
shops belonging to BUTCHERS. In nearly all these concerns, whether small or spacious, it would be almost impossible to suggest any improvement. There is one belonging to Duval, in the Rue Tronchet, just at the rere of
the Madeleine, well deserving of an express visit. An
entire house is appropriated to make a shop, and nothing
intervenes between the floor and the roof. Over the front,
as emblems of the trade, you see gilded ox-heads and the
horns of deer displayed. You enter on a floor neatly
matted, or in summer sprinkled with white sand. The
meat lies on slabs of white marble, or hangs from hooks of
polished steel, and the scales are sheeted with porcelain.
Stools, well padded, and covered with green leather afford
you a seat. On the shelves, and in the recesses, bouquets
of flowers and pots of the choicest exotics gratify your
sight and smell. A fountain with a rock-work basin ex-
hibits gold fish and scarlet carp. The cashier is a handsome female, elegantly attired. The aspect of the place
tends to excite an appetite, for no idea of an impure or
disgusting nature can be suggested by anything in your
view. The front closes with lattice rails, which admit the
air, and the meat in warm weather is covered with a gauzy
kind of canvas which excludes the flies. If you admire
a nice plant or bouquet, it is intimated that you can have
it at a certain price, and the fish will be sold if you fancy
any of them. Any articles you purchase are succeeded
next morning by a fresh supply. One word, however, as
to the Parisian butchers' shops. Never lodge very near one,
unless you are satisfied to lie awake from about four o'clock
in the morning. The beasts are all slaughtered at the public
"abattoirs," the carcasses are conveyed to the shops on
strong and loudly-rattling carts. The work of cutting up,

2 G

cleaving, sawing, chopping, then commences, and to sleep within fifty yards of the place, is out of the question.

The transition is natural from the butcher's stall to the poulterer and fishmonger. Their shops are far inferior in arrangement or appearance to those of the flesh venders, but the fowls in France are uncommonly fine, which is ascribed to the feeding being *finished* with maize and milk. I would back Paris against London for a Christmas turkey or pair of fowl. Truffles are an addition seldom seen at our tables, but a splendid turkey would be considered in France, a very ill-treated bird, if it went to the spit unaccompanied by the honors of a truffle-stuffing. I may here incidentally mention that I have seen flocks of turkeys at *St. Germain en Laye,* and also in different parts of Normandy and Brittany, feeding eagerly on haws picked from the foot-stalks and crushed in wooden troughs. What numbers of turkeys might be fed in Ireland by a similar process! Fish, in Paris, is scarcely ever of first-rate quality, and it is always dear. They eat many kinds which we seldom touch. Carp, tench, and perch are frequently to be seen at table, and the gudgeon is used to an extent calculated to surprise a Dublin man, in the vicinity of whose city it is most abundant, but at whose repasts it is unknown.

THE SEINE.

The Seine, which at Paris is a considerable river, not being affected by any tide, and also being protected from the access of such quantities of filth as are conveyed into the Liffey by our public sewers, presents always a clear, and sometimes a limpid, appearance. The banks are a great school of practical patience. There may be seen numerous anglers watching the floats of their lines, and tranquilly awaiting the bite of some unwary member of the finny tribe, whilst hours are absorbed into past time, but without pastime—not even "one glorious nibble" rewarding their perseverance. I have sauntered along the quays of Paris for an hour or two almost every day, and never saw but one capture, which was a small eel. The proprietor of the rod and line seemed very proud of his solitary achievement, and it was evident that he regarded it as an unusual occurrence.

Persons who rescue others from drowning at Paris receive from some public fund, either police or municipal, a reward of twenty francs (16s. 8d.) I have been credibly informed that it is not an infrequent arrangement between two scamps, that one is to fall into the river, and then the other takes a heroic plunge, seizes the sinking victim, and emulates the skill and courage of Cassius, when "from the waves of Tiber he bore the troubled Cæsar." But the modern Cassius and Cæsar, if the reward is attained, devote it to a gastronomic sacrifice, and feast sumptuously on what was so nobly acquired. A young female on the Quai Voltaire, having excited suspicion by falling too frequently into the river, was told that no reward would be given for any future salvage; consequently the subsequent wettings of her garments were reserved for the washing tub.

TREES AND FLOWERS.

Perhaps the most general taste in France, amongst all classes and conditions of people, is for ornamental trees and flowers; you see them everywhere. On the Boulevards you find rows of the Oriental plane, acacia, horsechestnut, hickory, catalpa, maple, and various other trees. Every nook or corner, not required for some industrial or

domestic purpose, is planted. The yards of horse repositories or forges have trees or scandent plants trained on
the walls; and in private residences, and the enclosures
belonging to public offices, trees and flowers abound.
Balconies and window-stools display boxes and flower-
pots wherever the aspect is favorable; and even in northern
aspects the hardy ivy is encouraged to push its verdant
tendrils. In the palatial gardens and public parks, Flora
appears to be not merely the presiding, but the monopoli-
sing deity. Great care is bestowed on the cultivation of
those places; but it is worthy of remark and imitation on
the part of strangers, that where an enormous population
have free access, without any distinction of age or class,
no trespass is committed—the blossoms are unplucked,
and the boughs unbroken. Flower shows are very frequent in Paris, and are always certain of attracting a
numerous and fashionable assemblage. I have attended
on many such occasions; and my candid judgment of the
gardens and horticultural exhibitions I have seen is, that
profusion and mediocrity appear to be their leading characteristics. I can freely and fairly acknowledge that
many of the choicest productions of our gardens, our best
fruits and finest flowers, have been originally derived from
France; but our cultivation, whether of trees or plants,
results in a decided superiority. However, I have seen a
vast deal worthy of admiration in their horticulture, and I
hope that speedy improvement will attend their future
labors. I shall now close my horticultural remarks with
an anecdote which I ascertained to be strictly true.

A PRETTY THIEF.

In 1864 there was a show of fruits and flowers in the Rue
de la Chausée-d'Antin, and the proprietor of a suburban

nursery exhibited a collection of *orchides,* grown and blown to perfection. One flower was of surpassing size and beauty, and was deservedly considered the gem of the exhibition. On the second day, a young woman of prepossessing appearance, whose attire and manner indicated that she belonged to the industrial class, appeared to be quite enchanted by the splendid orchis, and her encomiums, and perhaps her good looks, attracted the attention of the exhibitor. He paid her some gallant compliments, and ventured to inquire her name.

" Monsieur, it is in the catalogue."

" Then, Mademoiselle, it must be 'Rose;' you are indeed worthy of the same designation as the pride of our parterres."

" Monsieur is right in his conjectures as to my name, but he is mistaken in the comparison by which he compliments me so greatly."

" May I persume to ask where Mademoiselle resides ?"

" I live, Monsieur in the Rue d'Amsterdam, No. —."

" I indulge the pleasing hope that Mademoiselle may permit me to have the honour of calling on her."

" Monsieur confers a great honour on me, I shall have much pleasure in receiving his visit."

The horticulturist became completely enamoured ; he redoubled his compliments, and eventually requested Mademoiselle to remain in care of his flowers whilst he procured some ice and other delicacies for her refection. When he returned, Rose had disappeared, and with her his magnificent orchis had departed. The plant remained, but the stem was severed near the root, and the display of its loveliness was adjourned for at least twelve months. Furiously indignant, he denounced the pretty Rose as a thief. Proceeding quickly to the Rue d'Amsterdam, he found that the numbers of the houses stopped short by one of the number mentioned by her. He was despoiled, and had no available remedy. Towards the close of the next day, he was contemplating his stand, lamenting the loss of its greatest attraction, and recounting to his sympathising friends the circumstances of the spoliation, when a box and a note were delivered to him by a porter, who had been employed to convey them from a neighbouring street. The note was as follows :—

" MONSIEUR,

" You displayed too great a temptation to an ardent admirer of beautiful flowers. From the moment I beheld your orchis I determined that its artificial reproduction should not fall to the lot of any rival *artiste*. In the accompanying box you may behold your flower ; and if you place it upon the stem, it will not wither for a considerable time. Receive, Monsieur, the assurance of my lasting respect and gratitude.

" ROSE."

The box contained an artificial orchis, so exactly resembling the stolen flower, that it would deceive the closest observer. It was placed upon the stand, and passed off admirably. The fair delinquent was not detected—indeed the search for her was not rigorously pursued—but copies of the abstracted orchis gained a general and deserved pre-eminence amongst the artificial flowers which graced the fashionable female dresses of the succeeding season.

FRENCH WIT.

Some of the lighter literary productions of the French press afford to a reader abundant instances of pithy and witty expressions. A stranger who has not been habituated to the language, and accustomed to think in it as well as to speak it, will be very likely to allow many sparkles of conversational wit to escape his notice, and may consequently impute more dulness to the social circle in which he mingles than he is justified in ascribing. I am sure that many ebullitions of genius totally escaped my observation, but I recollect an expression addressed to me by a cab-driver which I cannot omit relating. I had walked down the Rue St. Florentine towards the Place de la Concorde, when in turning the corner at which I had arrived, the driver accidently let his whip fall. It lay just at my feet, I took it up and handed it to the owner, who respectfully touched his hat and said, " I thank you, sir ; I hope that whenever misfortune (*malheur*) meets you, he'll lose his whip."

FRENCH SILVER.

I often thought, during my Parisian sojourn, that the instability of human dynasties was strongly evidenced by a handful of French silver, a coinage which has been left to public currency from the end of the last century. I met with coins of the old Republic, of Bonaparte, First Consul; Napoleon, Emperor; Louis XVIII., Charles X., Louis Philippe, the French Republics again, and Napoleon III. The silver coins of the Republic immediately preceding the last empire, have on the obverse, " Liberté. Egalité. Fraternité." I remarked to a shopkeeper in the Rue de Bac, that it was very strange the Imperial government left the coin of the Republic still in circulation. He took up a five-franc piece, and said, "*Liberté point. Egalité point. Fraternité point.*" The forcible wit of his expression consisted in the double meaning which may be assigned to "*point.*" It signifies a full stop or period, but taken as an adverb, it may be understood to denote " Liberty, not at all ; Equality, not at all ; Fraternity, not at all."

THE HOTEL DES INVALIDES.

There is no institution more worthy of a visit from a tourist than the Hotel des Invalides at Paris An additional interest has been imparted to it since the remains of the first Napoleon have been deposited in a magnificent mausoleum immediately adjoining. In the front of the building, ranged along the terrace, and also on the eastern and western sides, were a considerable number of cannon, captured in war. I saw guns of Russian, Chinese, Dutch, Austrian, Prussian, and Moorish origin; but amongst them all I do not believe that the English artillery would find an old acquaintance. When you enter the church, your attention is immediately arrested by the flags of various nations pendant from the walls to your right and left, and placed there as captured trophies. On the left hangs an English flag. I asked, on four different occasions, and of different persons, where this color had been taken, The invariable reply was "Leipsic." I thought this very extraordinary, having always supposed that no English were at Leipsic, except a troop of the Rocket Brigade, and certainly they did not carry a color.

The Hotel des Invalides was under the direction of the Minister of War; and in the library of the War Office I have seen several rolls and registries of its former inmates. In such as relate to the period between 1700 and 1775, Irish names are not infrequent; Byrne, Bryan, Carty, Cavanagh, Dunne, Delany, Keogh, Kelly, Corcoran, Quin, Purcell, Redmond, Sullivan, &c., appear to attest the services and sufferings of the Irish Brigade. There are not many "O's"; and I am inclined to believe that in several instances that prefix was laid aside purposely. Scotch names occur, but not at all in such frequency as

Irish. Of the occupiers of this splendid military asylum, I can safely affirm that I found them extremely civil, and by no means reserved in their communications. They were proud of their Institution and of the profession with which it was connected; but their conversations exhibited the human character in some thoroughly prejudiced phases. I did not meet amongst the veterans even one individual who had served under "The Emperor," and only three or four who had ever seen him; but all were well versed in the traditions of his military achievements. I had become intimate with Monsieur Turpin, the librarian of the War Office, who understood English perfectly, and he appeared to enjoy, as much as I did, frequent visits to the Invalides, and the peculiar feelings or sentiments expressed by the old soldiers, especially regarding the policy adopted by Napoleon, and the political and military operations to which he had recourse for the extension of French power throughout the world. It was almost an article of faith amongst them, that Napoleon was never conquered by any of his numerous adversaries. They could not admit that he ever committed a military mistake, or was guilty of a moral wrong. In Russia, he was repelled by the frost and snow. At Leipsic he suffered a reverse by the premature explosion of a mine. At Waterloo he was sold. At Paris he was betrayed. It was politically expedient for Napoleon to imprison Ferdinand of Spain, when he entered France as a suitor for the hand of his sister, Pauline; but it was infamous to send Napoleon to St. Helena. It was a noble idea for Napoleon to collect the choicest works of art from every capital on the Continent into the museum of the Louvre; but that their original owners should take them back was *robbery*. It was glorious to recollect that the victorious eagle of France had triumphantly entered Madrid, Lisbon, Berlin, Rome, Vienna, Milan, Naples. Munich, Venice, Hamburg, and Moscow; but that the European powers should ever think of returning the visit— that the Russians should have threatened to shell Paris from the heights of Montmartre—that the Prussians should have encamped in the Bois de Boulogne, and the English in the Champs Elysées, was a degradation, an insult never to be forgotten nor forgiven. After all, perhaps, these Frenchmen are fair specimens of human vanity, of human resentments, and only think and speak as we would think and speak if we had, like them, to revert to a series of astonishing military successes, terminating in our complete discomfiture.

CHAPTER XXXIII.

GAIN PREFERRED TO GLORY——CURIOUS INSCRIP-
TION——FORMER GAMBLING——AN ASSAULT——
FRENCH CHARITY——A LETTER TO HEAVEN——
FATHER PROUT.

WHEN a stranger surveys the military asylum for the
maimed or aged soldiers—when he beholds the triumphal
arch (*l'arc de l'Etoile*) at the higher termination of the
Champs Elysées, erected at the almost incredible cost of
£417,812, to commemorate the achievements of the
French armies—when he contemplates the column in the
Place Vendôme, towering to the height of 135 feet, and
cased with bas reliefs, of which 360,000 pounds weight of
captured cannon supplied the material—when he observes
large and frequent bodies of troops marching with beat
of drum to various posts—when he finds it impossible to
glance at any crowded street, or enter any place of public
resort or recreation, without beholding the uniforms of,
perhaps, every branch of the service, he is almost forced
to the conclusion that the bent of the French disposition,
and the genius of the nation, is essentially military. However, I believe that an observant and reflecting mind will
notice many points in the French character of an unmili-
tary tendency. Whenever a campaign or expedition becomes

the subject of conversation in a French circle, the first con
sideration is, How much will it cost, and what shall w
gain ?   Solferino and Magenta are prized more as havin
annexed Nice, than for the laurels they conferred on Frenc
valor.   I frequently visited the triumphal arch to whic
I have already adverted ; and on one occasion I was struc
by the remark of a Frenchman in reference to the enor
mous sum it cost, and also to the surprising fact, tha
although the names of more than ninety victories are in
scribed on its interior walls, *not one of those places wa*
then in the possession of the victorious power.

CURIOUS INSCRIPTION.

On the 15th of August, 1864, the birth day of the first
Napoleon, the fete of the Bonaparte family was celebrated
by various public demonstrations.   The rails surrounding
the base of the column in the Place Vendôme were
decorated with violet-colored ribbons and wreaths of
Immortelles.   Amongst them I observed a large oval
tablet richly bordered, and bearing an inscription in Italian,
which I transcribe and translate, leaving its applicability
to the character of the first Napoleon to the calm and
dispassionate judgment of all acquainted with the history
of Europe from the time of his appearance at the siege of
Toulon to the subversion of his power at Waterloo—

"A Te, essere il piu maraviglioso della creazione, il cielo conceda quella
pace che ti negò la malvagita degli uomini."

"To you, the most wonderful being of the creation, heaven grants that
peace which the waywardness of mankind denied you."

FORMER GAMBLING.

Gambling houses, formerly so perniciously abundant in Paris, have been rigorously suppressed by the government for a considerable time past. High play is carried on still in various phases of society, but as it is furtive and illicit, its dupes and victims are very limited compared with the thousands who were ruined when the vice was tolerated by the public authorities. The Palais Royal was, about forty years ago, the head-quarters of Parisian gaming, and every season produced a crop of suicides. The usual course was for the ruined gamester to pledge or sell his watch or trinkets, buy a pistol at a gunmaker's shop in the piazza, charge it, cross the rails into the parterre, and blow out his brains; but such incidents did not stop the play; they merely produced a few shrugs of the shoulders, and the observation, " His game is up."

There is an old gentleman in Dublin who resides so near my house that I see him almost every day. About the time to which I refer, he was in the confidential employment of a most respectable firm of solicitors, and one morning he was apprised by the senior partner that it was intended to send him to Paris, to have certain deeds executed. He was to be allowed liberally for his expenses, and to be permitted, as a reward for his previous good conduct, to spend ten days or a fortnight in the French metropolis. He arrived in Paris at night, arose early next morning, and betook himself at once to the business with which he was entrusted. He was so fortunate as to find all the required parties, and in a few hours had all the deeds perfected. He then went off in quest of amusement, and having met an acquaintance, was ultimately brought to the Palais Royal, and entered one of the principal gaming-houses. He looked on for a while, an then ventured a stake of a few gold pieces ; he won, trie again, and was successful. He continued to play wit such good fortune, that at the termination of the sitting he had won upwards of one thousand pounds. He wer to his hotel, took some rest, paid his bill, and set off wit all haste for Dublin. His employers were surprised at hi speedy return, and he told them what had occurred, addin that *he would not trust himself another night in Par*: His was a solitary instance of good luck and prudence; fo with thousands of others a similar gain would have onl; been the precursor of final and irretrievable ruin.

AN ASSAULT.

At the suggestion of an intimate friend, who was in Paris during the time of my residence there, I shal mention an incident of an extraordinary and very disagreeable nature, arising entirely from an expression used by me to a young woman possessed of considerable persona: attractions, but also having a most fearful and ungovernable temper, without the least intention on my part to excite her feelings. I went into a shop in the Champs Elysées, to purchase some stationery, snuff, postage stamps, &c., and was supplied by the young woman, to whom I handed a twenty franc gold piece for her to take four francs and give me the change. Belgian silver coins were at the time very freely circulated; but Swiss silver was considered to be alloyed most unreasonably, and when recognised was invariably rejected. The damsel gave me eight pieces, each of two francs, and I observed that on two of them the Helvetian or Swiss designation was impressed. I immediately remarked that Mademoiselle had been subjected to a Swiss deception, (*une tromperie*

Suisse,) when she exclaimed, "Accursed Englishman, you are a liar," at the same time throwing a heavy canister at me, knocking off my hat, and following up that hostile proceeding by flinging a flask of oil in the same direction. The latter did not strike me, but broke a large square of glass in a side window looking into the Rue de l'Oratoire. Her brother-in-law, who was proprietor of the concern, seized her, and prevented any further violence; but the abusive language continued for some minutes. Finally I succeeded in getting the Swiss silver replaced by two pieces of French coinage, and left after declaring my intention to prosecute my assailant. The proprietor contented himself by declaring that the affair was a mere "mistake;" and he certainly seemed more annoyed by having his window smashed than by the misconduct evinced towards me. Subsequently I was informed that the young woman had been engaged in some courtship or amatory correspondence with a Swiss, who had terminated the affair by an abrupt departure without any previous notice. The angry damsel referred my expression, not to the money, but to the man, and I relinquished any attempt to make her responsible for the treatment I had received in consequence of her hasty "mistake."

FRENCH CHARITY.

In the foregoing observations I have not hesitated to refer to some faults, vanities, and unreasonable expectations which attracted my attention during my residence in Paris. I shall now offer a few remarks and a little narrative connected with one of the noblest virtues that can elevate and adorn human nature, and which I believe to exist in the French character to a degree far beyond what would be imagined by the travellers whose brief visits enable them to take only transient or superficial views of French society. There is no civilized nation more charitable than the French. They have no legalised and established system of poor laws, but their cities abound with benevolent institutions, and the requirements of helpless age or unprotected infancy are never disregarded. There is no lack of charity in any class—even the rag-pickers will share their slender means in alleviating human suffering. Amongst the more affluent there is very little mediocrity of religious feeling; they are generally devout or indifferent, but very few are uncharitable. The means of relief for the suffering of indigence are almost always administered through religious agencies; and the mercy that is manifested in a generous and unostentatious succour of the poor, exemplifies very frequently the words of Shakespeare—

> " It blesseth him that gives and him that takes."

For many of those who were indifferent to religion, but disposed to charity, have been themselves caught, reformed, and reconciled through the energies which they employed for relieving the necessities of others.

A LETTER TO HEAVEN.

Connected with the subject of French charity, I shall introduce the narrative of an incident of 1864, and I had several interviews and conversations of a very agreeable nature with the little heroine of the tale.

In one of the small old streets which adjoin the market of St. Honoré, upon the upper floor of a house built some centuries ago, the family of a poor workman were struck by a most fearful affliction. Not only had the wife been unable to rise from a bed of sickness for a considerable time, but the husband, the only support of her five children, had, by a sudden accident, been so disabled as to be stretched in utter helplessness and acute suffering. What was to be done? Where were the helpless creatures to find subsistence?

Amongst the children of this hapless couple there was a little blue-eyed, fair complexioned girl; she was lively, intelligent, and interesting, and had been for a short time attending a public school; but now she was obliged to remain at home to give her puny care to her sick parents. Afflicted by the misfortune of her father, and assailed even by hunger, she instinctively sought a remedy.

"When you are in trouble you should apply to the Good God; the sister at the school tells us so. Well, I shall address the Good God. I shall write a nice letter, such as my mother made me write to my godmother last Sunday. I have a bit of paper and a pen."

No sooner said than done. Whilst her parents are in an uneasy slumber, she scribbles a note abounding in blots, in which she implores of the Good God to restore their health, and to send some bread for her little brothers and herself. Then she slips out, runs at once to Saint-Roch, and supposing that the alms-box for the poor was the letter-box of the Good God, she approached it with timidity, and in the hope that she was not seen.

At this moment an aged and respectable lady was leaving the church. She was behind the little girl, and seeing her approach the alms-box stealthily, and supposing her actuated by some culpable motive, she caught hold of her arm.

"What are you doing, you unfortunate child?"

2 H

The little girl, surprised and affrighted, cast down streaming eyes, but being kindly and mildly questioned the lady, she recounted her sad story, and showed letter which she wished to send to heaven.

The good lady, moved with compassion, consoled poor child, and taking the paper, said—

" Leave me your letter ; I take upon myself to forwa it to its destination."

Then she immediately added, " But have you put yc address, to receive the answer ?"

The child, who looked upon the lady with the utmc astonishment, answered, " No, Madam ; but the sister my school tells us that the Good God knows ever thing."

" And she has told you the truth, my child," said tl lady, smiling ; " but those whom He may charge to deliv the answer may not know as well as He does."

The child then stated where her poor parents lived, rt ceived two francs from the lady, and with a joyous heai betook herself back to the wretched garret.

In the morning she found at her door a large hampe containing clothes, provisions, and some money. : label was affixed, inscribed, " The answer of the Goo God."

A gentleman named M'Carthy, eminent for his medica skill, and also much respected for his generous an benevolent disposition, soon after, at the instance o the charitable lady, visited the poor sufferers. He wa: one of those Irishmen whose talents and worth attaine to high professional positions in Paris. He speedil cured the man, and considerably alleviated the suffering: of the woman. He allowed me to accompany him two or three times whilst attending the humble denizens of the garret, from whence charity had removed misery and despair, and on those occasions I found the little girl fully convinced, and most earnestly insisting, that the answer of the Good God must have been brought *by one of His angels*.

CHAPTER XXXIV.

FATHER PROUT.

I HAD, during my residence in Paris, the supreme gratification of being honored with the intimacy of the Rev. Francis Mahony, whose *nom de plume* of " Father Prout" is suggestive of a complete union of learning, wit, and poetic power, without the slightest alloy of pedantry, acerbity, or vanity. I was a very frequent visitor at his apartments in the Rue du Moulin, and was never denied admission. If he was writing, I did not accost him, but sat down, taking up a newspaper or book, and remaining silent until he found himself at leisure either to chat at home, or to saunter out through the parks or gardens, museums or libraries. I repeatedly thanked him for the unrestricted access thus granted, and his invariable reply was " Come whenever you please, you never interrupt me." He was the correspondent of a London evening paper, *The Globe and Traveller*, and I do not think that he relished the occupation, for his conversation scarcely ever indicated a political tendency, and I never knew him to introduce a topic involving political or religious differences. At the time to which I refer, the war was raging between the northern and southern states of America;

and the only opinion that I ever heard Father Mahony express on the subject was not favorable to the cause of either side as regarded its merits, but to the effect, that whatever might be the issue of the contest, the belligerent states would never become again united in firm and enduring friendship. He formed this conclusion from the deadly hatred and vengeful denunciations evinced by great numbers of Americans of both parties who were then in Paris, and amongst whom the females were the most uncompromising and persistently truculent in their expressions. It remains for time to confirm or confute his prediction; I pass to one or two anecdotes of this gifted and amiable individual, which I hope my readers will consider interesting. I had made an appointment with him to have a ramble in the French capital, or its environs, and twelve o'clock was the hour fixed for its commencement. Some unforeseen circumstances, however, delayed my arrival at his residence until another hour had nearly elapsed. When I apologised for my failure in punctuality, Father Mahony said that he had employed the interval in jotting down suggestions as to the direction which our proposed saunter might take, for my consideration and decision. They were as follow :—

To the Bois de Boulogne shall we wander to-day,
  Or visit the tomb where Napoleon réposes,
Or ascend Notre Dame, from its tow'rs to survey
  The scene unsurpass'd which that prospect discloses ?

From Boulevards crowded our steps may diverge,
  If we wish at the Bourse* to see bright or long faces,
As some bubbles rise, or as others may merge
  In the vortex where Hope vainly looks for their traces.

* The Parisian Stock Exchange.

Shall we seek the Pantheon's vast edifice, where
  An echo to thunder converts every sound,
From vaults* in whose precincts the bones of Voltaire
  Were so carefully stow'd that they cannot be found ?

Or the Luxembourg Palace, with gardens, where grow
  The roses so varied, throughout the whole year ;
And you see on each side statued queens in a row,
  Their costumes antique looking cold and severe.

To the Louvre's magnificent halls shall we hie,
  Where art's choicest gems require days to explore them :
Where dynasties past seem around us to lie,
  Whilst emblems Imperial are triumphing o'er them ?

Shall we visit St. Cloud, and continue our course
  To Versailles, where a palace exemplifies all
That monarchical pride from its serfs could enforce,
  Till their patience exhausted accomplish'd its fall ?

If at Sevres we pause to admire for awhile .
  Its plastic productions of classical taste,
We shall see the sole work that the Pompadour's smile
  Ever sanction'd that was not impure and debased.

We should not forget St. Germain, and its claims
  On a stranger's attention   *   *   *

The last place mentioned in this unfinished production
was chosen ; and after viewing the tomb of James the
Second of England, the church, to the vaults of which the
mortal remains of many French monarchs had been
consigned, the old palace, and the exquisitely beautiful
scenery of its vicinity, I prevailed on my estimable friend
to become my only guest at the Prince of Wales' (*Le
Prince de Galles*) Hotel and Tavern, where we had what
he designated "a sumptuous dinner," the entire charge

* The door of this vault, when clapped, produces a noise fully equal to
the report of a heavy cannon. The general opinion is, that the bones of
Voltaire were abstracted and burnt, soon after the restoration of Louis the
Eighteenth.

for which was defrayed by seven francs (5s. 10d.) How sumptuous!

During another stroll I happened to express very great admiration of the poetic productions of Gray; and in reference to his " Elegy written in a country churchyard," ventured to term it the finest composition of the elegiac class in the English language. Father Mahony praised it highly, but disagreed as to its merits being superior to every other production of the kind. He then stated that about the middle of the last century, a native of Dublin, named John Cunningham, who was a comic actor, published a volume of poems, and dedicated them to David Garrick. They were chiefly pastoral, but amongst them was an " An Elegy on a pile of Ruins," composed, he believed, on Rosslyn Abbey and Rosslyn Castle; and he then repeated several verses which I considered very beautiful, and which he declared to be equal, in his estimation, to the poetic merits of Gray's Elegy. I asked if he could lend me the work, and he replied that he had never seen it except at a public library in Cork. Soon after my return to Dublin I saw on a bookstand at Aston's Quay, a copy, which I purchased for a shilling, and thus became enabled to quote the verses to which my very learned friend ascribed such excellence. They are extremely alliterative—

> In the full prospect yonder hill commands,
>   O'er barren heaths and cultivated plains ;
> The vestige of an ancient abbey stands,
>   Close by a ruin'd castle's rude remains.
>
> Half buried, there, lie many a broken bust,
>   And obelisk, and urn, o'erthrown by Time ;
> And many a cherub, there, descends in dust
>   From the rent roof, and portico sublime.

Where rev'rend shrines in Gothic grandeur stood,
  The nettle, or the noxious night-shade, spreads ;
And ashlings, wafted from the neighbouring wood,
  Through the worn turrets wave their trembling heads.

There Contemplation, to the crowd unknown
  Her attitude composed, and aspect sweet !
Sits musing on a monumental stone,
  And points to the MEMENTO at her feet.

Soon as sage ev'ning check'd day's sunny pride,
  I left the mantling shade, in moral mood ;
And seated by the maid's sequester'd side,
  Pensive, the mould'ring monuments I view'd.

Inexorably calm, with silent pace
  Here TIME has pass'd—What ruin marks his way !
This pile, now crumbling o'er its hallow'd base,
  Turn'd not his step, nor could his course delay.

Religion raised her supplicating eyes
  In vain ; and Melody, her song sublime :
In vain, Philosophy with maxims wise,
  Would touch the cold unfeeling heart of TIME.

Yet the hoar tyrant, tho' not moved to spare,
  Relented when he struck its finish'd pride ;
And partly the rude ravage to repair,
  - The tott'ring tow'rs with twisted Ivy tied.

The eight verses which I have quoted from "An Elegy on a Pile of Ruins," are not consecutive in that production. It may appear extraordinary that Father Mahony should make such long quotations with perfect correctness, but to those who knew him a misquotation or deficiency of recollection on his part would seem far more surprising.

CHAPTER XXXV.

A FRENCH LAND MURDER—IRISHMEN, FRENCH
ECCLESIASTICS—ALGERIAN PRODUCTIONS—BIRD
CHARMING—BRITTANY—CHATEAUBRIAND.

WHILST sojourning in Paris I became acquainted with an
avocat, named Vanneau, who practised in a provincial
district, and who came to stay, for a few days, at the
boarding-house in the Rue de l'Oratoire in which I was
located. He had been recently engaged in defending
persons charged with criminal acts, and narrated a case
by which it appeared that Ireland had not a monopoly of
land murders. A M. Deneubourg had purchased, at
Cambray, a piece of land near Ewars, occupied by a
farmer, named Potiez, who had offered for the property,
but was outbid by Deneubourg. In the evening of the
day of sale, the two men, on their way home, met at a
house of entertainment at Ramillies, and some very angry
language passed between them. They left the house, and
in some time Potiez returned to Ramillies, and stated
that they had been attacked on the road, that he had saved
himself by flight, but he feared Deneubourg had been
murdered by the villains who had assailed them. On

proceeding to the place described, Deneubourg was found horribly murdered. His head was smashed to small pieces, and to a club which was found near the body a portion of his brains and two of his teeth were adhering. There were no footprints on the soft ground except what corresponded to the shoes of the deceased or of Potiez, and the dress of the latter was marked with blood. Various other circumstances fully indicated the guilt of Potiez. He was convicted, but was not sentenced to death. The French jury found him guilty of the murder, *under attenuating circumstances.* I asked Monsieur Vanneau what attenuating circumstances could the jury discover in so brutal a murder, and he gravely replied that they thought an accepted offer for the purchase of the property, outbidding that of the occupying tenant, was a very strong provocation and a natural incitement to revenge. He then added that Potiez was fortunate in being tried by a jury on which there was not *a landed proprietor or an auctioneer.*

IRISHMEN—FRENCH ECCLESIASTICS.

I met in Paris with some Irishmen holding ecclesiastical appointments there, and I gratefully recollect their kind and hospitable attentions. One of them, Pere M'Ardle, was attached to the church of St. Sulpice, which was much frequented by Irish, English, and American Roman Catholics. His duties consisted in the celebration of Mass, hearing confessions, visiting the sick, &c.; but he never preached, the pulpit being reserved for clergymen who could deliver sermons in French with the ease and fluency incident to their native language. The side aisles of the church were appropriated to persons of respectable appearance, who were expected to pay six sous for each chair provided for their accommodation. The chairs were under the management of some female attendants, who were most persistent in collecting the chair-rent. On Whitsunday, 1864, a soldier entered one of the aisles and took possession of a chair, without the intention, and probably without the means, of paying for its use. He was immediately required to pay the usual charge, or to leave the aisle and join the general crowd in the centre, and he obstinately refused to adopt either course. Whilst the altercation was proceeding, the Curè of St. Sulpice had entered from the street, and was passing quietly to the sacristy to make the necessary arrangements for preaching the sermon. He touched the soldier gently on the shoulder, and whispered, " My friend, pay her trifling demand ; here is what will enable you to procure the same accommodation for a considerable time." Slipping a five-franc piece into the soldier's hand, he passed on and discharged the duty which he had undertaken. On the next Sunday, (Trinity,) the Curè was confined to bed by a severe attack of bronchitis, and another ecclesiastic preached, and afterwards went to the apartment of the invalid to afford his sympathy and express hopes of a speedy recovery. The Curè almost immediately asked him if he had observed a soldier amongst the congregation, to which the other replied that there were more than a dozen soldiers listening to the sermon, and they subsequently came to the sacristy, where, on being asked what they required, they replied, " Only the money." On being told that there was no money for them, they expressed some anger and great disappointment, as they had been led to believe by a comrade that they would get five francs each.

On one occasion I was a spectator of a procession of French bishops from the college of St. Sulpice to the church. Amongst them there was one Irishman, Monseigneur Cruise; he was the bishop of Marseilles.

ALGERIAN PRODUCTIONS.

From the abundance and variety of Algerian productions which I beheld in the Parisian markets, it appeared to me that the country from which they were supplied possessed great capability of soil and climate, and received a high degree of cultivation. The finest Muscat grapes, both as to size and flavor, melons, pomegranates, shaddocks, and all the lesser varieties of the citron tribe, almonds, brinjals, sweet potatoes, and what was a very novel sight to an Irish eye in October, splendid strawberries, met my view in several shops entirely appropriated to the sale of Algerian commodities. I confidently hope that French enterprise will be eventually far more successful in Africa than it was on the other side of the Atlantic. Few of the most valuable productions of the West Indies are indigenous. They were first introduced by the French into St. Domingo, and that island was the first to escape from European ownership. When the sugar-cane was brought from Egypt, the coffee bush from Arabia, and luscious fruits and stimulating spices from various lands, the negro was imported from Africa, to be eventually the master of all. However, the stain of slavery does not attach to the French rule in Algeria, and from all that I was able to learn of their government there, I know no reason why all who are desirous of the substitution of civilization instead of piracy and tyranny should not wish it to be permanently successful.

BIRD CHARMING.

In closing my Parisian recollections, I wish to notice what was termed "Bird Charming" in the gardens of the Tuileries. There was a silly notion amongst some people there that by the agency of animal magnetism, or by some peculiar power, the feathered tenants of the woods and shrubberies of the palace became familiar with particular persons, and the subject was specially mentioned in *Le Monde Illustre.* It was certainly very curious to see the sparrows flocking about a person, eating from his hand, and perching on his hat in expectation of the crumbs which he was distributing; but it was far more extraordinary to see the woodquest (*le pigeon sauvage*) come from his lofty nest, alight at your feet, then perch on an adjoining rail, and pick the crumbs from between your fingers. Still the "charming" was a misconception. The birds were in a place where they felt secure; they were not shot at or frightened, but they were petted and fed, and accordingly became familiar. I had no magnetic or mesmeric influence, but I had some nice bread, and they came down and eat from my hand, and some sparrows even took morsels from between my lips. *Le Monde Illustre* noticed two occasions on two consecutive days, when the birds were plentifully fed, and their feeders were described in terms, of which the following is a very literal translation :—

"A young man of genteel demeanor, his head uncovered and slightly thrown back, called the birds, which came fluttering around him, and took, even from between his lips, the morsels of bread which he offered them. We wished to discover the secret of this curious proceeding, and returned at the same hour on the following day. We experienced a great disappointment; for, instead of a man young and prepossessing, we beheld 'a charmer,' *old and wrinkled, no sparkle in his eye, no expression in his looks.* He began by throwing into the little railed arbours some morsels, quickly devoured by the bold sparrows. Then, having gradually attracted them, he kept in his hand a further supply of bread, and from the thickets of shrubs, and from the surrounding trees, finally from all quarters of the garden, birds of various species came flocking and fluttering around him. Attaining to a degree of *crescendo* between him and his feathered guests, he finished by having them perched on his shoulders, and picking the crumbs from between his lips."

Who could the individual have been, thus designated as old, wrinkled, unsparkling, and inexpressive? Oh! I hope that none of my readers will suppose or suspect that such terms were applied to me. I should prefer being considered "a young man of genteel demeanor," but if the other description appears more suitable or probable, then —" What can't be cured must be endured."

BRITTANY.

I left the French capital after a very agreeable residence of eighteen months, and, previous to returning to my native city, availed myself of an invitation from a kind and hospitable friend to pass a month with him at a delightful villa in Brittany, about a couple of miles from St. Malo. Amongst the people of this locality, I observed a vast dissimilitude to the corresponding classes in Paris. Display, and the excitement incident to the metropolitan requirements of frequent and varied amusements, appeared to have very slight attractions for the Bretons, whose pursuits and habits were mostly directed to the acquisition and enjoyment of public advantages and domestic comforts. Their soil did not appear to me to be superior to the generality of that which I have seen in the southern half of Ireland; nor did I consider their climate more genial during the time of my visit, which comprised the latter half of August and the next half of September. Their exports of orchard fruits, butter, eggs, and poultry, from the port of St. Malo, were enormous in quantity, and, I believe, unexceptionable in quality. The external appearance of their firkins and other packages was extremely neat and cleanly, and the butter was liable to inspection previous to its shipment. I was informed by the English Consul that the exportation of butter amounted in the year to twenty-five thousand firkins, and the fowls exceeded one million. On the lands which I had opportunities of viewing in Brittany, I saw very large crops of rape, the seed of which was intended to be crushed for the production of oil, and I have been in three concerns where the rape oil was filtered through charcoal, and thus clarified and qualified for our use as " Colza oil." Buckwheat *(blè noir)* is considered a valuable crop, and is much used for feeding poultry. The sugar-beet (*betterave jaune*) is often to be seen, but is generally mistaken by strangers for mangold wurtzel. But the most extraordinary production is one which we could cultivate fully as well and as profitably as the Bretons can, if we were permitted on any terms. I have seen many acres, even on one farm, thickly covered with tobacco growing most luxuriantly. Why cannot we see it on the Irish soil? Why is it utterly prohibited here?

During the wars of the French Revolution and of the first empire, St. Malo was a port almost exclusively appropriated to the outfit and employment of privateers. Few of their cruises were eminently successful ; but the greatest prize stated to have been acquired was a large ship, belonging to the English East India Company, which was captured in very foggy weather between Jersey and Southampton. The cargo consisted of the choicest Indian produce, and there was also a very large amount of specie on board. This affair realized an ample fortune for the proprietor of the privateer, who retired from any further speculation in or connection with maritime operations, whether forcible or otherwise, and invested his gains in the purchase of a fine estate in the vicinity of St. Malo.   During my visit I was at several delightful entertainments given by families with whom my friend was on intimate terms ; and at one, in St. Servan, a conversation arose relative to the great injury inflicted on the commercial navy of the Northern American States by Southern privateers.   One gentleman stigmatized such proceedings as utterly disgraceful, and insisted that no nation should ever promote or even countenance nefarious attack on private property, and the consequent ruin of unarmed and non-belligerent parties. I was much amused when, on our way home from the repast, my friend informed me that the indignant denunciation of privateers was uttered by the possessor of the estate acquired by the capture of the Indiaman, the grandson of the proprietor of the fortunate cruiser.

The religious tendencies of the people of St. Malo formed a very great contrast to those of the Parisians.   In these pages I shall not intentionally introduce a word of a controversial or sectarian nature ; but I may remark that whilst in the metropolis, public and private works and commercial avocations were unscrupulously pursued on Sundays ; whilst the bricklayer, carpenter, and slater, plied their trades, and numerous carts supplied them with building materials, the provincial town was as still and as quiet as the most rigorous observer of the Sabbath could require in our cities or towns. I went into St. Malo on a Sunday when the procession of Corpus Christi passed through the principal streets, and it appeared to me to produce amongst all classes most devotional effects. The thoroughfare was covered with freshly cut grass and short sprigs of evergreens. Young females dressed in white headed the procession, carrying baskets of flowers, which they occasionally strewed, whilst flowers were abundantly thrown from almost every window. I firmly believe that demonstrations of any inclination to impede or offend the numerous sacerdotal functionaries engaged, would have excited the general populace to a very prompt and violent manifestation against the offenders. I feel equally convinced that any similar religious or ecclesiastical demonstration in Paris could not pass through any street of that city. It would be overwhelmed by mob violence, not from its connection with any particular creed, but from the popular dislike to any form of religion whatever.

CHATEAUBRIAND.

Whilst at St. Malo I visited the tomb of a man, the great attributes of whose character, and the extraordinary incidents of whose life, have been recently made the subject of a most interesting lecture, delivered by my truly learned friend, Professor Robertson, and published, amongst several others, by Mr. Kelly, of this city. I allude to François-René, Viscount de Chateaubriand, who was born at St. Malo in the year 1768, and during a life of eighty years witnessed the outbreak and many of the horrors of the French Revolution; who had, for his personal safety, to undergo exile and penury, until his literary acquirements and productions procured for him the friendship and respect of strangers, and relieved him from indigence. Then, having been enabled to return to France, he published some romances, and also works of a serious description, by which he acquired a high and lasting reputation. Subsequently, having travelled in Greece, Asia Minor, Syria, Palestine, Barbary, and Spain, he made the results of his travels the subject of a most interesting Itinerary. In 1821 he was sent as ambassador to Prussia, and in 1822 was appointed to a similar office at the British Court. Towards the close of the reign of Louis the Eighteenth, he became the French Minister of Foreign Affairs, but did not continue long in office; he died in 1848 at Paris, and his remains were conveyed to St. Malo. I have mentioned Chateaubriand as an illustrious and highly gifted man, and my readers will be greatly surprised when I add—He sleeps in a nameless tomb.

In his life time the municipality of St. Malo had, at his request, granted a solitary rock in the bay of that seaport for his place of sepulture. There his coffin was deposited in a grave cut out of the solid stone, and surmounted by a granite cross, which marks the last resting-place of one whose reputation was far more than European. It bears the short and simple inscription of "Here lies a Christian." (*Ci git un Chretien.*) I believe, however, that the omission of the name has caused all who have seen the tomb to enquire who was its occupant, and has not tended to render him forgotten, or his memory unappreciated by his countrymen.

The foregoing notice of this celebrated native of St. Malo had scarcely been put in type when I received a copy of *The Tablet* newspaper, containing a communication from a French correspondent relative to the inauguration of a

Chateaubriand memorial at St. Malo, on Sunday the 5th of September last. I presume to insert it in these pages, as strongly confirming the opinions I have expressed, and being likely to please and interest the reader by its intrinsic merits.

" *A Statue to Chateaubriand.*—Yesterday (Sunday) the inauguration of the Chateaubriand Memorial took place at Saint Malo. All the papers are full of recollections of the author of the *Genie du Christianisme.* Chateaubriand lived at a time when the evils of revolution had left the strongest emotions in all hearts. There was a drama in every man's life, a romance in every one's history. The very air was full of a floating, vague poetry of sufferings and regrets, and disappointed hopes. Nature and misfortune combined to make Chateaubriand a poet. A dreamy, unhappy childhood heightened the sensitiveness of his feelings, and religion itself was to him as poetry was—emotional. He saw his mother die, heard her last prayer for himself, the child of her affections, for his welfare, temporal and eternal. From that day he submitted to the Church's dominion. "I wept," he says, "and I believed." He then travelled in America, and the ocean and the wilderness revealed to the young man a new kind of poetry. He went to Philadelphia to salute Washington. Subsequently he travelled into the far West. Returning to Europe, Chateaubriand endured the miseries of exile. That was the most unhappy part of his life. It was then that he commenced authorship. We next hear of him at the siege of Verdun, on the surrender of which place he found himself without resources. After many vicissitudes of fortune he reached London, and betook himself seriously to literary work. The remainder of his history is too well known to need recapitulation here; I therefore return to the *fête* of yesterday. The town of Saint Malo is small but curious by reason of its sombre mediæval aspect, its granite houses, its narrow, winding streets, and its absence of greenery—not a lawn nor a shrub being visible anywhere. Chateaubriand's native townsmen retain a lively recollection of him, and welcomed the day with enthusiasm. A large number of strangers also paid their respects to the tomb of the author of *Les Martyrs.* The emotion was general when the procession reached the summit of the "Grand Bé," and came in sight of Chateaubriand's monument. High above the waves was an iron railing and a cross of stone, nothing more. Its simplicity was touching and effective. Chateaubriand perhaps yielded to a feeling of pride, in wishing to be buried thus on that elevated spot, with nothing in sight but the immensity of the heaven and the immensity of the ocean :—

' Cœlum undique et undique pontus.'

Be that as it may, the people of Saint Malo have done honour to themselves in honouring Chateaubriand. We may apply to him his own words about Bossuet, ' His genius will stand like the mighty figure of Homer, always seen through the long vista of the ages. If sometimes it is obscured by the dust of a falling century the cloud soon disperses, and there it is again in all its majesty, only overlooking new ruins.' "

CHAPTER XXXVI.

THE ARRAN ISLANDS—CIRCUIT REMINISCENCES.

On my return from France, I found that my son, Frank Thorpe, had accepted the appointment of medical officer in the Islands of Arran, which lie at the entrance of Galway Bay; and at his earnest desire I proceeded to visit him, without the slightest expectation of deriving from the trip any pleasure, except that resulting from our meeting. On my journey, as I reverted to the scenes and associations which, in distant and foreign lands, had been almost invariably agreeable, I felt convinced that I was certain of finding, in the lonely insular locality to which I was going, the most striking contrasts. The passenger communication between Galway and Arran was effected by a sailing vessel of very moderate dimensions, but bearing the dignified appellation of "The Yacht." She had one small cabin for the reception of all ranks, sexes, or ages; and as the weather was neither wet nor cold, I preferred a seat astern, and having procured a reeling-line from one of the crew, amused myself by capturing mackerel until I had acquired a couple of dozen. There were four lines in operation during a run of about thirty miles, and for five hours the catching of mackerel was incessant. The skipper said that the bay was swarming with them, but net-fishing was only followed in the vicinity of Galway town, as the transmission of large quantities by sailing boats was considered extremely hazardous. If the capability of Galway Bay for supplying enormous quantities of mackerel, herrings, and occasionally pilchards, shall ever be made available, results may be obtained immensely advantageous to local interests, and most important to the general community. I may revert briefly to this subject whilst detailing some incidents of my sojourn amongst the Arran islanders.

No traveller ever arrived in a locality to which he could be supposed to attach a more slender expectation of being gratified by what he might see or hear, or by the treatment he might receive during his stay, than that felt by me at the commencement of my visit to Arran. I was impressed with a paramount idea, that I was to spend the time in a bleak, sterile region, and amongst a population destitute of almost every habitude or quality imparted by civilization. I could not possibly have formed a more erroneous opinion, for I never stood on any spot, in any of the islands, without having in view, whether near or distant, scenery sublimely picturesque; and I found the people, without even an individual exception, unpresuming, unobtrusive, civil, obliging, intelligent, and industrious. The adults of both sexes generally indicate in their personal appearance the effects of constant manual labor, and of occasional privation, but they are mostly tall, vigorous, and active. Many of the youthful females are decidedly beautiful in features and figure, and there is no scarcity of very pretty children. The aggregate population of the three islands exceeds four thousand; and although Irish is the language generally spoken, I did not meet with any who could not converse in English. Schools connected with the National Board of Education are numerously and regularly attended ; and although the generality of the men and women appear to be attached to, and contented with the locality in which they live, there is a great desire frequently expressed to qualify their progeny to engage in industrial pursuits or trading employments elsewhere.

There are no forest trees to be seen in any of the islands except a few stunted sycamores. I saw two or three pear-trees, which had been planted close to walls, but their growth appeared to have been checked by the saline atmosphere and shallow soil, and they produced no fruit. On the hills I found a great variety of indigenous flowering plants, which were very handsome, and in the rocky dells there were several kinds of convolvulus of very rich florescence. The Madagascar Periwinkle seems to be perfectly acclimated, and blossoms profusely; and I was greatly surprised to find a very abundant growth of hops, the introduction of which is ascribed to the monks, by whom the numerous old ecclesiastical structures were formerly occupied. The tillage of the islands comprises potatoes, mangold-wurtzel, vetches, rape, clover, oats, and barley. The potatoes almost exclusively planted are round, white tubers, generally small, but numerous, and they are termed " Protestants." A perfect stranger might be startled by hearing a direction given to put the Protestants on the fire, or to roast them in the glowing turf ; but the proprietor of the Atlantic Hotel, in reply to an observation of mine, said that there was no offence intended, for *they found the Protestants very palatable.* The tillage crops are sometimes greatly devastated by caterpillars and grubs ; and I have frequently heard the abundance of those pernicious insects attributed to the great scarcity of sparrows and other small birds. Starlings are occasionally seen, but I never observed a swallow. Gulls and other marine birds are very numerous, amongst which the Ospray or sea-eagle is a conspicuous object. The raven, crow, rook, or jackdaw cannot be found; but there is a bird which I thought extremely handsome, very numerous, especially in the North Island. It is the Chough, which in addition to plumage dark and glossy, like that of the jackdaw, displays a beak and legs of bright scarlet. It is said that this bird was formerly to be seen in flocks at various places on the English coast, especially Dover cliff, and that now it cannot be found in any part of the United Kingdom except the Arran Islands. I should regret its extinction, for I know it to be handsome, and it is reputed to be harmless.

I recollect reading, although I am unable to specify in what work, that frogs were not indigenous to Ireland. It was stated that in the reign of Elizabeth, a person connected with the University of Dublin, then recently established, brought from England a crock or jar of frog spawn, which he emptied into a ditch at Beggars' Bush, near Dublin, and that in his importation our present community of amphibious croakers and jumpers originated. The probability of this statement is strengthened by the fact, that frogs are not to be seen in the Arran Islands.

I believe that there is not a salmon fishery in Great Britain or Ireland more abundant than the one at Galway. I have there seen from the bridge the fish in such numbers as I should have considered incredible if described. These myriads of salmon entered Galway Bay from the Atlantic, and passing the islands, proceeded about thirty miles to the river where they appeared in such enormous quantities. I therefore think that I should mention a most extraordinary fact, that whilst I was at Arran, I saw, in a morning stroll, five men drawing a seine net at the entrance to Kilronan harbour. They took some herrings, a few flat fish of various kinds, some whiting, some pollock, and a salmon of about twelve pounds weight. I was desirous of purchasing the latter, and they readily sold it to me for two shillings; but they all assured me that they did not know what kind of fish it was, and that they had never seen one before.

The quantity of land capable of tillage in each island is very limited, and consequently affords employment only to a small portion of the population. Fishing in the bay, with boats rather poorly equipped, or drawing seine nets in the creeks and entrance of the harbour, and cleaning and drying the produce, are followed by many during the favorable weather; but the principal employment of a very considerable number of both sexes is gathering of the seaweed, and converting it into kelp by calcination. I believe that all other industrial occupations are of trivial importance to the Arran people compared with the production of kelp. The capability of Galway Bay to be made a fishing station of immense importance has never been denied; it can produce an abundance of the choicest piscatory delicacies, and frequently becomes, through its entire extent, replete with mackerel or herrings. I venture to express an opinion, that the greatest obstacle to the development of such advantages is to be found in the feeling of indifference, perhaps I might use a stronger term, on the part of the people belonging to the various adjoining localities, to each other. I have heard, in Arran, frequent expressions of contempt for the Connemara fishermen, of dislike to the Clare people, and of utter detestation of those belonging to the Claddagh at Galway. On two occasions, in the South of England, I saw a great

fleet of boats, comprising vessels from Cornwall, Devon-
shire, Hampshire, and Kent, co-operating amicably and
efficiently in surrounding a shoal of mackerel or pilchards.
On narrating these occurrences to some Arran fishermen,
I was told "it would be impossible to bring about such a
state of things there; and that, even if others became
agreeable, the Claddagh fellows would rather sail through
the nets of other fishermen than join in taking as much as
would fill every boat."

Whilst I was at Arran some cases occurred of severe
typhus fever. There is no hospital in any of the islands.
The habitations are, with three or four exceptions, thatched,
and without any upper story. The invariable course
adopted was to nail up the door of the patient's apartment,
to take out the sashes of a window, and render it the sole
means of external communication. The medical attendant,
clergy, and nursetender, had no other means of ingress or
egress, and I never heard any objection made to the system.
My son contracted the disease, and although ten days
elapsed before a medical gentleman arrived from Galway, he
surmounted the fearful malady. I spent each night in his
apartment, and during the day he was tended by a nurse.
Almost every night I heard some gentle taps outside of
the vacant window, and on going to it I would be told,
"My wife is afther making a pitcher of whay fur the poor
docthur; you'll find it on the windystool," or "I brought
you two jugs of milk, to make whay fur yer son; they're
on the windystool." When the crisis had passed, and
nutriments or stimulants were required, I would be told,
"We biled down two chickens into broth for the docthur,
I hope that it will sarve him." Rabbits, chickens, and
joints of kid were tendered for his use, and even a bottle
of "rale Connemara potteen" was deposited on the

window-stool. The people were all kind and anxious; and when he became able to walk out, he was cordially saluted and congratulated, but no person would approach him if they could avoid it. They were all dreadfully apprehensive that he might impart the direful contagion. I brought him home as soon as possible, but he and I will always remember most gratefully the unvarying kindness and sympathy we experienced in Arran.

CIRCUIT REMINISCENCES.

Some friends of the Leinster Circuit have suggested that a few descriptive notices of my personal recollection of scenes in court, convivial evenings at the Bar-mess, or other amusing incidents of the period between 1827 and 1840, during which time I had attended every Assize Court held in Wicklow, Wexford, Waterford, Kilkenny, and Tipperary, might not be unacceptable. The subject is one in which the pleasures of memory are mingled with numerous regrets; for of all those whose learning and talents excited my respect and admiration, or whose wit and conversational powers rendered their society invariably delightful, very few remain. Of the judges whom I remember, I considered Chief Baron O'Grady (subsequently created Lord Guillamore) the most amusing public functionary that I ever had seen. He came our circuit but once during my time. At Wicklow he presided in the Crown Court; and amongst the cases for trial there were four or five for sheep-stealing, and they were all convicted. Sheep-farming was at that time so prevalent in Wicklow, and considered so important by the class of persons who were summoned as jurors, that an accusation of sheep-stealing almost invariably eventuated in conviction. Towards the close of the assizes, a member of the Militia band then stationed at Arklow was put forward for trial on an indictment for the manslaughter of a comrade, whom he had killed with his sword on a sudden altercation. The case appeared fully to warrant a conviction, but the jury, without even retiring, acquitted the prisoner. Mr. Scott, the senior counsel for the crown, expressed an indignant disapproval of the verdict, upon which the Chief Baron observed, " Mr. Scott, the prisoner is not yet discharged, and you can get a conviction immediately if you only indict him for *sheep-stealing*." When we proceeded to Wexford, the Chief Baron, as Record Judge, had but two short cases to try, and when they were disposed of, he engaged in the trial of criminals. A woman named Hester Carroll, who had been for some time a pest and disgrace to the town of Enniscorthy, was put forward, charged with a robbery of a gold watch and chain, and upwards of twenty pounds, from a farmer, who had become intoxicated in her society. She was found guilty, and when the verdict was announced, a sergeant of constabulary, who had been the principal means of her detection, advanced to the table in the Record Court where she was standing, to take away various articles which had been found in her possession ; whereupon she sprang at him, tore his face fearfully, and bit his hand very severely. When she was disengaged from her intended victim, and held so as to prevent further violence, the Chief Baron pronounced the sentence of the court in terms which seemed to me and others of his hearers to be an imitation, in style and assumed solemnity, of that incident to a capital offence. After some preliminary observations on the heinous nature of her crime, and the certainty of her guilt, and the tendency of her conduct in court to prevent any mitigation of punishment, he concluded in the following words—" The sentence of the court is that you, Hester Carroll, shall be taken from the place where you now stand, to the gaol from whence you were brought, and from thence that you shall be transported for the term of seven years to such penal settlement or colony as his Majesty's government may direct, and may God have mercy upon those who shall have to manage you there."

A prisoner was tried before him at Wexford on an indictment for highway robbery, and although the evidence amounted to a strong probability of his guilt, the verdict was an acquittal. Richard Newton Bennett, who defended the prisoner, immediately applied to the Chief Baron to order the man to be liberated, to which the other replied, " He will be discharged from custody, Mr. Bennett, to-morrow at noon. I shall set out for Waterford in the morning, and I wish to have a couple of hours start of your client."

In my early professional days the law in reference to njuries to growing crops of vegetables was very imperfect, and although taking potatoes, turnips, &c., out of the owner's ground was considered a very serious trespass, the offence could not be treated as actual larceny. Some pro-ceedings at Waterford, in reference to the abstraction of turnips, were held to be insufficient to sustain an indict-ment, and a deputation of the Grand Jury sought a con-ference with Chief Baron O'Grady on the subject. One of them asked his Lordship if the delinquents could be made liable to punishment under the *Timber* Act, to which he gravely replied, " Certainly not, unless you can prove that the turnips were *sticky.*"

Charles Kendal Bushe had been a member of the Lein-ster Bar; and when he had attained the distinguished position of Chief Justice, he frequently selected his former circuit as a Judge of Assize. Amongst the members of the Bar he was not merely respected and admired, but beloved. Portly in his personal appearance, he was dignified without ostentation, witty without sarcasm, learned without pedantry, and his judicial duties were discharged with impartiality, patience, kindness, and humanity. Kilkenny was his native county, and amongst the gentry of that place his family had been long established. The judges on circuit usually invite two or three barristers to dinner daily in each town; and I had the very agreeable honor of being an occasional guest of Chief Justice Bushe. I recollect a conversation relative to the criminal calendars of that time compared with those of the previous century. The Chief Justice said that the name of his family had been introduced into the charge of a judge to the Grand Jury of Kilkenny, about the year 1760, in terms far from complimentary. There were then organised bands or gangs of freebooters, who plundered and maltreated the proprietors and tenants of estates, unless a certain subsidy, called rapparee rent, or blackmail, was paid for their forbearance, and concealment and subsistence afforded whenever required. He said that the Agar family, (pronounced *Eager,*) the Floods, and the Bushes had become contributory to the marauders, and sheltered them from capture. Rumors of such an arrangement having been circulated, it was alluded to by Baron Dawson telling the Grand Jury of Kilkenny that their county was *eager* for prey, *flood*ed with iniquity, and that every *bush* sheltered a knave.

Having given the Chief Justice's anecdote in reference to three names, I may mention that my own name has not passed scotfree. At our Bar-mess, the Hon. Patrick Plunket was one evening insisting that I should sing a particular song. I begged to be excused, but he persevered, and continued exclaiming " Porter! Porter!" I said that "although I was ' Porter,' he should not make a *butt* of me." He replied, " I dont want to make a *butt* of you, I only wish to get a *stave* out of you."

Judge Torrens often came on our circuit, and generally dined twice at the Bar-mess: one dinner being the customary banquet given by the Bar to the judges at Kilkenny, and the other being by special invitation at Clonmel. He was always desirous on such convivial occasions of obtaining some vocal contributions, especially of a comic character. His favorite song was " The Wedding of Ballyporeen." He was Judge of the Record Court at Clonmel in 1833, and immediately after taking his seat at the commencement of the Assizes, was applied to by the late Mr. Brewster, to fix a day for the trial of a case, the parties to which, and their witnesses, had to come from the most distant part of the country, namely, Ballyporeen. The Judge made the order sought, saying, in a playful tone, " Is Mr. Porter engaged in this Ballyporeen case?" " No, my Lord," replied Brewster, " I regret that I have not the assistance of my learned friend."

" Most unquestionably," said his Lordship, " he ought to be in it."

There were some attorneys present who heard his remark, but they were not aware of the origin of his suggestion. Perhaps they ascribed it to a very favorable opinion of my professional capacity, or to a feeling of personal friendship ; but I found it subsequently productive of several record-briefs, which I might truly say were obtained " for a song."

In 1836, the Attorney-General (Richards) appointed me to a Crown prosecutorship on the circuit. In the afternoon of a day next before the opening of the Assizes of Clonmel, in 1838, I was sitting and noting a brief, whilst about a dozen more were lying on my table, when I was informed that a gentleman wished me to grant him an interview. Acceding to his request, I desired the servant to show him up, and I immediately perceived that he was an ecclesiastic. I proferred him a chair, and he proceeded to inform me that he was the Rev. Mr. Coony, a Catholic curate in a parish the name of which has escaped my memory; but it was near Clonmel. He was young, and zealous in advancing the religious interests of the flock with which he had recently become connected, and stated it was much to be regretted that the Catholic church of his parish was so completely out of repair as to require almost a total renovation. That he had been encouraged by the character he had heard of me to appeal to my generous and charitable disposition for a subscription towards rendering the church suitable and safe for his numerous poor parishioners. I was inclined at the time to have a little fun with his reverence, and said, " Well, sir, when you have your church repaired, I suppose you will make it as available as possible to the religious and moral improvement of your people."

" Certainly, sir ; we shall endeavor to do so."

" You will urge them to abstain from fighting and killing each other, from administering unlawful oaths, serving threatening notices, burning houses, houghing cattle, or plundering firearms, and even from excessive drinking."

" Assuredly, sir, it will be our duty to do so."

" So you come to me, to persuade me to cut the ground from under my own feet, by subscribing to further your acknowledged intentions. I am a prosecuting counsel on this circuit, and on the table before you I have a profitable assortment of murders, conspiracies, and attempts to murder, abductions, threatening notices, and faction-fights. You would render my vocation worthless by inculcating the observance of law and order, quietude, and temperance. It would be much more reasonable that I should be asked to subscribe to a society for the distribution of blunderbusses and pistols."

" Oh !" exclaimed the astonished priest, " may heaven grant that I shall never again hear such expressions from human lips."

" Well," said I, " suppose we effect a compromise. You expected to get a pound from me. Will you let the poor Crown prosecutor off for half-a-sovereign ?"

" Mr. Porter," said he, " I now feel convinced that you were jesting ; for, if you really felt as you spoke, you would not give me a farthing."

I gave him the half-sovereign. We walked together to " The Ormond," where we had some biscuits and wine, and parted on most friendly terms.

For a considerable time previous to my retirement from the Leinster Bar we had a junior member of that body whose name it is unnecessary to mention fully. He had been the adjunct or drudge of an attorney-general, and was consequently known amongst us by the designation of " Tom the Devil." I have heard that in his earlier years he had been a midshipman on board the " Orwell," a splendid ship belonging to the East India Company, and that for some special service which he undertook and accomplished under most dangerous circumstances, the Directors had allotted him a reward of one thousand guineas, on the acquirement of which he returned home to Ireland, and applied himself to the legal profession. He was greatly liked amongst us, and none relished his society more than I did. He frequently became my chum on circuit, and on one occasion, at Clonmel, he asked me to convey, in reference to a personal quarrel, the most liberal offer perhaps ever made to an adversary. There was an individual whose conduct and character were by no means questionable, as they were fully ascertained to be thoroughly disreputable, and he came to our lodgings whilst I was ordering breakfast. He was accompanied by another person who had been concerned, as a second, in a recent hostile meeting, and he stated that he wished to have an interview with Mr. ——, meaning my chum, "Tom the Devil," who was still in bed in a small adjoining room. I went to the door and said, "Tom, here is Mr. ——, who wants to see you." He jumped up, and without adding any other garment to his night-shirt, put his feet in his slippers and entered the sitting-room; then turning to the applicant he haid, "What do you want with me?"

"Mr. W——," was the reply, "I have been informed that on several occasions you have insinuated various matters prejudicial to my character, personal and professional; and I deemed it necessary to have a direct explanation as to whether you have expressed such injurious insinuations."

Tom replied, "You have been altogether misinformed. I can solemnly affirm, indeed I can safely swear, that I never breathed any *insinuation* whatever respecting you." The other bowed and seemed evidently gratified, but Tom continued, "I admit that I have spoken of you, but not indirectly. I have not hinted or insinuated, but plainly stated that I considered you a low, mean, ignorant, pettifogging blackguard. That is my explanation; and now, sir, if you will only wait until I draw on my boots, I shall feel much pleasure in kicking you down stairs."

2 K

I stepped forward, and implored the interrogating party and his friend to retire. I said that the apartment was mine, and that I would not allow any further altercation there. I succeeded in getting them away, and then I said to my candid chum, "This is a most unpleasant affair to occur in my presence. It may be highly injurious to me, for it will produce a challenge and a hostile meeting."

" He wont fight," observed Tom. " They are gone down the street, and as you are dressed, slip on your hat, and follow them. Tell the rascal to make no further row here, but to start at once for Milford, where I'll meet him. Tell him that my brother gave me forty pounds yesterday, and if he fights me I'll give him twenty, and, by ――, *I'll pay for his funeral into the bargain.*"

I declined carrying this liberal offer. I may add that there was no challenge sent, and the party against whom there had been *no insinuation* immediately retired from the profession. I cannot call to mind any further reminiscences connected with the Leinster Circuit. I regret that, whilst I was a member of it, I did not keep a regular diary.

In the foregoing pages I have mentioned occurrences and personal observations incident to my sojourns in France, Germany, Spain, and England. In all the cities which I visited, I found the people by no means indifferent to the reputation of their respective localities, or disposed to impress strangers with the opinion, that they had arrived in a place where vulgarity, dishonesty, and brutal violence habitually prevailed; and where to the worst and most appalling crimes there had been publicly accorded

" A local habitation and a name."

It would seem specially reserved for Dublin, my native city, to record by public inscriptions, and to insert in the list of our metropolitan thoroughfares, that within the municipal precincts there may be found a COW-PARLOUR, a PIGTOWN, a CHEATER'S LANE, a STONEYBATTER, a CUTTHROAT LANE, and a MURDERING LANE. It may be said that these places are mostly of small dimensions, but they appear in Thom's Official Directory in the same type, and fully as conspicuous to the eye of a stranger as the most populous and important of our streets or squares. Within my memory Skinner Row has been metamorphosed into Christchurch Place, Dirty Lane has become Bridge-foot Street, half of Exchequer Street has been converted into Wicklow Street, and French Street has been elevated into Upper Mercer Street. Surely the same authority that effected such alterations ought to substitute other names for those which cannot be retained without continuing to impute to our city that it contains places specially appropriated to low, vulgar, dishonest and sanguinary practices. During my tenure of magisterial office I found the city of Dublin capable of very favorable comparison with any other place of similar extent and population; and I consider the names to which I have referred most unjustifiably false and defamatory. The designation of one of our bridges has lately been changed, and it is to be henceforth made conducive to the memory of Grattan. The motives of those who proposed such an alteration were undoubtedly patriotic and praiseworthy; but identifying the truly illustrious orator and statesman with a bridge across the Liffey will not, in the present state of the river, tend to keep his name in *good odour*.

Since my return home I have lived in such retirement and quietude that I cannot refer to any incident worthy of insertion in these pages. In concluding these " Gleanings and Reminiscences," I have to assure my readers that I have sedulously endeavoured to minister to their information or amusement. If I have succeeded, their approval will impart great happiness to the closing years of my life; and having done my utmost, I trust that they will accord me a favorable criticism, for which I shall be deeply grateful.

PORTEOUS & GIBBS, Printers, Dublin.